HARDPRESS.NET
HOME OF HARD-TO-FIND BOOKS

Memoir of the Late James Halley, A.B., Student of Theology
by William Arnot

Memoir of the Late James Halley, A.B., Student of Theology

William Arnot

Engraved by Schf. Burton.

You ever grateful friend.

James Halley.

PUBLISHED BY JOHN JOHNSTONE, HUNTER SQUARE, EDINBURGH.

MEMOIR

PUBLISHED BY JOHN JOHNSTONE, HUNTER SQUARE, EDINBURGH

MEMOIR

OF THE LATE

JAMES HALLEY, A.B.,

STUDENT OF THEOLOGY.

BY THE

REV. WILLIAM ARNOT,

MINISTER OF ST PETER'S PARISH, GLASGOW.

SECOND EDITION.

EDINBURGH:
JOHN JOHNSTONE, HUNTER SQUARE;
LONDON: R. GROOMBRIDGE; HAMILTON, ADAMS & CO.
AND J. NISBET & CO. GLASGOW: M. OGLE & SON;
W. COLLINS, AND D. BRYCE.

MDCCCXLII.

ENTERED IN STATIONERS' HALL.

Edinburgh : Printed by JOHN JOHNSTONE, High Street.

NOTE TO THE SECOND EDITION.

THE first impression of the following Memoir having been disposed of in the course of a few weeks, a Second Edition has been prepared with the least possible delay. The whole has been revised, and several additional letters have been inserted.

As the volume necessarily contains many statements of fact which readers at a distance cannot immediately verify, it has been deemed inexpedient that it should remain anonymous. Accordingly the Editor has assumed the responsibility. At the same time he takes this opportunity of stating, that the friend referred to in the Advertisement to the First Edition, on whom, had he remained in Edinburgh, the principal share of the biographer's task would have fallen, is the Rev. James Hamilton, of the National Scotch Church, Regent Square, London.

GLASGOW, *April* 1842.

ADVERTISEMENT TO FIRST EDITION.

THOSE who knew Mr Halley will find the following Memoir an accurate representation, so far as it goes. They will observe many things that they knew in the original, but they will also miss many. Although it is chiefly a reflection of his mind from his own familiar correspondence, and not a portrait depending for its accuracy on the skill of another, it wants the breathing and colours of life. Books can never fully supply the place of the living man—least of all the living friend. The very best things in a friend are such as cannot be spoken—far less written. But while friends will not find here every feature of the departed, they will gladly recognise those that have been recalled and recorded. Those, on the other hand, who never knew him, and so cannot fondly cherish the memory of the man, may yet be instructed by his advice, and reproved by his example.

The 'Life' of such a person, in such circumstances, must, to a certain extent, be a 'Life and

Times,' otherwise it loses more than half its value. Accordingly the Editors have spoken, and allowed him to speak freely of good and evil, in opinion and practice, wherever it appeared. In stating facts or administering censure, they are not conscious of having been actuated by uncharitable motives; but they do not cultivate the charity which, in times of difficulty, would hide salutary truth. To have withheld all reference to living persons, would have been to leave the book without meaning, and without value. In cases where no good was to be derived, and some evil to be apprehended, from publishing names, they have been suppressed. Names have been freely given wherever there appeared no positive impropriety in giving them. This principle has been adopted, to relieve the reader, as much as possible, from the unintelligible mystery of asterisks, and the annoying ambiguity of initials. In regard to those things which may possibly wound the personal feeling of some, the Editors have only to say, that, while it would have been far more agreeable to themselves to have withheld them, they were not at liberty to suppress statements of truth where there appeared a prospect of exposing erroneous principle or checking unrighteous action.

To students of divinity and ministers of the Gospel, the Memoir is affectionately and respectfully com mended, in the hope and with the prayer, that it may be blessed as the means of stirring them up to greater diligence in their holy calling. At the same time, it is hoped that many an inquirer in private life may see his own 'natural face' in the glass of Mr Halley's experience, deriving from it warning, and instruction, and encouragement in the good ways of the Lord.

The Memoir has occupied a greater proportion of the volume than the Editors expected, and consequently, it contains fewer of Mr Halley's more formal compositions than was originally intended.

As to the execution of the work, the lenient judgment of the public is needed. Of the two persons on whom it devolved, one was called to a sphere of arduous labour in a distant part of the kingdom, before the work was begun. Notwithstanding his removal, the whole has been submitted to his judgment, and he has divided the responsibility of inserting facts and documents, but the labour of preparing the Memoir for the press has necessarily fallen upon one. It has been done at broken intervals snatched from the bustle of a city minister's charge. This is mentioned, not to pacify those who may see in the Editor's department any positive evil, but to bespeak the indulgence of those who may desiderate a greater amount of good.

December, 1841.

CONTENTS.

MEMOIR, &c.

CHAPTER I.

' I WILL remember the works of the Lord; surely I will remember thy wonders of old. I will meditate also of all thy work, and talk of thy doings.'—Psalm lxxvii. 11, 12. It is in the spirit of this declaration that we propose to lay before the public the following Memoir of a departed friend. It is only upon the principle acknowledged in this verse, that we expect the book to be either pleasing or profitable. We claim attention to the record that follows, not on the ground of our own affection for the subject of it ; for in that we could not expect others to sympathize : not on the ground of stirring incidents in the narrative ; for to these it makes no pretensions : not even on the ground of the extraordinary talents possessed by the deceased ; for this of itself would not repay the reader's pains and our own. We present the narrative as an example of the ' work' of God, whereon the reader may profitably meditate. We ' talk' of the dead, because we are persuaded that the living, for their own profit, may

A

see in his life and character much of the 'doing' of
the Lord.

To the reader who, by familiarity with the current
literature of the day, has acquired a taste for something novel and startling in every page, we have nothing to offer.   To the scholar yet in the ardour of
youth, thirsting after knowledge, we have an example
to hold out for instruction, and a warning to proclaim
for reproof.   To those who are prosecuting their studies with a view to the office of the Gospel ministry,
we write a lesson which they would do well to read.
But we do not exclusively direct our regard to any or
to all of these classes.   Like Wisdom in the Scriptures,
we seek to ' lift up' our voice over a wider sphere.
' To you, oh *men*, I call.'   We address the lost of
every class, while we present to their inspection the
experience of one whose loudest cry was, What shall
I do to be saved ?   We have something for the scholar ; and more for the professional theologian ; but
most for the sinner seeking peace with God through
the Lord Jesus Christ.   We take this method of per-
petuating and spreading a record of our friend's experience, because, though it finds no place in the page
of this world's history, it will be accounted ' great in
the kingdom of heaven.'

Like many of his countrymen who have attained to
eminence, James Halley inherited from his parents
neither rank nor wealth ; yet he obtained through
their means a more substantial portion—an early education.   Intelligent and industrious, they retained, in
a high degree, that which was once universally the
characteristic of the Scottish people—they made the

education of their children the principal object of their care. James was their eldest child. He was born at Glasgow, January 17, 1814. At six years of age he was sent to an elementary English school, where he continued about one year. When between seven and eight, he entered the grammar school. The usual course of study at that seminary was five years—four under one of the masters, and the fifth under the rector. Although always a clever boy, there was nothing in Halley's progress during the first two or three years, that strongly drew the attention of his instructors. From a low place in the early period of the course, he rose gradually year by year, till he was dux of the fourth year's class. This place he maintained, under Dr Chrystal the rector, during the fifth and last year. Both teachers retained a strong affection for their pupil ; and Mr Douie, the only survivor, still delights to speak his praise.

With a high and rising reputation, he entered the University of Glasgow in October 1826, before he had completed his 13th year. During the first session, in the Greek and Latin classes, he maintained his character ; but having come into competition with young men of mature age, he held but a secondary place in the annual distribution of rewards. At the time, it was matter of regret to him that he was sent at first to the senior classes, because it placed him necessarily lower on the prize list ; but he afterwards came to be of opinion that the method adopted by his friends was ultimately the most advantageous to himself.

During the summer of 1827, an accident befell the scholar, which seriously retarded his studies for a time.

Having gone to reside for a few days with a relative in the middle ward of Lanarkshire, he was amusing himself riding in a cart along with another boy, when the horse became unmanageable and ran off. The cart soon upset, and both were thrown with great violence to the ground. It was found that Halley had received a severe injury in the head. The blow took effect chiefly on his right eye. It was some time ere medical assistance could be obtained; and then, by some unaccountable mismanagement, no blood was let until the patient was brought back to Glasgow. There he was placed under the care of an eminent oculist, who succeeded in partially restoring the sight of the eye; but it was then found that the organ had been driven from its axis by the violence of the contusion; and no sooner did the patient begin to see with both his eyes than he saw every thing double. In these circumstances, the restoration of the injured eye did no good. Whether this defect could have been remedied is not certain, for there was no opportunity of trying it. In the process of healing, it was found that the pupil had been fatally injured, and the sight irrecoverably lost. He could always distinguish with it light from darkness; and even by much straining could sometimes detect the form of an object; but for all practical purposes it was totally useless ever after. The preservation of his life at this time has a place in the enumeration of the special mercies of God, which he inserted long after in his diary.

Having lost much of his vacation by this accident, and being weakened in strength by the illness which accompanied it, his friends judged it expedient that he should rest, or be but partially employed during the next session of college. Accordingly, with the view of affording him a wholesome exercise without too much fatigue, they enrolled him in one class—the Greek. This season he soon attracted the notice of the eminent professor who then held the Chair, the late Sir Daniel K. Sandford. From this time the Greek became Halley's favourite study. He devoted himself to it with the utmost enthusiasm ; and this predilection he ever after retained. Perhaps the predisposing cause of his choice is to be sought in the peculiar talents of his teacher. Long after, when the teacher had passed off from the stage, the pupil, himself just ready to follow, enumerates, with equal accuracy and elegance, ' the light of Glasgow college now gone down,' among the objects of memory's fondest regard. Certain it is, that Sir Daniel succeeded in raising the standard of classical acquirement among the youth of Scotland, and the effects of his labours are still widely felt. At the close of the session, Halley obtained the highest honours of the class.

Having been recruited in strength, and his health fully established by the summer vacation, he entered college next session as a second year's student, taking the Greek and Latin classes. In both, we believe, he obtained the first prize.

In 1829, adopting the usual custom of the university, Halley enrolled as a student of logic, but still prosecuted his study of Greek in the public class, and maintained his position against several eminent competitors.*

* As a student's position in a class is altogether a comparative thing, giving no certain indication of the absolute amount of his attainments ; and as the standard of classical education in Scotland is not rated high by our English neighbours, we think it proper to mention the name of one of

In the logic, which was his main business this session, he entered on a new walk. This period of his studies was interesting to his friends, as affording a test whereby to ascertain whether his genius were of that contracted kind which excels in one subject, but can adapt itself to one only. Hitherto his studies had been almost exclusively in the Greek and Latin classics. In that department he had attained the highest honours that were open to him in a Scottish university; and now that he had begun to turn his powers in another direction, it was soon made evident that his genius was of that expansive character, which can apply itself to any subject, and excel in every subject to which it is applied. In the logic class, under the efficient superintendence of the professor, Mr Buchanan, he met with the kindest encouragement, and the most ample scope for the exercise of his talents. In the daily oral examinations, and in the weekly written exercises, his superiority was as distinctly marked as it had been in the languages; and again, at the close of the session, the highest honours of the class were awarded to him.

During this winter Mr Halley passed with great credit what is called the Black Stone Examination, in Greek.* The list of books given in was altogether

Halley's class-fellows during this session—Mr Archibald C. Tait. Immediately after leaving Glasgow he entered a student of Balliol College, Oxford. There he soon attained the very highest honours, and was elected a Fellow at the earliest period allowed in the order of promotion. That distinguished scholar will not account it any dishonour, to have it told that he stood second to Halley, when side by side with equal ardour they pursued their favourite study under the auspices of Sir Daniel Sandford. We have been informed that Sir Daniel, several years afterwards, laconically introduced Mr Halley to an eminent scholar in Edinburgh, as 'the man who beat Tait.'

* It is a rule in the University of Glasgow, that all the students of philosophy must be examined every session on the subject of the preceding year's

unprecedented in extent; and yet the examinators found him at home in every portion of it. There is in this department always a keen competition among the more eminent students, which excites much interest throughout the university. Mr Halley obtained the highest prize.*

Though employed in a very extended course of reading for this examination, and performing at the same time all the exercises of the two public classes, he yet found leisure during this session for another extraordinary feat of scholarship. This was nothing less than writing a Greek play—an original plot with all its parts complete, after the model of the tragic drama. It extended to 800 lines. This performance, done at intervals of a most laborious season, shows a familiarity with Greek iambics scarcely ever attained in modern times. It was examined by Sir D. Sandford, and mentioned by him in terms of highest admiration at the next general meeting of the university.

During the following winter, 1830–31, in the ethic and mathematical classes, Halley's course was the same that it had been in the logic and Greek—diligent application throughout the session, rewarded by the highest honours at its close. The only extraordinary work in which he was engaged this year was reading for his degree. The degree of Bachelor of

study. A logic student is examined in Greek; a moral philosophy student in logic; and so on. The student cannot get his attendance at any class certified as a part of his curriculum, until the professor of the preceding year pronounce himself satisfied with his proficiency. The bottom of an antique chair in which the students sit, is literally a black stone, and hence the name by which the examination is known.

* Three prizes are given. And it is remarkable that the gentlemen who obtained the second and third on that occasion, Messrs Tait and Smith, are the same two to whom we allude elsewhere, who very soon after became Fellows of English colleges, the one in Oxford, the other in Cambridge.

Arts may be obtained by students when they have attended the ethic class; but the common practice in Glasgow is to delay till the following year, when they may pass all the examinations, and obtain the degree of Master at once. Halley was induced to deviate from the usual custom, and take his Bachelor's degree this year, in order to have the opportunity of competing for a prize given by the Marquis of Lansdowne, Lord Rector of the university. His lordship, at his installation, had announced his intention of giving two prizes of £50 each to the best men in the examination for degrees in arts, the one in physics, the other in classics and morals. By applying thus early for his degree, Mr Halley was enabled to compete in the latter department, and he easily obtained the prize.

The next class in the course is the natural philosophy. It is remarkable in Mr Halley's case, as being the only department of study in college upon which he entered without obtaining a first prize; and yet, when the circumstances are known, his standing in that class is as honourable to his genius and industry as any position he occupied throughout the course. By this time he had conclusively determined to enter the Divinity Hall, with a view to the office of the sacred ministry in Scotland. It was necessary to attend the natural philosophy class before he could be enrolled as a student of divinity. And as a four years' course of theological study awaited him, he could not then afford to lose a season. Thus he was compelled to attempt the natural philosophy with a very deficient preparation. He had attended only the junior class of mathematics, which is wholly elementary: and though he had manifested his usual talent in mastering the business of the class, he had not reached those higher departments that are necessary in the solution of the problems prescribed in the physic class.* Accordingly he was obliged to carry on a private course of mathematical reading to enable him to perform the exercise of the day. Problems were prescribed by the professor on the supposition of that amount of mathematical knowledge being possessed by the students, which is indicated by a two years' course of previous study. Thus, a student who entered when he was master only of one year's course, had not only to solve the problem prescribed, but first of all to feel his way forward among the arcana of pure mathematics, in search of an instrument which he might afterwards employ in the solution of the problem. This is the kind of difficulty with which our student had to struggle ; and in this way he held on throughout the session with so much success, that he obtained the second prize. The gentleman who on that occasion stood before him, was Archibald Smith, Esq., junior of Jordan Hill, who very soon after was senior wrangler at Cambridge, — the first Scotchman, it is said, who has obtained that honour.

During all this period, his principal source of maintenance was the product of his own exertion as a private tutor. A very considerable portion of his time —always four, and sometimes five hours a-day—was taken up in this way. This very materially enhances his merit, in maintaining so high a position in all the classes. It is not easy to perceive how he was able to overtake all his engagements ; and yet there is no

---

* At that time the Professor of Mathematics was laid aside by age, and the class was taught by assistants appointed from year to year.

reason to believe that his health was injured during that period by successive exertion. He possessed great buoyancy of spirits. He was in no danger of wanting exercise from lack of inclination for amusement; and he always found leisure to join his companions in getting that inclination gratified.

We have said that by this time he had finally chosen his profession. Indeed, to devote him to the ministry, had from the first been the design of his parents, and it had been in accordance with his own boyish inclination. It is to be regretted that we have no record of the progress of his views on this subject. We cannot now trace any of the steps by which he advanced from childhood's unmeaning desire ' to be a minister,' up to those sublime conceptions of the office, and ardent, yet humble desires to be invested with it, which appear in his letters toward the close of his life. In him the work of the Spirit was as the wind which bloweth where it listeth, and we hear the sound thereof, but know not whence it cometh nor whither it goeth. The successive stages of the process could not be traced by others, and probably were not observed by himself. But though we cannot by searching find out those paths of the Almighty that lie in the deep, we can in this case clearly see the ' end of His ways.' He was led, though by a way which he knew not, to a right view of the ministry, and a hearty dedication of himself to the service of God in the Gospel of his Son. This is one among many instances of good resulting from the early dedication of a youth, by his parents, to the Christian ministry. Doubtless much evil has resulted from the practice. The evil, however, does not lie in the dedication at first, but in an obstinate adherence to it, when it has become evident that the youth, on attaining the years of understanding, has neither the fitting talent nor the right spirit. The prayers of parents, and the preparatory studies, may be blessed as the means of fitting a young man for the ministry; but the determination, if the subject of it is in child-hood, should always be made with the reserve, that if it shall afterwards appear that grace is not given him, he shall not be forced into the office uncalled, unqualified, to the loss of his own peace, and the injury of the Church.

At the period to which we refer — the summer vacation after he had finished his course of philosophy —we cannot speak with any degree of certainty as to the state of Mr Halley's religious views. It is certain that he had begun to think seriously of his future procedure, and that now in his matured judgment, he had a strong conscientious preference of the profes-sion chosen for him in his childhood. His adherence to it at this time shows that he had more than secular interest in view; for it must have been plain to him-self that his prospects of advancement in the world would have been much higher, had he abandoned it and devoted himself to scientific and literary pursuits. But, though a pretty decisive judgment had been formed, we incline to think that at this period there was not much of the spiritual enlightenment which he afterwards attained. It was at this period that one of those who now make these particulars known, first became acquainted with him, and he remembers well that Mr Halley, on his first introduction, being asked what he intended to do next session, replied in a

jocular air, ' I intend to be a *divine man*,'—meaning
that he was to be a student of theology. The impression then made on the writer's mind, was unfavourable
as to the depth and clearness of his religious views.

About the same time, he began to take part in the
work of Sabbath school teaching, in connection with the
Calton Association for Religious Purposes. Whether
any thing more than a sense of its propriety, in reference to his destined profession, induced him at first
to begin this work, cannot now be ascertained ; but
it is certain that in prosecuting it, he soon found out
a better reason, even a desire to save the lost,—he
soon felt himself constrained by a stronger motive,
even the love of Christ. In the capacity of a member
of this Association, he drew up a small catechism of
Scripture doctrine for children, which has been stereo-
typed by Collins of Glasgow, and is now very extensively used in Sabbath schools.

In November 1832, Mr Halley entered the theological classes. There are three chairs in the faculty of
theology—Hebrew, Church History, and Systematic
Theology. It is usual with students to attend them
all during their first session. Mr Halley attended
them all, and obtained the highest prize in each.

In the Hebrew class he found the standard of excellence was not high. The teaching and the learning were superficial. Suddenly called to the office,
without having time to prosecute those peculiar studies which are necessary for the efficient discharge
of its duties, the professor was placed in a difficult
position. Apparently distrusting himself, he could not
inspire his pupils with confidence. It is dangerous
to put questions where the answer elicited may lead

the interrogator beyond his depth, and so the routine of the class was to the students very easy, but very dull. While they respected their professor for his general intelligence, and were won by the kindness and affability of his manners, they sympathized with him in the embarrassment of his situation. Soon after, his patrons relieved him from the necessity of teaching Hebrew, by transferring him to another chair. Mr Halley read some Hebrew afterwards in private, but in the class no scope was given for the exercise of his extraordinary powers of acquiring a language. An essay, prescribed on Hebrew syntax, he wrote, and obtained the prize.

In the ecclesiastical history class there was no teaching, and no examination. Lectures were read twice a-week, at which the students were compelled to attend, but in which they felt no interest. The only exercise prescribed or allowed was a prize essay once a-year. This prize Mr Halley obtained in each of the sessions that he attended the class.*

In the divinity class, conducted by the late venerable Dr M'Gill, the lectures and examinations were more varied and more interesting. Mr Halley always regarded this professor with the greatest respect, and often, long afterwards, enumerated his example and

* We are not conscious of any unkind feeling towards the *persons* concerned, and we strive to avoid severity of expression as far as the interests of truth will permit. We object to the system by which professors are appointed. It has now begun to be observed as an anomaly, and felt as a grievance, that the Church has no control over the appointment of those professors who are to guide her future ministers in the studies peculiar to their profession. The evil has now proceeded so far, that some remedy must needs be devised and applied. If either a minister of the Crown, or the close corporation of a Scotch university, shall nominate to a chair in theology, a person evidently unfit to teach, the Church has the power, and she ought instantly to exercise it, of relieving the students from the necessity of attending the class and paying the fees.

instructions among the special mercies of God. Dr
M'Gill was a man of an eminently devotional spirit,
and the elevation and fervour of his daily prayers
often diffused a hallowing influence over the Divinity
Hall. His lectures were not confined to speculative
theology. He knew, that to make his students familiar with the science of theology, would be of no avail,
if the power of the Gospel was not felt in their hearts.
Acting on this view, his teaching often assumed a
character too practical for mere speculators. But we
remember the respectful and earnest attention with
which Mr Halley, during the fourth session, listened
to his course of Lectures on personal religion, and the
duties of the ministerial office ; and those who were
most intimate with him, could perceive that he was
not a forgetful hearer.

There is so much of sameness in the four years'
course of theology, that after the preceding notices of
what the classes were, we do not think it necessary
to trace his progress through them from year to year.
We shall now notice, without precise regard to the
dates, some of the events illustrative of his talents and
character, that occurred during the period.

Numerous prize essays were prescribed in the various theological classes, for nearly all of which he
wrote ; and, so far as we know, every effort made
was successful. Besides these, there were university
essays open to all the students. Of those that were
gained by Mr Halley, we have no record before us, but
we know that he obtained the university silver medal
for exercises in theology in two different sessions. The
subjects were, *The Samaritan Pentateuch*, and *The
Authenticity of the first two chapters of Matthew.*

To illustrate the versatility of his genius, we may here mention an exploit on which he was often inclined to make merry. In the summer of 1834, he enrolled as a student in the botanical class. This was done chiefly with a view to benefit his health. The garden in which the lecture-room was situated, lay at a distance of about two miles from the place of his residence, and the hour of lecture was from eight to nine in the morning. This secured for three months a system of early and regular exercise. It happened that, during that session, a gentleman, whose name was not given, empowered Dr (now Sir William) Hooker to offer a gold medal for the best essay on *the natural history and uses of the Potato*. Halley had not paid much attention to the study of botany, and the prescribed subject of the essay did not at all lie in his way ; yet, he determined to write by way of amusement, and as he said, ' to beat the medicals.' The result was, a treatise extending to 172 closely written quarto pages. It was pronounced the best, and the interloper carried off the medal, fairly won from the medical students on their own proper field. Whether this achievement had found its way into the Farmer's Magazine, we cannot tell, but it had nearly procured for him a reputation of which he was not desirous. One day a stranger was ushered into his room, announcing himself as an Irish agriculturist, who had devoted considerable attention to the failure of the potato crop. Having heard that Mr Halley had been studying the same subject, he had waited upon him to hear the result of his researches. Mr Halley received his visitor with due politeness and gravity,—laid aside his folios, and entered with all becoming solemnity into the comparative merits of late and early planting—of whole sets and single eyes; and after a long consultation dismissed his visitor, greatly delighted with the interview.

On several occasions during his theological course, Mr Halley had opportunities of trying his gifts in public speaking.   The first effort which attracted the notice of his fellow-students, was a speech in a debating society in the spring of 1834, on the question of Church Establishments, then lately raised and exciting an intense interest throughout the country.   On this question the members of the society deviated from their usual method of debating, merely as an exercise of their powers.   This was a real debate.   It was a conflict of opinion, in which the combatants spoke what they felt.   The speakers felt that the question must have a momentous practical result.   Sportsmen though they were at other times, on this occasion they thought more of the game than of the chase.   After a careful muster of the forces in private, Halley was chosen to open the debate on the side of the Establishment. This he did to the full satisfaction of his friends, in a long and most elaborate oration.   It was thoroughly prepared and committed to memory.   This secured a clear and close argument throughout, and yet in the manner of it there was all the freshness of an unpremeditated harangue.   After a debate of three nights, it remained his right to close with a reply.   The reply was skilful and effective.   At the vote, the affirmative was carried by a very large majority.*   This being his

---

* It is necessary to remind the English reader, that the principle of admission into the Scottish universities is thoroughly liberal.   All are admitted on the same terms.   There is as great a variety of opinions on Church polity in the university as in the city.

first public appearance as a speaker, it was much noticed by the students, and in this walk, as in others, it was
evident from the first that he was destined to excel.

Several opportunities were afterwards afforded him
of exercising this talent, especially in the election of
lord rector of the university. In the election of Lord
Stanley, in 1834, his influence was predominant. As
the first of a series of Conservative triumphs, it was
an important era in the politics of the university.
The sudden triumph of Conservative principles in the
university at that time, has never been understood by
statesmen. It was no change of view in secular
politics. Previous to that date, the students belonging to the Church of Scotland were generally liberal,
and they threw their influence into the liberal scale.
At that time liberalism in State politics came to
be generally identified with voluntaryism in Church
politics. Upon the instant, the members of the
Church held in abeyance their (still unchanged) opinions on secular polity, and sided with that political
party who seemed most to side with the Church of
Scotland. Politicians should know this. Nor do we
ask them to take it on our word. We tell the story,
and leave them to learn from it. After Lord Stanley's
term of office—two years—had expired, Sir Robert
Peel and Sir James Graham were successively elected, by overwhelming majorities, over the most distinguished Liberals that could be opposed to them.
There was much gratulation among the Tories. Aged
professors came forth from their seclusion—attended
the dinner of a political club that had been established
among the students—announced themselves, amidst
the cheers and laughter of the audience, 'old tough

B

inveterate Conservatives'—and paid 'a debt of gratitude' to the young gentlemen who had 'burst asunder the thraldom of external domination, and shaken
off the fetters imposed on them from without.' * The
joy was very great, but it did not last long. In an
evil hour, Sir James Graham came down to Scotland,
and gave his vote and influence, as Lord Rector,
against Dr Chalmers, who was a candidate for the
Chair of Theology. There he touched the Church of
Scotland in the most tender point—he touched the
liberties of her people in the person of their most
distinguished defender. The series of Conservative
Rectors was immediately broken. At the next election, the Marquis of Breadalbane, a decided Liberal,
but an intelligent and uncompromising defender of the
constitution of the Church, was triumphantly chosen,
in opposition to the highest name that England or
Europe knows. The spell was broken. The Peel
Club dwindled into insignificance, and fell to pieces ;
and the 'old tough inveterate Conservatives' were
obliged to retire again within the cloisters of the college. Conservatism fell in the university at the very
time when it was consummating its triumphs in the
country. These are the simple facts, and they are
notorious in Scotland. The lesson they contain is very
plain. The Church of Scotland, as she has done in
generations past, will still ' oppose all deadly,' without inquiring whether they be Whig or Tory, who
attempt to infringe the liberty wherewith Christ has
made, and the constitution of the country has *acknowledged*, her free.

* Report of Principal Macfarlan's Speech at the Peel Club Dinner, in
the ' Glasgow Constitutional,' 25th December 1839.

A portion of Mr Halley's time, during the last three years at college, was occupied in performing the duties of librarian in the collection attached to the Divinity Hall. In this station he had an abundant opportunity of exercising his extraordinary power of memory. His habits of accuracy, and his extensive knowledge of books, were also made available for the benefit of the students in their resort to the library. One incident connected with this office should be noted here, as it made a deep impression on his mind at the time, and he often spoke of it with much interest long afterward. The affairs of the library were administered by a librarian and a committee of twelve, chosen annually by the students from their own number. Several periodicals had been introduced which lay on the table, and were read by the students when they had occasion to lounge in the library for an hour, between the dismissal of one class and the commencement of another. Among others more appropriate, *Blackwood's Magazine* had some way or other found a place. In process of time a considerable portion of the committee came to be of opinion that *Blackwood's Magazine* should not be there. Being nearly equally divided, they had made several contradictory decisions, at different times, according as the contending parties happened to have a majority present. At one time, by a majority of one, the magazine was condemned ; at another, by a casting vote, the magazine was recalled. At last an appeal to the constituents—all the students in the hall—was mutually resolved on. A meeting was arranged, and Dr M'Gill, the professor, agreed to preside. The whole matter was argued at length. The one party quoted (no very difficult task) passages

from *Blackwood*, to prove that it was not a fit book to
be selected to lie on the table as the special delight of
divinity students ; the other party palliated, and urged
all sorts of arguments in its favour.   At length a vote
was taken, and *Blackwood* retained by a very large
majority.   This decision made a strong impression on
Halley's mind.   Doubtless he felt it in some degree as
a personal defeat.   It was a failure where he was not
accustomed to fail.   With good arguments and a good
cause, and his fellow-students for an audience, he
had gained before this triumphs for himself, as well
as righteous decisions on the questions in which he
was interested.   In this instance he had to endure a
double disappointment—the loss of personal influence,
and a wrong decision on a cause which he had much
at heart.   After such a course of uninterrupted success, it is not surprising that he should have been at
times somewhat imperious in his rule, and somewhat
impatient of restraint.   He was at this time piqued at
the apparently successful opposition made to his own
paramount influence in college, but he was penetrated
by another and a deeper feeling—even sorrow at witnessing an erroneous and discreditable decision on a
question that affected the tone of religious sentiment
prevailing among theological students.   It was evident to those who had an opportunity of observing,
that long afterward, when the resentment had wholly
subsided, his judgment .of the merits of the case still
continued the same.   He kept a list of those who
voted with him in the minority, with the view of
marking how far his own judgment was confirmed by
their future character.   On the blank leaf of one of
his latest journals the list is found written out, headed

by the emphatic title—*The fourteen.* The formal defeat was in this case, as in many others, a substantial victory. Such was the moral effect of the contest, that soon after all agreed to give up *Blackwood.* It was discontinued by universal consent, and has never since made its appearance in the library of the Divinity Hall.

During the session of 1833–34, the most prominent public matter in which he was concerned, was the University Church of Scotland Society. We insert a brief account of it in his own words, from a letter written to a friend in the country. The language is severe; but it tells its own tale, and the reader may judge for himself whether the severity is merited :—

' GLASGOW, 24*th February* 1834.

' My dear Chalmers,—. . . . . We formed in November, immediately after our Stanley triumph (which was most superb), a University Church of Scotland Society, whereof the first meeting was held in the Greek class-room. The Voluntaries felt bound to get up a counter association, and applied for the same room. Sandford referred them to the Faculty, which learned (and most courageous and well principled) body, through fear of alienating the Voluntaries —to whom, of course, they refused the room—kicked us out of college. We remonstrated in a savage memorial, which will amuse you. They replied in a contemptible, shuffling " finding," giving every reason for their conduct but the true one. The whole matter, of which I shall tell you more fully when we meet, has marvellously enlightened me on the principles and character of public men. We have since met in the Tron Church session-house, and have discussed, since our commencement—Scripture argument for Establishments (Stevenson) ; Arguments for them from

Experience and Utility (Jos. Patrick) ; Refutation of the Leading Objections to Establishments (Halley) ; Argument from Scripture for Presbytery, as opposed to Episcopacy (Arnot) ; History of Patronage (Mac-Corkle) ; Argument against Independency (James Hamilton) ; and next Thursday we are to have a history of Presbytery, by Stark.

. . . . 'Stark's essay was admirable, and elicited, from several members, marks of strong approbation. Next Thursday we have James Morrison as essayist —subject, History of Christianity in Scotland from its Introduction till the Reformation. A fortnight after that we are to have a miscellaneous debate on Patronage,—each member to state his own views, and make his own motion. I hope it will be spirited, and tend to raise the character of the society.

'Talking of debates, the formal ground on which the Faculty expelled our society from college was, that it disapproved of all meetings for the discussion of questions of temporary excitement and political controversy ; and yet, a few days ago, the University Forum, the chief debating society of the year, discussed the question of the right exercise of the royal prerogative in dismissing the Melbourne ministry, and is next Friday to debate the point, whether Irish Church property should be alienated to State purposes. Of course the Faculty are silent. *Heu prisca fides !* Honesty and consistency for ever !

' JAMES HALLEY.

' Mr Wm. Chalmers.'

As yet, Mr Halley had never printed any of his compositions. About this time a communication was made to him, through a common friend, from the editor of the Presbyterian Review, requesting an occasional article. He entered into the proposal with great willingness. We shall give his own answer to the suggestion from the same letter that is quoted above :—

‘ I come next, in due course, to notice your important communication about the Presbyterian Review. I mentioned the matter to Stevenson, who, with characteristic modesty, treated the thing as altogether out of the question. Whether it be that I have more impudence, more self-conceit, or a more correct perception of the merits of the case, I shall not say ; but for myself I am disposed to treat your statements somewhat differently. Be it known to you, then, that I am a great admirer of the Presbyterian Review, and a greater admirer of its editor ; and if I thought I could write any article worthy of admission to its pages, would regard it as a very high honour to have any lucubration of mine appearing therein. I did not need your hint about the editor's having the prospect of paying his contributors ; for so highly do I approve of the publication, that I should be most glad to lend it any aid I can, and to place myself at the *command* of its editor, without price, prayer, or reward. If, therefore, he ever thinks it worth while to ask you again about Glasgow contributors, you may tell him you know one stripling, that knows a good deal of Greek, some Latin, and a moderate quantity of Hebrew,—has a smattering of logic, moral philosophy, and divinity,—and has bestowed some pains on Biblical criticism, and the Voluntary question,—who would be delighted to lend him a hand. Greek and Logic are decidedly my *fortes ;* and so works on subjects connected with these I should like best to review ; and in subjects connected with theology, I am best up to Biblical criticism, the Voluntary and Socinian Controversies, and the Christian Evidences.’

In reference to this at a later date, he writes to the same person,—

'GLASGOW, *9th July* 1835.

'My dear Chalmers,— . . . . I may tell *you*,—
what, however, you need not tell Mr Dunlop,—that,
for the same reason which prevented me from writing
you, I have not written one line for his periodical.
But having looked at Mitchell's Acharnians, being
assured I have something to say on them, and being
now really very resolute in the way of working when
I take on hand any thing definite of this sort, I do
most solemnly assure you, that a paper on said comedy
shall be in Mr Dunlop's hands on or before the 11th
day of August—probably long before it. The book
I have for some time had by me, having got the loan
of it from Sir D. K. Sandford, who has reviewed it in
the "Edinburgh" (*ergo*, by the way, I must try to
write something decent on it) ; so I shall not need to
avail myself of Mr Dunlop's permission to draw on
his resources.   J. H.

' *Mr Wm. Chalmers.*'

This article was his first effort in reviewing. It
appeared in the Presbyterian Review for September
1835, a few weeks after a similar critique in the
Edinburgh Review, from the pen of Sir Daniel Sandford. It is saying enough for Halley's article, that
it is almost as lively, and quite as learned, as the production of the brilliant and accomplished Professor.
If many of our readers were adepts in the minutiæ
of Greek criticism, we could adduce from this review
specimens which would make them wonder that one
so young should have read so much, and studied the
canons of syntax and prosody so profoundly. But
since Mr Halley was so much known as a classical
scholar, and since we are precluded by our plan from
giving evidence of his erudition, we shall introduce,

in the Appendix,* an extract as closely related to Greek learning as the plan of the work will admit. The learned reader will perceive from it how much at home he is among the institutions of Sparta, and the literature of Athens. It will, moreover, be generally interesting as a specimen of his first composition intended for the press.

His next contribution to the ' Presbyterian,' was one on which Mr Halley bestowed unusual care—a review of Haldane on the Romans. To qualify himself for writing it, he read or consulted on the first five chapters almost every commentator on whom he could lay his hands—some of them cumbrous and forgotten books. But it was his turn of mind. He could not sit down in comfort to write on any theme until he knew how other men had viewed it. † His vigorous and independent mind often drew from their own facts and arguments, conclusions different from

---

* Appendix, A.

† The entries in his diary of this date, for eight successive days, are the following :—

' *Monday, March* 21.—Two weeks shamefully omitted, chiefly, perhaps, because little was done. . . . On Romans I failed most miserably, having done nothing. I resume it this morning after prayer, and hope to go on to-morrow and following days with vigour.

' *Tuesday*, 22.—Besides class, library, and teaching—Romans, with Calvin, Tholuck, Stuart, and Haldane, as also Wardlaw on Infant Baptism, 8½ hours—practical reading and devotion, ½ hour—miscellanies, 1 hour.

' *Wednesday*, 23.—Romans, 4½ hours—practical reading and devotion, ½ hour—examining a passage in Hebrews, ¾ hour.

' *Thursday*, 24.—Devotion and practical reading, 1 hour—Romans, 7 hours—Greek ex., 3 hours.

' *Friday*, 25.—Devotion and practical reading, 1 hour—Romans, 8 hours—Greek ex., 2 hours.

' *Saturday*, 26.—Devotion and practical reading, 1½ hours—Romans, 6 hours—miscellanies, 2 hours.

' *Monday*, 28.—Devotion and practical reading, 1 hour—Romans, 9 hours.

' *Tuesday*, 29.—Devotion and practical reading, 1 hour—Romans, 10 hours.'

what their authors designed; and great part of his
originality consisted in the orthodox application of
materials collected for heterodox purposes.   Of this
system of extensive reading, the *tendency*, doubtless,
was to give his productions a pedantic air; but its
actual effect with him was to render them singularly
accurate.   In the case of many men much reading is
a source of much plagiarism.   In Halley's case it was
only the source of much learning.   In the present
instance a sifting investigation of the earlier chapters
of the Romans was repaid by sound views and unal-
terable convictions on the subjects of original sin and
free justification, and resulted in an article where these
truths are asserted with equal precision and cogency.
It is an essay which does not deserve to perish.   In a
periodical which contains some of the ablest theological dissertations by the present race of Scottish ministers, there is none where the erudition is more exact,
or the argument more conclusive.   Indeed, one of our
soundest theologians, as he read it in ignorance of its
authorship, declared that he was glad the Church of
Scotland contained a minister capable of writing such
an article.   Halley bestowed more pains on the preparatory study than on the actual composition of this
paper.   It was written in haste to meet the emergen-
cies of periodical publication,—and having no opportunity to correct the press, it was a subject of great
annoyance, aggravated by an almost painful puncti-
liousness, that typographical errors had repeatedly
marred the meaning.   Nevertheless, so instructive
had he found the study, that he always reverted with
pleasure to the weeks bestowed on it, and felt a special
favour for the performance itself.   It was published
in the Presbyterian Review for May 1836.

During the summer of this year—1836, Mr Halley and three of his friends in the Divinity Hall, formed themselves into a little society for the investigation of theological subjects. As all its members found signal benefit from its meetings, it may be good to tell how they were conducted. Their object was thoroughly to indoctrinate the members in the different *loci communes* of theology. At each meeting the next subject of examination was fixed, and books were assigned to each member, which he was expected to read and to master for the common good. For instance, if the subject were the Atonement, one of the brethren undertook to make himself acquainted with the work of Archbishop Magee; Smith's Scripture Testimony was assigned to another; Stevenson or Symington to a third; and, perhaps, some heresiarch to the fourth. On the day of meeting they assembled early at the house of one of the party; each came furnished with a list of questions suggested by his reading; a plan was fixed; the doctrine was defined; the direct arguments in its favour were adduced; objections were discussed and refuted; and information of all sorts was mutually contributed. This scheme of study had many advantages. By a mutual compact each was committed to a certain amount of labour, and during the recess of college, when there are many inducements to idleness, the members were constrained to read many books and master many subjects, with which it is commonly agreed that students of theology ought to be acquainted, but which, from the want of an immediate inducement to study them, they too often postpone indefinitely and never overtake.

Mr Halley was a member of two other societies,—

one for the delivery of discourses, with the view of
improvement in the style of pulpit address,—the other
for prayer, the devotional reading of the Scriptures,
and practical conversation on the passage read.   In
both, his clear intellect, his extensive learning, and his
growing grace, were exercised for his own profit, and
for instruction to his friends.   By the members of both
societies, scattered now over this and other distant
lands, he is still held in affectionate remembrance.

During the whole period of his course in the Divinity
Hall, he had been steadily advancing in the matter of
personal religion.   Along with his study of the Bible
as a theologian, he carried on a system of searching the
Scriptures for the truth as it is in Jesus.   While he
was preparing for preaching to others, he continued
seeking for himself pardon and peace with God
through the blood of the covenant.   The first notices
written by himself with direct reference to his own
spiritual state, occur at the conclusion of a letter on
Biblical criticism, addressed to an intimate friend resident in the country.

'GLASGOW, 3d July 1834.

' My dear Stevenson,— . . . . I most sincerely
sympathize with your bodily illness, and still more
with your statement of the obstacles to personal piety.
Your remarks read me a severe but wholesome lesson.
If there ever was a being whom his own instability
and dissipation of mind were irrecoverably ruining,
I believe I am he.   I feel constant cause to complain
of myself for light-headedness and light-heartedness,
when seriousness is most of all an imperative duty.
I am grievously averse to every thing like spiritual
meditation ; on these things I can read sometimes,
but I cannot (rather will not) think.   To those heart-

communings which, above all other things, if done in a prayerful frame, God's Spirit is most likely to bless, I am little better than a total stranger; indeed, the only exercise of this kind (if it can be so called) in which I can find satisfaction, is the repeating by myself passages of Scripture, psalms, and paraphrases, in which I fear there is too much parrot-work. All this betokens a most diseased state of mind. I thank you, therefore, for your hint about meditation, and for your counsel that I would repair to a higher counsellor. These advices you cannot too often repeat, or rather, not often enough for my need of them. In conformity with your example, and thoroughly agreeing with your remark on intercessory prayer, I have set apart a small portion of this day to engage in that exercise for you and myself; and I propose to do the same next Sabbath.

'I shall expect, as usual, a letter from you next week, along with your sermon on the Divine Omniscience. Till then, believe me to be, your affectionate friend,   J. H.

'*Mr James Stevenson.*'

Mr Stevenson, who had the best opportunity of knowing him about the period to which this letter refers, gives the following account of his religious progress:—

'On Friday the 24th of October 1833, I returned to Glasgow, and spent two days with Mr Halley. The communion was on the 26th. He was then in a more serious frame than I had ever seen him before. He employed a considerable time in preparation for the Sabbath's solemnities. He read the Scriptures, and a little treatise on the Lord's Supper, with the view of assisting him in the work of self-examination. We prayed together. There was an unwonted fervour in his prayers, and great apparent enlargement of heart. I only recollect one subject on which we conversed.

It was the duty of caring for the souls of relatives. He lamented that he had never yet been able to open his heart to those who were dearest to him, and urge upon them the necessity of seeking salvation. If I were to fix on the period when a decided religious change was effected in his character, I would be disposed to point to this period, the autumn of 1833 ; but my opportunities of judging were imperfect, and I would not speak with confidence. True, immediately after the time I have condescended on, he was involved in all the bustle of the contest for the office of Lord Rector ; but though not then on an arena favourable for bringing out manifestations of Christian character, I remember nothing that he said or did inconsistent with it."

Besides the usual labours of a Sabbath school, Mr Halley had for several years conducted a senior class in Calton, to which he devoted a very considerable share of his time and regard. Among other things, he wrote out for them, and read at their meetings, a series of lectures on the Christian evidences. During the busiest season of his college duties, the weekly essay was written ; he never would allow any thing to come in the way of it. The following notice of the class from one of his own letters, will be interesting to the reader. It is addressed to the same person from whose letter the last quotation is made.

' GLASGOW, 23d *July* 1834.

' My dear Friend,— . . . . I may say just now, that it (a promised visit) must be about the beginning of a week, and I must deny myself the pleasure of hearing any of your clergymen. For I do not wish to miss my senior Sabbath evening class more than two Sabbaths ; and I believe we shall be at least two away on our projected excursion. You see I can get nobody else to *write* lectures for me; and they say they will not hear lectures, which I offered to *write*, *read* by any one else. I have, therefore, to give them a vacation; and the shorter it is the better. . . . .

' I am ashamed of myself, when I find you complaining of spiritual indifference. My mind has always been exceedingly securalized. On no subject am I wont to display much warmth; and it is only saying that I am depraved, to say that this coldness is most felt in religion. I can hardly conceive the earthly means that would inspire me with the ardour necessary to a good soldier of Jesus Christ; nothing intermediate, I almost think, could effect such a change, —nothing short of a *direct* operation of God the Holy Ghost. For his influences I have great need constantly to pray. I feel in myself a remarkable aversion to speaking of religion except where I cannot help it. There is only one kind of exercise of this sort that excites any feeling in me at all,—it is, conducting that senior class; and, when I feel myself there among a few immortal beings, earnest to obtain knowledge relative to the Bible, and one or two of whom, through the labours of Tait, I have some cause to regard as children of God,—I do sometimes feel a little the importance of my situation, and seem to myself to see something of the benefits of religion. The influence which, once or twice, I have felt the conducting of these exercises exert on my mind, has made me conceive the idea of a Divinity Hall Home Missionary Scheme, which I hope to discuss with you when we meet. Might not a few students of divinity, joining in a society to visit among the poor *one hour* daily, and meeting to pray for and report the progress of their labours, feel themselves *twice* blessed in such a work? More of this again. J. H.

' *Mr James Stevenson.*'

The visiting society mentioned in the concluding sentence was instituted, and continued in operation for some time; but it was necessarily broken up when the members of it left town.

During the two or three last years of Mr Halley's residence in Glasgow, there was perhaps no subject on which he entered with so much zeal, as the business of the College Missionary Society. In 1834 he was secretary, and the following year president. The institution had existed for a number of years; but at this period, chiefly by his exertions, and those of his immediate predecessor, a new vigour was infused into all its operations. Instead of a meeting only at the commencement of the session to institute proceedings, and another at the close to distribute the funds, the meetings were held first once a-month, and then once a-fortnight, alternately for hearing an essay and for prayer. The society collected and bound into one all who knew the meaning of the prayer, " Thy kingdom come." Many a friendly conversation on the state of the heathen, and the means of reaching them, was heard at these meetings by the younger students who went in to listen, and many a salutary impression left. We shall afterwards give evidence, from his own letters, of the interest Mr Halley took in the proceedings of the society. Those of our readers who were in the habit of attending, will remember how much they were solemnized by his prayers, and instructed by his addresses. It was at these meetings that his growth in grace could be best perceived. Those who were accustomed to mark something of dictation and *hauteur* in his manner, when he gave his opinion on other subjects, were surprised and delighted to observe a chastened childlike humility when conversing on the things that pertain to the kingdom of God. When engaged in an object directly religious, he laboured under a strong sense of personal unworthiness, which produced a very marked effect in softening and subduing his tone. His genius, when thus divested of its sterner attributes, was peculiarly attractive. Many who, on witnessing his literary triumphs, had been convinced only that his head was enlightened, saw with delight in the meetings of that society, evidence that his heart was renewed. Having often in the class-room admired the scholar, in the missionary meeting they loved the man.

At these meetings one of the most pleasing parts of the business was the correspondence maintained with societies and individuals engaged in missionary operations in different parts of the world. The reading of draft letters for approval before they were despatched, and of the answers which were returned, gave a vivid interest to the proceedings of the society, rendering the meetings a scene of enjoyment to piously disposed students, as well as a source of instruction. With the twofold purpose of illustrating the character of a society in which the subject of this Memoir was so deeply interested, and of affording instruction and warning to our readers on the subject of Christian missions generally, we subjoin a specimen of the correspondence. We select two letters which contain distinctly expressed opinions regarding the society and its proceedings, by two persons holding prominent and influential stations in the Church. Both were addressed to the secretary, in answer to official communications, and both intended to be communicated. We assume, therefore, that it is perfectly accordant with the intention of the writers, to give the public the

c

benefit of their opinions. We give the letters in the order of their dates,—the one from the Rev. Dr Macfarlan, Principal of the university in which the society was instituted,—the other from the Rev. Dr Duff, missionary of the Church of Scotland in India. The first we insert entire; of the second an extract.

Glasgow College, 17th March 1835.

'SIR,—I have to acknowledge your letter of yesterday's date, inclosing Report of the Association of Students for missionary exertions, and conveying their request that I should become a contributor to their funds.

'It has long been my decided and avowed opinion, that such exertions on the part of students are premature and injudicious.

'The object of their attendance here is to acquire the information, and form the principles, the application of which, in after life, will enable them to pursue valuable ends by worthy and effectual means. To anticipate the period of such exertion, appears to me not only unbecoming the station they now occupy, but full of danger to their future character and usefulness. However laudable may be the purpose of their association, it requires no small share of judgment and observation to select those means of promoting it which are at once safe and effectual.

'These views receive additional confirmation even from the appropriation of the funds stated in the report, the objects of which are not by any means all equally entitled to support.* Holding, as I do, such opinions, you will at once perceive that it is impossible for me, in honesty and consistency, to comply with the request of the association, by adding my name to the list of subscribers.

'I trust you will receive this explanation as a proof

* The objects to which the funds were appropriated that season were the following:—General Assembly's Schools—Gaelic School Society—Irish Society—Serampore Mission—and Glasgow Missionary Society.

at once of my deep interest in the real welfare and improvement of the students attending this university, and of the personal regard for yourself,—with which I am, Sir, your most obedient servant,

' *Mr James Halley.*   D. MACFARLAN.'

' *Pitlochrie, 7th March* 1837.

' MY DEAR SIRS,—Your interesting and welcome communication safely reached me, though, judging from its date, considerably later than the ordinary course of post ; and when it did reach me, I happened to be engaged with some urgent matters that wholly engrossed my time and strength, otherwise you would have had an immediate reply.

' I had once expected to have been able to meet your association in person,—in which case much could be advanced that cannot well be committed to writing. But it was a constitution shattered beyond hope of recovery in a tropical clime, that drove me from the field of labour ; and ever since my arrival in my native land, I have been buffetting with the dregs of tropical disease. In this way, rocked by discipline, and cradled by disappointment, I have been unable to overtake a tithe of what I had originally proposed to myself. But as it is the ordination of Heaven, I trust I have learned to submit in patient resignation, —ever ready to adopt the language of my Saviour and Redeemer,—" Even so, Father, for so it seemed good in thy sight."

' In the midst of the thunder of clashing interests, and the lightning of angry controversy in this distracted land, oh, how sweet, how refreshing to the soul, to enter the quiet haven of devotion, and there hold communion with the great I AM, and the Lamb slain from the foundation of the world, and the Holy Spirit that enkindles with the fervour of divine love! It is this feature in the organization of your society, —effective as it is in other respects also,—that inspires me with the purest joy. An alternate meeting is devoted, you say, to Christian fellowship, prayer, and the reading of missionary intelligence. God be praised who has put it into your hearts to unite in such hallowing exercises. If such meetings were more general, they would be the rallying centres of hope to a divided Church and a bleeding world.

' You advert to the chilling influence of academic pursuits on the growth of piety in the soul. Most keenly have I felt it myself. How is it to be obviated ? By constantly falling back on the touching and search-ing simplicity of God's own Word, and constantly besieging a throne of grace with the honest effusions of a heart thirsting and panting after the love of God. Without the unceasing recurrence of such soul-reviv-ing exercises, I have learned, from sad experience too, that even religious pursuits,—whether these consist in replenishing the intellect with divine knowledge, or in the multiplied duties of the ministerial office,— that even such pursuits may drain up the fountain-head of spiritual vitality, and cause the Plant of Re-nown in the soul, for a season at least, to droop, and wither, and decay.

' You complain of indifference to religion in general, and missions in particular. Oh, it is this indifference which I fear may eventually prove the ruin of our land, if God in mercy do not send some trumpet-peal to rouse us from our lethargy ! The work of missions is so peculiarly a Christian work, that neither its prin-ciples nor its objects can be rendered perfectly intelli-gible to any but God's own children. Indifference to religion in general must, therefore, produce indifference to the missionary cause. These are related as an an-tecedent and consequent—as cause and effect. If the souls of men have not yet been awakened to a sense of sin and danger,—if they have not yet been sanc-tified, they cannot be susceptible of any spiritual im-pression from any quarter whatever. And if they are not thus susceptible, no sense of spiritual wants or maladies can possibly affect them,—no spiritual miseries however dreadful, — no spiritual dangers, however appalling,—no spiritual cries for help, however piercing,—*can* produce a vital sympathy, a deep and enduring impression, a keen and heart-stirring concern for the spiritually wretched. To arrest the attention of such persons in a vital manner, and secure their sympathies and their exertions in behalf of the perishing heathen, we must first arouse them to a lively personal concern for the salvation of their own souls. To achieve this end, the soul must be brought in contact with the imperishable Word of God ; and to this union of the soul and the word, must be applied the " baptism by fire,"—the lifegiving of the Spirit of God. Then would darkness be suddenly exchanged for light, and coldness for warmth, and deadness for vitality, and impenetrable hardness for the quick and ready susceptibility of every moral and spiritual impression. Then would the bare statement of dead and dying men—miserable men, daily sinking into perdition—cause these awakened susceptible spirits to rush forth instantaneously to the relief of the perishing. . . . . . Yours, &c.,

' ALEXR. DUFF.'

It may be instructive to our readers to compare these two letters, and contrast the principles which they embody. Both writers refer to the same subject, and both speak out very plainly. The thing spoken of is the Association of Students for the reading of essays, conversation, and prayer in regard to Christian missions ; and for collecting money, which was distributed once a-year by the votes of the contributors, in aid of several missionary operations at home and abroad. This thing the Principal pronounces to be ' full of danger to their future character and usefulness.' Of the same thing Dr Duff writes,—' God be

praised who has put it into your hearts to unite in
such hallowing exercises.'   There is a strong contrast
here ; and we leave the Christian reader to infer the
lesson for himself.   Our direct object in introducing
the letters is to throw light on the character and future
conduct of the subject of this Memoir.   It is well
known that there are two contending principles within
the Church of Scotland, the supporters of which are
called respectively Evangelical and Moderate.   We
know of no sample which could give to readers at a
distance a more distinct idea of the difference between
the parties than the above two letters.   There are ex-
ceptions, in some instances pretty strongly marked,
but the amount of them is not such as to affect the
accuracy of the general rule.   The Evangelical is quite
in character when, looking on young men's missionary
meetings, he calls them ' the rallying centres of hope
to a divided Church and a bleeding world.'   The
Moderate is quite in character when he is avowing his
' opinion, that such exertions on the part of students
are premature and injudicious.'   The reader of the
following pages will be at no loss to perceive to which
of these classes Mr Halley belonged.   We cannot
point to any one day in which his choice was made,
nor to any one circumstance that formed the ground
of his judgment.   Having been brought to know the
truth of the Gospel by the teaching of the Holy Spirit,
he found that the religion which pervades Dr Duff's
letter, wherever it might be exhibited, exactly coincided with his own ; while the religion which pervades
the other letter, wherever it might be exhibited, alike
opposed his judgment and offended his taste.   His
judgment against the principles of Moderatism in the

Scottish Church, which latterly was so stern and severe, was of course formed and strengthened by a series of facts illustrative of its character that came under his observation. Of these facts, the reception of the above letter was one of the most important and effective. His predilection for evangelical doctrine did not originate in it; but it is well known among his friends that his repugnance to the opposite doctrine was much strengthened by it. By such exhibitions of it, he was convinced that its distinguishing principle—operating with greater or less effect in the conduct of different individuals—was at variance with the spirit of the Gospel; consequently, he could not but dislike it; he was constrained to exert all his faculties to counteract its influence.

Cherishing a feeling of respect for the Principal, from whom he had formerly received marks of kindness, Mr Halley did not often or publicly speak of this letter, but he continued to the end of his life, when occasion offered in private, to refer to it with aversion and regret. It did not escape his acute judgment—indeed a very ordinary intellect might easily perceive it—that amid much pomp of expression, the letter is as inaccurate in philosophy as it is defective in religion. To require of a body of young men, at various stages of their education, and at various ages, from fifteen to twenty-five, that they should attend to the business of their classes, and rigidly abstain from missionary exertions, is certainly not wisdom, though it come from an academic chair. Confine the religious affection, and, lest it should go out in a wrong direction, do not allow it scope for exertion at all, during the whole period of a youth's attendance at the uni-

versity !   You would rigorously debar a youth from
taking any part in exertions to promote Christ's kingdom, during the whole period spent at college acquiring information and forming principles !   And
will the youth whose character has been formed thus,
begin at the word of command, the day he leaves
college, to be a zealous advocate of missions ?   Vain
thought.   Even the wisdom of this world can see the
folly of such an expectation.   Tell a youth of twenty
at college, that all exertions on behalf of missions on
his part are premature and injudicious—Mr Halley
was twenty-one years of age when he was formally,
officially told this by the head of the university—and
if he has felt the power of the truth, he will answer,
' I have been bought with a price, and I must glorify
God ; I must work while it is day, for the night
cometh.   To check the outgoings of my affections
now, were to seal them up for ever.'   Such, practically, was Mr Halley's answer ; and the answer contains more sound philosophy, as well as more practical
religion, than the document to which it refers.

We repeat, that this manifesto from the head of the
university, warning the students under his care against
the danger of meddling with missions, was one of the
facts illustrative of the principles and practice of the
Moderates which made a deep impression on Halley's
mind.   Since that time, events have occurred in the
Church of Scotland which make it more important
than ever to judge accurately between the two classes.
Our departed friend formed his judgment without
hesitation, and vigorously acted upon it throughout.
We have dwelt on this matter of the missionary society with the view of showing, by an example, to

readers unacquainted with the circumstances, that his judgment was formed on sufficient grounds.

In May 1835, Mr Halley attended the meeting of the General Assembly.   A letter, written immediately after his return, contains a graphic sketch of its proceedings.   From symptoms that had even then begun to appear, he declares his conviction, that Patronage would soon become *the question* within the Church. Of Dr Duff's speech, which he missed, he speaks in the following terms :—

' I went to the Assembly with Tait on Monday last, at 12 noon, having deferred my departure from six in the morning to that hour, in consequence of his urgent solicitations, which were chiefly exerted by a certain difference of two shillings on the coach hire.   This turned out to be " pound-foolish," although " penny-wise ;" for we lost Duff's speech—a noble burst of enthusiastic appeal, which made gray-headed pastors weep like children, and dissolved half the Assembly in tears.   Nothing could exceed our vexation ; for the prospect of hearing Duff had been to both of us the main inducement to attend the Assembly.'

During the same summer, proposals were made to him for the employment of his talents, by two different societies in Glasgow.   Although he accepted of neither, we think it right to notice the proposals, that we may have an opportunity of recording the grounds on which his decision was formed.   We find a brief account of both, written by his own hand, in a letter to a friend. In explanation of the first of these, it may be necessary to premise, that the Church Building Society of Glasgow were in the habit of placing a missionary in the district where they intended to build a church,—that he might visit the people, and have the nucleus of a

congregation ready, by the time the building should be
finished and the minister appointed.   It was one of
these stations he was invited to occupy.   In reference
to it he writes,——

'GLASGOW, 12th *June* 1835.

' My dear James,—— . . . . Before I received your
letter, I had declined to become the Calton or Bridge-
ton missionary.   I deliberated long, and very painfully, before I came to this decision; but I still think
it was the right one . . . . You will say that I overrate
the sacrifice; but I think not.   I am far behind in
doctrinal and practical theology, although, perhaps,
above par in criticism; and I found (on the most
moderate calculation) that five hours a-day would
scarce suffice for the mission.   Now, this is a very
great cut in one's time, and the labour would produce
lassitude, &c.   Now, I see in the very strongest light
the necessity of a profound theology.   I have not lost
sight of the new Glasgow erections,——I could cheerfully live and die a minister of one of them.   But, if
ever I hoped to be useful in any charge, especially a
nascent one, it struck me very powerfully that variety
of topic and illustration is indispensable.   Had I gone
into the mission, I could not have attained this in the
interim.   Had I failed in conducting it well, any character I have would have been gone.   Had I done it
well, I should have been urged——perhaps prevailed
upon——to take license sooner than I ought, and have
been launched on active duty, without a deep-laid
foundation on which to repose.   I thought, therefore,
I should best serve the Church of Scotland, and,
through her, the cause of God, by abandoning this
prima facie opportunity of doing good, and striving
to arm myself for the combat more effectually.   I have
gained, however, something of impulse by the offer,
and (I trust) some good by the meditation it induced.
The offer has almost compelled me to work; for how

severe will be my reflections, if, after having resigned
one walk of usefulness for the sake of another, I
neglect that other also ; and I have learned something
of the weakness of my own faith, and of my need of
Divine assistance. By the blessing of God, therefore,
I think the whole matter may be for my profit, although I have been obliged to relinquish the immediate exertion.

' I need hardly say how thankful I was for the
promptitude and extent of your consideration of my
difficulties ; and for your very kind offer of aid, if I
should bind myself to the work. You will give me
credit for this, although I have been obliged to come
to a different determination. In proof of it, I beg to
submit to you another matter which promises usefulness, both present and future, though not of the
kind certainly which I had contemplated. It was
mentioned to me by Mr Lewis, confidentially, not by
authority, but yet so as to show that it was nearly as
good as a formal offer. I have whispered it to none
but you ; let me know your sentiments on the thing.
The Educational Society want a missionary, to leave
Glasgow in a month,—visit Edinburgh, Dublin, London,—Prussia for six months, under Professor Zahn,
—Switzerland, Holland, and France, —inspect and
estimate the modes of instruction pursued,—send occasional reports home,—publish when he returns (at
the end of 12 months) an account of his tour,—and
become Director of the Society's Normal Seminary.
He thinks there is every chance of its becoming a
Government appointment, if the thing in any measure
succeeds ; and he states, that the immediate remuneration from the Society will be about £250 per annum.
Of course, he presses very strongly the thought, that
no situation of higher utility can be conceived, than
one which aims at the regeneration of Scottish education on the basis of Christianity. *Prima facie*, I am
averse to this,—partly because it requires a sudden and

total surrendering of the course of usefulness I had marked out for myself, and partly because I think I am ill-qualified.   Let me hear what you think of it,— what you would do yourself in such a case ; and be assured that your opinions carry the highest value with me, notwithstanding the somewhat equivocal way in which this has been displayed by recent circumstances.'

The grounds of his decision in declining the offer of the Church Building Society are very characteristic. He was ' behind in doctrinal and practical theology.' He had already attained enlarged conceptions of what the office of the ministry is ; and, in his own estimation, he was ill prepared.   This was the habit of his mind in every thing.   His maxim was literally αιεν αςιστευειν—whatever he did must be thoroughly done. He had got into the habit of aiming at the highest point.   In nothing was he contented with a measure of preparation that would pass, so long as there was a possibility of ascending another step.

In the matter of the Educational Society, he was guided by the same general principles.   The thing that ruled his decision in both cases, was a desire to enter the ministry at the earliest period, and with the best possible preparation.   There is a short reference to these proposals in the following letter, written after he had finally declined them both :—

' GLASGOW, 9th July 1835.
' My dear Chalmers,— . . . . Suffice it, by way of introduction to an epistle apologetic, to say, that, as I do not keep copies of my letters, I knew not that my last one had been written on February 24 ; and being occasionally somewhat oblivious, my memory had

made a very "unceremonious preterition" of the promise to write fortnightly.'

. . . . ' Now for my excuses. *First*, when I was in Edinburgh, I probably told you I had the offer of a mission in Glasgow, which a society, who are building a new church, wished me to undertake, with a view of getting up a congregation. I lost a week thinking on this ; it haunted me every where ; I could not work till I had decided on it.

' *Secondly*, no sooner had I refused this offer, than another came, which, but for apologetic purposes, I would not mention, and which must be strictly *entre nous.* The Glasgow Education Society want a man to go to Edinburgh, Dublin, London, Prussia, Holland, Switzerland, and France,—to examine schools, and to report, and thereafter to take charge of their seminary here. This job, sweetened by £250 a-year, with prospects of more, was offered me ; and Lewis and Stow pressed it very hard upon my acceptance. I was long tortured about it ; fearing, on the one hand, to refuse a walk of usefulness which Providence seemed to be throwing in my way; and, on the other, to run the risk of never engaging in the work of the ministry. At last, two days ago, chiefly on Dr Macgill's advice, I declined to go.

' *Lastly*, a Central Committee of Churchmen was formed on 17th June, to give harmony and vigour to the labours of the several parochial and Church Societies, and I was made a secretary. In forming new societies in parishes where none exist, attending meetings, &c., nearly half my time has been spent since I was compelled to take this laborious office.'

The earliest of his journals that have been preserved, begins with September 1835. We insert the first entry entire. We have never met with a more beautiful specimen of the blending together of ' prayer and pains,' in due proportions. We commend it especially to the notice of students, as an example, in God's good providence, set before them for imitation, of what it is to be at once ' diligent in business,' and ' fervent in spirit, serving the Lord.'

　　　　　　　　　' GLASGOW, 10th *September* 1835.

　' In former years I have more than once attempted to direct my studies according to some regular system of rules, but have always, through inconstancy, so miserably failed, that shame compelled me to destroy every record of these fruitless endeavours. I still, however, see the importance of systematic labour in so great a work as that of preparation for the holy ministry ; and I have, therefore, resolved to make one more attempt, of which, even though I fail, I shall preserve the memoranda, that they may at least increase my repentance. I have set myself to the task of laying out my time, after special prayer to the God of all grace for his guidance in framing, and his strength in executing a scheme ; and I here record it as my most deliberate, humble, and earnest desire—a desire forced upon me by many sad experiences of my own weakness and folly—to renounce all self-dependence, to walk in reliance on a heavenly power, and to be always praying with all prayer and supplication, that I may be strengthened by the Divine Spirit in the inner man. May I follow on to know and love the Lord ; may my understanding of divine truth be improved, and my feeling of its importance deepened and increased.

　' I have found too minute a subdivision of time generally an evil, begetting a constraint of which one is impatient, and rendering it so difficult to act up to the prescribed scheme, that one is often tempted altogether to give up exertion in sullen despair. I shall therefore state *generally* what I am to do in a *week*, giving myself full latitude to apply on one *day* to this, and another to that, as convenience or necessity shall dictate.

' In sleep I shall spend *six* hours daily, and no more; in meals *one* hour. These, multiplied by five, and deducted from the days between Monday and Friday inclusive, will leave in these days, 85 hours. These shall be disposed as follows :—

		Hours
' (*a*)	Devotion, and reading the Scriptures,	5
' (*b*)	Divinity and Sermon-writing,	10
' (*c*)	Inquiry into the Scripture meanings of " Pride,"	10
' (*d*)	————— Poor Law question,	10
' (*e*)	Copying old Essays (the reward of indolence), practical reading, and miscellanea,	15
' (*f*)	Teaching (during September),	7
' (*g*)	Divinity Hall Library,	4
' (*h*)	Meetings of Church and Sabbath School Societies, &c.,	6
' (*i*)	Church and Sabbath School business,	4
' (*k*)	German,	10
		81

' The first five of these departments are to have, *at least*, the time above specified ; the last five, *at most*. Saturday shall be spent in the preaching society, in preparing for my Sabbath classes, and in making up for deficiencies during the week.

' Every evening, beginning with to-morrow (Friday the 11th), before going to bed, I shall insert in this book a statement of the books read by me, and of the work done ; and every Saturday evening I shall sum up the whole, and compare the result with my plan. I shall also inscribe in the other end of this book, a list of the books I read, with their sizes, and the date on which I finished them, or left off reading them.

' And may I have grace given me to be found faithful ; and the praise shall be (not mine, but) IIis, who worketh all things according to the counsel of his will. J. II.'

The record that follows, marking the number of
hours given to each department, would not be generally interesting.   Here and there, some very characteristic notices occur, especially in the way of recording
and complaining of deficiencies.   Ere the first month
is done, one of the entries concludes thus :—' Very
far and very lamentably deficient.   " O let Him help
send from above." '   In the middle of October, the
routine of the journal is broken by the following
reflections :—

' The above record, which now, after a sad inter-
ruption, I survey on October 19th, shows how unfit
I am for any good work, and how unable to adhere
to my resolutions.   After reviewing the whole, and
thinking and praying over it, the following remarks
suggest themselves to my mind :—
' 1. I am of so light and buoyant a spirit, that the
thought of my solemn responsibility sits on me very
lightly ; and this is one great cause of my failure.
2. I am too much engaged with bustling out-of-door
employments—in Church, Sabbath School, and Protestant Societies ; and this may be a second cause.   I
see, too, that it is as difficult nearly to get quit of this
as the other.   3. I am indolent, almost beyond conception ; having almost spent every day more time in
sleep than I had prescribed.   This is doubly an evil ;
as it wastes time, and as, by making my body heavier
and less firm, it renders me languid even when awake.
4. That if I continue in the same habits, I shall never
be qualified to preach the Gospel, is evident ; and it
is as clear, that I display little of its temper, when thus
destitute both of diligence in business and of fervency
in spirit.   5. If I am rescued from such evil ways,
it can only be by God's sovereign grace, for which I
pray, and to the leadings of which, as it comes through
the Holy Ghost, I desire to resign myself.'

We shall insert here two or three of the more ordinary entries, as a specimen of the style he employed.

' *Tuesday and Wednesday, Nov. 3d and 4th*, were chiefly spent in letter-writing and other trifles. No important work done; and every thing good almost wholly neglected. Shall I resolve again? I dare not, but I will pray.

' *Thursday, Nov. 5, 1834.*—Read " Hopkins on the Vanity of the World," and engaged in the exercises of devotion, one hour; read Tracts, &c., on the Popish Controversy, two hours; studied on the " Pride " * subject, six and a-half hours; library, class, and teaching, as usual. These, of course, I need not enrol; but, apart from these, I have always twelve hours of disposable time, of which, with divine aid, I shall try to make a good use, and to keep a regular account.

' *Friday, Nov. 6.* — Devotion, &c., one hour; Popery Tracts, &c., three hours; attended a sermon on Popery, two hours; " Pride," five hours, during two of which, however, I was very listless and sleepy.'

Considerable portions of this journal are written in Greek. Of date December 1st, there is a curious illustration of his literary habits. Intending to conclude the short entry with the prayer from the 20th Psalm, ' Send thee help from the sanctuary, and strengthen thee out of Zion,' he has written it in the first instance, as accommodated to himself, in Greek prose; but perceiving afterward that they would run into verse, he has so transposed and altered the words, as to compose a hexameter, without in the least altering the sense. The whole note stands thus :—

' *Dec. 1, 1835.*—Still very deficient. Devotion, &c., one hour; Oberlin—Church and Protestant busi-

* A Prize Essay on which he was engaged.

D

ness, four hours; visiting the sick, nearly two hours—
ω σθενος εξ ιερου πεμποι, ισχυν τε Σιωνος.'

Under date the 18th of December, there is a solemn
personal covenant, wholly written in Greek. It appears
that this language was chosen as a more certain mean
of ensuring secrecy; for at this period he was not at
all willing to speak of his own religious state. There
was at this time a marked shyness on the subject of
personal religion, especially in presence of the members of his own family. Although it is accessible only
to a limited class of our readers, we venture to insert
the document entire. It will be interesting to scholars
as a literary curiosity; and to those scholars who have
attained ' the beginning of wisdom,' it will appear possessed of a more powerful charm. Those who, amid
many temptations, are 'holding on to know the Lord,'
will like to see some of the secret strugglings of one
who has gone before them and entered into rest.

' *Dec.* 18, 1835.

' Εκ της ημερας εν ῇ τα προγεγραμμενα τῳδε τῳ
ϐιϐλιῳ παρεδωκα, ουδεν πανυ περι των πεπραγμενων
συνεγραψα. Χωρις της περιστασης μοι αργιας, τουτον
σχεδον άπαντα τον χρονον αιτιαν ϐελτιω η γλυκυτεραν του
μηδεν ώδε παρεντιθεναι ειχον, αλγησας πλειστα και
συνεχεστατα την κεφαλην, ώστε μη δυνασθαι τοπαραπαν
αγαθον ότιοῦν ποιεῖν. Αλλα νῦν, δια το πολυ του Θεου
και Σωτηρος εμου ελεος, αναπαυλαν τινα και αναπνευσιν
ειληφα,——και ευχας λιτας τε εμας ανανεοῦσθαι χρηζω,
ώς σθενος και επιθυμιας όσιας και φρενα μη οκνηραν και
πνεῦμα ζεον ελεησας διδοιη,——και χρησιμον εμε ποτε και
πολλοις ευλογητον καθισταιη εν τη βασιλειᾳ του Κυριου
ἡμετερου Ιησου Χριστου. Ω Θεος, μη μοι δωρημα του

Ἁγιου Πνευματος ἀρνησῃ—ἀλλα ἐκεινον χαριτος και
ἀληθειας πληρή πεμψῃς—και ἐν τῃ πονηρᾳ καρδιᾳ τῃ
ἐμῃ ἐνοικισῃς. Ἐλθε, ὡ ἐλθε, ὑψιστε, και την φυσιν ἐμου
μεταλλαξον,—και ποιέι ὁπως παντα σπουδαιως πραξω,
ὡσπερ τῳ Κυριῳ, οὐχ ὡσπερ ἀνθρωποις—παντα ἐν τῳ
ὀνοματι του Κυριου Ἰησου, χαριν δια τουτου Θεῳ και τῳ
Πατρι ἀποδους. Μηκετι ὡς ἀσοφος περιπατησω, ἀλλ᾽
ὡς σοφος, ἐξαγοραζομενος τον καιρον, ὁτι αἱ ἡμεραι πονηραι
εἰσι και ὀλιγαι μαλα. Δος, ἑνεκα Χριστου. Ἀμην.

Τῆς ἐμῆς καρδιας πολλα ἐξετασας την φυσιν, και
τας αἰτιας της ἐμης ἁκαρτιας ἐξιχνευσας, εὑρισκω (ὡς
γε φαινεται) οὑτω μικρα τα πεποιημενα, δια τε μηπω
ἐμαυτον τῳ Θεῳ παραδωκασθαι—ὡσπερ πολλοι των
ἀγαθων πολλακις παρεκελευσαν—παραδοσιν καταγραπ-
την τινα και κυριως ὀνοματι ἐσφραγισμενην. Νυν οὐν,
τουτο πεισαμενος ταμαλιστα, ἐμαυτον Θεῳ ὑψιστῳ ἐν
Ἰησου Χριστῳ παραδιδομαι, ῥημασι μεν ὀλιγοις χρωμ-
ενος, θυμον δε ἐχοντα φερων, και Θειαν ἀρωγην και δυνα-
μιν οὐρανοθεν αἰτουμενος. Και συ μοι, ὡ Θεος, ἀληθως
ὑπηρετουντι σοι δος το πνευμα, ἱνα τουτο, ὡς ἐναντιον σου
ὡν ἐν ἁπλοτητι και εἰλικρινειᾳ Θεου ποιησω.

Παντα τα ἐν ταις της παλαιας και της καινης δια-
θηκης γραφαις περι τον Θεον και την της σωτηριας ὁδον
ἀκινητως δεχομενος,—ἐμαυτον Θεῳ μονῳ ἀληθει, Πα-
τερι, Λογῳ, και Πνευματι ἁγιῳ, ἑκουσιως, σπουδαιως,
και ἐκ πολλης ἐπιθυμιας παραδιδομαι σωθησομενον ἀπο
της ἁμαρτιας και της γεεννης ὑπο Χριστου Ἰησου, ὡσπερ
ἐν τῳ εὐαγγελιῳ δυστηνοις ἀνθρωποις ἀποκαλυπτεται.
Ὁμολογουμαι πανυ ἀχρειος και ἀποβλητος ὡν, και τουτο
εὐ ἐμαυτῳ συνειδως, προς τον Σωτηρα ἡκω,—ταπεινωθεις
δε και ἐμαυτου κενωθεις, εἰς τους ἐκεινου βραχιονας ἐμε
ῥιπτω, και ἐκεινῳ παν το ἐλπιζομενον παραθηκην ἐγχει-
ριζομαι, πεπεισμενος ὁτι τουτο καλως φυλαξει εἰς την
ἡμεραν ἐκεινην. Και Πνευμα αἰτουμαι Ἁγιον συν ῥιπαις
ἱκνεισθαι βελτισταις και εὐμενεσιν, ὡς ἐν ἐμοι τοιουτο

φρονημα, οἰον εν Χριστῳ Ιησου γενηται, παραστησαι μὶ
ἁγιον και αμωμον και ανεγκλητον κατενωπιον αυτου.
Ἰκετευω δε, ὡς πνευμα υἰοθεσιας Θεος εμοι δοιη, ὡς τᾶι
ἁγιον εν τη εμη καρδιᾳ σπειροι, απο σθενους εις σθενος
αγοι, εστ᾽ αν, το εσχατον, απταιστον φυλαξας, και εις το
την αυτου δοξαν αποφαινειν ισχυν πορισας, στηση κατενωπιον της δοξης αυτου αμωμον εν αγαλλιασει.   Ταις
του ῥηματος αυτου πειθομενος επαγγελιαις, την εμηι
ψυχην, ὡς πιστῳ κτιστη, Θεῳ παντοκρατορι παρατιθε-
μαι, τῳ δυναμενῳ υπερ παντα ποιησαι ὑπερεκπερισσου,
ἁ αιτεῖν η νοεῖν δυναμαι.   Και δη ἡ χαρις του Κυριου
Ιησοῦ Χριστου, και ἡ αγαπη του Θεου, και ἡ κοινωνια
του ἁγιου Πνευματος μετ᾽εμου ειη προς αιῶνας αιώνων.
Αμην.*   J. H.

* Since the day on which I committed the preceding record (a prayer
also written in Greek) to the pages of this book, I have written no account
of what I have been doing. Besides my besetting indolence, almost the
whole of that time I have had a better reason for inserting nothing here—
at least one that better satisfies my conscience—a severe and incessant
headache, which made me wholly unfit for any good. But now, through
the great mercy of my God and Saviour, having obtained, as it were, a
rest and breathing time, I feel bound to renew my prayer, that He would
in mercy give me strength, and holy desires, and a mind not slothful, and
a fervent spirit,—and yet make me useful, a blessing to many in the kingdom of our Lord Jesus Christ. Oh God, do not deny me the gift of the
Holy Spirit; but send him full of grace and truth to dwell in my evil
heart! Come, O come, Most High! and change my nature; and enable
me to do all diligently, as unto the Lord and not unto men,—all in the
name of the Lord Jesus, giving thanks unto God, even the Father, through
him. May I no longer walk as a fool but as wise, redeeming the time,
because the days are evil, and very few. Give, for Christ's sake.—Amen.
   After a diligent investigation into the state (nature) of my heart,
and a strict search for the causes of my unfruitfulness, I find (at least so
it appears to me) that the reason why so little has been done lies in my
never yet having dedicated myself to God—a dedication written out and
solemnly subscribed with the hand. Now, therefore, fully persuaded of
this, to God Most High in Jesus Christ I dedicate myself—using few words
indeed, but with a willing mind, asking divine assistance and power from
heaven. And thou, O God, while I truly wait upon Thee, give me the
Spirit, that I may do this as before Thee, in simplicity and godly sincerity.
   Firmly receiving all that is revealed in the Scriptures of the Old and
New Testaments concerning God and the way of salvation, to the one true
God, Father, Son, and Holy Ghost, willingly, ardently, and with full purpose of heart, I dedicate myself, to be saved from sin and hell, by Jesus
Christ, as in the Gospel he is revealed to miserable men. I am myself an
outcast altogether unprofitable; and with full knowledge thereof, I come
to the Saviour,—humbled and emptied of myself, I cast me into his arms;
I consign all my hope to his keeping, persuaded that he will preserve it
safe until that day. I pray that the Holy Spirit may come with influences
good and gracious, to beget in me that same mind which was in Christ
Jesus, and present me before him holy and blameless, and without rebuke.

Our direct object in introducing the above is to throw light on the *religious* character of the writer; but it may serve very well also as an evidence of his scholarship. Any person acquainted with the language will perceive that he is quite at home in employing it. In applying the Greek to express his own thoughts, there is no stiffness—no straining. The idiom is accommodated to the thought, and the words flow with all the ease and freshness of a vernacular. In some places, there is great eloquence of expression, and certainly much solemnity and grandeur in the thought.

After this the daily record continues uninterrupted for a time, and then after an interval of several weeks the following occurs :—

' *Feb.* 18, 1836.—After special prayer for divine aid, I commenced the study of the Epistle to the Romans. I mean to devote, by divine aid, five hours of each day to it; and I earnestly pray for the Spirit's teaching. I have resolved also to resume my entries in this book; and to read, once a-week, the minute of 18th December, and the self-dedication it contains. —" Ye are not your own." '

Under date 11th June 1836, after making some necessary alterations in the plan of his studies, he writes,—

' In setting out on this plan, I desire to go on in the strength of God, for I have none of my own;

I pray that God would give me the spirit of adoption, implant every holy emotion in my heart, and lead me from strength to strength, until at last, having kept me from falling, and given me power to declare his glory, he present me spotless in the presence of his glory with exceeding joy. Trusting to the promises of his Word, I commit my soul as unto a faithfulCreator, to that Almighty God who is able to do exceeding abundantly beyond all that I can ask or think. And now, may the grace of the Lord Jesus Christ, and the love of God, and the fellowship of the Holy Spirit, be with me for ever.—Amen. J. H.

"neither know I what to do ; but my eyes are upon
Thee." I desire to take three mottoes,—two of them
from the Word of truth, and one from a servant of
God in whom that Word dwelt richly,—
  ' " The time is short."—1 Cor. vii. 29.
  ' " Ye are not your own."—1 Cor. vi. 19.
  ' " If we are in danger of running to any excess at
all, much better, since we can live only once, that we
exceed in diligence than in indolence in the service of
that great and adorable Master, who did not spare
himself in our cause, but loved us and gave himself
for us."—*Dr Hamilton's Remains*, i. 205–6.'

The journal is continued, with very little interrup-
tion, up to the 6th of September; but we have extracted enough to let the reader see the character of the
whole. At one time there is a record of abundant
labours—then a few days of comparative recreation,
followed by severe reproaches against himself for time
misspent. But the prevailing feature — the distinguishing characteristic of the book, is the spirit of
prayer that runs throughout. He never stops with
his complaint and his resolution ; these are in every
case followed up by an attempt to ' trust in the Lord.'
We conclude the notice of this journal with one of
the many short prayers that are interspersed through
its pages :—

'Oh God ! I flee to thee to cover me from my own
folly. I know that it is not in man that walketh to
direct his own steps ; teach thou me in the way which
I should go ; guide me with thine eye. O give me,
even yet, to be brought back to thee, and made an
instrument of advancing thy glory.'

At an early period of this summer, Mr Halley
formed the resolution of spending the succeeding win-

ter in Edinburgh. Subsequent events led him to look back on this as the most important step in the course of his life ; and long afterward, when tracing to it as the immediate cause, the first commencement of his disease, he was wont to speak of it with great thankfulness, that he could review the motives which led to it with an approving conscience. It is certain that the prospect of enjoying the instructions and friendship of Dr Chalmers, was itself one strong inducement to repair to Edinburgh ; but it was not in his case the only, or even the chief consideration. His primary object in making the change was to escape at once from the whole mass of miscellaneous avocations in which he was involved, that he might devote all his time to the proper studies of his profession.

About this time he had begun to direct his thoughts more closely to the work of the ministry. As the prospect of entering it drew near, he looked upon it more narrowly,—he applied to it, as it approached, that extraordinary intensity of thought which he brought to bear on every subject in which he was interested ; and the result was, such a magnifying of the office, as to produce a deep sense of his own unfitness for undertaking its duties. Knowledge in his case seemed but the discovery of his own ignorance. He attained a very high conception of what it is to be an ambassador for Christ, and, as a consequence, felt that he was far from being thoroughly furnished for the work. Not that he was unconscious of his own talents and acquirements. The distressing sense of unfitness which began to press upon him at this time, did not, strictly speaking, spring from a low estimate of the talents he possessed, but from a high estimate

of the work in which these talents were to be employed.
It was not a judgment that his powers were mean absolutely, or in comparison of others ; but a judgment
that they were mean when compared with the task
which lay before him.   To serve God in the Gospel
of his Son was the object on which his heart was set.
It was now drawing near the time when he should be
called to begin that service.   The apparent magnitude
of the object increased as it approached, and the feeling which pervaded his mind at the prospect was,
' who is sufficient for these things.'   In these circumstances, his design was not so much to go to Edinburgh, as to leave Glasgow.   It is difficult for those
who have not known him, to form any idea of the
multiplicity and variety of objects which at this time
engaged his attention.   In Glasgow he knew, and was
known over a wider circle than any other person of
his age.   A very clear head made every body apply
to him for help, and a very kind heart made him help
every body who applied.   The resolution of removing
to Edinburgh was adopted as the means of breaking
loose from all these entanglements, that he might
devote himself wholly to studies more directly preparatory to the exercise of the ministry.

CHAPTER II.

———

FROM the period of his removal to Edinburgh, the biographer's task becomes comparatively easy. In an uninterrupted series of letters, we find his subsequent history written by his own hand. Henceforth we shall do little more than present a series of extracts from his letters and journals in the order of their dates. Even where a blank is left in the history, we shall not be very careful to fill it up minutely from other sources. Our object is not to write a narrative of his life, for the events of it were not very remarkable ; but to present a picture of his mind. It is not the external history of the scholar and the invalid, but the internal history of the Christian, that we wish to delineate ; and that delineation we shall lay before our readers almost wholly in lines traced by his own hand.

The following notice of his removal, dated at Edinburgh, 4th October 1836, is inserted at the end of the book in which he kept a record of his studies at Glasgow :—

'During the remainder of September I was very variously occupied. I had to wind up my connection

with many societies, to bid farewell to many friends,
and to prepare for my removal to Edinburgh.   Read
Walton's Hooker and Donn, and some other trifles.
Expended nearly a week on some domestic concerns.
And finally, left Glasgow on Monday the 26th September, for Edinburgh.   Settled myself in lodgings
on Tuesday, and spent the rest of the week chiefly in
calling on friends, and copying into short-hand some
old notes on the Gospels.   Went to Aberdour on
Saturday morning, and sojourned there till Monday.
Returned to Edinburgh on Monday evening, and now
(Tuesday) have nearly all arranged for my winter's
campaign.   I mean to keep a statement of all my
work in another book, beginning to-morrow.   And I
pray the Head of all good and holy influence, that I
may be enabled, with a new scene, and a new record,
and new facilities for labour, to have new dispositions, and more vigorous resolutions, and a more
self-renouncing, faithful, and energetic spirit.

'J. H.'

The first entry in the Edinburgh journal is of the
same date, and we insert it to show the spirit in which
he commenced his labours there.

'EDINBURGH, 4th October 1836.

' I have bought this book, with the purpose of recording in it the amount of labour I perform.   By the
help of God, I hope that it will not prove so awfully
humiliating a document as my former diaries.

' I would commence my work in Edinburgh, with
the deep—may it be a practical—conviction, that of
myself I can do nothing; and with the prayer, that
the Strength of Israel would be my strength.   May He
guide me in the selection of the topics of my studies,
in the manner of prosecuting them, in the formation
of all my religious opinions, in the cultivation of a religious spirit.   May He enable me to redeem the time.

May He anoint me with the Holy Ghost. May He enable me to live near himself, to serve him with my whole heart, and to be refreshed by his grace. May He have mercy on me, deliver me from myself, and hold me by his right hand. J. H.'

In a letter to his father, dated 6th October, we find a beautiful example of the manner in which he reduced to practice his own strong resolutions about redeeming the time.

' I have been doing some little work since I came. Copied a number of notes on the Gospels. Have had a most sickening job in shortening an article of my own for the Presbyterian Review: I am now copying it. I have hit on a new plan of redeeming an odd corner of time, which bids fair. I infuse my own tea, and it stands by the fire 15 minutes before I drink it. During that short space, I have begun committing passages of Scripture to memory. Yesterday I managed the first chapter of Ephesians; this evening (I had some friends at breakfast, and so lost the morning time) I have got ten verses of the second chapter. In this I hope to persevere. I have risen generally between six and seven since I came to Edinburgh.

' Hoping to hear soon, and wishing you every blessing, I am your affectionate son, J. H.'

Those of his fellow-students who knew him best will read a lesson in this little extract. Of all his acquirements, there was none which excited the admiration of his friends more than the extent and accuracy of his knowledge of the Scriptures. They perceived his acquirements, and set them down to the account of a prodigious memory. His memory was certainly extraordinary; but he was more indebted to his diligence than to it. Of, these two elements of success, the more important is in the power of every one.

The next letter exhibits a feature of his character of which we shall have many examples hereafter—an intense feeling of sympathy with his friends, hallowed and solemnized by religion. It is written to a friend in Glasgow who had sent him an account of the death of a young person, a scholar in a Sabbath class.

‘ EDINBURGH, 18*th October* 1836.

‘ My dear A———,—I owe you many thanks for your brief appendix to M.’s letter. So simple and unaffected an account of the transition from earth to heaven in one whom I had known, and, so far as I knew, loved, quite melted me. I read it with heart and eyes full. And for several hours after I had perused and reperused it, I wept and prayed by turns,—imploring a like end for you and myself, and the members of both our classes, and all our friends and brethren, specially those who are either already in the ministry, or looking forward to its holy labours. . . . . It was faith triumphant. And I cannot tell you the complication of feelings which mingled with my tears over it. I hope there was gratitude to the God of all grace, who had brought, as it were, under my own eye, so beautiful an instance of one who knew the power of Christ’s resurrection. We read the strong confiding words of the subjects of formal religious biography often as something romantic and far away from us ; and I was, I trust, thankful and impressed for the Word, in its upholding energy, being thus brought nigh me. There was wonder at so plain an exhibition of what the faith of Christ could do for one in a sphere so humble. And there was deep and bitter humiliation at the thought, that it is not more than three months since I—oppressed often with fears

of my own state, and seldom, if ever, privileged to feel
that I am reposing on Christ—pretended to teach one
who was far abler to teach me in every thing truly
spiritual.

' I am averse, generally, to a too confident assumption, that those who are gone, are gone to glory. But
here I feel no need of guarding my words. Take
them for yourself, and impart to —— and ——
the consolation which Paul gives you,—" Them that
sleep in Jesus God will bring with him." And John,—
" There shall be no night *there*." Is it not a thought
almost too great for us to entertain,—yet one which,
through the tender mercy of our God, we may *dwell
upon*,—that, among those who are walking in white,
—for the white linen is the righteousness of Christ
wherewith the saints are clothed,—is the recent subject of our anxieties and prayers ? It is something
too mighty for us fully to realize ; yet *it is true*.
Dimly as you may see it now in the first freshness of
your sorrow, it *must* comfort you. And, as unceasing prayer makes it clearer to you, and a more composed mind grasps it more firmly, it will put off your
sackcloth, and gird you with gladness. O what an
honour to have been an instrument in converting or
establishing such a one. For what is our hope, or
joy, or crown of rejoicing ? Your true friend, J. H.'

The next letter, addressed to a near relative, explains
itself. The statement with which it opens is peculiarly
valuable. It is expressed with the utmost simplicity
and tenderness. We are persuaded that very many
of our readers will perceive its lesson to be applicable
to themselves, and feel the reproof it contains.

' EDINBURGH, 20*th October* 1836.

' My dear ——,—The postscript of your letter of
last Friday requested me to write you before the
sacrament,—a request with which I gladly comply. . . .

'What I inferred was, that you wished my letter to have some bearing on the approaching dispensation of the holy Supper. I feel very unable to advise you; so greatly do I feel that I stand in need of counsel myself. It is the more difficult for me to say anything seasonable, as, from feelings which were natural, but by no means vindicable, you and I, dear as we are to each other, have never conversed much about the things of our peace. True; I have sometimes tried silently to turn your thoughts that way by putting books into your hands; but the constraint of *nature*, and our inborn aversion to speak of eternity, or to think of it, have kept us from pouring out our souls to each other in familiar converse. Probably, a great reason of this reserve on my part, was—my fear that counsel coming from me might have its edge taken off by some unguarded ebullition of temper, or some particular in conduct, quite inconsistent with the sincerity of a Christian profession. This reason did not exist in reference to my class, so to them I could speak freely; but to you, who knew and saw me narrowly, I was naturally, but criminally, afraid to do so. I would like now, by the help of God, to make up for thus failing in the highest office of brotherly love; and I have all along contemplated it as one of the advantages to be obtained by living at a distance, that I could rise, in writing, to that freedom for which I had not fortitude in speech. Ought it not to be reason of deep humiliation to us both, that this best intercourse is so late in beginning, that we have given such provocation to the Son of man to be ashamed of us when he comes in his glory.

'The preparation of the heart in man is from the Lord; and it is not many minutes since, when you were engaged in the forenoon service, I was entreating Him that you might have it. Our great duty, then, is to seek to the Lord with confession and supplications. Daniel's prayer, in the ninth chapter of his prophecy, may be seasonable. Some of the Psalms, such as the 78th, which speak of Israel's backslidings, may help us to conceive the heinousness of our own ; and they may profitably be followed up by some such entreaties as those in the 79th Psalm. We can never go wrong in reading and meditating on the 51st, and the 130th. In fact, we must be humbled ; for receiving Christ truly is called, in Scripture, a *submitting* to his righteousness, and God deigns to dwell only with him that is humble. That our transgressions should be ever before us, is a needful preliminary to our being made to hear joy and gladness.

' But we must not stop here ; and we ought to be instant in prayer for each other that we may not stop here. A true view of sin, indeed, always involves a reference to Christ. If we are not at first enabled to mourn for our sins as his crucifiers—for our convictions are generally, in the first instance, selfish—we are at all events brought to see our need of him, and soon learn to view our sins in the light of his cross. Let us both strive to do this—to look unto him— exalt him in our view as a perfect Deliverer—and throw ourselves upon his work and free mercy. This is no easy thing : I am often fearfully apprehensive that I have never achieved it. I hope you have done it in simplicity, and can sometimes enjoy the comfort of it. Still we must not regard this comfort as the test and measure of our fitness to sit down at his table. Oh, it is a great thing to have it ; for then how joyful might we expect to be made in his house of prayer ! But he may give us, *in* the ordinance, a comfort which we could not bring *to* it. And the great question to settle in going, is—whether we see ourselves to be *utterly lost* without Christ, and are *willing now* to commit our souls to him in well-doing. If we are not willing to do this, then we have no right to assume the badge of discipleship. But although we have not warm affections,—although we have

many doubts and fears,—yet, if we have hungering
desires after Christ and salvation, and a real willingness to be the Lord's in covenant, we may come,—and
the larger the expectations we come with, the better.
—Your affectionate ——,   **J. H.**'

The two following letters, both addressed to one
person, are wholly occupied with an effort to minister
consolation to a wounded spirit.   They combine the
solid doctrinal instruction which you expect in an
elaborate treatise, with the ease and freshness which
you expect in a familiar epistle to an intimate friend.

'   EDINBURGH, 31*st October* 1836.

' My dear ——,—I have this moment received
your mournful letter of Thursday last.   I feel most
deeply that to such a case I cannot speak ; for I am
a child. . . . .

' Generally, I would say,—cherish your convictions
of personal guilt and ruin ; but endeavour, by prayer
for the Spirit's guidance to Christ, for a sight of the
Saviour in his fulness, for a believing view of him as
the Lamb of God who taketh away the sin of the
world, to escape from that dark despondency which
now involves you.   I would not put your soul in peril
by speaking soft things, much as I long and pray for
your release from the spirit of bondage.   Yet I may
lawfully, in the hope that the Divine Comforter will
turn it to good account, remind you that *your case is
no new one,* and often before has the mercy of God
been signalised in the deliverance of those who had
been so compassed about with his terrors, as to think
almost that he had forgotten to be gracious.   Read
the 88th Psalm, the few last verses of the 31st, and
the 77th, with *prayer*, or (if you will not call it so)
with such poor, yet earnest cryings to God as your
heart can utter.   Then, after you have seen what
others felt under legal terror, try next and see what

was their hope : with this view, read that most evangelical Psalm, the 89th, and the precious declarations
of Divine compassion in the 86th. *Never lose hope
while these remain.* Then turn to Christ, and see if
it is not a *faithful saying*, and worthy of all accepta-
tion, that Jesus Christ came into the world to save
sinners,—*even the chief.* Remember Paul, who was
a blasphemer, and a persecutor, and injurious, whom
Stephen's dying words did not move,—yet who is now
before the throne. But you will say that you cannot
realize to yourself the faithfulness of this saying, nor
feel that Christ came to save you. It were a glorious
privilege if you could,—and we must daily aim at it ;
but remember, that our warrant to come does not lie
in our own states, but in Christ's free offer. Do you
feel that you are the chief of sinners ? labouring and
heavy laden with guilt ? having your whole head sick,
and heart faint ? Then *such* as you Christ came to
save. Grasp at the promise ; and, while you look to
your own exceeding sinfulness to lay you very low
before God, look still more to Christ's sufficiency of
atonement and grace. Isaiah xlv. 22 ; John iii. 14,
15. Do not ask, " Am I believing ?" at least, do not
ask that yet ; that will come afterwards ; but *look to
Him,* and be saved.

  ' Our convictions are almost all in the first instance
legal. By stedfast looking at your own sins, and
prayer for the true use of the Spirit's office, John xvi.
8, 13, try to get impressed on your contrition the
character of having respect to *all* sin, in its defilement
as well as consequences,—of leading you to Christ,—
and, above all, of a deep and permanent feeling of
unworthiness and self-renouncement. There is yet
good hope in Israel concerning this thing. I rejoice
in your expression that you have nothing, and stand
in need of every thing. Cherish that feeling, but let
it not be alone. Add to it those brought out in the
121st Psalm. I cannot enough impress on you the

E

necessity of letting the hideous spectacle which every inward look discloses, lead you to turn your eyes on the *Just One.* We declare unto you *glad tidings.*— Yours, &c. J. H.'

'EDINBURGH, 8*th November* 1836.

'My dear ——,—You had no need of making any excuse for writing me by post. It will be long before I complain of receiving too many letters from you.

'I need scarce say, that I had anticipated the request you made; and that, though no such request had come, it was my determination to have made your case a subject of special prayer at the Lord's Table. I am now happy to tell you, that I never enjoyed so refreshing a communion, and never had my soul so much drawn out to intercede for others. Your condition, indeed, is never out of my mind; I cannot tell you how often I recur to it every day in the way of ejaculation for your good; and it was my first, and best, and most earnest request on Sabbath— yea, my very heart's desire and prayer — that you might be saved. And I may add, that, amid the heaviness and sorrow of heart which the dark character of your letter caused me, I was cheered by the thought that surely the Lord had not forgotten to be gracious, and that he meant our present intercourse for good. With ——, I think your present convictions cannot be of Satan; although I have no doubt it is his policy to tinge them with despair. Do try to preserve all that is essential in them; and, by the Word of God and prayer (for I know no other means), to keep up the impression that you are by nature a child of wrath. But oh! do not dissever this impression from a view of Christ as the author of eternal salvation, and of the promise of the Spirit's working to cleanse you from all your pollution. " From all your filthiness, and from all your idols, I will cleanse. A new heart, also, will I give you, and a new spirit will I put within you." "He hath received gifts for men, *even for the rebellious*, that the Lord God might dwell among them."

'You tell me I have mistaken your case. Very possibly I may; for the heart is deceitful above all things, who can know it? And if we cannot understand our own errors, it is little wonder that we misapprehend one another's frames. Yet, if I remember what I wrote (hasty as it was), I think it contained some such *general* references to divine truth *in Christ Jesus*, as might be useful in any case of dejection. Adam, the author of the "Private Thoughts," which you have seen, a man of singular Christian experience, speaks strongly of the evil of dwelling on sin *apart from Christ;* and this was just the thought which, however weakly, I wished to bring before you. You cannot think too much of your sin, its vileness, its ingratitude, its desperate folly; it should be ever before you; but by no means allow yourself to rest here; pray for strength to lift up your eyes to the brazen serpent, however feebly or languidly at first, yet in some way to lift them, and look to the Holy Spirit for opening your eyes, and giving earnestness and intensity to your gaze at the Saviour. True, those whom I mentioned had deep spiritual views of sin; but did their views of it *begin* so? if not, the same gracious Power that deepened theirs may deepen yours, and make them the means of leading you to Jesus. There is danger of your *sullenly* resting in your present feelings. Why will you not know that the Gospel is a *joyful* sound—glad tidings of great joy?

'You say you do not *despond* enough. I would rather say, you are not *humbled* enough; and *therefore* you *despond* too much. You are out of humour that you can find no righteousness in yourself; and have not learned against hope to believe in hope—to submit yourself to the righteousness of Christ. Yet

to this submission we must come : " Lord, help me,
or I perish." And then Christ, full of grace and
truth, replies, " O thou of little faith, wherefore didst
thou doubt ?"

' You did not rave when you wished for a place at
——'s feet. What are you, which she once was not ?
Was she not lost, although now in her Father's house ?
Is the Lord's hand shortened ? or his ear heavy ?
No ; he still says, " I have seen his ways," evil, rebellious ways, " and will heal him." Your expression,
that you are " *hell-doomed*," pierced me through with
many sorrows. Believe me, it is the result of pride ;
" *hell-deserving* " was the right word. I want the
fact expressed by this last word to be deeply impressed
on you : " Father, I have sinned, and am not worthy
to be called thine;" *but remember the Father's answer*.
To use the other word, is to *blame* your Maker : far
be this from you.

' You speak of ——, and say, " If the righteous
scarcely," &c. Yes ; it is a solemn truth. Where
will you or I appear without Christ ? But who made
her or any one righteous ? " The Lord our righteousness." Why not " *our* righteousness ?" Is it that
heaven is full ? or grace exhausted ? or Satan more
mighty than the Captain of our salvation ?

' You are unwilling, alas ! to read or pray. " The
Spirit also helpeth our infirmities." If you knew the
grace of Him who sends that Spirit, you would call
on him. " Before they call, I will answer ; while
they are yet speaking, I will hear." You will perhaps say that these promises are not for you ; they
are for all who can lay hold on them,—or rather, to all
who will come to him in whom they are yea and amen ;
and him that cometh he will in no wise cast out.

' My dear——, I am very inexperienced, and almost
terrified at my own boldness in advising you at all.
But I have not done it without prayer ; and I hope
the words I speak are not my own.

' In fine, think of these words : " Ye have sold yourselves for nought," to how profitless a service ; " but ye shall be redeemed *without money*." Don't wait away from Christ *till you become* better and worthier to go ; but go to him *that* you may be made better.——Ever yours, J. H.'

From the 5th of October, the day on which he commenced his studies in Edinburgh, there is a tabular record of the occupations of every day and every hour. The very sight of the thickly-studded pages is enough to show any one that it is the diary of a laborious student ; but he continued to be dissatisfied with his progress. Of date the 27th November, there is a break in the columns, and the following is inserted :——

' " Cut it down, why cumbereth it the ground." Acknowledging how justly this sentence might have gone forth against me, and praising that grace which has hitherto spared me amidst unparalleled unfruitfulness, I have sat down this evening seriously to consider my ways. The record contained in the preceding pages might give ample grounds for the humiliation of a whole lifetime. I pray that God the Spirit would use it, and all my past shortcomings, as the means of making me truly broken and contrite in heart. And now, after solemnly requesting His guidance, and in dependence on His strength alone for the fulfilment of my resolutions, in order, for the future, to walk more worthily of my calling as an aspirant to the holy ministry, I resolve,

' 1. To read through the entire Scriptures,—the New Testament in Greek,—in six months, beginning from Monday next the 21st November.

' 2. To read, with special prayer, every Monday morning (when at home), the Scripture denunciations which I have collected against indolence.

' 3. To be occupied in study *eight* hours every day

(except Saturday, on which some relaxation *may* be taken), exclusively of the *six* hours devoted to classes and teaching ; or, failing the *eight* hours, at least to come as near it as sitting till *four* in the morning will make me.

' 4. To beware more of the snare of visiting.

' 5. To endeavour habitually to remember that "the time is short," and that " outer darkness " is reserved for the servant who buries his talent.

' These things, by God's help, I promise to do.

' J. H.'

The following letter, addressed to a former fellow-student, we insert nearly entire.

'ABERDOUR, 26*th November* 1836.

' My dear James,—Your letter of the 11th reached me on Wednesday the 16th. It is not from want of earnest desire that I have not answered it sooner ; but, having bound myself to do a certain amount of work, I have never found the tale accomplished, till the morning was so far advanced, that I knew you would much rather want a letter than have it so untimeously written. To-day, however, being Saturday, I have fairly escaped from Edinburgh and labour ; and, after walking to South Queensferry from Edinburgh, and from North Queensferry to Aberdour, enjoying a while of Chalmers, and drinking tea at the manse, I find myself with some minutes at command, and to you I cheerfully devote them.

' And, first, after thanking you for your letter generally, I have to thank you especially for your dietetic hints. Sorry I need them. The one which vetoes medicines I have been obliged sadly to transgress. . . .

' Next, as to the more important matter of mental health. My progress in reading has been sadly retarded by this conversion of my stomach into a kind of medicine chest. However, since I came to Edinburgh, I have read, " Whewell's Br. Treatise" (twice) ;

" Chalmers' Works," vol. 3 (half twice) ; " Memoir of Mary Jane Graham" (twice) ; " Bagot and Porter's Discussion" (cursorily) ; " Adam's Private Thoughts" (carefully) ; " M'Laurin's Sermon on Glorying," &c. ; " Swift's Sermon on the Trinity ;" " Melvill" (nearly all) ; " Owen on the Person of Christ ;" half a volume of " Atterbury ;" " Cooke and Ritchie's Discussion ;" and some parts of " Dods on the Incarnation," " Hall's Contemplations," and " Calvin's Institutes on the Supper." I was much struck with " Mary Jane Graham" and " Adam" as practical books. Speculatively, " Owen " is good, but very lumbering ; yet I am sensible of having got some new ideas by reading him. " Dods" is the noblest work I have looked into for many a-day ; I do not know where I have seen such massive and satisfying theology,—although on some minutiæ I differ from him. I am sorry and ashamed to say that I have not yet overtaken " Pye Smith's Scripture Testimony," and " Wardlaw on Socinianism." I find I get on very slowly and very languidly. I do not know when, even in regard to a decent knowledge of systematic divinity, I shall be at all fit to preach ; and every thing else is wanting. I have written nothing but a sort of pastoral letter to the class in Calton,—making the main subject C.'s death, which impressed me more than any thing I recollect.

' I am delighted to learn, although it was no more than I expected, that all went so well about your steps towards settlement. I shall have the greatest pleasure in observing the time you mention for prayer and devout exercises, in connection with your trying circumstances. The truth is, intercession for you and my other friends and brethren is the only enjoyment I have that can be called spiritual ; and I gladly embrace the opportunity. Otherwise, I am fearfully dull and dead ; in this exercise, I often feel. On our communion Sabbath I hope I felt a good deal. I may mention, that every Sabbath evening, at half-past eight, being the time when Morrison may be expected to commence his prayer before dismissing the class, I engage in prayer for them. I shall be happy to learn that you can *often* join me, then in prayer for them,—but especially for myself, that the Lord may have mercy upon me, according to his loving-kindness, and either purify me for his service, or withhold me altogether from touching the ark. More and more I find my need of your prayers. . . .

' I breakfasted (*solus*) with Dr Chalmers on Thursday. As we walked up together to College,—the class hour is eleven,—he invited me to come often at nine o'clock. I made, as in duty bound, some excuse about his time ; αυτιχ' επειτ' επαμειζετ', " I'll not let you off in that way,—I'll propose a minimum to you ; you must come at least once a-week." So you see, wonders have been effected, either by my knowledge of what has been doing in Glasgow by Collins, &c., or by Mr Colquhoun's introduction.

' Monday last, I heard Sir ———— ————'s introductory,—" On the Advantages of Metaphysical Study." Clearly and elegantly written, and sometimes profound in thought. Especially was I pleased with his proof, that mental cultivation is better than mere knowledge of facts,—that " the chase is always better than the game." Two things in the lecture I heard with horror. First, after a flourish about the fact that metaphysics is the only science in which Scotland has given its name to a school, whom did he pitch on as the great renovator of the science, and founder of that school ? Why—*David Hume.* And for what reason ? Because his scepticism drew out master minds in reply. *Ergo*, by this most *logical* professor's ratiocination, Priestly was the great founder of modern Trinitarianism, because he gave occasion to Horsley to demolish him. Secondly, he laid down, broadly and unequivocally, the principle, that man, in regard to temporal things, is, and ought to be, *his own end.* . . . . .

' In fine, " I commend you to God, and to the word of his grace," as the best evidence of my warm affection.—Ever yours in love, J. H.

' *Rev. James Stevenson.*'

The above letter contains the first distinct intimation of his illness. At that date there was no pulmonary inflammation, but there was a continued derangement of the functions of the stomach, aggravated by hard study, which was secretly generating an incurable disease. Even at this time, some of his friends became apprehensive, and counselled a relaxation of study; but he continued till long after to be insensible of danger. He did not take alarm till too late for retreat. His imprudence in this matter, and its consequences, add another to the many warnings addressed to ardent students by the mistakes of those who precede them; but we shall afterwards have an opportunity of expressing it in his own words.

The distinct testimony which this letter contains regarding the enjoyment to be derived from intercessory prayer, is worthy of special notice. In connection with the promise so warmly expressed, we are enabled to insert, from a letter of a later date, addressed to the same person, the following notice of the manner in which it was fulfilled :—

' I attended to your request in regard to Christmas day. I devoted from seven to nine to meditation and prayer connected with your settlement. To fill my mind with your wants, I read Psalm cxxxii. and most of the Epistles to Timothy, with some sections of " Bridges' Christian Ministry," and then endeavoured to spread your case before God. I hope you have been largely watered with the dews of the Spirit, and that

hitherto you have been upheld and strengthened even
beyond all our asking.   You find a place in my daily
prayers, and I hope I am not forgotten in yours.'

The sufferings of his friends made a deep impression
on his heart, and never failed to draw forth the warmest
sympathy.   The first part of the following letter has
reference to a family mourning the illness and approaching death of a child :—

' EDINBURGH, 15th *December* 1836.

' My dear C.,—Your letter of Monday last reached
me on Tuesday morning.   Its mournful announcement
and request affected me much.   I need not say how
willingly I *immediately* complied with your solicita-
tion. . . . .

' You and Mrs B. will pardon my suggesting one
single thought.   If the child is removed, I would try
to do away repining by a look at the experience of
Jacob.   " All these things," said he, " are against
me ;" yet, *at that very moment*, all were for him.
His Joseph lived ; and Benjamin's removal was but
the earnest of his own entrance on the rich land of
Goshen.   Let your kind-hearted friend, if she should
ever feel inclined to adopt Jacob's complant, consider
the *reality* of his case, and endeavour (it is a noble
exercise of faith) to trust that *all is for her.*   Let
her dwell on the thought.   The very dwelling on it
may be part of God's means for giving it reality.   Her
views of duty in regard to her remaining children may
thus acquire impressiveness ; and a mighty influence
may be exercised on them, if they but see their mother
comforted, day by day, in the midst of her sorrow,
with the hope, that their sister's death may give a
commencement or a powerful impulse (as the case
may be) to their spiritual life.   The Lord grant that
her sorrow may thus be turned into joy !   May the
stroke (if it has indeed fallen), and may its near ap-

proach (if it has not), be made the means of adding to all that is lovely in that most interesting family, the worth and beauty of character which belongs to those who know that they have here no continuing city, and are truly seeking one to come.

'Pray excuse the brokenness of these hints and wishes. If they cannot testify to wisdom and spiritual understanding and discretion, they will at least bear witness to my concern. One thing more. When the result is known, whether favourable or unfavourable, let me know it; it will give point and application to those prayers, which I hope not soon to interrupt or abandon. And pray, for my sake, and for the sake of the Church of which I am to be a minister, give me also some account of what you are doing to stimulate me, or some hints to guide me, or (what most of all I need) some incitements and directions in the cultivation of practical godliness. . . . .

'I was much refreshed by what I saw of my old class. I met them three times,—on Friday the 2d, Sabbath the 4th, and Friday the 9th. The two Friday meetings were about a little society in aid of missions which they were forming among themselves. They kindly left its full organization to be accomplished in honour of my visit. I got a glimpse just, in the hand of one of them, of a pastoral letter which I had sent them, and was pleased to see it was well thumbed. So they have not quite forgotten me. . . .

'Moreover, when in Glasgow, I did about the most melancholy thing that ever I did in my life. I addressed a meeting, from the chair of the College Missionary Society, *for the last time*. The first public meeting was made in time to catch me in the west; and I actually took farewell, with feelings of humiliation and regret utterly indescribable, of one of the best-beloved scenes of labour I ever entered. The meeting was not large—about fifty; but some of the speeches were very noble. My own situation, as speaker there *for the last time*, was somewhat affecting; and in touching (as was my custom as president) on some of their topics, and alluding to my own long farewell, I was more thoroughly overcome than I recollect ever to have been. I had some comfort in feeling that I was not alone. . . . . Your ever affectionate J. H.'

Not one, we believe, of the fifty who constituted that meeting, will have any difficulty in recalling the scene, when this notice of it meets his eye. They are widely scattered now. Some of them are missionaries in different parts of the world. From that little meeting, two or three at least have already gone to preach among the Gentiles the unsearchable riches of Christ. The speeches truly were noble; for it had pleased God at that time to fill with missionary zeal some of the most gifted minds among the youth of the university, and the society presented the noblest field on which learning and eloquence could be allowed to expatiate. We feel assured, that not one of these fifty will ever come to regard that meeting as "full of danger to his character and usefulness;" but that each, from the station which Providence has assigned him, will look back to it as a season both of pleasure and of profit—a time of refreshing from the presence of the Lord.

From a very miscellaneous letter, written in a lively familiar style, to a fellow-student, we extract several items that throw light upon this period of his history. The members of the College Missionary Society at Glasgow had requested him to write the draft of an address, which they intended to print and circulate among the students. It is this address that is referred to at the beginning of the letter.

'EDINBURGH, 20–21*st Dec.* 1836.
' Three o'clock, A.M.

' My dear Morrison,—Your parcel came on Saturday, and was given to Hamilton same night. He is well, and has written a most racy article on Buckland, which you'll see in January's Presbyterian Review. His mother, &c., are all well; glad to hear of your happiness; and hugely amused with my account of your nightly incarceration. The address, so cruelly demanded by you, I have written, *et voila.* It has one advantage, viz., that it keeps quite clear of the former ones. You, and I suppose every body, will set it down as a weak and rather impudent effort at homethrusting. If that is the general opinion, burn it without ceremony. . . . .

' As soon as possible, after getting this, go to Great Hamilton Street. Tell my sister that, in laying out my hours for to-day (which, by the way, *jussu* Todd's Student's Guide—a noble book—I am trying to do every night for next day), I inserted *two whole hours* for writing her a long letter, and *one hour* for the address, of which I thought I had the matter so well concocted, that I had no more to do than write it off. But when I began, *hei mihi! qualis erat, quantum mutatus ab illo!* I mused, burned, erased, altered—needed to write a second copy; in short, have been at it from half-past nine, when I finished my tea after coming in from teaching, to this most untimeous hour. Although not the least sleepy—as my handwriting may witness—I am too much jaded to write her as I would like; so, with this apology, ask her to be patient till next week, when I shall have an opportunity. I might have told her all this, and what follows, in a separate note; but I chose to give it you, that the family in Great Hamilton Street might be cheered by a visit from you. Say, too, that I must have my alarum clock. . . . Anent the *packing* of the clock, T. will put the *pendulum* into his trunk or carpet-

bag.   As for the rest, if Janet thinks it will be secure
enough sewed up in a bit of pack-sheet, good and well.
If not, she must get the wright, *meis sumptibus*, to
make a rickety deal-box for it. . . . .

' You ought certainly to renew your assault upon
Blackwood.   For condemning evidence against it,
read any of the late articles on Alcibiades, which may
be taken quite as a sample of the work, for I learn
they are from ——'s own pen.   I look back with
great pleasure to the part I took about *Blackwood.*

' By the by, what think you?   I am not so un-
popular every where as in Glasgow Divinity Hall.
In my absence, on Thursday the 8th, I was chosen a
curator of the Edinburgh Theological Library.   The
law is, that Dr Chalmers proposes 36, from whom the
students select 6.   At the top of Chalmers' list, *literis
majusculis*, stood—James Halley.   And, in the vote,
the *two highest* were — Smeaton, 81 ; Halley, 80.
Arn't the Edinburgh folks really φιλοξένοι?

' Moreover, during my absence I was elected a
member of committee of the missionary society.   This
is to be no sinecure.   The society is not known in
college.   To make it so, I proposed an address.   Of
course, I was named to write it, on the plan of giving
every man who devises a good thing the trouble of
working it.   *Item*, I have been hooked in for an
essay, the man who was appointed last year for it not
being at hand.   It is to be read on Saturday, 7th
January.   Subject—" The promotion of religion at
home no reason for neglecting foreign missions."   If
I write these two articles as slowly as I have done
your Glasgow address, I shall have little else to do
for a fortnight.

' We have succeeded in forming a prayer-meeting.
We meet, for the first time, next Saturday night *at
eight*, in my room.   You will not forget us in your
meeting ; and I, who am to open ours, will not forget
you. . . .

' With kindest love to all, and scarcely any headache, even now at four o'clock,—I am ever yours
affectionately, J. H.

' *Mr James Morrison.*'

This letter exhibits a most lamentable want of care
in regard to the preservation of his health. Already
he had got severe warnings ; but the moment the illness passed, he seems to have been insensible of danger.
It is most melancholy to trace these records of the
process by which his health was undermined,—sad to
find a student by his candle from eleven in the evening
to four—the very period which Providence provided
and intended for the stillest rest and most refreshing
sleep—and writing, meantime, in a strain of playfulness about an alarum clock, as an artificial means of
counteracting the tendency — in these circumstances
necessarily strong—to sleep when the morning is advanced. All this, too, with ' Todd's Student's Guide'
in his hand ! Bought wisdom may be good ; but,
alas ! in such a case, the buyer does not get the benefit
of it. He has paid too high a price.

The following reflections in a letter to his sister,
dated 2d January 1837, acquire a melancholy interest
from subsequent events. Now that he has been laid
with the clods of the valley, it is pleasing to find that
he cherished such thoughts, and so tenderly expressed
them, before he had any apprehension of an early
departure :—

' So poor ——— ——— is gone, the chief companion
of our infancy. Do you know I am often led to
think very mournfully of the departure of some of
our nearer stays. I can hardly bear the thought,
which often occurs to me, that, in the common course

of providence, I must by and by lay my father's head
in the grave.   Only one thing half reconciles me to
it, that I do believe it would kill him to lay mine
there.   And yet, if I were sure of my own peace being
made with God, I could contentedly lie down with
the clods of the valley to-morrow, provided it would
detach him in some degree from his fond idolatry for
his children, and lead him to lean, *entirely* and *implicitly*, on a mightier arm. . . . He is now an old man
—*sixty* next Sabbath-day.   Let me send him, with
an earnest prayer, as his birth-day present, these texts
of Scripture,—and may the Holy Spirit give the commentary :—Isaiah xxxviii. 18, 19 ; xlvi. 4 ; Psalms
lxxi. 18–20 ; lxxiii. 26 ; xcii. 13, 14.'

The following letter will explain itself :—

'EDINBURGH, 26*th January* 1837.
' My dear John,—Many thanks for your kind attention to my interrogations and commissions. . . . .
Very thankful for your hints on Forgandenny ; only
they were too few.   Your journal I hope some day to
see.   Isn't ——— ——— a fine specimen of a humorous,
quietly-sarcastic, sensible, kind old Scotchman ?   He
is intensely Scotch,—quite a Perthshire τεττιξ. . . .
' Your questions in theology are happily so indefinite, that it does not much wound my conscience to
postpone answering them. . . . To confess the truth,
I am not able to answer either.   I have not yet
studied Heb. ix. 28 with any care ; although, on a
superficial view, I am disposed to take "sin" quite literally.   On verses 16 and 17, I could scarce say what
view I advocated in my essay,—so completely does
one forget, *for general use*, the knowledge acquired
only *for a special purpose*.   But I have often been
miraculously brought out in debate, when, if set up
versus nobody, I could not have spoken three minutes.
So here, if you tell me any objection to my views, any
difficulty I have left untouched, or, if touched, left

unmitigated, very probably I may get something to say.

' The other subject you mention, I feel to be very momentous, and can only wonder at your asking me about it, when you had A. and M. beside you, who are so far my seniors in Christian wisdom. However, since you have sent so far for suggestions, I shall do what I can ; and if you find you knew it all before, the coincidence of opinion will at least fortify you.

' From what you say, I understand there is no outward obstacle to your friend's engaging in the preparatory studies for the ministry ; and the cause of God in our land has much need of the *directest* aid that can be rendered by any one " of respectable talents and good principles." I regard this destination, then, as *a priori* desirable. The main point, in order to render it desirable *in the present case and circumstances*, is the nourishing of these " serious impressions " you mention into something deep and decided. Let this be your great aim, to lend your friend what aid you can towards being truly a Christian, and then you can urge him to devote himself to the life and work of a *minister*.

' Now, for the promotion of this grand object, you will of course direct him especially to " that Light which lighteneth every man that cometh into the world," of the spiritually born. For a subordinate help, you will find a very good, because a very serious and a very short one, in " James's Anxious Inquirer Directed and Encouraged,"—a small publication of the London Tract Society, which I have looked into with great pleasure. This will help to give substance and definiteness to his views. If more of this kind of reading is felt to be desirable, I should feel inclined to point him next to " Guthrie's Christian's Great Interest,"—a book remarkable for its plain and home-coming character. ' After " Guthrie," it might be well to warm him with " Baxter's Saint's Rest."

F

'One remark on the manner of reading these. I feel, often, perhaps generally, in reading practical works, that I do it in a kind of *professional* way. I mark the suitableness to a common mind of the way in which this or that truth is presented, and the force of this or that appeal ; and, instead of applying it (as is my ostensible object) to my own soul, I resolve, forthwith, to use it some day for behoof of the souls of others. Thus, fifty times in a single sitting at prac- tical and experimental works, I find myself reading for others rather than myself. Meantime, my own soul is starved, while I am filling my barns with the choicest of the wheat for my neighbours. The same evil appears in a different form at other times,—in an attempt to *get up* some state of feeling which is *pro- per* to me as a minister, rather than to *cultivate* it as a thing *necessary* for me as a sinner seeking salvation. Against this you must warn your friend. Let him beware of *getting up* (ὡς εἰπεῖν) certain emotions as due to his views, hypothetical as these may be, of the sacred office. Let him forget, for a time, the thought of his professional destination, and read solely as a sinner seeking a Saviour.

'Should his views of sin and of Christ become so decided, as to lead him to more direct intentions as to the ministry, then the books for him are " Baxter's Reformed Pastor," and " Bridges' Christian Minis- try ;"—" Baxter," if he is not very patient and in- dustrious, but impressible ; " Bridges," if he can be brought to read a book of detail,—both, if he would have impulse and detail united.

'But, more than mere reading on the subject *direct- ly* do I judge it important to give him some practical notion of the kind of work to which the ministry would bind him,—some taste of the pleasure of doing good. If he is not a Sabbath school teacher, you can- not too soon make him one. Any comfort and suc- cess he may enjoy will be worth a thousand arguments;

and, although the want of these *ought not* to turn one away, yet their presence, when graciously given, will be felt as sweet earnests of usefulness in a higher sphere, and as obligations to go on in the attempt to occupy it.

'Once more, you would do him good by placing him, if not there already, under an energetic and affecting ministry. Those that strike me most are, ... Any of these ministers would profit such a one much; which of them to recommend, you will fix from considering his temperament.

'And now, you will say that I bind heavy burdens, and grievous, on your friend's shoulders, while, with my own fingers I would not touch them. Alas! the truth is, I have not touched them. But the advice may be sound, although the adviser has been too much a trifler to profit even by his own contemplations.

'And yet, what need have we to avoid this trifling. I do little enough when fully able; but since I last wrote you, I have been able for little or nothing. From Wednesday the 4th to Saturday the 7th January, I was confined to the house by cold, and sore throat and chest, not very bad, but so bad that I durst not go out. Under it, however, I had to write half my missionary essay, which went off very well on the Saturday morning to about 100 people. Then, next week I wrote a sermon. On the 17th, my birth-day, I had planned some great doings; when lo! two days after, back came, with double force, this influenza, and I have been two whole days and three halves *in bed*. I am now quite convalescent; but absolutely prostrate in strength, and am working little or none. Very thankful that all cough is gone, and nothing wrong but weakness. One practical lesson I learnt, —the inefficacy of death-bed repentance. Even with my slight illness I tried to think, but absolutely *could not.* It will be madness, if, with this *felt experience*, I do not work while it is *day*.—Yours ever, J. H. ‘*Mr John Mackail.*’

It appears from this letter that application had been made to Mr Halley for advice regarding a young person who was inclined to devote himself to the ministry. The fact of such an application having been made to one so young, shows the high estimation in which his judgment was held by his friends; and we are persuaded, that none who read the letter will think their confidence misplaced. The counsel he gives should be pondered by those who aspire to the office of the ministry; and even those who have already entered into the office may gather instruction from it. The young man alluded to died soon after.

As a specimen of the style of Mr Halley’s more formal compositions on a religious subject, a portion of the missionary essay referred to in the above letter will be inserted in the Appendix.* It has somewhat of an academic tone; and right that it should, seeing it was written for a society exclusively composed of students. Scholars will perceive a chaste and simple eloquence pervading it; the uneducated reader will have no difficulty in understanding its argument; and Christians of every class will feel it a warm effusion of love to men, from a heart that is constrained by the love of Christ. We shall also insert entire the sermon referred to in the foregoing letter. †

With reference to the illness mentioned at the close of the last letter, the following entry appears in the journal, of date 27th January 1837 :—

* Appendix, B.   † Ib., C.

' Being now, by Divine mercy, recovered from illness, and seeing a serious need for amendment, and more zealous labour,—especially seeing that I have hitherto neglected my promised study of Socinianism, I deem it right to engross the following *intentions* (with the name of *resolutions* I dare not dignify any of my designs) :—

' 1. To rise daily as soon as may be after 7.

' 2. For the sake of health, to walk at least an hour before breakfast.

' 3. Always to retire by 1 A.M.

' 4. To make it my endeavour, five days a-week, to study 7 hours, besides class and teaching.

' 5. To be more regular in adhering to *stated times* for prayer; 7, or soon after, in the morning; 11 at night, or such others as experience may show to be preferable,—*only*, to be *regular*.

' 6. As I have promised to write on the Person of Christ in the Presbyterian Review for May, I must read largely on it. To this, *almost* exclusively, I propose to devote the ensuing seven weeks, *from Monday*, 30th *January, to Saturday*, 19th *March*.

' 7. For the Presbytery of Edinburgh I must also prepare a homily on Rom. viii. 1. On this I would like to consult Brown of Wamphray, Fraser of Allness, Henry ; and read Rawlin on Justification, and the Lime Street Lectures on Justification and Sanctification. This must be done at little sections and corners of time ; but it must be done by February 22. Therefore ουχ εδρας ακμη. Σπευδωμεν, εγκονωμεν. The cause is noble ; the man most impotent. May he be merely an instrument in a mightier hand. May the Holy Spirit, the fountain of grace and truth, lead, guide, and strengthen me with might according to his glorious power.'

In an entry of a later date, it is recorded, that the unexpectedly early publication of the Presbyterian

Review rendered it unnecessary at that time to write on Socinianism. From other records, it appears that he had read largely on that subject, and taken many notes. He contemplated a very elaborate article; but having deferred the execution of it at that time for the reason just stated, he was never afterwards able to resume it.

Notwithstanding the announcement of recovery contained in the preceding extract, it appears from the journal that he never enjoyed good health during the whole of that winter and spring. The account of his daily labour is frequently interspersed with notices of interruptions from headache. The following may be inserted as a specimen of the short notices which frequently occur :—

' *Sabbath*, 26*th February* 1837.

' Forenoon, North Leith : Mr Buchanan on John xvii. 9, first clause. Afternoon and evening,—could neither go out, nor read, nor meditate, nor (alas !) collect my thoughts to pray, by headache.

' ὡς αμενηνα ταυτα τα σκηνη· φαινεται ολιγον εις χρονον, ειτα παμπαν αποιχεται. Ειη μοι, δια Χριστου, δομος, αχειροποιητος, αιωνιος εν τοις ουρανοις.* Αμην.

' J. H.'

At this period there occurs another of those eager pleadings addressed to a person in a state of spiritual despondency, of which we have already given several examples. It is no piece of composed theology. The reader will perceive at a glance, that his whole soul was in it. In combination with strict doctrinal accuracy, there is the most tender affection, and a wrest-

* How fleeting these tabernacles ! They appear for a very little time, and then vanish away. May there be to me, through Christ, a house not made with hands, eternal in the heavens. Amen.

ling eagerness of appeal. It contains ' thoughts that breathe, and words that burn,' on a subject which ought to animate the heart, and fire the tongue of man—even the life of a brother's soul. The book referred to is ' James's Anxious Inquirer.'

' EDINBURGH, 28*th* *February* 1837.

' My dear ———,—Partly from engagements, necessarily undertaken to interest A———, and let him see as many good things as I could,—and partly from headache, which has returned on me in some force, I have been prevented from sooner taking pen in hand, to answer at large your two notes of the 2d and 22d February. And now, it is very late (half-past twelve), which I just put in as an additional apology to that of spiritual ignorance, if I fail to do you any sort of justice. You will, however, readily believe that I am seriously anxious to do so,—and that I do not make the attempt without the preparation of some sort of feeble prayer.

' First, then, as to the only noticeable point in that of the 2d. . . . . I think you will see, that, if not in the best, at least in some fair and intelligible meaning, you are one of those whom James addresses. Read, then, the book ; and read it carefully ; I am convinced it contains a message from God to you. But you say you are " in a state of perfect torpor, spiritually dead." God forbid. But, suppose it to be so, surely you do not need to be told,—at all events you have only forgotten it, and will at once admit it when I recall it to your remembrance,—that the new creation, the washing of regeneration, and the renewing of the Holy Ghost, the origination in the soul of a true faith in the Saviour, may be the *end* of a long course of *serious inquiry*, made under impressions which did not themselves directly contain any saving element. Such was the case with Mary Jane Graham, Halyburton, and thousands more. Now you must not expect to possess, as a preliminary, to justify you in using a book addressed to people of a certain character, or as a kind of qualification for reading the book, that spiritual liveliness to which it is in truth *intended to conduct you.* It were happier, doubtless, if you had that life already (yes, it were a glorious blessing, for it is the germ of life eternal); but is it not still a happy prospect, that an honest, persevering use of the means of arousing and guiding you, will *land* you in that glorious blessing? Don't think all is over if it is not at the *beginning* of the process; pray and strive that it may be given you *even at the end.* James finds you, we shall say, just under some concern for salvation; he wishes to be the means of leading you to spiritual life. Do try to follow him, or rather the Spirit, who, in answer to prayer, will apply to you the sayings in which James is a follower of Christ. Surely He will not deny you his grace.

'As to your letter, you needed not to ask me to use gentleness. My heart fills whenever I think of you. You complain much of indifference, caused in part by your not being much alone. There is just one way of making all work together for good—tell God of your temptations; and remember, for your encouragement, that He who so often retired to a mountain *apart* to pray, will not be insensible of the difficulty in the way of your keeping in a serious frame, and will give grace for your need. You feel, likewise, the workings of a carnal mind. And do you not regard it as your enemy? Forewarned is forearmed. Knowing its being within you, O cultivate a spirit of godly jealousy,—not of empty and peevish complaint. Let your complaint, like David's, be made to God, and seconded by a steady eye on your own heart, and a firm hand on the reins of it. Stimulate yourself by those passages of Scripture which speak of the glory yet to be revealed. Let watchfulness and self-denial be brightened by the reflected light of the heaven to which they are the appointed way.

' Be diligent,—*it is really worth while*,—especially in reading the Word and prayer.

' Beware lest any root of bitterness springing up trouble you. I mean, be earnest against allowing any sin. See if it is not some one root that has hitherto marred your comfort.

' I think you would be wrong to pray for fresh convictions. Don't *prescribe means* to God. Pray for the *end*—a believing view of Christ—the salvation of your soul. ' " Help my unbelief" in any way Thou wilt,'—should be your hourly cry. Oh! be instant; " Why stand ye here all the day idle ?" Go in to the vineyard. And may the God of peace, &c.—Heb. xiii. 20, 21.   J. H.'

Yet with all the suffering which at this period he endured from headache and other effects of a confirmed dyspepsia, and notwithstanding the melancholy tone that pervades many of the entries in the journal, he exhibited throughout great energy of mind, and when occasion offered, the utmost liveliness of disposition. To illustrate the versatility of his talent, and the readiness with which he entered with enthusiasm into any subject that might be brought before him, we insert the following hasty but clever exposition of the dilemma. It is contained in a letter to a fellow-student at Glasgow, who had sent queries on several subjects connected with the study of logic.

' EDINBURGH, *7th March* 1837.

' My dear John,—Your letter of 2d February was very acceptable. You evidently, however, over-estimate the hints which my last was meant to convey.*

---

* Regarding a young person about to enter the ministry, contained in a preceding letter.

. . . . As to the dilemma, the task is hard, especially after the sneering parenthesis of that knave A——. But here goes.

'First, then, I take the true dilemma always to conclude *alternatively*, never categorically ; and I apprehend that each of the alternatives afforded must be a true ελεγχος of your adversary, so that he is equally transfixed on all. This seems to me to result from the name *dilemma* or *trilemma*, &c., which implies a choice of alternatives,—and to be necessary, also, to distinguish it from ordinary hypotheticals which have one or both premises compound.

'In its general form it may be thus expressed :—

'If A is B, C is D ; and if E is F, G is H :

'But either A is B, or E is F :

'∴ either C is D, or G is H.   (α)

'This general *form* may be modified (although the essence of the things is unchanged), by the antecedent or consequent *terms* in the various proposals being identified. Thus, we may have,—

'If A is B, it is D ; and if it is F, it is H :

'But A is either B or F :

'∴ it is either G or H,—which is, by the by, the form of that one given in Whately (from Demosthenes) about Æschines being either inconsistent or unpatriotic ; and of the numerous dilemmas made by men in all ages, in order to show, by an alternative conclusion, that their opponents are either rogues or fools.

'Again we can have,—

'If A is B, C is B ; and if E is B, G is B :

'But either A or E is B :

'∴ either C or G is B.

'But it is obvious that these, when expanded, are really of the form (to use Algebraic language) of the expression (α)

'Founding on that expression (α), and on the subjoined formula (β)* of the *modus tollens*, I would define the dilemma to be " a compound hypothetical and disjunctive syllogism ; in the major whereof two conditional propositions are conjunctively laid down ; in the minor whereof the antecedent members of these two propositions are disjunctively (*mod. pon.*) *affirmed;* or their consequents disjunctively (*mod. tol.*) *denied ;* and which concludes (*mod. pon.*) by a disjunctive affirmation of the consequents, or (*mod. tol.*) by a disjunctive denial of the antecedents.

' This definition, which, though hurried, is, I hope, correct, may help to guide you. I have not time to show, but you will easily see it in individual cases, that every pretended dilemma which concludes categorically, is just a plain sailing compound hypothetical. It has none of the dilemma's *grasp.*

' Do let me hear soon of your progress. Pose me with some more logical difficulties.——Ever yours in love,   J. H.'

During his residence in Edinburgh, several pastoral letters were addressed to the Sabbath class in Glasgow. We give one of these as a specimen of the style in which they are written.

' EDINBURGH, 31*st March* 1837.

' My very dear Friends,——Three months of constant, though not severe illness, must form my excuse for the seeming neglect of which I have been guilty. The same excuse is partly in force still. But although I am not conscious of such vigour, either of mind or body, as gives me much hope of saying any thing that may be peculiarly fraught with instruction, still, as I have begun to write, in obedience to the constraining power of a strong affection, and not without endeavouring to hallow what I have to say by prayer, I

* (β) If A is B, C is D ; and if E is F, G is H :
   But either C is not D, or G is not H :
   ∴ either A is not B, or E is not F.

have some trust that God will enable me to speak to your hearts, and will use me as the happy instrument of provoking you to greater love to Him who gave himself for us. The truth is, that reflecting upon our close and dear relationship,—which Providence, while it has *outwardly* dissolved it, will never (I trust) wholly abolish from our thoughts and feelings ; and recollecting that the season is now very nigh, at which the churches in Glasgow are wont to remember the death of Christ, I felt that I could not let pass a time of such holy impression, without beseeching you once more to suffer the word of exhortation.

'And let me begin by congratulating those of you, who, by sitting down at Christ's table, have openly declared yourselves to be among the number of his friends, on your near prospect of renewing this solemn declaration, and again, in the name of the Lord, displaying your banners. May I take it for granted, that, on former occasions, you have found a season of communion to be happy, *because* it is holy?——that you have felt, as it were, the chords of your heart—some deeply seated principle in your nature—thrilling in sweet and solemn answer to your Saviour's reasonable demand, " Remember me?" Then let me invite you again to draw refreshment from this well of salvation—again to seek your happiness in engaging to be the Lord's. Let me urge you to think well beforehand of the various uses you may make of this sacred service. Let great searchings of heart precede your approach. Let all your sins be mourned over. Let your besetting sins especially be detected and brought to light; while the holy emblems are in your hands, pray and resolve peculiarly against them ; yea, let these deadliest enemies of your souls, which would not that God should reign over you, be dragged forth and slain before him. Let those duties, in which you are weakest, be sought out ; and go to the feast that is spread for you, with the humble, grateful expectation, that the flesh which is meat indeed, and the blood which is drink indeed, will give you a better strength than your own in which to perform them. But, while you attend earnestly to all these, oh! forget not the main object—to remember Christ. Let the remembrance of Him who bare our sins in his own body on the tree, be the great means to which you look, and which you pray the Holy Ghost to bless, for making you more dead unto sin, and alive unto righteousness. Let these words follow you through all the service—" Truly our fellowship is with the Father, and with his Son, Jesus Christ." And if you find it hard, as the " ignorance that is in us" will often make it, to comprehend what is meant by so high a fellowship, ponder well our Saviour's explanation of it, in answer to a question of Judas the brother of James : " If a man love me, he will keep my words ; and my Father will love him, and we will come unto him, and make our abode with him." Mutual love, then, is the bond or element of this communion. Strive therefore, beloved friends, that the love of God may be shed abroad in your hearts, through the Holy Ghost given unto you ; so shall you know the blessedness of a true and fruitful communion with the Father of your spirits. And let me beseech you, that, when you are seated in the banqueting house, and the King comes to offer you of his bounty, this shall be one of your petitions, that he who now writes to you may be enabled, on the very next Sabbath after your communion, to appear as an acceptable guest at the same table. Yes ; it is the same table. Though spread in different spots of this wilderness, it is yet covered with the same heavenly fare, set forth by the same bountiful Provider, presided over by the same Master of assemblies, and common to the whole family in heaven and earth that is named by the name of Jesus.

' To those of you who have never yet taken your seats at it, I intended to have said something of the *duty* which lies on us to engage in this service, when we understand its nature ; and of the *privileges and blessings* which we lose, by missing this supper of the Lamb.   But I must leave these topics to the superior practical knowledge and experience of him who now watches for your souls.

'Let me now thank you, as I have often blessed God, for the refreshment which your letter afforded me.   I hope such refreshment will very soon be given me again.

'My constant feeling towards you is expressed in 1 Sam. xii. 23 ; my constant request from you in Rom. xv. 30.   And now, may the God of peace, &c., Heb. xiii. 20, 21.—Ever yours,   J. H.'

The journal, during March, is occupied with brief jottings of his study.   Omitting these records of a scholar's labours, we extract the following, to show the spirit in which these labours were prosecuted :—

'*8th April* 1837.'
' " Cut it down, why cumbereth it the ground ?"
' " Lord, let it alone this year also."

'Though so long, in great forbearance, spared by the great Master of the vineyard, I am lamentably unconscious of any production of greater fruit.   Never can I sufficiently adore the mercy which has thus patiently yielded to the Saviour's prayer, and given me time to improve, ere the execution of the merited sentence.

'And why has this time been hitherto so lost and trifled with ?   Because God was not enough in my thoughts ; and the indolence of nature was allowed to run its course, undisturbed by any steady contemplation of a judgment to come.

'The first, second, and third thing, which I need, in order to my improvement even as a student, is a close operative conviction of responsibility,—more of the feeling that God and eternity are near me ; more of the sense of walking before the Almighty; in a word, more of practical religion; and of it especially in that ingenuous and powerful form in which it appears, when the love of Christ constrains us to live not unto ourselves. God grant that I may be " bought with a price;" and may his Spirit teach me that holy gratitude, which will make me his in energetic self-devotion, and impel me to glorify God in my body and in my spirit, which are God's.'

Three days after this date there is a scheme of study containing some modifications of former schemes in regard to the distribution of time. Annexed to it are the following *rules*:—

' 1. Continue instant in prayer.

' 2. Meditate daily on the shortness of time, the sin of burying the talent, and the grace of our Lord Jesus Christ.

' 3. Read every Sabbath evening, with special prayer, the Scripture denunciations of indolence; and sometimes on Monday, this and the former minute.

' 4. Review on Saturday night, or Monday morning, the work of each week.

' 5. Never sit later than 1, nor lie longer than 7.

' 6. Avoid more the snare of visiting.

' All which, may the Holy Spirit, for Christ's sake, enable me to observe and do. J. H.'

As our principal, though not our only design, in laying these pages before the public, is to stir up those who have lately entered the ministry, or are now preparing for it; we shall withhold nothing from Mr Halley's letters or journals which contains the expression of his judgment regarding the qualifications for the sacred office. With this view the following extract is presented:—

' EDINBURGH, 20*th April* 1837.'

' I was refreshed above measure by your account of
the conduct of the —— towards ————. It was
beautiful exceedingly—a precious reward for all your
labours and anxieties.   You have now something of
sight to stimulate your *faith*, great cause to bless God,
and great encouragement in going forward to a more
weighty and more public ministry.

' I am often tempted to rush into it under very different feelings,—those of indignation at such conduct
as that of ——.   It is often to me a matter of bitter
sorrow, that the ministry of the Word in Scotland
should be abandoned to men who do not seem to understand so much as the proprieties of their station ;
or to the forward and bustling, but ill-furnished, like
———— and ————, whom before I can trust and
respect so thoroughly as I would like to do every
brother in that work, there must be an entire reversal
of the principles of my moral nature.   These feelings
often tempt me to hasten on, as if an *intellectual* perception and conviction of the ministerially *fitting*,
with some energy of character, were all that is needful.   But wiser and better thoughts revive a severe
self-condemnation, and tell me, that although I may
not " do the same things," yet surely I, so unprofitable
and unsanctified, have no right to judge another.

' J. H.'

In an entry in the journal, of date the 24th of
April, there is the following notice of an accident, to
which he often afterwards recurred in his attempts to
recount the mercies of God :—

' On Saturday, I experienced a deliverance, for
which I desire to bless God.   Leaping carelessly, with
a strong impulse, from a high wall, I was so stunned
with the shock, and my lungs so collapsed, that I was
several minutes speechless, unable to utter any thing

but a hollow inarticulate murmur. In gasping for air, I thought this must be something *very like death.* However, I was mercifully restored ; and apprehend nothing worse than a few days of pain in the spine and general languor.'

The following hasty notes of the Assembly of 1837 are peculiarly interesting at the present time. The playful strain of expression is, in the circumstances, perfectly natural, and does not detract from the value of the sentiments which the letter contains. The reader will observe the measure of Dr Bryce pretty accurately taken, at a time when he was not so notorious as he is now.

' EDINBURGH, 26*th May* 1837.

' My dear Arnot,— . . . . . Thank you enormously for your letters. Can't go over them seriatim. φιλτατον Ιαχωζου χαρα will do ; although, you ninny, it would not come into an iambic line. 'Twas well you kept your old light ears away from those awful trumpets that *blow up* the Commissioner from Holyrood to the Tron. When you're moderator, I'll second the reforms. And yet I am not quite sure but that *kingly splendour* ought to be turned into such a channel.

' Isn't it glorious for the Church that there was so little bickering *intra fores* about the moderatorship ? The house, I am told by those who were present, acted with a cool resolution quite unexampled, on a subject on which almost every member of it must have felt so strongly. They gave W——— a very short tether, to be sure ; and they were right ; for to have let him discuss the subject at large, would have been like the letting out of water. Replies and duplies would have come ; and hot ones too ; and yet no opinions modified or changed. So it was admirable tactics to vote at once.

' Man, Duff gave them, on Wednesday, a horrid

G

dressing on this controversy—"squabbling about a piece of paltry precedency ;"—and the malicious interpret it into a very savage hit at Drs —— and ——, when he spoke of them as making the " billows lash the sky, to float a feather, or to drown a fly." His speech was noble, but butchered much, as to effect, by that dry cold body, Dr Bryce from Calcutta, following it with an hour's prosing. Duff's former speech was followed by a solemn prayer from Dr Gordon ; and how different the grand impression !

' Yesterday, a capital brush on Church Extension. Dr Chalmers let the Government alone in his report ; but Dr M'L. touched it a bit in moving some resolutions. Why put that man forward, with his inveterate Duke-of-Gordon-dinner Toryism? Then followed Mr Colquhoun, very ably. . . . .

' Anent my own motions, which you ask so kindly about. Unless health absolutely compel it, I must remain in Edinburgh, for the loaves and fishes, till the end of July. Then, every body is peremptory that I go to the country. Ever thine, J. H.'

' *Mr Wm. Arnot.*'

During the months of May and June he continued his studies, although the disease was steadily gaining ground. At last, about the beginning of July, in obedience to the positive injunction of his medical adviser, he consented to try the effect of a residence in the country, and complete relaxation from labour. A letter written after this determination was formed, exhibits more fully than any of an earlier date, the process of heart-searching to which he had long been subjecting himself in the prospect of entering the ministry. It is addressed to a friend in the country, whom he intended to visit immediately on leaving Edinburgh.

'EDINBURGH, 3d *July* 1837.

' My very dear Friend,—Accept my best thanks for the truly kind and sympathizing letter, which reached me, by M.'s parcel, about the time that you would reach F. I am sure, if sympathy and tender affection could cure a cough, I should soon have as clear a larynx as any one in Edinburgh.

' To take up the most important matter (that is, to myself, for I must be selfish here) to which your letter alluded, let me thank you for the delicacy and gentleness with which you reminded me of my hints about " mental disquietudes." I did not know of any hint but the last, and an old quotation from Shakespeare, which you yourself good-humouredly turned off in your answer; otherwise I should certainly have been more sparing of them. If that mode of keeping you in suspense had made you angry, I could not have blamed you. How much, then, must I be pleased to find you treating the matter so very kindly, and begging me to " judge coolly and rigidly, whether telling you would do me any good." After all the thought I can give the subject, my opinion is, that it *may* do me good. Unable as I am, after repeated efforts, to judge for myself, I must have recourse to some friend.

' I prefer to put the question in a general form: " Dare any one, who has serious doubts of his own conversion and interest in Christ, enter upon the work of the ministry ?" It will at once occur to you, that no one in such a state could enter on the work ; that serious doubts would inevitably work too strongly in his mind to permit him ; but we must not forget the influence of long cherished desires and prospects, which might be enough to bind or silence even the keenest feelings of self-reproach. Viewing it, then, as a *possible* case, could any circumstances justify such a step ? And here, my friend, you will wonder what can have brought my views of it to so low a pitch, as that I should even ask the question at the head of this page. Certainly it were most accordant with the general strain of my religious *opinions*, to meet it with an instant negative. But *feeling* comes in here to aid opinion ; the supposed case is *my own ;* I am, and have now for a considerable time been, in doubt about my personal interest in the Redeemer ; and, although I see not how one in such a case can preach to edification, I feel a lingering desire after the work of that office to which I once thought I had, *by the will of God*, devoted myself. Many considerations (although almost all, I confess, earthborn) conspire to keep up this lingering feeling. Friends expect me to preach ; I have laboured for it ; in my own poor way, I have prayed for it ; Providence has seemed to smile on *some* steps in my progress ; I have sometimes even thought that I felt my heart burn within me to declare the glad tidings ; but would any of these give me comfort in preaching what I durst not call, and do not feel to be, a tried and experienced salvation ? I have been thinking, as I told you at the time, that the offer made me two years ago to go to Germany, was a providential hint to leave a profession for which I was unfit; and I have been interpreting this two months' illness, which has kept me entirely aloof from my preparations for license, much in the same way. I do not abandon hope ; but I greatly fear. As to many things which I have said and done, very unlike the sayings and doings of the ungodly, I can see, in the retrospect, some of them accounted for by a cool sense of *duty*, or even of what was *proper* to my station ; many fervent prayers referable to sympathy, and a vast deal of good-looking actions the fruit of the subtle sin— hypocrisy.

'Write me your thoughts on the whole matter, and as soon as you can ; and above all, pray for me, that I may be enabled so to repair to the blood of sprinkling, as to obtain the comfort of a felt union to the

Saviour. . . . . Dr Alison—whom I allow to be my *dictator*, while *I weigh* the advices of non-professional friends—has ordered me, for the cough, on which the last month has effected scarcely any improvement, to leave Edinburgh by the middle of July. . . . .

' Write soon, and tell me the welcome news that you are to be at home. Do not treat me too tenderly as to my doubt. That is your extreme. Try to be quite faithful. Your most affectionate, J. H.'

In reply to this letter, his friend urged that it was nothing new he was about to undertake ; that already in Sabbath schools and otherwise he had been preaching Christ and delighting in it ; that his arguments against accepting license to preach applied with equal force to what he had already been doing. In reference to this, we find Mr Halley, four days afterwards, writing to the same person,—

' EDINBURGH, *7th July* 1837.

' . . . . And now, my dear friend, let me thank you for that very affectionate part of your letter which related to the cause of my mental disquietudes. I was much impressed by it. I hope, by the nourishing of these impressions, I may be profited. You will rejoice to learn that I feel it has done me some good. Were I to enter into argument with you on the subject, I would say, that you have *proved* one of two things, (the sad difficulty is, *which ?*) *either* that I should never have begun preparation for the ministry, *or* that I should now finish it by undergoing the vows of license. I am more apt to draw this disjunctive conclusion from your premises, than your own categorical one. But I will not argue on the point. I have seen, in some cases, with what perverse ingenuity a despondent person can reason against himself; and I would not expose myself to the temptation. While I cordially thank you for the

letter, let me entreat a peculiar place in your prayers.
Be importunate for me, for I can never reach that
myself, that in this matter I may be guided aright;
and that the "great concern" may be all well,—my
spirit saved in the day of the Lord Jesus.

'That you may be more and more blest, and more
and more happy in his service, is the earnest desire of
your affectionate friend,   J. H.'

In this extract the reader will not fail to observe a
remarkable combination of ardent feeling and sound
judgment.   Oppressed by a sense of want and unworthiness, as his bodily health declined, his spirit
was sinking under an increasing weight of despondency—*feeling* led him to despond ; but knowing that
this power of arguing against himself might be a ' perverse ingenuity,' he determined to guard against the
danger.   Uncertain where the exact line of duty lay
between the extremes of presumption and despondency, he did as all who have been led by the Spirit
before him have done ; as David—' Out of the depths
have I cried unto thee, O Lord ;' and as Paul,—
' Brethren, pray for us.'

By this time Mr Halley had become very much
reduced in strength ; most of the symptoms which
usually indicate the existence of pulmonary disease had
appeared,—the night perspirations, the chest pains,
and the cough.   His appearance was altogether that
of a consumptive patient.   Urged by his friends, and
beginning himself to be alarmed at the character of
the malady, he at last broke off all his engagements
in Edinburgh, and left it on the morning of the 15th
of July.   His first retreat was with one of his former
class-fellows in Strathearn, in the immediate neigh-

bourhood of Perth. During the two weeks spent there, his health was very much improved. His strength increased ; his appearance became fresher ; and the symptoms of disease were alleviated. The change had a very marked effect in elevating his spirits. During the journey from Edinburgh he was very cheerful. As soon as he arrived at his destination, and without any rest, he had himself seated on a chair below the shade of a tree, and wrote there a poem in Greek hexameters, commemorative of an incident that had occurred in the stage-coach. The verses—forty-three in number—were sent immediately by post to a friend in Glasgow.* They have been preserved, and though of no consequence themselves, are valuable as a proof of the amazing facility with which he could express *impromptu*, in the language and numbers of Homer, the common incidents of the day. In this he appeared the scholar. On the same evening he was enabled to exhibit, in a remarkable manner, a more precious gift. Having been asked to conduct the worship of the family, he prayed with a fulness and unction altogether beyond what he was

---

* The incident, though very trifling in itself, was strongly impressed on his mind by the circumstances in which it occurred, and he often afterwards referred to it. The following note of it, written by his fellow-traveller, on a part of the same sheet which contained the original verses, may be interesting to some of our readers :—' Halley is engaged on a heroic poem, which goes into the third page. I must give you the facts on which it is founded.—Coming from Edinburgh, he sat on the driver's seat. I sat right behind him, and two other gentlemen were on the same seat with me. One of them was intelligent and polite. We got acquainted with him, and talked not a little. The day was warm. *Clegs* (grey blood-sucking insects) were abundant. One alighted on the neck of said gentleman's coat —low, towards the shoulder. Halley has an utter abhorrence of the insect ; and no sooner had he seen it perch, than he was smitten with an immoderate desire for its destruction. " Stop," says he, with the utmost eagerness of tone and gesture ; " sit still, sir,—there's a *cleg* on your coat." Whereupon he brandished a heavy peeled knotty stick around his head, and came thwack down, right across the middle of the gentleman's cheek. The scene that followed cannot be described in prose : the *cleg* escaped. The assailant attempted an apology, but, meantime, I had lost my gravity, and the begun apology terminated in a laugh.'

wont to attain ; and his attainments on ordinary occasions were great.   The prayer was remarked at the
time by those who heard it ; and it was discovered,
by a reference made to it in a letter long after, that he
had felt himself more than usually free, and looked
back to it all his life as a time of refreshing from the
presence of the Lord.

At the end of July Mr Halley was removed to Tillicoultry to spend the month of August, under the
hospitable roof of his kinsman, the Rev. Mr Anderson,
minister of the parish.   While there, his health was
apparently still farther improved.   We are enabled to
give, in his own words, an account of his progress in
the earlier part of August.   Although the letter is
written in a somewhat playful strain, it is inserted
almost entire.   It exhibits great buoyancy of spirits,
at a time when there was much to make him sad.

' TILLICOULTRY, 10th *August* 1837.
' My dear John,—You talked so heroically in your
note the other day about your preference of letters to
pence, that I am impelled to test the sincerity of your
gloriation, by this speedy infliction of a postage.   A.,
in the kindness of his heart, insisted that I should
write each week to some of my Glasgow friends an
account of my state and progress.   Last week, having
an opportunity, by the hands of cousin H., I wrote to
J. ; but this week, having no such opportunity, I have
resolved to amerce you in the sum of 9½d. sterling
money, as a punishment (though too slight a one) for
the shortness and rarity of your communications.

' In answer, then, to the supposed " How d'ye do ?"
of all you folks in Glasgow, I have to say—" Better,
on the whole."   My cheeks have unquestionably filled
up considerably ; and my legs and arms are getting a
little less like pins, and more like the fins of a human

animal. The cough abated very much during the warm days ; but yesterday's east wind brought it back nearly (not quite) as it was when I left Forgandenny. The breathlessness is so far reduced, that I can walk faster on a level ; but it afflicts me much in any attempt to ascend. The perspirations are much less than formerly. The rheumatics are a good deal quieter, though not defunct. But the inward pain in the chest, connected with the cough, was, this morning, fully worse than I ever felt it. I must confess frankly, that so long as this remains, I have no great faith in the general improvement of appearance, as regards plumpness, &c., which mere regimen produces, and therefore do not consider my recovery at all so far advanced as my countenance would lead one to suppose. But it is, I think, advancing ; and I hope, by the Divine goodness, will go on to its completion. I am even beginning to entertain hopes of being *physically* (alas! how little *morally !*) able to preach in a few months, and of not needing so long a recline upon the shelf as A. was prescribing for me. Yet I believe I have more need to pray for strength to curb the impatience of my disposition, and for preparation to be taken away in mid-time of my days, if such a decree should have passed respecting me. I confess myself to know far too little of submission ; but I see its necessity in all events ; and my great desire is to be found not an unwilling learner.

'You can't expect news from a *solitaire*. Yet I have one piece of news for you. On Friday afternoon, who should step in but James Hamilton, as a deputation from Edinburgh, to know how I was getting on. He stayed the night with us, and visited Alva Glen in the morning before breakfast, where he caught four botanical rarities. Afterwards, he and I walked to Dollar (2½ miles), and he ascended to Castle Campbell, wherewith he was greatly delighted. We walked back—which, I hope, conveys to you a due idea of my valour. In the afternoon he went off jubilant to Edinburgh.

' In most resigned obedience to the commands of Arnot and the other authorities, I am doing nothing that can be called study. Scottish Guardians, Records, Christian Instructors, and the Edinburgh Almanac, have been my chief companions. Besides doing justice to these, I have read two very good sermons by Mr Glen of Benholme, entitled " Comfort and Counsel for Sea-Faring People," Hurrion " On the Knowledge of Christ Crucified," and the Presbyterian Review for August.

' Let me hear from you soon, and long. I am sure I give liberal measure, whether in Greek or English.

' My pupil, J. M., has gained *ten* prizes in the Academy ; W. R., four. Rejoice with me at this.

' *Vale et vive.*   *Tuus semper,*   J. H.'

' *Mr John Mackail.*'

On his return to Glasgow, about the beginning of September, the state of his health became a matter of most anxious concern to his numerous friends. The plans for the approaching winter, so far as at that date they had been suggested, are shortly mentioned in the following letter to a minister in the country.

' GLASGOW, 16*th September* 1837.

' My dear James,— . . . . . Since I wrote you from Tillicoultry, my health has a good deal improved. I have about doubled the meagre stock of flesh which clothed my bones when I took up my residence there. My general strength has grown so much, that I can now walk about ten miles in a day without much fatigue. The cough, however, and pain in the chest, continue with but little improvement ; and I am much pained with stitches over half my body. Twice, during my stay at Tillicoultry, I made a run to Edinburgh to see Professor Alison. On both occasions,

he assured me that any attempt to preach, for many
months to come, would be attended with much danger, and strenuously urged me not to spend the winter
in Scotland.   He spoke at first of a voyage to Madeira,
but afterwards recommended Jersey, or the south of
England.   I just wait the leadings of Providence, to
see whither I must go.

' I had thought of coming to see you towards the
end of this month, previously pledging and engaging
myself to keep by myself, and not interrupt your
studies.   My principal view was to have enjoyed,
under your ministry, the communion of the body and
blood of our Lord.   I am still anxious for this, and
may perhaps accomplish it.   The only barrier is the
earnestness of many friends that I should leave Scotland before September closes.   But this, I think, is
impossible at any rate.   So that I *may* be with you at
that solemn season.   At all events, although I cannot
fix a day, as my complaint varies much with the weather, I hope to be at Newton manse in the course of
next week, or the one following.

' I could say much more, but leave it till we meet,
as the writing posture is not a salutary one.

' Only let me explain that defect which you notice
in my letters—a want of such spiritual remarks as
might serve the great end of mutual excitement to
diligence in Christ's work.   The reason is most humiliating—the barrenness and deadness of my own soul.
I feel little disposed to account for this, as I do for a
certain intellectual feebleness of which I am often conscious, by physical causes ; but am compelled to refer
the whole to an evil heart of unbelief, in departing
from the living God.   This has cost me, when I was
able to reflect at all, many sad reflections.   It threw
a chill over my mind in sickness, and obscured my
view of Him who is the hope of Israel, and the Saviour
thereof in time of trouble.   It gave a bitter flavour to
almost all my thoughts.   Especially, it pressed me

with doubts and fears about entering on the ministry
at all, and has led me to view my present sickness as
a confirmation of these doubts. From such reflections
I have only been relieved by excluding thought altogether. On the subjects from which I ought to draw
my comfort, my mind wanders.

'In a word, I have been taught impressively how
frail we are, and that he who trusteth in his own heart
is a fool. Yet, if I have any reliance at all, it is in
Christ's blood and Spirit.

'Ever your affectionate friend,   J. H.'

'*Rev. James Stevenson.*'

We request the attention of every reader to the
latter part of the above letter. We think it exhibits
an instructive example of Christian humility. Those
who had an opportunity of knowing the natural disposition of the penitent, will not fail to recognise the
wonderful work of God in so completely subduing his
spirit. It was not naturally meek. There were in
his conduct many traces of an imperious disposition.
In matters connected with secular knowledge, he was
not easily induced to yield. When challenged, he
maintained his point always with great boldness,—
sometimes with obstinacy. It required, indeed, no
small degree of courage to oppose him. But in the
matter of personal practical religion, any one might
rebuke him with perfect impunity. In this he would
submit to the meanest. The moment you introduced
the idea of his own relation to God, all his pride of
intellect was subdued—the imperiousness of his disposition vanished—and he was ready to esteem every
one better than himself. This visit was accomplished;
and the invalid enjoyed for a few days the hospitality
and faithful instructions of a fellow-student, now a

minister of the Gospel, whom he had always respected as a counsellor, and loved as a friend.

As the season advanced, the symptoms of his disease became more strongly marked, and towards the end of October, it was determined that he should spend the winter in a warmer climate. The resolution, and the immediate occasion of it, are announced by himself in the following hurried note, addressed to Mr James Hamilton :—

'GLASGOW, 24*th October* 1837.

' My dear James,—Dr Watson, whom I saw after my return, gave me a more serious view of my complaint than my former advisers. He denounced Jersey as a half measure, and very strongly recommended Madeira. The same day a providential opening appeared for my getting abroad. . . . . I have resolved, then, to go to Madeira, fully aware that this affords me the only chance (if I may so speak) of longer days. I feel some trust (would it were more) in God, and that all will be well. I greatly need your fervent and constant intercessions for a spirit of submission, for unshaken faith, for a lively hope, for a sense of the Divine favour. . . . .

' I have met with much unlooked-for kindness. " O magnify the Lord with me." Farewell—perhaps for ever ; but wherever I am, believe me still your affectionate friend, J. H.'

The providential opening referred to in this note, was an offer of a few gentlemen in Glasgow to defray the expense of his journey and residence in Madeira. While this act speaks much for the Christian liberality of those who gave, it is also a substantial eulogium on the character of him who received. It shows how highly his life was valued in his native place, where his talents were best known. Still farther to the credit of both parties, it should be told, that this munificence was not wholly, nor chiefly, an act of personal friendship; it was done on public grounds.   One at least of his benefactors, and that, too, the one who bore the heaviest share of the expense, had never seen Mr Halley till the day before he sailed.   In this instance, those rich men, who are in some degree enabled to account themselves stewards of the gifts of God, gave of their substance, not so much to save the life of a friend, as to preserve for labour in the vineyard, one to whom the ten talents had been committed by the Sovereign Lord.   A very considerable sum was expended.   It was not an act of common benevolence. It had the character of a contribution in behalf of the Church of Christ.   It was a gift brought to the altar.

The preparations for departing were very speedily made.   At the conclusion of a letter written two days before sailing, occurs the following sentence, which gives some indication of the state of his mind in leaving his native country :—

' My heart has been much shaken within me ; but now all is plain.   My prevailing feeling is, that, *if ever I return*, it will be under tremendous obligations to labour more abundantly.'

The same sentiments are more fully expressed in another letter written on the following day :—

' My hopes of life are not very sanguine.   I never calculated on being a long liver; would that my expectations had more influenced my conduct.   I am not one of those who can look back with much pleasure on former experiences.   I have been a transgressor from the womb; and but for the freeness of the outward call I should faint.   But I have been wonderfully supported.   I can now look forward with some composure, if God should appoint me them, to the weary feverish nights of the confirmed consumption. Let me entreat you to pray, that, if the outward man is destined to perish, the inward man may be renewed day by day. I feel with Manoah's wife (Judges xiii. 23), that, " if the Lord were pleased to kill me, he would not have showed me all these things." So many of his dear children are deeply interested in my recovery, and so many prayers (I have reason to believe) are presented for it, and so many of those who labour in his cause have exerted themselves to render me comfortable in my exile,—that I do hope he has some work for me to do yet in his Church. But I look to him for strength to do, or to suffer all, and to be ready to depart whenever he calls me. In a season of much perplexity I have peculiar need of your prayers. I do not forget you in your labours and trials. May you be a blessing ; and may the blessing of him that is ready to perish come upon you.'

Ardently desiring to recover, that he might preach the Gospel, he had a pretty strong hope of getting benefit *through* a residence in Madeira ; but his expectation all the while was '*from* the Lord.'

CHAPTER III.

———

On Saturday, 28th October 1837, Mr Halley sailed from Glasgow, accompanied by his sister. His route was from the Clyde to Dublin, and thence to Falmouth, the station of the packet to Brazil. We insert, from a letter to his father, a brief account of these first stages of the journey.

'FALMOUTH, *4th November* 1837.

' My dear Father,—I ought certainly to have written you yesterday, as I promised to write immediately on arriving here, and we got ashore yesterday morning. But I was very much knocked up with our voyage, and thought I would be better able to do it after a night's repose.

' We have much cause, then, I am happy to say, for thankfulness, on account of the state in which we have been enabled to finish this first part of our voyage. We reached Dublin on Sabbath morning, having been twenty-six hours on board the *Mercury*. Janet was very sick. I got to my berth before it reached that point with me, and was happily preserved. The steamer was very full; and the heat in our berths was almost suffocating. But a little fresh air on Sabbath morning (which was a shining one) set us all right again, and we got ashore in tolerably good spirits. By the steward's advice, we went to the " Imperial Hotel," which he said was good and very moderate. We found, however, that his views of moderation differed from ours. Nevertheless, we were certainly very comfortable. On Monday, it rained so much, that we could do no more than take our places in Wednesday's steamer for Falmouth ; but on Tuesday we had a good clear sky, and saw a little of Dublin. After Edinburgh, it did not greatly please us. . . . .

' On Wednesday we left Dublin by a car for Kingstown, where we were to find out steamer for Falmouth. An exquisitely Irish scene occurred at the harbour, —three or four boatmen trying severally to make a prize of us. Janet promises you a full description of them, in a journal of remarkable incidents, which she is always vigorously threatening to commence, but has never yet actually begun.

' Our fellow-passengers in the *Leeds* (for that was our vessel's name) were just two students of Trinity College, Dublin, with whom, during daylight on Wednesday, I had much interesting chat. One of them, named Johns, turned out to be a botanist, and a correspondent of Sir William Hooker. On Wednesday night it became rough, and on Thursday blew a storm. We were all in our berths tolerably sick ; but, through a port-hole, I could see the waves a good way above the paddle-boxes. Though very inferior in accommodation, the steamer proved an excellent sea-boat. We got round the Land's End about midnight on Thursday ; at half-past one we passed the Lizard lights ; at four, we lay to at the mouth of Falmouth harbour, waiting for the day ; and at eight, by advice of Mr Johns, who came on shore along with us, we stepped on board a nice four-oared boat, which came out to see if any of the passengers chose to put up at the Green Bank. I took care to make sure, by inquiry, that the charges were more moderate than those

H

of the Imperial ; and we see every prospect of being comfortable for the next week.   When I first came ashore I was very much exhausted, every bone and muscle being racked by lying on my back so long, under such fearful pitching ; but a good breakfast and a tepid bath set me much to rights.   I now cough little. The weather, though cold yesterday, was mild to-day ; and Janet and I had a very pleasant walk of nearly two hours. . . . .

' During Thursday night, when we were at sea, other steamers were putting back into Falmouth through stress of weather.   I mention this, that you may join in thanksgiving to Him who sitteth on the floods, for our safe arrival.   God willing, our vessel sails next Friday at ten.   You will remember us then, and we will not forget you.   Of course, we shall write whenever we can ; and meanwhile, praying that every good thing may rest and abide on you,—I am your ever affectionate son,   J. H.'

The following short extract is interesting, as indicating the tone of his mind when on the eve of departing from his native land.   The letter is addressed to a gentleman in the south of Scotland.

' FALMOUTH, 8th *November* 1837.

' My dear Sir,—I can really hardly see any right that I have to inflict a letter on you from so great a distance.   My apology must be, that, having been unable, from the vast amount of things I had to do, to write you, as I promised, from Glasgow, this is the next best measure to which I can resort.   So busy was I while at home, and so occupied with the kind visits of friends, that, for days together, I really had not ten minutes which I could call my own.   Now, however, in the solitude (for such it is to me) of an English inn, and just waiting the sailing of the *Madeira* packet, I remind myself of Prometheus, when his being *bound* gave him time enough, and to spare, to tell the Oceanides his story :—

Σχολη δε πλειων η θελω παρεστι μοι.

' . . . . . Our places are taken in the packet—the " Lyra," Captain Forrester ; and on Friday next, at 10 A.M., probably before you receive this, we shall be once more on the " glad waters of the dark-blue sea."

' I do not go without hope of recovery, though I am far from sanguine. My right lung, it seems, is a good deal wasted ; but the case is not worse than others to which Madeira has been beneficial. Yet there is no doubt but I am every day getting perceptibly thinner. I now know a little, through increasing weakness, of their state, to whom the grasshopper is a burden. Still, there has been something so providential in the outset of this voyage, that I feel disposed to trust and not be afraid of its issue. " If he had meant to kill me, would he have shown me all these things ?" I am sure, at all events, I find a place in the prayers of not a few ; may I say, also, in yours ? Let me hint to you that I feel especial need,—besides the fundamental blessing of a secure interest in the Saviour,—of submission to the Divine will, and of the spirit of adoption.

' Be much in asking these for me ; and believe me to be, with every good wish for time and eternity, very sincerely yours,   J. H.'

' *Rev. J. Whitelaw.*'

While the invalid was hovering on the verge of his native land, waiting for the ship that should waft him away, it might be for ever, the current of his thoughts naturally ran back toward home and past enjoyments. Among the cherished objects that busy memory presented then, the Sabbath class seems to have been the most attractive. A pastoral address, written at Falmouth, and sent to his adult class at Glasgow, has been preserved, and we gladly insert it here.   It is a valuable document, and we present it entire.

'FALMOUTH, 9*th November* 1837.

' My dear Friends,—It is not unlikely that I now address you for the last time.   The disease which has compelled me to go to a foreign country in search of some relief, is one from whose grasp very few escape; and even should God work out for me so great and unusual a deliverance, and restore me to the place of my birth, there will lie on me so enormous and accumulated an obligation to enter on some labour in his Church, that I can scarcely expect again to raise my voice among you.   We stand, then, to each other, in circumstances of no common solemnity.   And I feel, that, in this position, I should fail in *duty*, did I not try to give once more to the truths of the Gospel all the impressiveness which our altered condition may impart to them, and to speak to you of the things of your peace, as one who enters to-morrow on a voyage, from which his first haven may be in eternity.   Nor can I think that I mix too much of human feeling with my thoughts on these high topics, when I tell you, that I would have felt a want of some reasonable and heartfelt *enjoyment*, if I had not, at this season, sent my affections back to that little scene of " opening the Scriptures," which was long one of their most cherished and sacred abodes.

' And now, my dear friends, in looking back deliberately to our intercourse, as far as it regarded the word of truth, I cannot see that I have now any other Gospel to declare to you, than that which, in much weakness, I formerly endeavoured to unfold.   These are my firm and unaltered convictions,—and I trust will be so to my dying hour,—founded, as I believe them to be, on the Holy Scriptures: that we are all lost and ruined, both in Adam and in ourselves; that

God, in free and sovereign mercy, hath found out a ransom ; that Christ bore our sins in his own body on the tree ; that the benefits of his mediation are apprehended and received by faith ; that this grace, along with all the elements of a new obedience, is the gift of the Holy Ghost ; that that good and free Spirit is given to all who ask him ; and that, having begun in them a good work, He will carry it on, in spite of all difficulties and temptations,—impart to them strength according to their day,—cleanse them at last from every spot and speck of earthliness,—and fit them for the pure and holy society of the kingdom that cannot be moved.

'This glorious salvation is in the offer of every one of you.   And I trust some of you know what it is to have embraced it as their own ; and have seen enough of the wretchedness of nature, and the freeness of grace, and the fulness that is in Christ,—to make them give themselves up, soul and body, to that beseeching Saviour, and lay hold of the everlasting covenant, and labour, by a holy walk, to prove themselves the disciples of a holy Master.   One thing, my beloved friends, is certain, that through this process *every one* of us must pass, ere we can become partakers of the inheritance.   This is the gate through which alone we can ever enter into the heavenly city. "Open ye the gates" is the divine proclamation.   O be persuaded to pass within : " Salvation hath God appointed for walls and bulwarks."

'But ye need not that I thus remind you what be the first principles of the oracles of God.   Let me rather take for granted, that you know and are convinced of the *absolute necessity of faith ;* and let me insist upon the desirableness of having something farther,—even a comfortable belief and confidence that this faith has indeed been wrought in you.   Many, doubtless, of those who are God's children, walk in darkness as to their acceptance with him, and have no

light on the evidences of their calling.   Many may be
saved, as by fire, without enjoying the sense of the
Divine favour here, until it fully burst on them hereafter.   But this is always their sorrow ; and their
cry is, " O when wilt thou come unto me ?"   " *Show*
us thy mercy, O God ;" "O visit me with thy salvation, that I may *glory* with thine inheritance."   They
recognise it as a fault in themselves, that they cannot
confidently say, " Abba, Father ;" and they long to
be delivered from this spirit of bondage.   And there
can be no reasonable doubt, that, if we have faith at
all, it is possible to make it out by its appropriate
marks and symptoms.   Otherwise, how should Peter
exhort believers to make sure of their calling and election; or Paul speak so confidently of his Hebrews as
partakers of the heavenly calling ; or our Lord command his disciples to rejoice that their names were
written in heaven ?   There *is* a way of ascertaining
that our state is secure ; and doubly blessed are they
who have found it.   They have the *security ;* and
have the *comfort* of feeling it.   But, if we lazily rest
without " giving *all diligence*," not merely to fix this
great point, but to ascertain it,——then, indeed, we may
be safe ; it is barely possible we may ; but we do not
know it ; and eternity is to us all uncertain.   For a
time we may walk quietly, and solace ourselves in a
general and easy belief in our state ; but, unless we
have ascertained on Scripture texts (such as, " By their
fruits ye shall know them"), our personal interest in
Christ,——our peace will be, if I may so speak, at the
mercy of every wind.   And oh ! to think of our sore
amazement, if it be found to fail us when we most
need it ; if, in the near prospect of death, we can only
faintly *hope*, but cannot say, " I *know* whom I have
believed."   Dearly beloved, labour after the frame of
mind which these words of Paul express.   Seek scrip-
turally and earnestly for the marks of a work of grace
within you.   And God grant that all of you may find

them,—not worthless counterfeits—but the genuine fruit of the Spirit, in all goodness, and righteousness, and truth. Finally, dear friends, farewell. I commend you to God. The God of all grace, who hath called us unto his eternal glory by Christ Jesus, after that ye have suffered a while, make you perfect, stablish, strengthen, settle you. To him be glory and dominion for ever and ever. Amen. So prays your sincere friend, J. H.'

The first letter written by Mr Halley from Madeira, containing an account of his voyage and arrival, never reached its destination. This want will be, in some measure, made up by extracts from other letters written soon after.

' FUNCHAL, MADEIRA, *Saturday, 25th Nov.* 1837.

' My dear Father,— . . . . Our last letter left us in the British hotel,—the only one, be it observed, in the *city* of Funchal. The house is huge, but nothing near half furnished ; and there was such a famine of blankets, that we had to be indebted to our fellow-passenger, Mrs O., for some of her ship-bedding, before we could be comfortably put up at night. Yet we had good enough living, though served up in rather an outlandish style by a little Portuguese waiter clad in white from head to foot,—barring always the butter, which, in Madeira, is shockingly bad. Our waiter, being in a *British* hotel, of course *pretended* to speak English, and made many desperate efforts, both to speak and to understand it ; his puzzlement and ours sometimes was extreme ; and we found out, by and by, that the only feasible way of getting any thing was, not to order it once, and in few words as at home, but to send Mr W. O., who is a most patient painstaking mortal, out to the stair-head, and let him talk over the matter rationally with Enrique (or Henry, for that is his name). Still, all things considered, we

were tolerably well ; only it was a clear duty to escape
from the " British" as soon as possible. . . . .

'You cannot imagine any thing more different than
the country to which we have come, from that which
we have left. In Glasgow you are now probably
walking up to the knees in snow; or else Great
Hamilton Street is one mass of mud. Here, with the
exception of showers yesterday evening, and this forenoon, every day has been continued sunshine ; on
Thursday, at noon, it was as warm as I ever felt it at
Tillicoultry. The thermometer has generally been
65 or 66 in the morning ; and as high as 70 during
the day ; while you are starving down between 32 and
45. We have no fires—not even fire-places, in any
apartment but the kitchen. And, although I sleep in
blankets, the people in health, such as our friend Mr
Small, are lying with no more than a sheet and cover-
let. Straw hats, white trousers, and white boots, are
the order of the day. The Portuguese oxen-drivers
have just a white shirt, white trousers, generally *one*
boot, and a queer nondescript kind of cap which just
covers the crown of their heads ; and these constitute
their whole equipment. There are only four wheel-
carriages on the island. The things which the oxen
draw are sledges of the rudest construction, the driver
carrying a wet cloth, which, every now and then, he
throws down before the sledge to prevent the wood
from catching fire, and make it slip more easily over
the stones. The roads are all made of round stones
from the brook, wrought together into a very hard
causeway, very like those of some of the smaller towns
in Scotland. I can imagine nothing rougher than it
must be to ride over them. Yet I see that, if I am
to get any exercise at all, I must frequently hire a
horse. The island is just made up of rocky hills, with
thin strata of soil, and you cannot go 100 yards in
almost any direction without meeting a pretty steep
ascent. It rises so abruptly out of the sea, that a

seventy-four can ride within pistol shot of the shore all round the bay. I went out yesterday to what they call a pretty level walk, and found an inclination like that of High John Street. So my walks will necessarily be short; but I shall try to make them frequent; and sometimes I shall venture on a pony. Though the soil is thin, it is very productive; every inch is occupied; and the most parched looking spots, which we would reckon unfit for any thing, wave with sugar-canes, or glitter with oranges.

' Of my health I cannot say much. The blister has certainly done much good, and has almost entirely removed the pain. The cough is much as when I left you. But I am beginning to flatter myself that my food is nourishing me better. We cannot expect, as yet, any decided change; and our effort, repeated every hour, must be to wait the Lord's pleasure—to be still, and know that he is God. . . . Mr Cadell offers to introduce me to two or three pious clergymen of the Church of England, who are here for health.

' Last Sabbath we attended the English church, of which a Mr Lowe is minister. Nothing can be finer or more fragrant than the entrance to it, which is fringed on either hand with Fuschias and gigantic Heliotropes. The chapel is very neat, and well filled; the preaching very ordinary, and scarcely any psalmody at all.

' And now, my dear father, with every good wish and prayer, I am your ever loving son,   J. H.'

Soon after he was settled in Madeira, Mr Halley began to keep a diary more strictly religious than any thing he had hitherto attempted. It was begun on the 1st of January 1838, and regularly kept up while his health was adequate to the exertion. It begins with a very solemn act of dedication to God. It is

not our province to start the question regarding the
propriety or utility of such an act of covenanting.
We are not careful to inquire how many have been
benefited by the use, and how many have been embarrassed by the abuse of it.   Our object is, to exhibit
the character of our departed friend as it was, and we
are not at liberty to withhold a feature so important
as the writing and adopting of such a covenant.   We
have already given a similar document written at an
earlier period of his progress, and it will be interesting to compare it with that which we now present.
We insert it exactly as it stands in the journal; confident that such a clear, scriptural, ardent exhibition
of a sinner's lost condition, and a sinner's only hope,
is calculated to convey instruction, and administer
reproof.   There is first a kind of preface containing
the reasons on which the resolution is grounded, and
then the form of covenant itself.

'FUNCHAL, 1st *January* 1838.

'" O Lord, our God, other lords besides thee have had
dominion over us ; but by thee only will we make mention
of thy name!"—ISAIAH xxvi. 13.

' Up to this time I have never attempted to keep
any thing that could be called a religious journal.   I
have kept records of study, with mingled notices of
frames of spirit ; but never a proper *diary*.   This
resulted, I confess with much humiliation, from the
absence or feebleness of real spiritual concern.   I
could not bear to look into my own heart ; still less
to register its sinful wanderings ; least of all, to have
the record always beside me, and to be incessantly
reminded by its presence of my utter vileness.   I was
too proud to be the chronicler of my own shortcomings ; and too blind and heedless to see the benefit

which might result from the remembrance even of failures and falls. (Psalm li. 2.)

'But now, by God's hand, eternity has been brought near me. With Job, I see that the graves are almost ready for me. And I trust that it is a work of divine grace, however feeble, that is now opening my eyes to the excellence of a scheme of Christian self-discipline so long and sinfully neglected.

'The example of the most eminent believers were enough to stimulate to the attempt. And a remark of Cecil, that we would do well to note our views and feelings in sickness, for our future instruction, as they are sure soon to vanish, strikes me as peculiarly applicable to my present state. God's chastening is upon me, under which even the careless pour forth a prayer. May he lead me by it to desires and meditations, which, if ever I recover, shall be profitable in the retrospect; and, if I die, shall, in the meantime, be filling me with good things.

'Unused, alas! to self-inspection, and prone to let my thoughts wander on the mountains of vanity, I shall probably for some time have little to record of my own feelings. But what I *do* notice, good or bad, I engage, for my own profit, and under a solemn sense of God's presence, to preserve here. And I resolve, additionally, in dependence on the Spirit of grace, to strive every day to bring my mind to some such definite contemplation of divine things, as I can commit to this journal; and, generally, to find my theme in a verse of Scripture.

'But, for this day, which, may God make much to be remembered in my eternal existence, I shall endeavour, by his help, to bind myself, in a written covenant, to be his. I do this, convinced that an explicit surrender of myself to God is both right, advantageous, and scriptural,—right, as a due acknowledgment of his propriety in me, and his numberless mercies in providence and grace,—advantageous, as a means of remind-

ing myself of my allegiance to him, a plea in prayer
(Psalm lxxxvi. 16, cxix. 94), and a stay in trouble; as
something which, in the hour of temptation, may be
quoted against my corruptions—of darkness, against
my doubts—of death, against assaults and fears ; and
scriptural, as Rom. vi. 13, xii. 1 ; 1 Cor. vi. 20; Gen.
xxviii. 18—22, xxxv. 14 ; Josh. xxiv. 16—27 ; Jer. l.
4, 5 ; Isa. xliv. 5 ; and the institution of the Lord's
Supper, abundantly show.

' Therefore, after a solemn, humble supplication for
His presence and blessing, I do here, with full and
deliberate consent of judgment and will, take the Lord
for my God, and give myself wholly up to him.

'2d *January* 1838.

' FORM OF COVENANT.

' Bow down thine ear, O Lord, hear me ; for I am
poor and needy.   I have no plea, but my own want,
and the infinite merits of thy Son.   For his sake, and
for thine own name's sake, O Lord, pardon mine iniquity for it is great; and turn not away my prayer,
nor thy mercy from me.

' Lord, thou mightest justly long ago have shut the
door of mercy, when I thought not of entering.   Thou
mightest have made me an example and monument
of thy terrible omnipotent anger.   For I have broken
thy holy, just, and good law; by the very bent of my
depraved nature ; by the general current of my pol-
luted, vain, and earthly thoughts ; and by special acts
of wilful and presumptuous transgression.   In my
daily walk I have been without thee; from my re-
creations I have excluded thee ; in my speech I have
not duly glorified thee, and maintained thy cause ;
in prosperity I have forgotten thee; in trouble I have
not . heard the rod ; opportunities of good I have
squandered ; thy Sabbaths I have abused ; and by thy
most melting calls I have been little, if at all, moved.
" Thou, even thou, art to be feared," but I have not

feared thee ; thou " art to be had in reverence," but I have not duly venerated thee ; in thy name should men glory, but I have not made my boast in thee ; to thee should every knee bow, but seldom, if ever, have I rightly worshipped thee ! Above all, I have been guilty of refusing to hear Him whom thou hast commanded all men to hear—to believe on Him whom thou hast sent ; of trampling under foot the Son of God ; and, both before and since the time when I faintly endeavoured to come to Christ, of grieving and quenching the Spirit, when he spoke through my own conscience and thy most holy Word. And all this have I done against the sacred majesty of the everlasting God,—glorious in holiness, inflexible in justice, immutable in truth, in wisdom most adorable ; in might most terrible ; in goodness and mercy unwearied and abounding ; against thine inconceivable love in the gift of thine only begotten Son ; against the grace of our Lord Jesus Christ ; against the influence and love of the Eternal Spirit.

' How transcendent, then, is that mercy which has continued me unto this day,—which has not cast me forth to wither and be burned ; but even now permits me to close with God in Christ in the terms of the new, the better, the everlasting covenant. There He, in whom it is humility to behold the things that are done in heaven, deigns to set his heart upon man, and to bind himself in an engagement to dust and ashes.

' Lord, with trembling, awful joy, I would lay hold of this thy condescension. I give myself from this hour to thee; be it unto me according to this word of thine,—" I will be your God." I give myself to God the Father, as his rightful property,—his prodigal, but now returning son ; to God the Son, as one of those lost ones whom he came to seek and to save,—a sinner needing to be washed in his precious blood, convinced there is no salvation in any other, and earnestly desiring to be clothed in his righteousness; and to God the Spirit, as a depraved creature, to be by him renewed, sanctified, built up, and comforted. And I take the Father to be my God, as he is the God and Father of our Lord and Saviour Jesus Christ; the Son to be to me the way, and the truth, and the life,—to be my Prince and Saviour, shepherd, friend, advocate, and forerunner within the vail,—to deliver me from wrath, and prepare me a place in the house of many mansions ; and the Spirit, as my light, teacher, and comforter, to prepare me for that place by his instruction, strengthening, and consolation.   In particular, should God be pleased to lengthen my days, I give myself, soul, body and spirit, to Him in the work of the ministry, in reliance on His own abundant aids, desiring to be filled with the knowledge of his will in all wisdom and spiritual understanding, and to be strengthened with might by his Spirit in the inner man, that I may preach among sinners the unsearchable riches of Christ.

' And will God in very deed accept and ratify this surrender ?   My goodness reacheth not unto thee; and though it did, all that is in the heaven and in the earth is thine ; and it is only thine own I have given thee.   And oh! how poor the offering ! maimed, halt, and blind! a corrupt thing, to Him whose name is dreadful among the heathen !

' But, O God of all mercy, may the altar sanctify the gift.   It is through Christ I venture to perform this reasonable service.   For his sake, take away all iniquity, receive me graciously, love me freely.   Make with me now an everlasting covenant, and cause it to be all my salvation, and all my desire.   Yes, Lord, thou despisest not any; thou *wilt* incline thine ear to hear me.   May this covenant be recorded and sealed in the book of remembrance; as a swift witness against me if I recede from its terms, and a sweet encouragement to hold fast the confidence and the rejoicing of the hope firm unto the end.   May it be applied by the Spirit, in subserviency to the word of truth, as a mean of warning, strengthening, stablishing, reproving, reclaiming, comforting me; may it lead me habitually to view myself as holy unto the Lord; may it be a ready argument against any sinful compliance; and, in the hour of trouble or of death, may it be used as a blessed instrument of maintaining in me a cheerful confidence and humble resignation. May the thought, that I formally gave myself to God, repress every murmur at his sovereign disposals, and fill me with the elevating conviction, that all things, even death, are mine,—for *God* is mine.

' And now, Lord, what wait I for? My hope is in thee. Accept me in the Beloved; and enable me, in simplicity and godly sincerity, to subscribe with my hand unto thee, according to the tenor of the foregoing covenant; wherein, if aught is wanting, do thou graciously supply it; if aught spoken unadvisedly, forgive it; and do for me exceeding abundantly above all that I ask or think: for the Redeemer's sake. Amen and Amen.

' FUNCHAL, 3*d January* 1838.

' I have now copied and read carefully over the preceding covenant. I believe it to be scriptural; and, imploring the blessing of God, I now sign it as his servant in Christ Jesus, on this 3d of January 1838.

' JAMES HALLEY.'

The entries during the month of January are almost daily, except when interrupted by severe illness. From these we shall present a continued series of extracts.

' *5th January* 1838.

' This day spent as yesterday; too much time probably given to express my feelings towards a fellow-creature, and certainly far too little to God.

' Mind, as well as body, enfeebled by a sleepless night. Thought in bed of dying; and felt how much

divine supports must be needed in the last agony.
Prayed for strength; but rather for prolonged life, if
it should be God's will, for my father's sake, and the
sake of the many friends who desire it. Did not feel
much fear: the Lord forbid that this should result
from insensibility; or, if it does, may he stir me up,
and give me the same calmness, yea, a better and more
stable, as the fruit of faith.

'6th January 1838.

'Miserably negligent of divine things. Why should
I compliment away a moment of the time which I
owe to God, and to my own immortal interests?

'"Then spake Jesus again unto them, saying, I am the
light of the world: he that followeth me shall not walk in
darkness, but shall have the light of life."—JOHN viii. 12.

'This is a more specific form of the promise that
"we should know, if we follow on to know the Lord."
It shows us the great way in which we ought to prosecute this knowledge,—following Christ, treasuring
up his sayings, and imitating his example. This will
not only give us light in regard to belief and duty;
but, if our walk is close with him, comfortably satisfy
us of our state. Why, then, do believers walk so
much in darkness? Because, for a time, they cease
from following Christ, or pursue their course with
fainting steps, and slow. If they followed on steadily
they would see "a great light" shining on their path,
the light of life, a quickening, encouraging, and guiding ray. Oh that I could say with David, "My soul
followeth hard after thee!" I would then know something of the joyful light which possesses and pene-
trates a heart at peace with God, and finding its rest
in the shining of his countenance.

'Sabbath, 7th January 1838.

'Day cold and stormy; so I had to confine myself
to the house. My affections were very cold; but

almost all my thoughts were given to religion.   Read part of Mrs Newell's life, and of Witherspoon on Regeneration.   Witherspoon very plain and discriminating.   Struck with a remark of Mrs Newell's (p. 69), that increased knowledge, if one is unconverted, may be the means of increased misery.

' " To the one we are the savour of death unto death."
—2 Cor. ii. 16.

' This awful proposition may be illustrated from the case of our most ordinary advantages.   He who, from heedlessness, rash rejection of prudential advices, dissipation, or any other cause depending on his own will, has lost the blessing of health, feels a more pungent sorrow than one who has all his days been subject to disease ; the abuse of a mercy thus punishing itself.   Thus, every gift of God, if abused, is the occasion of quickening remorse, and aggravating condemnation.

' But intellectual or moral gifts are peculiarly distinguished by having, in an eminent degree, this element of retribution in themselves.   The cultivated intellect is more capacious of the ideas, whether of pain or pleasure, than one which has not experienced the enlargement which education gives.   The man who has acquired an extreme delicacy of taste in art or literature, as he has more enjoyment from the *chef d'ouvres* in each, has also more pain in the view of what is rough and ill assorted.   And so is it in moral sensibility; the mind, as it grows in this quality, may be capable of more rapturous delight, but it is also exposed to intenser anguish.   The vessel is enlarged ; it can therefore contain more of the bitter as well as of the honeyed potion.   It seems, then, reasonable, and not repugnant to analogy, that, in another world, they who die in unbelief may suffer somewhat in proportion to their mental and moral capacities.   If so, how many unsanctified spirits that habitually forget God in the chase after distinction in literature or

I

science, shall find, that, in increasing knowledge, they have been increasing sorrow!   And how many, who boast of their sensibility, but lavish it all on the creature, will find that they have nourished it to a fearful acuteness!

' Lord, is all my acquisition of knowledge only to serve this sad purpose of vengeance?   Search and try me; show me my sins; give me true faith in the Lord Jesus; expand my heart with thine own love, shed abroad by the Holy Ghost; and guide me to glory.   For Christ's sake.'

' *Tuesday,* 16th *January* 1838.

' " Greater love hath no man than this, that a man lay down his life for his friends."—JOHN xv. 13.

' *Greater* love, certainly, than this measure of it, has never been exhibited by man; seldom indeed has the compass of human affection been so great.   A very few striking instances are on record, in the history of our whole species, of deliberate self-devotion in the room of a friend; and these have ever been regarded as reaching the acmè of human heroism.   But by no human standard can we measure the length and breadth of the love of Christ.   The love of Zaleucus to his son might serve as a measure of that still more wonderful devotedness which might be displayed for a more distant *friend;* but it fails, in this view, when we attempt to gain from it some conception of that generosity which could lavish its own life to save that of an *enemy.*   There is here no proportion at all; human affection might bring about the one result, something superhuman would be needed to produce the other. Multiply, by what co-efficient you may, the love of a father who maims his own body to deliver his son's, or of a friend who surrenders his own life in the place of one to whom his inmost soul is knit, and you can never come to the love of him who dies for his embittered foe.   (" But God commendeth, &c.")   'Tis like taking a multiple of a finite number to express infinity.'

'*Wednesday, 17th January* 1838.

' My birth-day. Spent in vanity almost wholly. Only a short season given to prayer and reading. Oh! my leanness !

' " We spend our years as a tale that is told."—PSALM xc. 9.

' A tale! often how interesting, how deeply enchaining! at all events how full of bustle and movement! Such, till about ten months ago, when the hand of God was laid upon me, were my years. I hurried from one occupation to another, without either time or taste for serious thought,—interested and zealous for the time in the pursuit which engaged me, and scarcely at all noticing that the descending current was carrying me down toward eternity. The tale was stirring ; one event pressed hard on another, and so it rapidly passed away.

' But a tale once told, how soon does it vanish from the memory! how suddenly do its images fade ! A dim impression is all that remains of that which once played so pleasantly round the fancy. And so is it with those twenty-four years which God has been pleased to give me. Their events are buried in the past eternity, never to arise, except in judgment ; and there, either to aggravate my condemnation (fearful thought), or to add to the glory of that grace which saves so great a sinner. The Lord in mercy turn them to the latter purpose ! Meantime a general impression is all that remains to me of these years of my pilgrimage ; and that is one of sin and sorrow, " vanity and vexation of spirit," unparalleled mercies abused, Emmanuel's love requited by neglect. " Return, O Lord, how long ?"—" O Lord, I beseech thee deliver my soul."

' May this new year of my being on earth (how

probably the last !) find me wholly a new creature. " Turn thou me, and I shall be turned, for thou art the Lord my God."—" O satisfy me early with thy mercy, that I may be glad and rejoice all my days !" —" Sanctify me wholly." And may " the God of all grace, who hath called me unto his eternal glory by Christ Jesus, after that I have suffered a while, make me perfect, stablish, strengthen, settle me :" To him be glory and dominion for ever and ever. Amen !'

' " The heart is deceitful above all things."—JER. xvii. 9.

' This I have most abundantly proved in the work-ings of my own heart. One most extraordinary in-stance of its deceit is, that whereby it persuades itself that bodily weakness is a sufficient reason for neglect of religion. Seldom, since I began to think of eter-nity at all, has my mind been so little impressed by it as during the few last days. And this I know I have tacitly excused to myself, on the imaginary ground that much serious thought would aggravate my dis-order. But *why* should it ? Or, even if it did, are a few hours of a sickly dying existence to be put in com-parison with the everlasting welfare of my soul ? Yet, in every evasion of religious thought on the score of weak health, the assumption is involved, that the one of these can compete with the other. If this is not the madness of self-deceit, where can it be found ? From this and all such manifest delusions of Satan, good Lord, deliver me.'

' " Behold, now I know that there is no God in all the earth, but in Israel ; now, therefore, I pray thee, take a blessing of thy servant. But he said, As the Lord liveth, before whom I stand, I will receive none."—2 KINGS v. 15, 16.

' The Scripture leaves us in no doubt about the propriety and acceptableness (through Christ) of thank-offerings. It commands us to " offer unto God thanksgiving" (Ps. l. 14)—" to offer the sacrifice of praise to God continually" (Heb. xiii. 15)—to " bring an offering, and come into his courts" (Ps. xcvi. 8) ; and those are commended, both in the Old Testament and the New, whose gratitude for spiritual mercies found a vent in liberality to the poorer saints, or to the sanctuary of God.

' Yet Elisha here rejects the gift of Naaman. And we thus seem forced to the conclusion, that it was not a mere expression of thankfulness, but intended in part as a remuneration for the service which the man of God had done him. Elisha resolutely maintains to him that the gift of God is not to be purchased with money or changes of raiment. What might have been accepted, had it come simply to attest the emotion of a grateful heart, is sternly refused when offered as a reward. It then becomes the fruit of a legal spirit, and acquires a taint from its parent disposition.

' Much of this legality—this *ex post facto* legality, if I may so call it—is found in Christians. When under strong convictions, they see with some clearness the enormous evil of sin, the hopeless condemnation (as far as human effort is concerned) under which it lays them, and the impossibility of making out, by deeds of law, either in whole or in part, a title to glory. Then Christ is revealed to their souls, and welcomed heartily ; they rely on him, and at first on him alone ; and they experience, partially, the blessed effect of having a weight of sin lifted from off their consciences. A lively gratitude succeeds ; but the remains of the old man mingle with it, and there is infused into it a tincture of the vitiating element of the legal, bargaining spirit. Salvation is too good, too great (they tacitly assume), to be so free. They must try to pay off some portion of the immense debt of gratitude they have incurred—to render some equivalent, forgetful that equivalents are out of the question, when the gift is everlasting life, and that that debt can never be lessened which stretches out

into the infinite. Thus many do partially " fall from
grace ;" " having begun in the Spirit," seek to be
" made perfect by the flesh ;" perform their duties on
a wrong principle, and so lose much of the comfort
they might minister. Instead of thanksgiving, they
dream of recompense ; and thus in many of their
efforts they are but beating the air,—losing of course
that at which they aim, and missing substantial good
which they might secure by running in the way of
God's commandments with a simpler intention.'

' Sabbath, 21st January 1838.

' " This day is holy unto the Lord your God ; mourn
not, nor weep ; for the joy of the Lord is your strength."
—NEHEMIAH viii. 9, 10.

> ' Sweet is the light of Sabbath eve,
>   And soft the sunbeam ling'ring there ;
> Those sacred hours this low earth leave,
>   Wafted on wings of praise and prayer.
>
> ' Season of rest ! the tranquil soul
>   Feels thy sweet calm, and melts in love ;
> And while these sacred moments roll,
>   Faith sees a smiling heav'n above.

EDMESTON.

' " It is good to be here " should be the language of
our souls, not merely when on the mount of ordinances, but throughout all the hours of that blessed
day which Jehovah has sanctified for himself. It is
good to be apart from the cares and turmoil of time ;
and, gaining this sacred eminence, to look abroad
upon eternity. And, were our hearts but right with
God, such meditation, though solemn, would be far
from sad ; the calm majesty that encircles the infinite would settle and compose the spirit, and we
should find a response within to that counsel of the
Levites to the remnant of Israel—" This day is holy
unto the Lord," &c.

' So far from having any tendency to throw a shadow over the mind, it is the native property of divine truth, when fully received, to minister peace and joy. If Christians, then, are under the dominion of habitual and prevalent dejection, it is not because they have too much religion, but because they have too little. Indeed, if our Christianity has never been to us the spring of a sensible satisfaction, there is too much reason to suspect it of spuriousness ; at all events, to conclude that it has but a very broken and imperfect sway.

' That joy, in some measure or degree, is an essential result of the possession of a true faith, is involved in innumerable declarations of Scripture. Joy is expressly mentioned among the fruits of the Spirit. It is Paul's desire for the Romans, that the God of hope may fill them with all joy and peace in believing. The Psalmist declares that praise is comely for the upright ; exhorts all lands to make a joyful noise unto God ; prays that the nations may be glad, and sing for joy, and that the daughters of Judah might exult in God's judgments ; counsels all worshippers to serve God with gladness, and come before his presence with singing ; and gives an explicit warrant to all that seek him to glory in his holy name. It is an apostolic precept to live rejoicing in hope,—to rejoice in the Lord alway ; and, to mark its importance, the injunction is repeated, " Again I say, rejoice." In a word, the announcement of a Saviour is "good tidings of great joy ;" his appearance was to give light to the people that walked in darkness ; the very name of his forerunner was one of gladness, and his disciples are directed to the natural issue of their faith, which nothing but its weakness prevents them from reaching, when Peter addresses these words to the children of the dispersion,—" in whom, though now ye see him not, yet believing, ye rejoice with joy unspeakable, and full of glory."

' Why, then, should our hands hang down, or our knees be feeble?   " Say to them that are of a fearful heart, Be strong, fear not "—" We declare unto you glad tidings, now that the promise which was made unto the fathers, God hath fulfilled the same unto us their children, in that he hath raised up Jesus again." " It is Christ that died ; yea, rather that is risen again ;" "in whom dwelleth all the fulness of the Godhead bodily."

' Besides the general reason for religious and sober joy, which is supplied by the grace that has been brought nigh unto us through the appearing of Jesus Christ, there are special reasons peculiarly applicable to all seasons of solemn festival, and, in particular, to that weekly rest which God's Word appoints and blesses.

' One of these may be drawn from that communion of saints, in spirit and purpose, which is one of the most refreshing of revealed truths.   To think that there is *one* great family called by the name of Jesus, scattered indeed through every nation, and kindred, and people, and tongue,—yet keeping the unity of the spirit in the bond of peace ; bowing around a thousand hearths, yet before *one* throne of grace ; praying in a thousand tongues, but the language of their hearts breathing *one* melody ; differing in bodily form and feature, but bearing one image and superscription on their souls ;—to think that on this day, especially, their hymns and prayers are all ascending, to be perfumed with Immanuel's costly incense, and to return in showers of blessing ;—surely this were enough to enkindle the coldest affections—to elicit a glad answer to the Levites' exhortation, " Mourn not, nor weep." To think that the living stones, found on every shore, from the icy mountains of the north to the islands of the southern wave, are being brought together to constitute one glorious temple, invisibly yet indissolubly cemented by the blood of the Lamb,—and that this day has a peculiar part to perform in consolidating the sacred edifice,—this were a sufficient reason for an angel's joy.

' And need we add that the Sabbath is joyful too, as the appointed emblem of the rest that remaineth for the people of God ? It is hallowed, not merely by the concert in worship of the saints on earth, but as the type and figure of their adoring repose in heaven. But how does our sin and corruption make the comparison to fail ! How " cold our warmest thought " to the service of those, his ministers, who are as a flame of fire ! How wretched our unbelieving doubts and fears, our half-confiding prayers, our stammering praises, when placed in contrast with the full tide of joy and gratitude which is poured from the lips of those who have exchanged faith for vision, and serve Him day and night in his temple ! Yet let the institution of the sacred day, as emblematic of its eternal antitype, elevate our aims, raise our affections, and fill us with a holy gladness. " The Lord is risen indeed," and gone to " prepare a place" for us,—a place of everlasting Sabbath and jubilee. Lord, bring me to that rest. Guide me with thy counsel, and afterward receive me to glory ! Amen.'

' Sabbath, 28th January 1838.

' Read the Scriptures, and Martyn, with some emotion, and came a little nearer than usual to eternity.

' " Deliver me, O Lord, from mine enemies : I flee unto thee to hide me."—PSALM cxliii. 9.

' How much do we lose from not having our minds constantly in the frame indicated in this prayer. So great is the number, and so overpowering the strength of our enemies,—of all those persons and influences that are adverse to the wellbeing of our souls, that no human power is adequate to our deliverance. Woe, then, to him who goes this warfare on his own charges !

' There is, first, the broken law pursuing the sinner to his destruction, demanding nothing less than the perdition of his soul, or a full equivalent,—and not to be diverted from this exaction by any ingenuity of excuse or palliation. It follows his every footstep, and threatens to engulph him in a lake of fire. There is, next, the prince of the power of the air, and all his subordinate thrones and dominions ; subtle and practised in working ruin, with ready access to his imagination, and skilful to spread those toils by which thousands already have been ensnared and taken. How is a feeble man to escape as a bird out of the snare of the fowler ? After these come the fascinations of a world lying in wickedness, of which it is emphatically said, that " all that is in it is not of the Father." And here we are liable to an especial danger. For, like those misguided friends who would have kept back the Saviour from his cross, and unwittingly marred a world's redemption, our friends may often be turned into foes, and the very attractions with which God has invested them be the means of estranging our hearts from him. And, in fine, our worst enemies are those of our own household, within our own bosoms,—the force of yet unsubdued iniquity maintaining its residence like a strong man armed. Without this our outward foes would want half their terrors. But this it is which gives the sentence of the law its bitterness, throws open the citadel of the heart to Satan, and clothes the world with many of its charms. And this we cannot of ourselves vanquish,—" Can the Ethiopian," &c.—" Who can bring a clean thing," &c.

' Thus beset and beleaguered by opposing hosts, whither can we betake ourselves ? Let David supply the answer,—" I flee unto Thee to hide me." " The rock of my strength, and my refuge, is in God." Does the law threaten us ? " In the Lord have I righteousness." Do the powers of evil molest us ?

" I have prayed for thee, that thy faith fail not." Does the world allure us? " This is the victory that overcometh the world, even our faith." Does it threaten us? " Be of good cheer : I have overcome the world." Do our own backslidings reprove us, and our iniquities, like the wind, carry us away? " The very God of peace sanctify you wholly."

' May I ever be enabled thus practically to use and apply his Word ; and, in every time of terror or temptation, thus to hide myself like a child in his father's arms : through Christ. Amen.'

The plan of these short records, it will be perceived, is this :——Some incident occurring is allowed to suggest the subject of meditation ; then a suitable text of Scripture is selected ; and the reflections written in the form of a practical comment on the verse. Perhaps it may be thought they are too formal for a diary. One reason of this is, that they are selections ; and the more elaborate have been chosen, because in this case the most valuable. The more familiar jottings regarding his own state have generally been omitted, because they are similar to each other, and not so well fitted to be generally useful. The short meditations that have been given, contain each an illustration of some important doctrine of Scripture. It is certain they have more the appearance of finished compositions, than the contents of a diary usually have ; but this is owing to the habit of the writer's mind. The same scrupulous accuracy of style runs through every thing he wrote. We are persuaded that serious readers will be so much occupied in applying the acute experimental religious instruction which these little essays contain, that they will have no leisure to criticise the form in which they appear.

To preserve the order of the dates, we insert here an extract from a letter to J. C. Colquhoun, Esq., M.P.

‘ FUNCHAL, MADEIRA, 5th *February* 1838.

‘ My dear Sir,—I am almost ashamed to take up my pen to write to you ; so long have I allowed the time to pass at which I ought to have made you aware of my state and prospects. Two things prevented me ; first, the hurtfulness of much stooping to a person labouring under pulmonary disease ; second, a strong desire to have something definite to say of myself before I should trouble you with a letter. The first of these impediments still operates so far, that I take only a sheet of the ordinary dimensions, instead of the gigantic expanse of paper which I *would* most willingly, and *could* most easily fill,—assured that you will regard the shortness of my epistle as inferring, not a diminution of gratitude to you, but an increase of wholesome care for that health which you have shown yourself so anxious to see restored.

‘ We left Glasgow on Saturday, 28th October, for Dublin, where we arrived next day ; sailed thence on 1st November for Falmouth ; and from Falmouth, on Friday the 10th November, for Madeira. We passed Porto-Santo on the afternoon of Friday the 17th, and anchored in Funchal bay on Saturday the 18th. Henry Cadell, Esq., of the Bank of Scotland in Edinburgh, who had been advertised by Alex. Dunlop, Esq., of my intended shipment, met us on the beach ; and, with the genuine zealous feeling of a right good Church-extensionist, aided us in getting settled. So full is the place of English invalids, that we were obliged to place ourselves in the only boarding-house which had at that time a vacancy. We think ourselves fortunate, upon the whole, in the place of our residence. . . . .

‘ The climate, although we have had a rainy season, as the Madeirans say, of unusual severity, is all that could be wished, and really exceeds my best expectations of it.   This has been such a day as Scotland will not know till June; and, after a short visit to Dr Renton's residence, I have returned home, loaded with heliotropes, geraniums, passion-flowers, and camelias, all blooming in the open air.   Only it must be admitted, that even after the *very heavy* rains are gone, there is so much moisture floating in the air, in consequence of evaporation, that it is sometimes trying to weak lungs.   Often, in the mornings, although we are in a dry situation, the rails of the stair within the house feel quite clammy and wet; and the state of atmosphere, by which this is caused, is pretty steadily indicated by that sure barometer—an increased difficulty of breathing.   The fertility of the island is altogether amazing, considering that it is just a thin mould, superimposed on successive layers of different lavas.   And the terraced appearance, which results partly from its structure, and partly from the labour of the natives to secure convenience of irrigation, renders the general aspect of Madeira peculiarly novel and picturesque.   Then the semi-tropical vegetation, —the orange, citron, lemon, banana, coral tree, magnolia, with cactuses and custard apples, excited at first a good deal of our attention, and served us with materials for some inquiries.

 ' The greatest hindrance, either to botanical pursuits (if I had cared about engaging in them), or to that physical exercise and enjoyment which constitutes much of my business as *a professed invalid*,—is the extreme steepness of the island.   A road is called *level* here, if it rises only one foot in five.   So that, I think, physicians, in sending consumptive people here, have a sly design to prevent their walking about much ; at least, they *are* as effectually prevented, as if the whole thing had been devised and adapted to that end.   Much motion, to a broken-winded man, is impossible without a horse.   And then the mode of

equestrian transport is so grotesque ; a Portuguese
attendant, clothed in their characteristic dress, almost
invariably accompanying you — giving your horse a
thwack on the hind-quarters with a stick, if he thinks
it is not going fast enough, and, if you move very
rapidly, seizing the tail, and, in this preposterous
guise, scampering along behind you.   In good weather, I go out in this style an hour a-day ; and have
got, along with the refreshment of the sun and air,
some useful lessons in riding, on roads more perilous
by far than any mountain track I ever saw in the
Highlands of Scotland. . . . .
   ' *Sed de meipso sat.*   A few words now on the state
of religion here.   Among the lower Portuguese, the
attachment to Popery, if we may judge from their
outward acts, is very blind and bigoted.   The higher
classes of them, at least those who think at all, are
said to be generally infidels; yet they make no scruple
of sending their younger daughters, who may happen
to be " *untochered*," into nunneries.   But the spirit of
Popery, Proteus-like, can accommodate itself to circumstances.   It does not exist here in its greatest
sternness.   The nunneries are accessible to strangers;
and a person who was in one of them the other day,
on a sort of conventual saturnalia, told me that the
nuns were busy singing and laughing; that there was
a good piano in the chapel, on which one played
cheerful airs to amuse the rest ; and that preparations
were going on for a supper and ball which the lady
abbess was to give on her re-election.   So there you
have the monster laughing.   Half of the priests, it is
said, are Deists ; and very ignorant the generality of
them must be ; for I saw a gentleman a few days ago,
who told me, that one of them, who is somewhat
more inquisitive than his neighbours, had borrowed
of him, and is reading, a Portuguese Old Testament,
—a volume which, till then, he had never seen.   The
vicar-general, who is ecclesiastical head of the island,

is a very liberal papist; insomuch that, on Christmas day 1836, he attended divine service at the English chapel.   Probably this was not so great an inconsistency as it seems, for the English clergyman is *high-church*, *i. e.*, fully half way to Popery. . . . .

' Inclusive of Mr Williamson, a Scottish licentiate, whom you met in the " Leith," and myself, there are here 15 or 16 *clergymen*—mostly invalids.   Of these not above six are evangelical; but among these are some of the excellent of the earth.   Mr Langford, an Irishman, and Mr Ashe, a most acute, intellectual, and spiritually-minded minister of the Church of England, strike me most.   A Mr Freeman, who is *high-church* in principle, is most meek and Christian in spirit. . . . Under Mr Langford's auspices, a prayer-meeting has been begun in his house, attended by from 40 to 50 people.   The sole clerical supporters of it, who have, of course, always to officiate, are Mr L., Mr Ashe, and myself.   Mr Kempthorne has occasionally attended; but all the rest (alas! for Zion!) either disapprove *in toto* of such things, or stay away because Mr Lowe disapproves.   One can have no sympathy with those who discountenance an attempt to remind the invalid population of the eternity on whose verge so many tremble.   There is also a clerical meeting of five or six persons for edification and prayer, in Mr Langford's, once a-fortnight, which I have attended with great pleasure and some profit.   So you see we have something of Christian friendship and fellowship here, and are enabled to declare " His praise in the islands."

' But the heart will seek homewards.   I long to hear something of what is doing in our own land. Can an M.P.'s duties admit of his writing to Madeira ? If they can, how it would rejoice me to hear from you.——Yours, &c.   J. H.'

The following meditation from the diary is a very

good specimen of the method adopted throughout,—
an incident suggesting the topic, and yet all the reflections founded on a text of Scripture.

'*Sabbath, 11th February* 1838.

' Heard Mr Lowe this forenoon from Gen. i. 31.
About two sentences of Christian doctrine, in which
were contained the two errors of baptismal regeneration and the sinfulness of our Lord's humanity.   In
the judgment, we, who were born in Scotland, will
have far more to answer for, than the poor Church of
England in Madeira, which scarcely ever hears the
truth.

' " Who shall change our vile body, that it may be
fashioned like unto his glorious body, according to the
working whereby he is able even to subdue all things unto
himself."—Philip. iii. 21.

' The agent in this change on our bodies, as the last
clause informs us, is Omnipotence ; and where such
energy is put forth, a mighty transformation need not
for a moment give rise to incredulous wonder.   And
how great that transformation! We shall be like Christ,
seeing him as he is ! The resurrection bodies of the
saints shall no more be " vile ;" for they shall resemble
the glorious body of him who is their head and pat-
tern.   But how little do we, how little can we, know
here, of his likeness ! It doth not yet appear what
we shall be.   But some distant hints are afforded us,
darkly, to shadow forth that coming glory.   The
transfiguration scene seems to have been given to the
disciples, to strengthen their faith, by foreshowing
their Master's exaltation.   On that occasion, " His
face did shine as the sun, and his raiment was white
as the light ;" whatever is bright, beautiful, and ethe-
real, being used to image forth the splendour of his
appearance.   And, in like manner, when he appeared
in vision to John in Patmos, " his countenance was
as the sun shineth in his strength ;" while yet the

beloved disciple could recognise him as like unto the Son of Man—that same Jesus on whose bosom he had leaned, and with whose sorrows he had mingled. In like manner, the new tenements, in which the souls of his saints are to have their eternal dwelling-place, will be bright and pure exceedingly, and yet the identity of their persons be fully maintained. Who knows but that the creative power, put forth in their reproduction in this exalted state, may operate in the way of collecting the very same particles which formerly composed them,—purged from all their dross and corruption, and from these constructing new and nobler residences for their now emancipated spirits? It may thus be literally true, that this " mortal shall put on immortality." That which here was " vile," the avenue of temptation, the minister of lust, the instrument of unrighteousness, may thus be " fashioned like unto Christ's glorious body." But, whatever the manner, the fact is an elevating and transporting certainty, that " where Christ is, there shall also his servants be,"—that, as his raiment was glistening on Tabor, so their robes shall be white in the heavenly Zion. Thus is the body " sown in corruption, but raised in incorruption ; sown in dishonour, raised in glory; sown in weakness, raised in power ; sown a natural body, raised a spiritual body." For, " as we have borne the image of the earthy, we shall also bear the image of the heavenly." Ειη μοι τουτο, δι Ιησου Χριστου. Αμην.'*

To account for the greater freedom and playfulness of the following letter, it may be mentioned, that it was written to a class-fellow with whom he had long lived on terms of closest intimacy.

' FUNCHAL, 14th *February* 1838.

' My very dear Friend,—" Better late than never," is the motto which I may now prefix to all my corres-

* So let it be with me, through Jesus Christ. Amen.

K

pondence ; and I am sure I will find in you a response
to the spirit of it—a satisfaction in hearing from me
even at the eleventh hour. . . . . We are forming an
acquaintance with the other inmates, chiefly by dint of
meeting each other in the *turret.* (This needs explanation ; but, in sooth, no explanation will convey to
you an idea of the whimsicality of Madeiran architecture. Be it known, however, that every house of any
respectability has, either superimposed on the roof, or
made into a separate edifice, an oblong room, with
windows all around it, in order to observe approaching
vessels ; the arrival of a ship being the only sort of
incident that ever occurs here. *Our turret* is a nice
little room, with a good many books, four green chairs,
a table, and a huge sofa,—whereof (the sofa) the use
has been most delightful.)

  ' Next in order, our out-of-door resources come to
be mentioned. The climate, in spite of a rainy season
of great severity, is delicious. True, it has sometimes rained so *bucketfully* for a week together, that
Senhôr Diogo (for such is my name) has not got out
during that time ; but then would come such a smil-
ing shining day, as you poor Britannics won't see till
May or June ; and the heliotropes, geraniums, and
passion flowers—blooming *sub Jove frigido*—would
make one think that Pindar had Madeira in view,
when he sung—" Ενθα μακαρων νᾶσον ωκεανιδες αυραι
περιπνεουσιν, ανθεμα δε χρυσου φλεγει."* The fertility
of the soil is amazing. It is just terraces of thin mould
on blocks of lava ; but every square inch bears ; and
under the vineries you may see undergrowths of pota-
toes, pumpkins, &c., &c. You would laugh to see
the infinitesimal spots which they inclose as fields ;
and still more to mark a Madeiran agriculturist with
a plough of most primitive construction, drawn by a
pair of little light-brown oxen, most philosophically

---

* Where the ocean breezes play upon the island of the blest, and flowers
of gold glitter in the sun.

sowing wheat and tares together. Apropos of the oxen, I may say, that they and mules are the only farm-servants from the brute creation. Cart-horses there are none, for this irrefragable reason, that there are no carts. The island is so steep, and the roads so rough, that wheel-carriages are quite out of the question. Two or three gentlemen have droskies, and the Portuguese ladies run to the balconies to see them, with as much zeal as they would to see a well-dressed Inglezina going to church. The internal transport of goods is effected by putting them in hampers on men's heads, or on sledges drawn by the oxen aforesaid. The same steepness which makes the island inaccessible to carts, renders it equally difficult to broken-winded men. Hence, whoever comes here as an invalid, if he wishes to get the benefit of that open air for which chiefly he is sent, must either keep, or frequently hire, a horse. Even on a horse, it is often a sad scramble. I have gone up places, which, at a little distance, looked like the face of a wall; and you cannot ride any distance without encountering some great ascents. The horses of course are used to it, and are very surefooted; and so are the men, one of whom runs after you wherever you go, and at whatever pace, clenching your horse's tail απριξ ονυξι. I generally ride an hour or more daily, weather permitting; and always feel my breathing the lighter the more I am out. *En passant*, I may say that I have got some good lessons in riding, both from the steep ascents, where, if one does not well compress his knees, he will infallibly slide back over the tail, and from riding a certain kicking pony, which, on various occasions, has manifested a strong desire to make me bite the dust. On one occasion lately he operated in this way rather curiously. A party of gentlemen went out, about a month ago, to ride along a road, which, during great part of its extent, is subtended by prickly pears—a coarse and very spinose cactus. Well, the gentleman (*not* Senhôr

Diogo) who rode this pony happened to get before the rest of the party. Turning round to look for his companions, he placed his hand—quite naturally—behind him ; but, unluckily, just on the spot where Mr Pony is rather touchy. Sundry vehement *funks* (a Scotchman may surely write in Scotch) were the immediate consequence, which duly deposited our hero among the prickly pears—a bed, compared to which, nettles would have been down. As he was emerging, the rest of the party rode up, and sympathetically inquired how he got there. Just as he had mounted, he replied, " Oh ! I was looking round, and just laid my hand on the pony *so*," suiting the action to the word. Of course the pony was not a whit less disposed to illustrate, with the closest accuracy, his previous performance; he repeated the experiment without a single demi-semi-funk of variation ; and so, once more, the simpleton sprawled. I think the *cleg* was nothing to this.

' Well, — but I wander from my theme ; for, in speaking of out-of-door resources, I meant chiefly to allude to *friends* and acquaintances. Inanimate nature ministers much to our delight and welfare ; but give me a man to talk to. In this respect we are very happy. My most valued crony is Henry Cadell, Esq., of the Bank of Scotland, in Edinburgh, who was Treasurer to the Church Extension Committee, and having been sent here by Sir James Clarke, was advertised of my coming, by Alex. Dunlop, Esq., met us on the beach, helped us to get settled, and often delights me with his visits. I need say nothing more of him than that he is a right-hearted Scotchman, every way worthy of being treasurer to Dr Chalmers' Committee. Then there are Messrs Ashe and Langford, evangelical ministers of the Church of England, both of a noble and devoted spirit. Ashe is a man of high talent and thorough orthodoxy, who commenced his ministry as a low Arminian, and was brought to change his views by reading the Scriptures; above all, a man of the most elevated spirituality, to whom you cannot speak without feeling that his conversation is in heaven. *E. g.*, I met him the other day at the funeral of the Rev. Mr Bond, another excellent man, and was remarking how heavily the stroke would fall on his friends, as he was taken off, not by his pulmonary disease, but by what I may call an incidental fever. —Ashe replied, " Why should they grieve? He has only *got the start* of us a little." How I envied his faith! Then there is the Rev. J—— S——, also an Anglican, who is eminent in another way; of vast reading, and great conversational power; a writer of verses in *Blackwood;* a hard student of Germanic criticism; but his theology tinged a good deal with the mud of that fountain. Yet he is truly liberal-minded; fond of discussion; confesses the parochial inefficacy of the Anglican system : and I think, if he were in Scotland, would vote with the extreme left in the General Assembly. Next, a Mr F——, Arminian in theology, but most mild and gentle in spirit; and his sister, a kind of female translation of his character. . . . . A Mrs O——, who came with us in the packet, is a great friend of Janet's. She has two sons with her, William and Louis ;—Louis, a young officer, who, poor fellow! will never see his colours again, being in the last stage of consumption; and William, the heir of a patrimony in the north of Ireland, who was intended for the army, but, having begun to think seriously on religion, resigned his commission to his brother. He is one of the most faithful and affection-ate sons and brothers I have ever seen. He seems willing to make any sacrifice, that his mother and Louis may be comfortable. And so intense is his fraternal affection, that after he had been made aware of the improbability of his brother's recovery, he was found (being of a very abstracted and absent turn) in the middle of the night, standing by Louis's bedside, and gazing on the pale and beautiful features of his sleeping brother. He maintains a very lofty standard of Christian conscientiousness; and though he has much to gain in religious knowledge, will find, I doubt not, an abundant fulfilment of the promises in Hosea vi. 2, 3, and John vii. 44. Mrs O——— is very clever; has travelled and seen much, and has a fine spirit, much subdued and mellowed by great family trials. Moreover, we have some *Glasgow* friends. . . .

' You wonder, I dare say, why I have not yet given a particular account of my health. Every thing in its order. I wanted to let you know first the causes in operation; a statement of the effects will follow. You have now some idea of the *moral* causes of cheerfulness and lively occupation; I shall now say something of the *physical* or *Rentonian* efficients of my health. . . . . Meanwhile, I am often filled with longings for the Presbytery of Edinburgh, and frequently feel as if, suppose I were licensed and yet not able to preach at home, I would gladly go to some foreign station under a warmer sun. You can't imagine how foolishly these thoughts sometimes engross me, and how sadly I think of those houses of prayer, in which, but for criminal indolence, which compelled me to delay, my voice might have sounded. But you must not think, from this, that the θυμον κατεδων* process is going on very actively. My besetting sin is light-heartedness and want of thought. And I have daily cause for lamentation that I am so apt to forget the solemnities of my state; and that, though pressed by the mightiest motives, I so little hold forth the word of life.

' The mixture of inability and inactivity, which operates to prevent me from doing the little good I might, is the more to be regretted, as there is scarcely any thing heard here of the truth as it is in Jesus. The minister of the English Church, though known

* Mind-consuming.

at Cambridge as a botanist and ichthyologist, and here as the composer of some pretty hymn music, is literally no divine. His theology, if it may be so called, is a compound of Arminianism and Popery. His views are what are called high-church, and nearly approximate to those of the Oxford Tract men; only he has not a grain of the fervour which marks some of them. I have heard him preach baptismal regeneration—the *necessity* of the sacraments to salvation—the notion that the virtue of the Lord's Supper lies " not in your faith, but in the consecrated signs"—the heresy that we are *not* justified by faith without works of law, &c., &c.; and with all this zeal for sacramental forms, I cannot say that I have ever heard him *fully* declare the Atonement of Jesus Christ, nor have I ever heard *one* forcible appeal to the conscience. With a congregation before him, 200 members of which are probably in the grasp of a fatal disorder, he edified us last day with a discourse on the folly of atheism, and with another, whereof the drift was to show, that " Anathema Maranatha," means—" excommunicated from the Church !" You will not wonder to hear that the people's state corresponds to these instructions. I have never witnessed a more intensely worldly spirit than among the English residents here : this, with gaiety, seems to make sad havoc with them. The Sabbath is much abused. Many of the English went to a ball on the evening of the 31st December; and what wonder, when just a week previously,—viz., on Christmas eve (Sabbath), the Rev. Mr T———, who is here for his wife's health, and often assists Mr Lowe, went to enjoy the music and spectacle at the Popish cathedral !

' The operation of high-church principles, which, if they be not purged out, will, I verily believe, be the ruin of the Church of England, will be best illustrated by a brief account of a prayer-meeting which is held at Mr Langford's. That zealous and excellent clergy-

man, who has been here three winters, was in the
habit formerly of holding such meetings.   Desirous
of doing so under the most favourable circumstances,
he asked Mr Lowe's aid, or, if not, at least his con-
currence and countenance.   The reply was, that "it
was not *ecclesiastical ;* if Mr Langford chose to meet
in the church, and read *the Church service*, Mr Lowe
would be very happy to give the use of the church
for that end ; but he thought it quite irregular to
meet in an unconsecrated place, and use *extemporaneous prayer."* Of course Mr Langford just set
on foot the meeting *suis viribus ;* and how many,
think you, out of 15 clergymen, assist in it ? why,
just Mr Ashe and myself. . . . . However, by the help
of God, the meeting continues ; and on good days is
attended by some 40 or 50 people.   I hope I have
learned something from the acute discernment and
spiritual understanding of Mr Ashe. . . . .
    ' With these occupations and enjoyments, blessed
be God, I have *never*, in the daytime, *known weariness.*   Sometimes, with my grievous incapacity for
sustained meditation, a sleepless night has passed
heavily away.   But on the whole, my comforts very
far exceed any thing of suffering that I have yet been
called to.   Probably you will wonder that I have so
long deferred saying any thing about my mental state.
The truth is, I have little to say.   Although eternity
has been brought so near me, I feel very much of a
body of sin and death still making my soul cleave to
the dust.   I have daily cause to mourn over levity and
worldliness of spirit, and wonder at myself for daring
to entertain imaginations and schemes which savour
of expecting a resting-place here.   I feel that I am
not " pure in heart ;" and how, then, I am often
tempted to ask, can I think to see God ? My only
refuge is to endeavour to look unto Jesus, in the exercise of the *direct* act of faith,——as being set forth
a propitiation for sins, through faith in his blood.

Iniquities so prevail against me, that I often see this but obscurely; but I dare not look any where else. I still need your prayers for faith and the *spirit of adoption*. . . . .

' And suffer me, my beloved friend, to exhort you, that you make full proof of your ministry. Every thing I have seen convinces me of the inexpressible advantage and blessing we enjoyed in being born in Scotland, and educated for the ministry under Dr M'Gill. I do think that, had the object been to devise a plan for the encouragement of careless men to enter the ministry, no more appropriate scheme could have been fallen on, than the system which prevails in the Church of England, in which prayer, by being in a prescribed mode, is rendered formal, and something nearly approaching to utter contempt is cast upon the ordinance of preaching, by running it so completely into a corner. Our sin is the greater, if the simple formula of our Church's worship—more suited, as I think, to the genius of a spiritual dispensation—do not lead us to conduct our labours in the newness of the Spirit, and not in the oldness of the letter. And while, alas! too many of Christ's professed ministers appear perplexed and bewildered if you remove their horn-book, and substitute the sacrament for Christ, and dwell in the outward form; may it be your happiness to know nothing but Jesus Christ and him crucified, to turn many to righteousness, and finally to shine as a star in the firmament for ever and ever. That this may be your course, I never forget to pray; and that " the God of peace, who brought again from the dead our Lord Jesus," &c., &c. . . . . . And now, my dear friend, farewell. You know to whom I commend you, with the truest affection. Ever yours, J. H.'

' *Rev. William Arnot.*'

This letter, all written on one sheet, is of very great

length.   The portions extracted above make up about
one half of the whole.   It is written with the utmost
neatness and accuracy.   Not a letter needs to be altered.   Every point appears in its proper place.   This
was his habit, exemplified in the most trifling note,
as well as in an elaborate essay.

In this and other letters which follow, the reader
will observe there are some very free remarks on the
species of Popery which is spreading in the Church of
England.   Although in some quarters they may give
offence, we do not feel at liberty to suppress such
passages as these.   It is no aim of ours to employ the
pen of the dead in stirring up strife among the living;
but we have a sacred duty to perform, and we must
go right through with it.   This is not a time to keep
back, through an overstrained delicacy, any evidence
that may bear upon that wide-spread heresy.   Mr
Halley had full opportunity of observing the developement of Puseyism among the English residents at
Madeira; and we feel it were an injury done to the
cause of truth to withhold the testimony of a witness
so competent.   We shall continue to present his evidence regarding the principles and practice of the
system.   When destructive error is prevailing, we are
bound to call as witnesses for the truth, those who are
qualified intellectually to understand the question, and
endued with moral courage to speak the truth plainly.

The following letter contains a pretty minute account of the state of his health.   He describes the
symptoms of his own disease, as he always did, with
as much stoical coolness as if he had been speaking
of a stranger; and yet it may be observed, that the
' proverbially deceptive' malady had some influence

in swaying his judgment. The hint toward the conclusion, about trying the missionary work in a warmer
climate, is eminently characteristic of the writer's mind.
He was 'full' of a desire to preach Christ, and 'weary
with holding in.' It is addressed to a minister in
Glasgow :—

' FUNCHAL, *Madeira, Feb.* 19, 1838.

' My dear Sir, — The kind and very active part
which you took in my transportation to this place,
fully entitles you to some account of the consequences
which have resulted from your friendly labours. I
did not write sooner, in order that I might have something pretty definite to say ; and I write briefly, lest
much stooping should defeat the very purpose for
which I sojourn in this strange land.

' My father and Mr R. will probably, ere now, have
told you something of our voyage hither, and of the
results of my residence here, up to the beginning of
January. All that I could then speak of was a very
slight degree of improvement, and I cannot speak of
much more now. Still there has been enough to
exempt the disease from the gloom of utter hopeless-
ness, although not enough, certainly, to warrant any
confident expectation of a recovery either speedy or
complete. Dr Renton, whose advice I enjoy, happened to call here the other day, when I was just
writing some account of myself, and he gave his
imprimatur to it in every particular ; so I cannot do
better than repeat it to the best of my recollection.

' When I came here in November, Dr R. examined
my chest, by means of the stethoscope, with great care.
He fixed at once, and confidently, on the very same
spots which Drs Alison, Peebles, and Watson, had
marked out as the chief seats of the disease ; but spoke
more strongly than even Dr Watson of the length to
which the malady had gone. " You have just about

one lung working; the right is almost wholly, the left partially *hepatized;* but no cavity has been formed, and it *may* be possible to bring you about *slowly,* by *care* and *active measures."*   As to *care,* Janet and I have done our best ; and the other measures have been sufficiently *active,* consisting of four blisters, two mustard plasters, and, whenever the skin was decently formed upon the blistered surface, constant irritation with tartar emetic ointment.   Three months of these things have made them and me excellent friends.   I am never above two days or so free from the tartaric irritation, and walk and ride about with it as composedly as if no such process were going on.   The effects have been, on the whole, favourable.   Dr Renton says, *quite decidedly,* that I can now inhale a longer breath than I could when he first examined me ; which proves that some part of the congestion or hepatization has begun to give way.   And if this much has been accomplished during a rainy season of almost unexampled severity, we may reasonably hope that the movement will not be retrograde when we come to really settled and genial weather.   Renton thinks it a good feature of the case that my build is naturally so strong, and that I have no constitutional tendency to pulmonary disorders.   Had such a tendency existed, he would have thought the case hopeless.   And it is a very favourable circumstance that I am quietly situated,—not in one of the large boarding-houses, where the inmates are fifteen or twenty strong, —and yet enjoy such various and pleasant society, that I have *never,* in the daytime, *known weariness.* But I am sensible that my ultimate recovery is still very doubtful—ετι ξυρου ιστατаι αχμης.   Long disease in the lungs may induce a tuberculous formation, for which there is no remedy.   But there is reason to believe that no such thing exists as yet ; and I cannot be sufficiently thankful to the Providence which sent me hither, and so delivered me from the fatal termination to which a Scottish winter would, before now, have brought my disorder. I have endeavoured to ascertain from Dr Renton what course he would advise me to follow, should I be spared till the time when the invalids usually leave this for Britain. He declines giving a decided judgment at present, till he sees how I stand the greater heat which we may soon expect. If it operates favourably, I presume, on medical grounds, he would advise me to pass the summer here. But the constant headache from which I used to suffer at home (insomuch that four months of 1835 were just one continued headache), are too likely to return under the excitement and heat of a southern summer. Of course, time alone can show how this is likely to be. I need not say, that all my own desires are on the side of returning home. Here, invalids are so unconcernedly spoken of as an article of commerce, and every thing, down to burial fees, is contrived so completely and remorselessly on the principle of fleecing them (or, as it is more gently expressed, making the most of them), that, even in the worst issue, I should not wish to die in Madeira. And, on the more favourable supposition of a recovery (which Dr Renton frankly tells me *must* be gradual and protracted), I have a great longing to deliver my remaining discourse before the Presbytery of Edinburgh, and be ready for any work to which Providence may call me. It must not be concealed, that Dr R. says plainly, that even should I live till the winter of 1838, it will be *out of the question to spend it in Scotland;* and this, no doubt, very much perplexes the question of my return in summer; for, if I were likely to need to come back here, it would be scarcely worth while to stir. But although I might be unfit for home labour, it is possible that I might be able to do something under a warmer sun ; and rather than continue a burden, any longer than is absolutely necessary, upon those friends who sent me here, I would volunteer into the foreign service of the Church. So far as I can at present see (although I am not confident in this opinion, for continued sickness enfeebles the mind, and makes one even more shortsighted than usual), I think, if it were the will of God, I might, from the influence of my college standing and other such causes, be more useful in Scotland than any where else ; but if I were not well enough to preach at home, and yet able to do even a little abroad, I should view it as a call in Providence to leave my kindred and my father's house. Now this could not be done without first obtaining license at home. On the other hand, if it is Dr Renton's judgment, after the lapse of some more time, that to return home would be just undoing what good has already been done, and that to remain here would give a more rational hope of ultimate recovery and usefulness, I presume my kind friends in Glasgow, who made you the organ of their benevolence, would approve of my acting on his counsel. . . . . . Yours with much respect and gratitude,   J. H.'

' *Rev. James Gibson.*'

As there is no letter preserved from February to May, we continue the mental history of the patient by another series of extracts from the Journal.

' *Saturday*, 10th *March* 1838.

' I have to record another mercy since my last entry in this book, viz., the arrival, on Tuesday last, of nine letters from Glasgow, some of which exceedingly affected and melted me. Blessed be God for such friends ; they add much to the mercies for which I must answer.'

' *Thursday*, 15th *March* 1838.

' Engaged in special prayer for an upward direction to my desires. Found a most humbling tendency in my mind to take up its rest here. Surely God is amply warning me that here I have no continuing city ; yet I go on as if earth were my home. Oh for more sustained solemnity of spirit ! oh for a heart in heaven ! '

'*Friday*, 16*th March* 1838.

' Again have I to speak of the Divine goodness in sending me most affectionate letters from Mr and Mrs Colquhoun and Mr Wilson, and favourable accounts, indirectly, of the state of mind in which my dear friend, Sir D. K. Sandford, died on the 4th February.

' Blessed be God for the kindness of friends, and for that good news from a far country which is like cold water to a thirsty soul.

' Surely in all things I may trust His grace. Yes ! I *will* trust and not be afraid. Felt some encouragement and comfort in drawing near to God, and committing myself to the Redeemer. Oh that I knew the blessedness of close communion with him—of being taken into the secret of his presence !'

'*Thursday*, 22*d March* 1838.

' Saw last night, in a Glasgow paper, mention made of the death of Mr George Forsyth, a student of divinity, of about my own age, and seemingly a far better life. "He that hath ears," &c.'

'*Friday*, 23*d March* 1838.

' This day month Mr Forsyth died, probably after a brief warning. My warning has been longer—so long as to leave no excuse for indifference. And it has been pretty explicit ; for I have always believed, and now (speaking as a man) feel convinced, that this disease of the lungs will carry me off. I *may* live for months ; but as to recovery, unless by some remarkable aid from on high, vain is the help of man. I record this, with the prayer, that the Spirit may make it effectual for keeping my thoughts upon God and eternity.

'I have often, while in perfect health, and with such an end far, very far, from my expectations, wished to die of consumption. And now that my wish is likely to be gratified, I see the ways of God in removing men from this world are more equal than I had imagined. If the man who is seized by acute and rapid disease has too little time to think—a chronic malady, to the corrupt heart, seems to give too much. If the one case is so pressing as to bewilder, the other is regarded as so little pressing that the poor patient delays his great concern. If the one is overwhelmed, the other is enervated. If the one is " consumed with terrors, as it were, in a moment," the other is flattered by hopes, and deluded by appearances of amendment. If eternity overpowers and prostrates the one by its near approach, it seems to recede and flee from the other.

'In thus speaking, I allude to the effects *naturally* produced in a depraved mind. The Spirit alone, in either case, can counteract them. And as every one best feels his own burden, I now see what special aids are required to keep a consumptive invalid from settling down into moveless lethargy.——Ειη μοι χαρις δι Ιησου Χριστου. Αμην.'*

'*Thursday*, 5th *April* 1838.

'I have been perplexed about the matter of duty in going home or staying here during the summer. May the Lord undertake for me, and show me by his providence what I ought to do, so that it may be done in confidence of faith !

'Finished Owen on Psalm cxxx.; and record, for the use and benefit of my soul, one short sentence from it,—" *Spiritual peace and sloth will never dwell together in the same soul and conscience.*"

'The perusal of this book has made me resolve more on *waiting* upon God. *Surely* joy *will* come ;

---

* May grace be given me, through Jesus Christ. Amen.

only let me be of good courage, and He *will* strengthen my heart.'

'*Friday, 6th April* 1838.

'" And I will wait upon the Lord, that hideth his face from the house of Jacob, and I will look for him."— ISAIAH viii. 17.

'*Patient waiting* upon God seems to be a duty to which I am now particularly called. Hitherto it has been often ruined in me both by impatience and by sloth. I have either *fainted*, and given up in a temporary despair, or (the more frequent case) I have limited the Holy One of Israel; and because spiritual comfort did not come just when I wanted it, or by the duties in which I expected to have found it, I have waxed froward and lost all the benefit. I see and deeply bewail the folly of such conduct. What am I that I should let my will loose upon those times and seasons which the Father hath kept in his own power? that I should prescribe a limit to the sovereign, all-wise, all-bountiful God? and fret, forsooth, because his disposals differ from those which my presumption and selfishness would have dictated?

' Blessed be his name, my eyes are now, in part at least, opened to the sin of this. I abhor myself, and repent in dust and ashes. And, in the strength of the Holy Ghost, I resolve quietly to *wait his time.* Meanwhile, during the season that the vision of his blessed reconciled countenance tarries, may he at least encircle me with his everlasting arm, and keep me from fainting. Oh for the attitude of the servant whose loins are girt!—the frame of silent, adoring, humble, hoping expectation! Lord, sustain and quicken me : raise me from the dust : visit me with thy salvation !

' And may I be taught also to *look* for Him in all ordinances and means; in reading his Word, prayer, praise, and Christian communion; in holy meditation ; in stirring up my heart to lay hold on him ; in

L

endeavouring to meet Jesus at his own table! Give
me, Lord, the preparation of the sanctuary for this
holy service, whenever thou permittest me to engage
in it.   Lift up the Redeemer, with power, before me;
and bow me down before the Cross of Christ.   Amen.'

'*Saturday,* 7th *April* 1838.

' " How precious also are thy thoughts unto me, O God!
how great is the sum of them!   If I should count them,
they are more in number than the sand."—PSALM cxxxix.
17, 18.

' Such, certainly, and more (if more could be said)
are the words of praise I owe to God my Maker.
May He give me this song in the night of affliction, to
extol and magnify his name for all his past and present mercies!   And how great is the sum of them!
Food and raiment, and support in comfort, *all my
days ;* many and endeared friends ; a most affectionate father ; a mother, whose memory is sweet ; a sister,
whose very life seems bound up in mine ; the dearest
and most devoted affection from many whom blood
in no way joined to me,—my pupils, my Sabbath
scholars, and others whom I love ; opportunities of
the best kind for intellectual improvement ; a mind
in some measure fitted to use them ; kind patrons to
notice and cheer my progress :—the blessing of an
evangelical ministry ; the prayers and instructions of
an evangelical professor of divinity ; the society of the
very *élite* of Edinburgh, as well as Glasgow, for piety
and talent ; in particular, the example and faithful
reproofs of . . . . :—success in almost
all my literary and professional undertakings :—many
deliverances at various times ; in particular, at Loch
Frochy, where I was nearly drowned from a fishing
skiff in 1826 ; in Rutherglen, where I fell unhurt
from the dickey of a coach ; at Glasford, where I
lost my eye, but had my life saved, in 1827 ; and at
Cramond, this day twelve months [wrong, it was on
the 22d], where I narrowly escaped death by an

unguarded leap :—a continued course for many years of health and high spirits, which enabled me, although sinning fearfully in the matter of indolence, to do something in study and in public exertion :—this sickness, which has thrown me inward (I hope in mercy) upon my own soul :—the kind sympathies of friends at its commencement, Dr Alison, Mrs Hamilton, Mrs Ramsay, and others ; Dr Watson's providential advice to come to Madeira ; the generous and prompt offers of Messrs ——— ; the kind sympathies of all :—our short voyage ; our location in a small boarding-house :—the unexpected abundance of Christian friends, Cadell, Bond, Ashe, Langford, Hull, Dr Smith :— . . . . Dr Renton's frankness as a medical adviser, and the goodness of many sympathizing friends :—the providential warnings afforded by so many deaths, especially those of Mr Forsyth and Sir Daniel Sandford—these make a sum of mercies which I cannot compute. And to these must be added another infinite—something far above and beyond our poor conceptions—in the promises and hopes of the Gospel.

'Surely goodness and mercy *have* followed me all the days of my life.' . . . .

'*Sabbath*, 8*th April* 1838.

' " What ! shall we receive good at the hand of God, and shall we not receive evil ! "—Job ii. 10.

' It is difficult for the flesh to say this ; yea, no one can truly say it but by the Spirit of God. I praise his name that in some poor measure I can, at this time, feel the excellence of such submission. When I think of the incident of 22d April 1837, when I was mercifully preserved from sudden death, and the altered feelings with which I can now look upon eternity, the Divine goodness appears marvellously displayed in this dispensation. My own impatient spirit might sometimes have been apt to think that it had been better then to die without all this languishing ; but, *ill* prepared as I am now, I was *worse* then, and so I can see great mercy in this protracted sickness. I " know (Job xi. 6) that God exacteth of me" far " less than mine iniquity deserveth ;" and I do, with some measure of heartiness, adopt as my own the prophet's resolution, "*I will bear* the indignation of the Lord, *because* I have sinned against him." (Micah vii. 9.)

'We have had a new trial to-day, in the arrival of the " Dart," which is to carry away from us unexpectedly soon, our dearest Madeira friends, in the —————— ——————. The want of letters, also, is trying to faith. Yet we know who it is that giveth bread to the hungry.'

'Sabbath, 15th April 1838.

'This is Easter-day, which many of the churches of Christ regard with peculiar veneration, as the day of his resurrection. I sat down at His table, with the solemn conviction, that, of the congregation who did so here to-day, one-half will never again meet on earth in the same way. If I can at all presume to judge of my own feelings, they were those of a sinner in need of every thing, coming to Christ, as a Saviour who can cleanse all sin, and bestow all grace, and hope, and joy. Had some enlargement of heart in commending to Christ, at his own table, those Christian friends with whom we meet no more ; and especially in asking for the —————— all joy and peace in believing. Surely the Shepherd of the sheep will keep them even unto the end.

'Tried to recollect and pray against my most besetting sins. I find, alas ! that their name is Legion. But as I did endeavour, in simplicity of soul, to give myself to Christ, I trust he will give me some gracious mark of his acceptance of so poor an oblation, in subduing sin within me, and making me more entirely his own.'

' *Thursday*, 26th *April* 1838.

' The ———s sailed.

' Oh God, it hath pleased thee to take from us the desire of our hearts, and the light of our eyes, as far as the temporal good of friends is concerned. May it please thee to be with them on the waters; may the Redeemer uphold them from sinking; may they be strong in faith, giving glory to thee. Be thou with them as the God of peace, guiding them to their home in safety, and giving them a happy and holy meeting with their friends. And may we, who are behind in this land of death, possess our souls in patience, and look for the mercy of our Lord Jesus Christ unto eternal life. Be thou far more to us than they could ever be; and, while the remembrance of them is sweet, may it also be sanctified. And give us a happy meeting—*here*, if it please thee; if not, at least *there*, where there is no night of sorrow or parting : through Jesus Christ. Amen.'

' *Sabbath*, 29th *April* 1838.

' Was confined in the forenoon, but heard Mr Lowe in the afternoon on Jude 11,—the character of Balaam, —a moral discourse, with various delineations of character, but scarcely a reference to the Cross of Christ.

' Through the important spiritual advantages I have enjoyed, I think I *do* see the central position which that Cross occupies in the scheme of divine truth. How great the responsibility which such knowledge involves! Oh that the heart were affected in proportion as the head is informed! Oh that I were made to glory in the Cross of Christ, by which the world is crucified unto me, and I unto the world! Oh for more of this wholesome crucifixion—of earthly desires destroyed, that the heavenly may grow! Lord, subdue me to thyself; captivate me to thyself; let me find my satisfaction solely in thee. "The Lord is my portion, saith my soul; therefore will I hope in him." " It is good that a man both *hope*, and *quietly wait* for the salvation of the Lord." " The Lord is faithful." Even so. Amen.'

We invite the attention of ministers of the Gospel to this last short extract. The reproof of unfaithful preaching is written in a tone of meekness, which shows clearly the power of renewing grace, softening the naturally ardent mind of our departed friend; but the reproof itself is more cutting far than if it had been presented in a strain of confident railing. Ministers who do not with all their hearts preach Christ crucified, should know that every inquiring penitent hearer feels the preaching to be miserable comfort, though few be able to tell where the defect lies. ' Woe is unto me if I preach not the Gospel ! ' ' A moral discourse, with various delineations of character,' will not satisfy souls that are longing for the living God.

The next letter is given as a specimen of the searching examination to which Mr Halley was in the habit of subjecting himself. It is certain that, sometimes during the course of his disease, he manifested a perverse ingenuity in finding out hard things against himself; but it may be instructive to read his own account of the process, even in those cases where he carried his reasonings too far. The prevailing sin is, not the excess, but the want of such self-examination ; and the keenness with which such a man searched his own sins, may rebuke the carelessness of the many who never concern themselves about the matter,— who heal their wound slightly, and cry Peace, when there is no peace.

To explain the allusion in the introductory sentence, the reader must bear in mind that the 1st of May was the day on which the annual distribution of prizes was made in the university of Glasgow. The 'light' of the college is the late Sir Daniel K. Sandford, Professor of Greek.

'FUNCHAL, MADEIRA, 2d May 1838.

' My dear A——,— I meant to have commenced the present epistle to you yesterday; but lost the opportunity, by means of falling into one of those interminable conversations with Janet, which you can so well understand; for many has been the time I have held them with yourself. It would have been pleasant, somehow (and yet I cannot tell how, for I weep as I think of it), to have begun it on the *first of May*,—a day once of no small excitement, in the anticipation, to you and me; but now—to *one* of us at least—a remembrancer of much unholy striving, with faculties, which, if better directed, *might* have glorified God. I could not help, yesterday, thinking of many friends; of the light of Glasgow college, now, alas! gone down; of poor Ivory and Mackintosh, to whom their rewards would lose half their sweetness; and of the current of reflection which I imagined was likely to carry Mackail, and Morrison, and Denniston,— perhaps even yourself in the midst of all your labours, and certainly my poor father,—to this distant island of the sea. Well! it is all over; but, I trust, *not* the lesson that " childhood and youth are vanity."

' Your much wished-for letter, dated 9th February, reached me on the 18th of April. If you knew the good it did me, and the inexpressible delight with which I have perused and reperused it, you would write oftener, and by a more direct way. . . . .

' God forbid you should ever be fully satisfied with your own preaching: then, indeed, one *might* mourn over you; but, meantime, as you are determined not to stand still, so I trust, by God's blessing, you will never be permitted to do so; but be content to cultivate a restless spirit of improvement and advancement in your holy art of winning souls *here*, in hope of the rest that remaineth *hereafter*. I am very grateful for your kind concern about me in regard to the one thing needful. It were well if all who inquire about my health had the same solicitude for my soul's prosperity. My heart was ever open to you, and I could always tell you more than I could tell any one else; but the time and manner of this inquiry have given me a greater willingness than ever to pour out to you all that I feel on the grand theme of my salvation. Yet I can only speak with stammering lips on this subject; for it is hard for another to imagine how the constant hurry of activity, in which I had for many years been involved, disqualified me for self-inspection,—how, while cumbered and troubled about many things,—*connected* even as these were with the kingdom of Christ,—I had forgotten the one thing, drifted away from my anchorage, and lost almost all ability to decide on the bearings of my course.

'Let me, then, with shame and sorrow, confess, that I am not yet out of that dubious and equivocal state in which I was when I last wrote you. I have a clear intellectual perception and conviction of the utter ruin of my own nature; every hour's experience painfully convinces me, that in me there dwelleth no good thing; I *know*—perhaps sometimes I *feel*—that by the works of the law I cannot be justified. My mouth *is* stopped; and though God were to cast me off for ever, I do believe that he would be clear in thus judging. Then, my judgment is equally satisfied on the leading outlines of God's scheme of recovery; in particular, that Emmanuel's atonement is enough for all sin, and any sinner who will receive him; that his righteousness, when relied on, is a sure title to glory; that his Spirit, dispensed to all who ask him truly, is omnipotent to make us meet for the inheritance. All this I receive as the word of the truth of the Gospel; and I try to found upon it a *surrender* of myself to this Saviour, and a constant looking upward for promised grace. Let me give a specimen of each: When iniquities prevail against me, as they *often* do, and I fall or rush into sins, *known* to be such, and therefore wounding to my conscience, I endeavour, as soon as I can, to bring them and lay them (in trusting supplication) on the head of the scapegoat—where the Lord hath laid the iniquities of us all; and again, when I am about to commence the perusal of any book, it has long been my habit to ask for spiritual light, that I may be able to separate between the chaff and the wheat, and that even secular knowledge (if it relates to this), or mental refreshment (if that is all I am seeking), may be sanctified in its possession and use. But, in such applications as these, of the two co-ordinate truths of atonement and spiritual aid for Christ's sake, I feel on all hands beset with snares, and so perplexed and bewildered, through the deceitfulness of sin, that I am often ready to take up Asaph's language in Psalm lxxiii. 22. In the first of the cases above mentioned, by way of example, I am often embarrassed by the thought, that this constant interchange of sinning, and then going to the Lamb of God, is, in effect, something very like making *Christ the minister of sin;* and this awful reflection is confirmed by the consciousness, that my reference to the cross of Christ is only made *after* I sin, and not *before* it; that it supervenes as a *cure*, rather than precedes as a *preventive;* and that, when I try to analyse my feelings upon *abstaining* from any thing *because it is sinful*, I rather find myself affected with its danger, than with the ingenuous and Gospel feeling, "*He* loved me, and gave himself for me." And, in the second case, I frequently want *confidence* in asking the Divine guidance, from a secret knowledge that my request may justly be refused, on account, either (1), of insincerity,—as when I ask a blessing on a book which I have previously determined to read fast, and finish by a certain time, whether it be digested or not,—or, (2), of exertion misapplied, as when I am reading a human exposition of Scripture doctrine or duty with too little reference to the lively oracles. Often, on such occasions, I have no resource but to say, " When my spirit is overwhelmed, then Thou knowest my path ;" and to confess myself all weakness, and helplessness, and misery. Now, what I have just given, is only a *specimen* of my hourly failures in appropriating Gospel truths. I do feel a sad want of simplicity and godly sincerity in resting upon Christ for every thing needful.

‘ It occurs to me also, that surely a steady dependence upon the Redeemer for righteousness and strength, did it exist at all within me, would produce an increasing love to Him, and more meltings of spirit when I think of Him as " The *crucified*." But of this growth of feeling I am in no wise conscious ; nor can any such emotion in me claim the character of intensity. Farther, I know that " this is the victory that overcometh the world, even our faith ;" and that, if faith were here, some conquests over a worldly spirit, and over besetting lusts and sins, ought in time to be manifest. Yet all seems to be at a stand-still in that respect. The sins that do easily beset me,—as indolence, censoriousness, spiritual indifference, &c., are still constantly leading me captive ; and, partly from the intensely worldly spirit of this place,—partly from the nature of my complaint, which, though it warns of death *long*, never warns *loudly*,—and partly from various subordinate temptations, I have been somehow, too frequently, looking back to this earth,—although I knew that its fashion passeth away, and my prevailing judgment was, that I had done with it for ever. In particular, I feel that even the mercies wherewith God has encircled me, have been thus made a snare to me ; and that the refreshment I experienced during the many hours I spent with our dear friends the ——, was often, through my exceeding sinfulness, made the means of withdrawing me from secret communings with my own soul and the Invisible.

' On the other hand,—for no tongue can tell how willingly I would be alive to any thing encouraging,— it is certain that I have of late thought more of eternity,—that an unseen world is never long out of my mind. I can look to death with some steadiness; and I have never lost hope. Only the prevailing tendency and character of my mind induces a fear that *insensibility* may have more to do with this than *faith.* Yet I pray to be delivered from this; I try to realize the truth that Christ has overcome death, and to view Him as the Captain of *my salvation;* and I can always mourn that I know so little of "the anchor of the soul." And, although I daily detect my thoughts wandering to and fro over the earth, just as if I had many days to spend in it,—and know the bitterness of having too many of my heart-strings twined round earthly objects,—yet I do believe that the leading desire of my soul on this side the grave, is to possess and hold fast a good hope through grace in reference to the other. But " my soul cleaveth to the dust ;" I can only look upward and say, " Quicken thou me according to thy word." . . . .

' In summer we shall have Madeira pretty much to ourselves. 'Tis a sad emblem—this island—of our mortal state. Our dearest friends lay among the strangers, and they are all on the wing. Mr Cadell, the ——, the ——, go probably next week ; the Freeman's, and Ashe, and Langford, soon after ; and probably our next meeting will be at the judgment-seat of Christ. We have just had time to value each other; and then the spell is broken. But, after losing the ——, which we did last week, other partings will be comparatively easy. Should the resting-place of my dust be within their reach, I am sure two are added to the number of those who will go to the grave to weep there. . . . .

'Shall I add, that, in our religious exercises with them, in commending them to God and to the word of his grace, either from natural affectionate feeling, or a temporary victory over unbelief, I had some comfort : I could even, sometimes, anticipate a meeting, without the biting reflection that I had neither part nor lot in it—in *our* Father's kingdom. And I can often see that every thing belongs to *faith ;* and feel, that, if I but knew myself a believer, I could rest every thing on that word, "The Lord *is* faithful, who shall stablish you, and keep you from evil." . . . .

'The God of peace be with you !—Your ever grateful friend,   J. H.'

We recur again to the journal, and present, at full length, another specimen of the manner in which Mr Halley, in his own practice, ' remembered the works of the Lord.'

'*Sabbath, 6th May* 1838.

' Heard Mr Lowe on John xvi. 12, 13, in the forenoon ; and John xvi. 30, 31, in the afternoon. Baptismal regeneration eight times inculcated ; scarcely any sound Christianity at all. I have to mourn before God over the criticising spirit in which I heard him. It was difficult to do otherwise ; but I ought to have remembered, " Who art thou that judgest another's servant ?"

' Blessed be God, my frame was better after returning from church. I had a sensible pleasure in thinking how many of God's dear children are *this day* commemorating the Redeemer's death in Edinburgh, and how faithfully His great Atonement would be preached to them. Sometimes I almost think that my soul longeth for these favoured courts of the Lord.'

' " Whoso is wise, and will observe these things, even they shall understand the loving-kindness of the Lord."— PSALM cvii. 43.

' " I will remember the works of the Lord."—PSALM lxxvii. 11.

' Such is David's advice and practice in regard to noticing the course of events in providence. It is a profitable study, if the Spirit deign to shine on it. Imploring his aid, I would now look back to *this day twelvemonths,*—the memorable Saturday on which I was taken ill.

' On the morning of that day, I breakfasted with my dear friends the Hamiltons,—Smeaton, Mackintosh, and John Cunningham being present. I conducted their family worship. The Psalm sung was the lxxiii., verses 24–26 ; and I remember, to this hour, with a glow of feeling, the happy way in which we sung it. I have no doubt that a majority of those who then joined in it were renewed persons ; and it was no ordinary privilege to hear God's children thus claiming and exulting in their relation to him. Since then, strange to say, I have formed some new and strong attachments upon earth. Yet some ties also have been broken. Surely *I am* more willing to be and to do nothing, if the Lord is pleased to say that he hath no need of me here. Surely *I do* feel more of a pilgrim spirit. But still, this sad gravitation earthwards, which nothing less can remove than that mighty power, which was shown forth in Christ, when God raised him from the dead. Oh for fresh and constant quickening !

' Then walked down with the Hamiltons to Newhaven, where, on the quay—how true an emblem of our short meetings here—we saw my dear friend John Tait, who was about to embark next Monday for New South Wales. In him, ever since I knew him, the grace of our Lord has been exceeding abundant. He has now, doubtless, entered on his work ; may

the Spirit of the Lord be with him!   And let me
be humbled by the reflection, that, while he, and
Chalmers, and Stevenson, and Arnot, and Sutherland,
and Smeaton, and others of my companions in study,
have obtained part in this glorious ministry,——it should
have been needful, on account of my indolence,
worldliness, coldness, and unholiness,——that the great
Head of the Church should not allow me " to be put
in trust with the Gospel." Let me kiss this—his
heaviest rod.   He layeth on me far less than my sins
deserve.

‘ Crossed to Burntisland, where, meeting Dr Chalmers, I was taken to his house, and spent the day
with him.   Thus were my last hours of comparative
health spent in converse with one, whom it is a privilege to have known—for he has been blessed of God
to many souls.   Little did I think, when I left him,
that we should never meet more on earth,——which now
it seems likely we never shall.

‘ I rode to Aberdour, faint and oppressed with headache.   Imagining that I had only some slight cold, I
went early to bed, took some medicine, and expected
to be well on the morrow.   However, it would not
do : I had to stay at home from church ; and, I recollect, occupied myself in bed in reading " Clarkson on
Faith."   On the Monday, along with Chalmers and
the Rev. Mr Robertson, I crossed to Edinburgh, *very
ill ;* took a long farewell of Tait, in which (alas ! how
vainly !) I spoke of holding the rope while he went
down into the missionary pit ; went to my lodgings,
and was laid up by an inflammation, which, though
slight at the time, met with so little resistance from
a broken constitution, that it has landed me first in
Madeira, and may ultimately bring me down to the
house appointed for all living.

‘ At the time when it attacked me, I little thought
of death.   The fair prospect lay before me of being
licensed, whenever I might wish it, to preach the

Gospel. But I was too little thoughtful in the prospect of so great a work; and I now see, in some measure, the Divine wisdom in preventing the effects of my rashness. I see, besides, that, had I begun to preach with such sickly lungs, probably the bursting of some blood-vessel, and a still more speedy dissolution, would have ensued. God, in kindness, stopped me, that I might have more space for repentance and preparation for eternity, ere I should go hence and be no more. O for grace to use it aright!'

We gladly give place to the next two entries—an example of self-examination. The most remarkable feature of it, is the clearness of judgment—the precision of thought that runs throughout. We have had exhibitions elsewhere of the Christian philosopher: here we have the philosophic Christian. We have been accustomed to think of minds imbued with the faith of the Gospel, applied to science and hallowing it: here we have a mind disciplined to the utmost by human learning, applying all its resources directly to matters of faith. It is, blessed be God, no rare thing to meet with piety equal to that displayed in the following extract; it is the strength of understanding, and logical precision of thought, here brought to bear on the subject of piety, to which we specially invite the reader's regard. Let those who, possessed of a knowledge 'spread wide, but thin'—a knowledge extending over many subjects, but not going deep into any,—are thereby emboldened to lay aside practical religious concern, as fit only for weak minds—let them read the meditation which follows, and judge whether they are the weak-minded who keep, or who cast off their faith. We have here a truly great mind bowing down in prostrate humility before God, and searching his Word : let the superficial sceptic read, and tremble.

'*Friday,* 11*th May* 1838.

' Having spent, on Wednesday, a sleepless night, I found my mind yesterday too feeble to make any progress in the work of self-examination on which I had entered. To-day, I have been much kept away from it by various engagements ; yet have been enabled to do a little. At no grand decisive result have I yet arrived. But the steps of my progress, hitherto, are these :—

' I reviewed, at considerable length, the Scripture testimony regarding justification, especially on these two points :—1. That it is by faith alone in Christ's righteousness and sacrifice ; 2. That it is, on the part of God, a complete and irrevocable act. Fully satisfied, *once more*, on scriptural grounds of these,— seeing the inexpressible blessedness of a believer's state,—and convinced that the grand question is, " Have I apprehended Christ by faith ?" I set about the inquiry whether I am indeed a believer—not in word only—but vitally and in truth. Two ways appeared of solving this :—1. Seeing whether, in my present sentiments and feelings, so far as I can *directly* observe and analyse them, there is any thing corresponding to the scriptural *descriptions* of faith, in its general *nature* 2. Ascertaining its presence or absence *indirectly*, by the appearance or non-appearance of its *fruits.* What appeared on applying these tests, I hope to record to-morrow.

' It is *a year to-day* since I delivered my two last discourses before Edinburgh Presbytery—a lecture on Haggai ii. 6—9, and a critical exercise on Heb. ix. 28. It has been a trial, difficult to the flesh to bear, to think that the end for which I delivered them will probably, now, never be accomplished,—my becoming a licentiate of the Church of Scotland. I pray God to sanctify to me this crushing disappointment. My

best desires on earth are withered. O that a longing for heavenly rest were to flourish in proportion !
Surely God has brought me into the wilderness, that
he may speak comfortably to me.'

Sabbath, 13*th May* 1838.

' Forenoon : Mr Guillemard on Rom. xiv. 7–9,—
an excellent sermon, on charity in judging of differ-
ences among brethren, and Christ's unalienable right
to the love and obedience of his professing people.

' Resumed my work of self-humiliation and self-
scrutiny.

' " Let us search and try our ways, and turn again to the
Lord."—LAM. iii. 40.

' 1. In my present feelings, so far as I can *directly*
observe them, is there any thing agreeing to the Scripture accounts of faith ?   In answering this question, I
would desire a spirit of especial caution ; for in nothing
is the danger of self-deception greater, than in *directly*
observing one's own feelings,—when it is very manifest on which side it is most desirable to obtain a
verdict.   It would be my prayer that I may keep this
in mind ; and that the *Spirit of truth* may preserve
me from deluding my own soul.

' Is faith, then, in the simplest idea of it, a *looking*
to Jesus for salvation (Isa. xlv. 52), as the wounded
Israelites *looked* to the brazen serpent for health ?
(John iii. 14.)   Surely, I look nowhere else ; my
hope is in Him.   Is it a *fleeing* to him as a *refuge ?*
(Heb. vi. 18.)   I feel as one beat out of every other
stronghold, and taking shelter with him as my hiding-
place from the storm.   Is it a *receiving* him as offered
in the Gospel ? (John i. 12.)   And how is he offered ?
As a *Prince* and a *Saviour.*   If I do not thus receive
him, it is the prime desire of my soul to be enabled to
do so.   Is it *submitting* to his righteousness ? (Rom.
x. 3.)   It is at least a matter of deep conviction and
heartfelt acknowledgment with me, that I have none

M

of my own. And God forbid that pride should hinder
me from being a beggar of his bounty. Is it *committing*
the soul to him? (2 Tim. i. 12.) "Lord, into
thy hands I commit my spirit." Is it *taking hold* of
his strength? (Isa. xxvii. 5.) Surely the *genuine*
language of my soul is, "Lord help me, or I perish."
Is it *hungering* and *thirsting* for his righteousness?
(Matt. v. 6.) "My soul fainteth for thy salvation."
Is it *trusting* and *confiding* in his grace implicitly, as
the centurion, the woman of Canaan, and the woman
with the issue, did in their respective distresses?
Though it were but as a grain of mustard-seed, this
trust is what I most long after. "*I will trust*," by
his Spirit's power, "and not be afraid." Yes, Lord!
I do trust thee, for thou art faithful who has promised,—Jesus Christ the same yesterday, to-day, and
for ever!

'So far, then, as *direct* observation of feelings can
go, I am rather drawn to the conclusion—the blessed
conclusion, (oh that I could draw it more decidedly!)
that I have some part in this most precious faith.
Yet the lines are not clear and strong. "Strengthen,
O God, that which thou hast wrought for us." Work
in me mightily; and put it beyond all doubt that I
am a believer,—a sinner relying on the finished work
of Christ, and born again of a seed that is incorruptible.
Amen.

' 2. In my conduct and feelings of late, have there
appeared any of the *fruits* of faith? For the tree is
known by its fruit. (1.) *Peace* with God? (Rom. v. 1.)
Some kind of quietness I have generally enjoyed;
although I cannot but look on much of it as spurious,
and the fruit rather of insensibility than of faith. Yet,
in all seasons of distress from sin, I have tried to "run
to the name of the Lord," as my "strong tower."
(2.) *Confidence in prayer?* (Eph. iii. 12.) Here I
come altogether short. I am either much afraid, or
(much more commonly) rash, and thoughtless, and

wandering. The only comfort is, I have always explicit *mental* reference to Christ's merits. Pardon, O Lord, the sins and abominations of my prayers! (3.) *Love* to God? (Luke vii. 43.) Here, again, I am forced to cry, "My leanness!" Seldom, if ever, can I trace any pure working of this glorious principle. My views centre so much in self, that I seem as if I had never really cared for God's glory. O for a heart to love him! O for the promise of the new covenant! (4.) *Love* to man? (Gal. v. 6.) I think I see more love to God's children, and would bless his name that so many of them care and pray for me. But my heart is, like too many invalids, occupied far too much with myself. Lord, have mercy upon me, and enable me to use opportunities of doing good to others. (5.) *Establishment* against temptations? (2 Cor. i. 21, 24.) My strength is indeed small; and a trifle, I find, is still powerful to turn me aside. One of my besetting sins, for which I desire to humble myself before God, has very great dominion over me; yea, rather, my masters are many. Inward temptations, I bless God, do not greatly afflict me. (6.) *Victory over the world?* (1 John v. 4.) Surely I am now less devoted to forming schemes for time; and my idols are *fewer:* alas! that I cannot say they are all dethroned. Yet I can say that I *abandon this world as the rest of my soul.* Lord, help me to live daily and hourly in the spirit of this good confession. (7.) *Joy?* (Psal. xl. 3; Rom. v. 11.) To this fruit of faith my heart has been entirely a stranger. Let me resolve, in the Spirit's strength, to wait till God, in sovereignty, is pleased to give me this joy. I cannot claim it; all my desert is eternal sorrow. Yet, possibly, weeping may endure but for a night. But even should this night extend over all that remains to me of life, I would pray for patience still to *wait* for him,—trusting that, through Christ, joy shall come in the morning of my entrance upon another world. (8.) *Hope?*

(Rom. xv. 13 ; Col. i. 27.)　Yes ; I have *some* hope for eternity.　Forbid, Lord, that it should be the perishing hope of the hypocrite.　Can I not say with David, " My hope is *in Thee ?* "　" To thee, O Lord, do I lift up my soul."　Yet this is faint and flickering ; and, through the defect of my faith, I dwell not, and live not, as I ought, among things unseen.

'In looking back over this list, I find that I can refer, in my experience, to nothing that can be called a *sure unambiguous* fruit of faith.　The most favourable are 5 and 8 ; and the first of these may be explained, perhaps, in some measure, by my plain perception of my present circumstances.　I have a *vast* amount of sin to set against all this—*much* of it so *wilful* as to have brought merited darkness on my soul.　But, knowing that, even in God's children, " the flesh lusteth against the spirit," I would not regard many workings of corruption as conclusive against a man, if he had *clear* marks of faith to show otherwise.　The present inquiry is embarrassed by want of *clearness* in my evidences.　Let this stir me up to *watchfulness ;* let me praise God that I am not left to utter despair ; let me beware of resting on this *examen ;* and let me look to the LAMB OF GOD.'

The next letter is of very great length, and on a great variety of subjects.　We extract only small portions from different places.

' MADEIRA, *5th June* 1838.

' My dear James,—The longest and most elaborate letter which I have yet written from Madeira, was indited on the 8th and 9th December, and addressed to yourself.　I had it committed to the Captain of the Portuguese packet, which sails (occasionally) between this and Lisbon, and he promised to put it in the post-office there ; but, as appears by yours of the 1st March, it has never reached its destination.　This is no small disappointment, as I had asked you to make my father master of its leading contents, and as my subsequent letters to him and Glasgow friends proceeded very much on the hypothesis that they were in possession of those introductory facts and first impressions which I had conveyed to you. . . . .

' You know on what my heart, amid many fightings without, and fears within, was set ; and, although I was often so indolent that I seemed without an object, yet *if* I ever had an *aim* at all for some years past, it was towards the service of God in the ministry. The present state of my lungs leaves me scarcely room to doubt that it has been His will to disappoint that aim.   At some times I have felt as if my soul could choose strangling and death, rather than life without preaching.   Yet Renton tells me, that, so far as he yet sees, I *may* live for some considerable time in favourable circumstances, but *can never* preach. When I came here first, and saw some who have been many years laid aside from any labour, I involuntarily shuddered when I thought how unfit, because of inward rebellion, I would be to bear the like : yet it is possibly the all-wise plan of the Father of lights thus to teach me to be still, and know that he is God. In the meantime, I labour—and no small labour it often is—to reconcile myself to a punishment which I once thought greater than I could bear—that of not being " allowed of God to be put in trust with the Gospel ;" and to persuade myself, that, if it is His will to spare me, he will provide some work for me, although it were only as a door-keeper in his house. As to any *probability* of being spared, I do not think that my chance admits of so favourable a designation.   I only continue to stay here so long as those who are his almoners enable me, because I take the decided advice of a plain-speaking physician to be such a providential hint as suffices to mark out our duty, although it cannot assure us of any result,—and because I wish practically to believe that " with God *nothing is impossible.*"   The freedom

from blood-spitting for a few days, and my partially
recruited strength, are, *pro tanto*, encouragements;
and a good augury may be drawn from the improvement of my breathing during any little heats which
the *siroc* has yet given us.   But the intense heat of
August *may* lower, or it may excite me, to an alarming degree,—in either of which cases Dr Renton
would send me home.   If neither of these happens,
and if I am enabled to exercise a moderate degree of
caution, the air is so mild in summer, that he appre-
hends no unfavourable change, and there is just a
possibility of improvement.   On this possibility he
advises me to stay.   If it were pronounced out of the
question that I should do more than stand my ground
in summer, I should directly come home ; for it would
then be evident that next winter would terminate the
contest, and I would rather (God willing) that it
should end on British ground.   No doubt it were sad
to leave Madeira under such an impression, and thus
deliberately resign all connection with this warm and
breathing world ; yet, if, by the abounding grace of
God, I had but a glimpse of "joy set before" me, I
think He would minister strength for that trial.   But
there is just a *possibility* of something more ; a "may-
be" which yet binds me to continue this experiment.
To be sure, unbelieving fear will often suggest, "What
if the experiment should stand still in summer, and
you should get suddenly worse at a season at which
removal would be madness?"   I can only answer this
question by turning it out of doors, as having too
bold and inquisitive a reference to those "times and
seasons which the Father hath kept in his own power."
And were I but sure of my union to Him, in whose
hands are placed the keys of death and the grave, I
could give it a more direct and triumphant answer.
O pray for me, that I may be able to say, "If I die
even here, I am not alone, for the Father is with me."
I very much need your prayers, and those of all who
love me, for repentance and the remission of sins, for

a spiritual discernment of God's design in chastising me, for submission, humility, faith, and a hope that entereth into that within the vail. . . .

' This digression ended, I go on with my schemes. If Cumming * has nothing you think would suit me, do you yourself know any subject on which I am qualified, or might qualify myself, to write, which might suit the present exigencies of our Church and country ? In the vast field of Christian truth there are surely spots as yet but little cultivated, which might yield a good and seasonable produce ? I have more time to *think* than I ever had, although my opportunities of *reading* are greatly curtailed, and that time I am anxiously desirous to devote to some useful purpose. Can you see no theme fit for this time, and fit for me ? The Oxford heresy, of which I daily see how it is eating out the vitals, and sucking the heart's blood (χλωρον αἱμα μου ῥοφεῖ ξυνοικῶν) of the Church of England, is a subject near my heart ; but on it I fear I could not write without documents, and a *corpus patrum.* Farthermore, is there no bookseller's job, by way of an Introductory Essay, or the like, which could be edged my way? You may enjoy my fertility in expedients : pray tell me, as well as you can, if any, and which of them is feasible. And, as a gift is doubled by being soon given, don't be long in arming me with your judgment.

' . . . . I came here a *red-hot* Presbyterian ; I am now *excandescent.* I have had something of an inside look at the Anglican Church, and have discovered more than I knew or suspected of its want of theological education, its feebleness of discipline, and its haughtiness of bearing. And, on this nearer inspection, I think we have a mighty deal less occasion to be overawed by its learning than I had formerly imagined. . . . .

* The Rev. James Cumming of Edinburgh, was then editor of the Presbyterian Review.

' Some of these Anglican clergy were truly excellent and estimable ; yet even in them I could observe the effect of that want of *direct divinity training* which is the greatest of that Church's deficiencies. . . . I now *glory* in the name of a member, and think it an honour even to have been on the way to become a minister of the Church of Scotland.   On the first Sabbath of May, your sacramental Sabbath, I could not help rejoicing in spirit at the power, and faithfulness, and touching tenderness with which I was sure the pure Gospel of our Lord Jesus was being proclaimed in Edinburgh.   " How amiable are thy tabernacles !   My soul longeth," &c.

' I had almost forgot to notice the breaking of my promise about collecting plants for you.   The ground is so utterly impracticable on foot, that I have done, and I fear, unless some marked improvement takes place, can do nothing.   It is easy to be generous *a priori* ; but I have found that broken wind and perpendicular rocks are about incompatibles.

' Shall I amuse you and Smeaton with some Greek ? I don't wish my "*si quid olium lusit*" to be quite lost ; so here go two stanzas, inserted in some copies of " Ken's Evening Hymn," and done into tragic trimeters sometime in January :—

1. ει δ' αυ καθ' υπνον θανατος εισβαλοι πικρος,
τι μ' αν ταρασσοι δειμα τοιουτου φρενας ;
φρουρουμενον τω σω μενει βραχιονος,
και περ με τυπτων, ουτι με βλαπτειν σθενει.

2. ζην γαρ το θνησκειν, το τε καμειν υπνος γλυκυς,
εαν μονον μοι πρευμενης παρη Θεος.
ευδειν γενοιτ' ουν, ειτε και θανειν εμοι,—
σως ειμι παντη, τω Θεω παντη ξυνων.*

* It appears that these stanzas are not found in the common editions of the hymn.   The substance of them is as follows :—If death overtake me in sleep, why should the fear thereof disturb my mind ?   Guarded by the might of Thine arm, although he strike, he cannot hurt me.   To die is to

' On comparing the solid contents of this letter with yours, I think this is not less than ten or twelve times its size, so you need not be disappointed if a long silence should ensue. You *ought* to write in simple charity, "looking for nothing again."

' I need not say, that, in the way of *study* I have done nothing since I came here. I have often been idle on principle; yet I have got through something considerable of not very heavy reading—more intended for the heart than the head.

' Be assured I can never forget my obligations to continue your affectionate brother, J. H.

' *Mr James Hamilton.*'

The next three letters are written very nearly at the same date, and refer necessarily to the same subjects—one to a minister in Scotland; another to a student of divinity in the Scottish Church; and the third a mark of tender affection to an aged parent.

' MADEIRA, 11*th June* 1838.

' My dear Munro,—I almost wonder at my own folly in commencing a correspondence with one with whom (although I trust our spirits were much congenial) I had never before maintained a communication by letter. But all my Glasgow correspondents have been so unaccountably silent about you, that, weak as I am, and far behind in writing to others, I cannot do justice to my own feelings of affectionate anxiety by any thing short of *recta via* sending you an epistle. It is meant, *observe*, to extract an answer, telling me all about your own state, physical and mental, your ministerial labours, troubles, and successes, and the general progress of "the kingdom" among you.

' And now I could tell you many queer things about this Madeira,—as how the peasant's caps only cover

live—oppressing disease is a sweet sleep, if God stand near propitious. Whether, therefore, I sleep or die, I am every where safe; for I am every where near to God.

the crown of their heads, and would puzzle a poor mechanician like myself to discover how they stick on; how the dogs and cats are generally to be seen *sans* tails and ears, by way of being made more beautiful,—in which case, I am sure, you will agree with me in thinking, the beauty is not in the object but in the mind; how there are no carts, but all the internal transport is effected either on men's heads, or by means of most primitive sledges drawn by oxen; how you scarcely ever see an equestrian, without an attendant accompanying him *pari passu*, being ingeniously *towed*—if we may use that expression of a land conveyance—by his horse's tail; how the nuns, in a certain convent here, had *a ball* on the 31st January; how the padres are so ignorant, that one of them borrowed a Portuguese Bible from an Englishman here, never having seen the like before; how it is confidently reported that the established faith is at such a discount, that, at the proper season, the priests are actually obliged to hire people to play the part of penitents; how the blacksmiths, *mirabile dictu!* work in white jackets; and how the resident English, with true and characteristic patriotism, reckon their invalid countrymen just a part of the traffic of the port, and generally resolve to make the most of them. All this, and more, I could tell you; but a profusion of such details, however amusing, could ill answer the feelings with which I think of you, and might jar with the associations which have been formed in your mind with him who is afar off upon the sea.

'You will like better to know how I am. In many respects, *well*. Goodness and mercy have followed me ever since I bade farewell to Scotland. Our passage was short and prosperous. The large boarding-houses being all filled, our lot was providentially cast in one where there was no crowd of light-headed and light-hearted people, but only two inmates besides ourselves, with minds subdued by much affliction, and with whom I could at any time converse of the things that are unseen and eternal, without the feeling that the theme was unwelcome. Although warned by a gentleman in Glasgow that I must make up my mind to want a religious circle, there being little probability of my finding many here with whom such sweet counsel could be held, — I have been in this most mercifully disappointed. Two thoroughly evangelical clergymen of the Church of England, Messrs Ashe and Langford—the former a deep Christian, amazingly elevated above human passion, and manifestly bearing the beauty of the Lord his God upon him—the latter warm in affections, and fervent in zeal, set up a meeting for prayer, in which, for a little, I was honoured to help them. There were four others, Arminian in theology, but amiable and serious in spirit, with whom it has always been a pleasure to associate; three or four lay friends, especially Mr H. Cadell of Edinburgh, were always ready to join in every sacred exercise; and there were many more among our acquaintances who were favourably impressed, and of whom one might well indulge the hope that they were something more than "borderers"—"not far from the kingdom of God." Farthermore, when we set up house, as, by way of economizing a little, we did a month ago, we found that a great many people, from whom we could not have expected such kindness, were seized with an appetite for giving and lending; so that, in this way, we have come by many necessaries and conveniences, from a tea-pot to a horse, for which we must otherwise have drawn on the funds supplied us from home. . . . .

' My decline has been, and is, very slow; for my constitution is of iron. But, looking calmly at all my symptoms, they have been aggravated since I came here. . . . Meantime, the doctor advises me to prolong the experiment; and I do so, knowing that if God has any thing for me to do, he can bring me back from the gates of death to do it; and having such confidence in the honesty of Dr Renton as to believe that, as soon as he sees the case to be hopeless, he will tell me so, and thus at once prevent me from expending the resources of others in a useless contest with death on foreign ground, and give me fair warning to return to Scotland, set my house in order, and lay down my head in quietness. There is yet a chance that the result may be otherwise; and my strength is to sit still, and await the working of a higher hand.

'Let my father know that you have heard from me, and that I remain just as when my sister last wrote to him. Farewell. Rejoice in your privilege of preaching. The Lord be with you! So prays yours most affectionately, J. H.

'*Rev. James Munro.*'

'MADEIRA, 13*th June* 1838.

'My dear Wilson,— . . . . Pray don't think me over-presumptuous in criticising thus freely the productions of men (Lectures on the Evidences of Revealed Religion), at the feet of many of whom I would be happy to place myself. Attribute it rather to the interest I take in the subject, having written myself, some years ago, 29 or 30 lectures on it for my class; and having thus been led, probably more than the greater number even of divinity students, to study the most direct and practical way of putting various portions of the argument. Possibly from a prejudice arising out of this, I felt also, in reading many of these lectures, that, admirable as they are in statement and reasoning, they are sometimes deficient in illustration.

'This matter over, I have to return again to the ever-trodden track, and tell you how I am. Happily, I do not need to enlarge much on it, as my symptoms have changed only in one material particular since I wrote Mr Colquhoun by Mr Langford. That change is, that for fifteen mornings now I have expectorated no blood. This is, *pro tanto*, an improvement, and

I am truly thankful to record it, as well as to add, that, in general strength, I seem at present to be rather making up. At the same time, these may only be the momentary fluctuations of a disease upon the whole incurable; they, as every circumstance in my lot, are a sufficient ground for gratitude, but will not bear the weight of hope. Indeed, with Renton's announcement, that, at the best, I can never expect to *preach*, all the best and holiest of my *earthly* hopes have perished. I can only be dumb with silence, and lay my hand on my mouth, in submission to that hand which has been pleased to wither them; but oh! even when one acknowledges the righteousness of the judgment, it *is* difficult to keep down a certain bursting sensation at the heart, as if all were gone which the soul cared for. This can only be effectually overcome by going a step farther, and getting so far, through grace, into the secret of the Almighty, as to see that he is *kind* in his chastisements. Oftentimes I think that I can feel and own this; but, when I analyse my own emotions a little farther, I find that I am tracing and (it may be) praising God's goodness, not in the affliction itself, but in some of those numberless mercies by which it has been surrounded and lightened. Thus, through the deceitfulness of sin, I find that many of my acknowledgments of mercy in this chastisement are spurious, or, if not *quite* so, at least leave me far short of that happy frame in which one can be said to " rejoice in tribulations." Yet, while many hopes are gone, and glad submission is not yet attained, I can have a positive enjoyment in this one assurance, that " with God nothing shall be impossible ;" that, if he has work for me, he will raise me up to do it; and if he has none, like the thief on the cross, I suffer " justly ;" and that, though the word of reconciliation may not be committed to me, I may yet have some name and place in his courts, as a door-keeper in the house of God. Meantime, I shall ever reckon it an honour and a blessing in providence that I was once on the way towards being a minister of the Church of Scotland. . . . . Very affectionately yours,   J. H.

' *Mr John Wilson.*'

' MADEIRA, *15th June* 1838.

' My dear Father,—You will not be disappointed although I should write you very shortly ; for I dare say you would be ready to excuse me although I did not write you at all. My general plan, you know, is —and must be—to give Janet the task of writing to all those whom she can with propriety address—such as yourself; and I only break through my rule just now, because I really feel it a grievous thing that you should be so long without seeing my handwriting; and because, when I have a kind friend actually going to Glasgow, I cannot send him to any one so deeply anxious to have the best information about me as my own dear father.

' The bearer of this is A. C. Ross, Esq., one of the medical men here. Dr Renton, you know, has been my regular attendant in this way ; and I begged Dr Ross to converse with him about my case, that he might give you a *professional* account of it—something more correct than I can hope to convey. He did so, and kindly offered to do more. He has just examined my chest very fully, and will be able to tell you all about the state in which he found me. I think for the last month I have been rather improving, at least it is a favourite symptom that I have now been sixteen mornings free from blood-spitting. But while this is matter of sincere thankfulness—and I hope you will feel it so—it will not justify us in entertaining any thing like fond or sanguine hopes. I must entreat you to beware of this as one of your besetting sins; you are apt to expect too much. Let us be thankful that I have been spared so long, and that God has put it into the hearts of our friends to desire and contribute for the continuance of this experiment; and let us not despair, for with God nothing is impossible.   Only let us prepare ourselves, by meditating on our own frailty and on His sovereign right to do what he pleaseth, and on the grace of that Saviour on whose shoulder the government rests, *for the worst* that may occur; and endeavour, by praying always with all prayer and supplication, to cast our burden upon the Lord, and to attain to that happy frame of mind which David describes, when he says of the righteous man—" He shall not be afraid of evil tidings; his heart is fixed, trusting in the Lord." My dear father, I hope *your* heart will be fixed in the same way, that you may be better able to bear the announcement, that there seems now to be no chance of my ever recovering so far as to be able to *preach*. I know this will be a sore stroke to you; but remember from whose hand it comes, and consider with how much mercy it has pleased Him to mix it.   What He may be pleased to do for me yet, we do not know; only let us *wait* with patience, and *pray* without ceasing, that whatever He does with our hope of usefulness or happiness here, He may at least, *through Christ*, give every one of us *one* hope—and that a *better*—even the hope of an inheritance incorruptible and undefiled. . . . . With constant prayers for your temporal and eternal good,—I am, dear father, your very affectionate son,   J. H.'

It was an era in the history of the invalid when his disease had advanced so far that it was pronounced physically impossible he should ever be a preacher. He had fondly clung to the hope of preaching so long as, on medical grounds, it could be considered possible.   The withering of that hope pressed sore.   Having, by the grace of God, been enabled himself to submit in patience, he strives, in the above letter, to make the sad announcement to his father in the softest form, and to fortify his mind by suggesting the consolations of the Gospel.

In the journal, of date 17th June 1838, occurs the record of a meditation on 1 Cor. vi. 11.

' " And such were some of you : but ye are washed, but ye are sanctified, but ye are justified, in the name of the Lord Jesus, and by the Spirit of our God."—1 COR. vi. 11.

' I take this to be one of the most comfortable verses in the whole Scriptures to a sin-burdened soul —one that feels its own vileness, and is almost apt to yield to the subtle taunt of Satan,—" There is no help for him in God." It is like the case of the converted and restored Manasseh, or that blessed " *whosoever*" in John iii. 15.

' " And *such* were some of you."—1 COR. vi. 11.

' These words—oh ! that it were with an adequate degree of shame and confusion !—I can fully appropriate. My impurity of heart ; my idolatry of the creature ; my covetousness of books if not of money ; my excessive use of some creature-comforts ; and, above all, my unbridled censoriousness of tongue, prove that the apostle's denunciation could be applied to me even at the present time, after all that I have seen of God's mercy, and felt of his judgments. Some appearances, of a very slightly more hopeful kind, having presented themselves in my health,—my sin, for a few days, has been an attempting to sit down, in my own schemings, with this world as my home, although God's work in it was ever designed as my labour. An earthliness of spirit, even greater than usual, has seized me ; and a desperate and almost frantic clinging to those whom I love below, and this has issued in a sad haste and dulness in every exercise of secret worship. I have trifled away in vain imaginations, till the lateness of the hour compelled me

to rush, as it were, into God's presence, and to offer
the Holy One a hurried and confused devotion. I
have awfully come short in reverence to the majesty
in the heavens. And it is a miracle of grace, that
the fire of God's jealousy has not, long ere now, burst
forth against and consumed me. May I not "account
that this long-suffering of our Lord is salvation; not
merely designed and fitted to lead me to repentance,
but a *pledge* of greater blessings yet in store, if I will
but hear his voice, and not harden my heart? Nothing, I know, but his own Spirit can effect this; but
He will not deny himself to a beseeching sinner. I
will flee, then, from myself to him. May he take of
the things of Christ—Christ's righteousness, atonement, strength, and fulness—and reveal them with
power to my soul! May he give me a cordial faith
in the Redeemer, and cleanse me from all filthiness of
the flesh and spirit; so that the remainder of this verse,
so full of grace, may be applicable even to me:—
" but ye are washed, but ye are sanctified, but ye are
justified in the name of the Lord Jesus, and by the
Spirit of our God." Amen and Amen.' . . . .
' The " *Lyra*," which brought us to Madeira seven
months ago, arrived here to-day, with the mail. . . .
' Went on board. Saw Captain Forrester, Mr
Burdwood, and many of the crew. They have been
mercifully dealt with; only one man lost since November. Mr B——, the surgeon, met me in Funchal,
and dined with us. His visit was a melancholy one,
as a tumour, forming on his brain, may cut him off,
by apoplexy, any day. Gave him " Augustine's Con-
fessions," which he promised to read for my sake.
" What are meetings here, but partings?" Saw, on
board the Lyra, a townsman, a son of Mr Farie of
Farme, on his way to Rio. Thus two atoms, floating on the great sea of time, came into a moment's
contact, and then—parted company for ever.

N

' Monday and yesterday I was only half my prescribed time at my systematic Scripture reading and
Portuguese ; being prevented on Monday by going out
to dinner and tea, and yesterday seduced by news-
papers.   To-day I accomplished languidly my tale of
Scripture reading, but spent only one hour on Portuguese ; the temptation was "Random Recollections."
Thus am I carried away by every wind.
' Yet God is not ceasing to plead with me.   To-
day he warned me by Exod. viii. 15, to take heed lest
I fall after the same example of unbelief as Pharaoh.
" When he saw that there was respite, he hardened
his heart ;" and I am too like him.   A gleam of hope,
in reference to longer life, is an intoxicating draught
with which I am not fit to be trusted.   Alas ! that
my lightness and earthliness of mind should almost
compel the God of mercy to deny my request, that I
may recover strength before I go hence, and be no
more !   O for *a fixed* heart—fixed on the hopes and
promises of His Gospel.

' Thursday, did my full work.   Friday, from various
interruptions, was thrown out entirely.

' Received, with thanksgiving to the Father of
mercies, admirable letters from Stevenson, Morrison,
Mackail, and Denniston.   I read, and wept, again
and again.   The Lord sanctify to me the possession
of such friends ; and, while every piece of intelligence
from them only makes me long the more to join them
in the work of our common Lord, may He give me
entire submission and resignation to his holy will.

' Have kept up my Scripture reading tolerably (not
quite) well these few days ; but have only on Wednesday done my devoirs to Portuguese.   It seems as
if to resolve any thing were the surest way *not* to do
it.   Have read Hannah More's Life, an important
lesson and example of the duty of working while it is

called to-day. Promptitude seems to have been her grand moral feature.

'Mr Lowe on Romans xii. 1, 2.

'According to the day of the month, it is a year to-day, and by the day of the week a year yesterday, since I formally gave up my study, and left Edinburgh for Forgandenny. I had then a suspicion that my disease was likely to pass all skill of medicine, but still had much hope that my exile from study would not exceed two or three months. Since that time the Lord has taken me apart; has He at all spoken to my heart in the wilderness?

'This solemn question, if answered in the affirmative, can only suggest a sad reflection on my deafness to the language of His providence. My goodness has been like the early dew; my repentances very constrained and imperfect; my faith weak and inoperative. I may regard it as of His special mercy that I have been spared during this year of trial; for, in the retrospect, I cannot set my eye on one season in which I could have yielded my spirit to Him who gave it, with any thing like *a joyful hope of glory*. In beginning this second year of my serious illness, I record it, as a witness against myself if I should be careless, that I do not expect to see the end of it in this world. Arise, then, my soul, and be doing! Get thee to the mountain!'

The following piece of scrupulous spiritual dissection, although in some parts similar to what has already appeared from the journal, we give entire. It is contained in a letter to an old and much valued friend.

'MADEIRA, 17*th July* 1838.

'My dear James,—Your very kind and welcome letter of the 30th May I received on the 7th of the present month, and read with much emotion. It has a peculiarity above the letters of my other correspon-

dents; most of them are in the centre of intelligence
about me, and are stirred up to write either by seeing
my friends or hearing from myself; yours has all the
merit and sweetness of a pure gratuity. . . . .

'But I proceed to more important matters.   I am
sick long ago of writing about bodily disease and its
symptoms; let me try to give you a sketch of my
mental history and state.   You know I have for many
years had a strong and intellectual conviction of the
truths of the Gospel, and possibly also such a view of
their necessity and connection, as might have operated
upon any heart but one hardened through the deceitfulness of sin.   This conviction I have always, through
mercy, retained; nor have I been harassed with so
much as one of those doubts, which many (even of
men in whom a good work was proceeding) have been
exercised withal.   This has arisen, probably, from
early religious education, and the gift of a tolerably
sober intellect; and therefore can be viewed only as
an aggravation of responsibility.   But I have never
been duly affected even with what I do most certainly
know.   I have always had a cold and hard mind;
and even the cross of Christ has had little power to
warm and melt it.   I have been very unfaithful in my
use of opportunities, very careless about maintaining
impressions, and am conscious of having quietly sur-
rendered myself to the sway of besetting sins, against
which I had often vowed, and was in the daily habit
of praying.   After repeated self-examinations, I have
never been able to satisfy myself of my state; and this,
too, with all the advantage of intensely feeling on which
side it was most desirable to have a verdict.   So long
as I look at *faith* alone, in the simple descriptions and
illustrations given of it in Scripture,——as trusting on
Christ, fleeing to him, committing a precious deposit
to him, leaning on him, and so forth,——and try, by a
simple act of introspection, to see whether these feelings are mine, I rise half persuaded that I have them;

but when I reflect, that "by their fruits ye shall know them," and seek in my life for the fruits of faith, I see all a blank; and if it should even seem that I am growing in any one thing, as I sometimes think is the case with regard to deadness to the world, I am soon brought to feel that this cannot be said to appear in a genuine Gospel form, but is, as much as may be, just a *rational submission* to what is inevitable,—a giving up the world because it is giving up me. Thus tossed and distracted whenever I have begun to seek for evidences of a union to Christ, I have, for the most part, followed the judicious advice you gave me at parting, to deal most with the direct act of faith,—" looking unto Jesus." But, alas! the dimness of my vision. The veil, I fear, is on my heart. And, although I am every day, almost every hour, pleading his blood for pardon, and the promise of the Spirit for strength, yet I cannot shut my eyes to the vast proportion of the *spurious* which enters into all these exercises. In particular, I am conscious that I seldom repair to the blood of Christ as a *preventive* against sin, as a motive to holiness, but only run to it *after* I have sinned for pardon and acceptance; (and is this being cleansed "from dead works?") and there is often a felt want of sincerity in my petition for the light and sanctification of the Spirit. Yet with all this, whether it be a merciful upholding, or a presumptuous delusion, (God grant it to be the former!) I have never once abandoned hope, or said to my soul that God had "cast off for ever." Still, in this one encouraging symptom, there is this sad defect, that it never arises to Gospel peace; it is only a vague indistinct hopefulness; and thus, "when for the time I ought to have been a teacher," I am still beating about the elementary truths of Christianity, and have sad forebodings that I may turn out to have "suffered so many things in vain,"—to be one of those who are " ever learning, but never coming to the knowledge of the truth."

And yet I see how *reasonable* and *glorious* a truth it is, that those have a right to rejoice in God who trust in his holy name (Psalm xxxiii. 21) ; but my trust is either so small, or such an utter nullity, that I cannot grasp this truth,—I cannot appropriate it.

‘ Thus I go on from day to day, not fearing death (which I am inclined to attribute to insensibility), but as far as ever from overcoming it ; and, wherever I start from, always brought back to the old point,— “ God be propitiated to me a sinner ! ”

‘ Can you minister to a mind so diseased ? If you can, pray write me. And oh ! try to stir me up ; for I find that indolence is still my besetting sin, yea, perhaps, more than ever ; and all is weak, frail, and out of joint.

‘ Yet (would you believe it ?) even in this state of confessed declension and inertness, I am often filled with a desire to preach. Indignant at the sad mixture of Popery and heartlessness with which the poor Church of England, in Madeira, is treated by one of these high-church heretics ; and vexed to find baptism substituted for the blood of Christ, I am often tempted to make Homer's wish my own,—*εἰ γάρ μοι δέκα μὲν γλῶσσαι, δέκα δὲ στόματ' εἶεν, φωνὴ δ' ἄρρηκ-τος.** And often do I long for the courts of the Lord in Scotland. On the first Sabbath of May, when we had more than the usual quantum of *baptismal regeneration*, I think I felt a real pleasure in reflecting with what power and faithfulness Jesus was being set forth crucified in the churches of Edinburgh, and how many of his dear children were there doing what he commanded, in remembrance of him ; and had I known that the same day was your sacramental season, I could also have wept for joy at what was going on in Newton.

‘ And now, my dearest friend, farewell. The Lord

* Oh that I had ten tongues, and ten mouths, and a voice that would not fail !

preserve thy going out, and thy coming in, from this time forth, and even for evermore.—Ever your grateful and affectionate friend,   J. H.

' *Rev. James Stevenson.*'

' *Sabbath*, 22d *July* 1838.

' From some increase of cough and pain, thought it imprudent to attempt going to church.   Read at home some of " Newton's Cardiphonia," with increased admiration of his Christian wisdom ; and studied, I hope not unprofitably, the 37th Psalm.   Many verses in it are deeply impressive.   Let me try to concentrate my thoughts on one.

' " Delight thyself also in the Lord ; and he shall give thee the desires of thine heart."—PSALM xxxvii. 4.

' This verse presents us with a specific against disappointment.   How often does God, in his wisdom, shatter our hopes and wishes, and leave us blighted and fallen, with but a faint sense that once we were able to feel so strongly, and aspire so high !   How often, through our perverseness, does it become necessary that He should answer our prayers, not in the palpable sense in which we offered them, but by terrible works in righteousness !   We know not what to pray for ; our wishes are frequently no fair representation of our wants ; and hence, in mercy, He denies a thousand little busy desires, in order to advance that, which, in our better moments, we would make our grand aim and object, the burden of our sighs, the matter of our prayers,—to be made holy. But as the process goes on, our desires become more assimilated to His ; our passing wishes flow in the direction of our habitual aim ; and thus the answer to our prayers, although not more *real* than before, becomes more *literal*—more *exactly accordant* to the *terms* of the prayers themselves.   Thus, it is easily seen how the promise of this verse is precisely fulfilled.   The more we delight in the Lord, the more do the desires of our heart mould themselves into an accordance with his will.   Delighting in Him, we desire what pleases Him; and as the one feeling increases, so does the other.   Hence it becomes consistent with God's glory, which it was not before, to bring these longings of our souls to a literal fulfilment. A harmony is established between what we wish, and what He wills.   And thus, the closer we live to Him, and the more we are transformed into His image, the greater, on obvious principles, is the probability of our obtaining manifest and recognisable answers to prayer.   Circumstances may occur to disturb this proportion between holiness and comfort; but, in general, it is a settled law of God's spiritual administration, and one which should stir us up to follow hard after him, that he who delights in God shall obtain the desires of his heart.'

We present, without any apology, the following letter.   Although the topics are trifling, the thing, as a whole, illustrates a distinct feature of character.   There is not only the fact of a very powerful memory, but the strong inclination to employ it in calling up past scenes with amusing minuteness of detail.   We trust even the gravest of our readers will not dislike to see such a specimen of the manner in which the disabled student tried at times to relax himself, while awaiting the issue of a protracted experiment in a foreign land. The letter is written at several different dates.

'MADEIRA, 28th July 1838.

' My dear Arnot,—My memory, which, you know, was always an affair of localities and particulars, has of late been very busily engaged upon old Scotland. In particular, the incidents of this day twelve months have passed before me in a lively review.   Permit me to remind you of them.   Soon after my last breakfast

at Forgandenny, you set off to negotiate about the
equipage which was to take us to Auchterarder. You
stayed long ; and several times I was despatched to
look up the grass avenue to see if you were coming.
At last, about one o'clock, you announced the success
of your diplomacy with Jamie Anderson. About two
we started—not without a parting blessing from ——,
—a blessing which I have not forgotten, as far as
prayers may go, to return to-day into his own bosom.
We had a cargo of books to leave at the village, and
with these you ran, under a commencing shower, by
a near cut, to the school-house. We saw Forteviot
at some distance, where my father spent his boyhood,
and those noble woods of Dupplin, at the mention of
which his eye brightens even yet. At Dunning we
left your chattels for Glasgow. Lord R., fat old gentleman in tights, at a gate. Little boy got into our cart
on the sly—medal round his neck—interesting child.
You pointed out to me the whereabouts of Madderty.
Dismissed Jamie Anderson at Ternaway. Remarked
on a cottage or two which can seldom see the sun.
Trudged along—you carrying my knapsack, like a
brother born for adversity. Sat a few minutes on a
little bridge about half a-mile from Ternaway ; but
soon moved on for fear of cold ; fine fresh Scottish
air. Faint and wearily pulled up the ascent to Auchterarder ; and came to anchor at M.'s father's about
half-past six o'clock. Astonished his hospitable mother
by my voracious demolition of her scones, to the utter
neglect of the *white* bread. Heard of James' feats of
study on a hay stack. Supped on a tumbler of excellent milk ; and after sanctioning the arrangement with
the dancing master for next morning, bathed my feet,
swallowed my cough medicine, and lay down to per-
spire and sleep.

' My disease, in its true nature, was then beginning
to develope itself to my own mind—perhaps also to
yours. Looking at it calmly, I am now much worse

than I was then. I could not now walk from Ternaway to Auchterarder, nor (as I did next day) from
Dollar to Tillicoultry, even although I had the advantage of Scotch bracing air to walk in, instead of the
soft enervating atmosphere which encircles us here.
But dark as the lesson is, I have seen something more
of myself since then ; and *surely* also much of the
goodness of the Lord in the land of the living. Take
the little boy with the medal, whom we saw on our
journey ; and suppose him, in the course of years, to
fall into consumption by misarrangement of his time ;
where, in all likelihood, would he find friends so
beneficent as to send him to Madeira ?

                           ' *Monday, 13th August* 1838.
' As I seem to myself now to have pretty well
reached the "*garrula senectas*" of my being, you will
forgive me for again indulging the reminiscences of
the past. Some day you may amuse Stevenson with
this sketch of what he and I did *this day four years.*
We rose very early from our couch in a little ale-
house at Traquair—self-dubbed an inn—walked to
the "Bush aboon Traquair;" then crossed the Tweed
to Innerleithen, by a nice new bridge, which, however, had the nuisance of a pontage, &c. I am out
in my reckoning—that was on the 12th of August.
Well, we spent the night of the 12th at Selkirk; and
on the morning of the 13th, after breakfast, sallied
forth on our *second* visit to Abbotsford, which the
descending shades had prevented us from fully survey-
ing the evening before. I cannot tell you all the
marvels we saw—from Archbishop Sharpe's grate and
John Knox's pulpit, to Rob Roy's dirk and sporran ;
or how odd it was to see the gate of the Old Heart of
Mid-Lothian built into the western wall, and into the
eastern some monument of Selkirk's grandeur, bearing
the chivalrous legend, " VP WITH YE SVTORS OF SEL-
KIRK ;" or how absurd we thought the inscription on
a garden door, " They heard the voice of the Lord God

walking in the garden in the cool of the day ;" or how we laughed at Sir Walter's supposed ignorance of Latin quantity, in thus epitaphizing his dog Maida,—

" Maidæ marmoreâ dormis sub imagine, Maida ;
    Ad *januam* domini sit tibì terra levis ;"

which ignorance, Lockhart, to the disgrace of his Oxford training, has appropriated to himself, by confessing that he, and not Sir Walter, indited the lines. Stevenson will also recollect that we made a large negotiation in gooseberries from the gardener's wife, and how we lay down under a hedge between Abbotsford and Melrose, to despatch the same, and skulk a shower. Arrived at Melrose; after some refreshment we made for the manse—Stevenson having a letter from Dr Mackinlay to the minister. There we dined with the old man and his lame son—no other than the original of Dominie Sampson. (*Both of these are since dead,* I hear.) With a true *cognoscenti* of a beadle we surveyed the abbey, and then took our leave; resumed our knapsacks, climbed the highest point of the Eildon hills (whence had one of the finest *champaign* views), visited Scott's grave at Dryburgh Abbey, and lay to at a respectable public-house in St Boswell's Green — the landlady whereof was not a little doubtful about receiving such suspicious characters at untimeous hours—for we had seen Dryburgh under the solemn twilight, and the sun was down long ere we reached St Boswell's.

' I would have gone farther, and told you how, the next morning before breakfast, we sat on the ruins of the old castle of Roxburgh, at the confluence of the Tweed and Teviot; and how, in Kelso, we got for 15d. the best breakfast that traveller ever saw,—kipper, boiled salmon, cold roast lamb, eggs,—not to speak of the vulgar accompaniments of bread and butter, and the divine beverage of tea;—but every pore admonishes me that the thermometer is rather better than 80 in the shade; and I must say " Vale" for to-day, resolv-

ing that, when I resume my pen, it shall discourse of
graver matters that concern the present or the future,
leaving these enjoyments of the past to be buried with
the years that witnessed them.

'*Saturday,* 1*st September* 1838.

' Do you know, I have for some time past entertained thoughts of preparing something for publication.
If this sickness is to be unto death, the only way I
can repay my father's anxieties and labours in my
behalf, is by leaving something in a state for being
published. Scarcely any thing that I have yet written
would bear the light, except posthumously ; nothing
of mine, indeed, is inherently worth it ; but adventi-
tious circumstances might bear it through ; and H. or
you, or whoever writes the preface, might warn the
critics—ανθρωπε, μη δρα τους τεθνηκοτας κακως.* On
the other hand, should it be the will of God to spare
me, although with broken health and a sealed tongue,
the most obvious instrument of usefulness to me is the
pen, and I would need to be casting about how to employ it. Tell me what you think of this. Tell me if
you think me mad or sober in indulging such imaginations. . . . .

' I have only room now to say, that my love to you
is still the same, or, if possible, greater than ever. The
Lord be with you. Your affectionate friend,   J. H.

'*Rev. William Arnot.*'

It is right to say, in explanation of the last paragraph, that Mr Halley had not the least conception of
such a book as his friends are now publishing. His
idea was, to prepare for publication some of his college
essays. He had actually begun to revise them ; but
the state of his health wholly unfitted him for long-
continued exertion, and no progress was made.

We continue the journal.

* Mortal ! deal not harshly with the dead.

' *Tuesday,* 31st *July* 1838.

' The end of another month ! " Lord, make me to know mine end, and the measure of my days, what it is ; that I may know how frail I am."

' Sent for to see, I fear on his death-bed, my landlord—a young man married only last November, and who, when I last saw him, about the beginning of June, seemed high in health and hopes. But God has brought him low, as it were, in a moment.

' The opening seems providential, for I went at his own request.

' Lord, in thy hands are the issues of death. If thou hast a design of mercy towards this youth, thou canst give speedy effect to thy truth, or canst maintain him in life till it slowly works its way to his heart. Do with him as seemeth good to thy supreme wisdom ; only deal not with him after his sins ; but fully awaken, and then graciously heal him. And as thou hast been pleased, in thy providence, to set before me an open door, and call me to be his spiritual counsellor in this trying season,—oh give me a wisdom not mine own, to see the exact point of his soul's disease, to apply the true Gospel remedy, to deal with him solemnly yet tenderly, to direct him always to Jesus, and to select such views of himself and the Saviour as may be best fitted to adhere to his enfeebled memory, and sink into his heart. May the Spirit of grace, for the Redeemer's name's sake, lead me and guide me, animate my prayers for him and myself, suggest, control, and greatly bless my efforts to instruct and direct him. And do Thou, in mercy, apply to my own soul the impressive truths which his sick-bed may disclose or lead me to enforce ; and may the fruit be seen, in my walking more with Thee, and more diligently preparing for my own removal. And now, " to Him that is able to keep," &c. Amen.'

' *Thursday,* 7th *August* 1838.

' Prevented by various causes, especially by a blister which I had on, on Sabbath evening, from writing till now.

' Poor Mr ―――― died on Wednesday, 1st August, at midnight, having seen me but twice, and expressed great anxiety for my third visit, which, however, was paid to his widow. He was much perplexed ; but seemed seriously asking, " What shall I do to be saved ? " and I would indulge the hope that God answered him in mercy.

' Saw his widow (not yet 18) on Thursday morning and Saturday evening ; and tried to be faithful.

' On Sabbath, sat down at the Lord's table, after a sermon from Matt. xxii. 35, 36, from Mr Lowe. Had less trembling than formerly ; tried to look to Christ as a free and full Saviour. Prayed for my friends, and against my besetting sins, with the elements in my hands ; and that I might be enabled to glorify God, whether in life or death.'

It does not appear that Mr Halley had any scruple in receiving the sacrament from the hands of Mr Lowe. Considering his strong opinions regarding the government of the English Church in general, and the doctrine of that particular minister, it is clear that his sentiments on the question of free communion were very liberal. It would be interesting to know precisely what were the grounds on which he acted in this matter, but there is no record of them in any of his letters or journals.

' *Monday,* 27*th August* 1838.

' Two more blisters, and intense heat, since my last entry, have prevented me from writing here.

' Pains lessened ; but cough much increased.

' Heard last week of my dear friend, Henry Cadell, being at the gates of the grave, and yesterday of the death of Louis O'Brien on the 11th June. What lessons for me ! Let me believe that it is not without some peculiar design of saving mercy that I am spared; and let me improve the moments for eternity. I have many difficulties and temptations: oh for a wisdom from above to guide me safely and righteously through!

'*Wednesday*, 29*th August* 1838.

' Made the other day, in bed, the following translation of a few lines of Merrick's 39th Psalm. "God of my fathers," &c. :—

' προγονων εμων θεος, ενθαδ᾽, ὡς κεινοι ποτε,
οδοιπορος παρ᾽ ἡμεραν στειχω μιαν·
ξενος, προς ολιγον εργα θαυμαζω σεθεν,
ευθυς δε προς δῶμ᾽ οιχομαι πανυστατον·
τι δῆτα λοιπον εστιν, εις ὁ,τι βλεπω,
πλην σου; τις ελπις, μη ᾽πι σου γ᾽ ηρτημενη.'

Two short passages, in a letter to his father, contain sentiments that should be read and pondered.

'MADEIRA, 4*th September* 1838.

' . . . . . . M. tells me about Patrick's Latin. I am much gratified by what he says; and I hope Patrick will be encouraged to do still better. I would not have you "seek great things" for him; but try and get him into a steady way of working, *on right principles of Christian obedience to his parents.* I now see unnumbered sins, even in those labours for which people used most to praise me. To work hard at school and college was often just my way of pleasing myself. Make it your prayer that Patrick may have grace given him to do all in a better spirit. He will now be back from Gigha, I hope much refreshed and improved; and I trust I shall hear that he is very diligent and very tractable, and fonder of his Sabbath school and Bible than every thing besides. He will find the indispensable use of these, if God should be pleased to do with his earthly hopes as he has dealt,

in his wisdom, with those which his brother once
cherished. . . . .

  ' I cannot flatter you by saying that I improve. All
that Renton can say is, that I have not lost much
ground. It is a favourable thing that nine blisters,
since 20th June, have not reduced my flesh. And
my blood-spitting has only been occasional, not constant, for three months now. But cough is worse, I
think, than ever. The difficulty of breathing rather
increases ; and pains are more numerous and quite
immovable. However, the heat has not fevered my
pulse. On the whole, I am not much worse, and feel
daily ground for thankfulness, although I can see no
solid reason for cherishing hope.

  ' I rejoice to find that you are trying to say, " Good
is the will of the Lord," whatever he may do with me.
But I fear you think too favourably of the state of my
mind. In myself, and for aught that I can do or have
done, it is all sin and sorrow. Those things which
have found me favour with men, I see to be but filthy
rags, when brought near to the law of God. I see
that if I am to be saved at all, it must be by the one
way—God's free grace through Jesus Christ our Lord.
I am not destitute of hope toward God, and I seek to
build it on the work of this Saviour. But it is faint
and low ; and I greatly need the quickening energy of
the Holy Ghost. Ask this for me in your prayers ;
and ask also the Spirit of adoption, whereby, in the
midst of trouble, I may cry, " Abba, Father." . . . .

  ' Your ever affectionate son,   J. H.'

                  ' *Monday*, 17*th September* 1838.

  ' Have resumed my pen, although both the weather
and my own indolence are adverse to its use, in order
briefly to mention, that I may improve them to my
soul's good, the events of this day twelve months.

  ' On Sabbath, 17th September 1837, I was at Roth-
say. Heard Mr Craig on Matt. xii. 33–42, and Mr
Begg of Liberton on 1 Cor. x. 1, 4. Spent the after-

noon in reading Dr Love's sermons; and closed the day by conducting the family devotions of a decent Highland family with whom I lodged.

'Next morning saw Denniston and Burns, for whose friendship and example I must give account. Walked to the Point-house, and was most kindly treated by Sir D. K. Sandford. In my then perplexity about my destination, he advised me, with much judgment and sympathy, to come here. With Professor Ramsay, he took me to see the site of the house he was to build. But God has already dissolved his own tabernacle of clay; and this his thought has perished. Wondrous mercy! that I live to record it.

'*Wednesday,* 26*th September* 1838.

'Received, with much emotion, a note from my excellent friend ———, accompanied by " Richard Alleine's Life and Letters," and " Taylor's Life of Cowper." Much humbled by an expression in the note —" God bless you with his best and choicest blessings." So my friends are, no doubt, hoping that the furnace is purifying me; while here am I, sinning, repenting, and complaining, and showing, in unmortified corruptions, that the dross is by far predominant, or rather, probably, that the metal is altogether base. Oh, it is sad thus to be falling short of the kind and charitable thoughts of God's children, dishonouring God himself, and (if one may so speak) rendering it impossible for him, in wisdom and faithfulness, to withdraw his heavy hand. An unholy and unhumbled heart *demands* more of the rod. Oh for the whisperings of the good Spirit to make me " hear it, and Him who hath appointed it!"

'This day two years I took one of the most decided steps of my short pilgrimage, in leaving Glasgow, the scene of much enjoyment, success, and kind encouragement, for Edinburgh, an untried field of exertion. To this step, under Divine Providence, I may in great part attribute my present illness; for it was a trans-

o

portation to a still more unkindly climate,——it removed
the restraints (slender enough at best) which existed
at home on night study, and it placed me, when illness
came, in a situation, in which, from aversion to giving
trouble, I was content to want many needful, or, at
least, desirable things.   But in spite of these effects,
I do not so much condemn this as nine-tenths of the
actions of my life.   So far as memory can replace me
in the circumstances, it seems to me that there was
less mixture of sinful motives in it than an accurate inspection could generally detect in others.   *Surely* my
main—my overpowering desire was to use the means
of securing a greater measure of fitness for the Gospel
ministry, than I could hope to gain amid the bustle of
my Glasgow occupations.   In this I was disappointed,
partly from ill health, chiefly from my own misuse of
opportunities ; but I can recall few desires which existed in me in greater simplicity.   Yet how tainted
must all have been, when even this was made, by
Infinite Wisdom, the means of chastisement.

'*Sabbath*, 30th *September* 1838.

'Heard an admirable discourse to-day, from the
Rev. Hardwicke Shute, on the necessity, evidence,
and acquisition, of the love of God, from 1 John iv.
19.

'On the Sabbath of last year, corresponding to to-
day, being the 1st day of October, I ought, according
to a promise made six months before—had I been
licensed—to have commenced my public labours in
Stevenson's pulpit.   But God scattered this imagination.   And it has probably been in mercy that I was
kept from touching the ark ; for I get day by day
such disclosures of my own unholiness, as make it
clear that I should have been most unfit for the
solemn duties of the ministry.

'Instead of being at Newton, I spent that Sabbath
at Killermont, reading the Bible and the "Life of the
Rev. Cornelius Neale," which, like every other Chris-

tian biography, was one continued reproach of my dulness and leanness.

'Endeavoured to recount my mercies and sins, with a view to self-humiliation.

'*Thursday, 4th October* 1838.

'. . . . . . This day twelve months I saw dear A. licensed; and got a word in season about my trouble from the Rev. Jonathan Anderson in the Presbytery house. In the evening, Dr Thomson, an old West Indian physician, was the first who distinctly pronounced me to be in consumption.

'I have thus now, for a whole year, known myself to be fatally diseased. How little has this knowledge impressed me! Lord, pardon my lightness, and teach me to live for eternity! Amen.

'On 16th October came to Socorro. On 27th do., burst a blood-vessel in my right lung. Much weakened. For three days no food. Confined to bed wholly for a week; to the house till now. Record it thankfully, that at the moment of the attack, I felt no fear, and was enabled to commit my soul to Christ. May grace be given me to do so daily!

'This day twelve months left Falmouth, and have never been so long confined as fifteen days till now.

'Hitherto the Lord hath helped us!'

The bursting of the blood-vessel noted above, was to his friends an alarming symptom of the progress of his disorder. This short note is very precious as a record of the hope that sustained him in his time of greatest need. At the moment of the attack he '*felt no fear.*' This of itself is abundant evidence against many of his own more despondent reasonings. Knowing, as he did, the state of his disease, and feeling, for the first time, a sudden and copious flow of blood from the lungs, he must have had a strong apprehension of immediate dissolution. In these circumstances he was enabled to commit his soul to Christ, and await the result without fear. This alone is enough to satisfy the reader that his hope was more steady and strong than the language of his complaints appears to indicate. His practice of aiming at the very highest attainments, which with him was an intellectual habit, gave a tinge to his expressions when speaking of his own hope. Those who did not personally know him should take this into account. His intimate friends know that he really possessed much more of the peace and joy in believing than a stranger would infer from the perusal of his letters.

He was much weakened by this attack for a time, but it does not seem to have much interfered with the activity of his mind. During the remaining two months of 1838, very little appears either in the journal or in the form of letters to his friends; but at that time he was not idle; what strength he still retained was employed in another way.

The two following letters give an account of the state of his disease at this period, and throw much light on a subject that lay near his heart—the religious state of the English inhabitants, and the means of bringing a preached Gospel within their reach.

'MADEIRA, 3d _December_ 1838.

' My dear James,— . . . . Thanks for your notes on Oxford ; you are not half so wild as I am against Newman and Co. If the English Church does not expel these fellows, I think the Church of Scotland will be utterly untrue to her Head if she symbolizes with it longer. I have read Newman " on Romanism and Popular Protestantism" twice ; thoroughly analyzed him ; and see the total want of bottom which characterises the scheme. But what is worse, I see its *pratiques* here. Here, in a community of dying men, have we whole sermons on baptismal grace, sacramental efficacy, and the like ; against prayer-meetings, as irregular ; against laymen praying with the sick ; and, *horrendissimum !* against the unrestricted reading of the Scriptures without a priest to interpret, —as if the besetting sin of the people here were an overstrained use of their Bibles. All this makes me quite overboil. And, by way of crowning the whole, last Sabbath (Langford having now come, and he and I having had some communings about reviving our prayer-meeting of last year) it was announced, as an extinguisher to all irregularities, that *prayers would be* READ in the chapel on Wednesday and Friday afternoons. Of course, the exhibition of such a spirit puzzles us as to our duty,—it becoming a question, whether we may not do as much harm by raising such evil feeling, as good by the possible effect of our addresses. Only it is a heavy thought, that if we abstain, there will be no preaching of the Gospel here at all ; and even the Word read in the lessons can hardly be expected to profit, when the people are sedulously taught not to attempt understanding and applying it for themselves. So much for high-churchism, which, from my soul, I abhor. This is the place for converting a man to our fathers' views of Black Prelacy. " By their fruits ye shall know them." Here endeth my philippic. . . . .

' And now, as to your other suggestions in the way of subjects for my weak and errant pen, I can only say, I hope they have deeply humbled me. To a mind that has any remnant of ingenuousness at all, nothing can be more distressingly humiliating than to find oneself so overrated. Indeed, my dear friend, I am *utterly unequal* to the task of writing profitably on any of the subjects you name. What am I that I should presume to write on Christian experience—to

lay my own theorizing on truths scarce felt at all, as a
model before the Church of God? Read a part of the
preface to " Abbot's Way to do Good," and you will
find remarks on inability to enter into the inner courts
of Christianity, which apply with far greater emphasis
to me. " Stated times for devotion" is the only subject named which I could at all illustrate, and here
every page would be a reproof and libel on myself.
But, weakened as I now am, it seems almost Utopian
to speak of putting my hand to any new effort. If I
do, you shall duly hear, though not probably for nearly three months, as the Dart and Vernon happen to
be here together, which spoils the alternation of our
conveyances. Meantime I read a good deal in a quiet
way, and much need your prayers that I may be found
watching. . . . .

' I dare not speak a word about my chance (as
ignorant beings must call it) of seeing out this winter.
It is wholly in God's hands ; and were the decision in
my own, I trust I can say unaffectedly, that I should
not wish it out of them again. It would be pleasant
to see you all again ; but then it would bind more
strongly so many ties to earth and its inhabitants.
But *He* will choose out the lot of our inheritance. O
pray that I may be strong in faith, and unreserved in
submission.—And believe me, while here, your grateful and affectionate   J. H.'

'Madeira, 1st *January* 1839.

' My very dear Friend,—I wish you very much happiness in the year which has now opened on us. . . .
I wish you also, from all my heart, what none of us
dare think of in reference to me—many joyful and
profitable returns of so solemnly impressive a season.

' Do not expect either a long or a good letter from
me just now. Somehow I am sadly out of the mood
in which I would wish to write any body, above all
to write *you* ; but, as my heart faileth with my flesh,

I know not when I may be in a better, so, having the opportunity of writing some one of my friends just now, and finding you to be the one that has the greatest present claim, I have resolved to give myself the pleasure, probably for the last time, of wishing you a *good new year.*

'Your most welcome letter, by Dr K., of the 17th September, reached me on the 14th October. I was both rejoiced and ashamed to find that you had taken the trouble of writing me at such length, in the midst of the many labours that must press upon you. Dr K. I have found a warm and truly Christian friend. He proposed to have a small prayer-meeting for private edification, which commenced three weeks ago. The members are, Langford, Dr K., Mr B., and myself. I hope to profit by it. K. is very zealous; anxious to do good, but rather tied up, as you may by and by have explained, if my paper serves; but he does what he can, and would willingly labour still more abundantly.

'Of my *health* you will have heard frequently since you heard directly from myself. I went on, much as when I wrote you, till the 27th October, when, in stooping, without any apparent cause, I burst a blood-vessel in the right lung. Lost two breakfast cupfulls of blood. Was confined fifteen days (the longest time, I am thankful to say, I have been in the house since I came to Madeira), and a good deal weakened. . . . . For a month past, however, this has been quite a tolerable evil, so I have bought an apology for a pony, and ride a little. Still, I do not stand where I was. My breathing is rather shorter; my sleep, always indifferent, has become very bad, and opiates only add to my restlessness; and my cough has increased very sensibly in frequency and depth. So I fear you and my other ardently attached friends, who were perhaps too willing to entertain favourable expectations, must really try to divorce yourselves from the hope of any considerable

prolongation of my life.   Renton, indeed, who examined my chest a fortnight ago, says the disease is
little more extensive than it was when I came, and
that I am at present in that peculiar state, in which,
with care and a good climate, I might hang on for a
good while; but confesses that a severe cold might
induce an amount of inflammation which no medicine
could check.   So that I ought to cherish the constant
feeling that my life is hovering between two worlds.
Yet you easily see that the possibility of living to see
another summer brings with it other possibilities which
draw away the mind from this steady view, such as
that of returning home; and then I perplex myself
with the difficulties which will arise about my future
disposal, through which God alone can cut a way; and
almost tremble as I think of the excitement of shaking
hands with those from whom I thought I had parted
for ever; and weep with joy and humiliation when I
muse upon seeing so many of my dear brethren in
college labour declaring, each in his own pulpit, the
glorious Gospel of the blessed God.   These are all disturbing forces; but yet, notwithstanding these, and in
spite of whatever to the contrary may appear to lurk
in what remains of my letter when I come to speak
of my plans (for *plans* you know I *will* be contriving
so long as I live), I trust I can say, without much
self-deception, that the steady tendency of my mind
is towards the remembrance of how short my time is.

'This would naturally lead me to say something
of my *spiritual health*; but here I must be silent.   I
have no right to trouble you with more complainings;
and I have not yet learned the " new song."   Your
remarks here were most welcome, and your solicitude
peculiarly pleasing to me.   I trust yet your excellent
advices and cautions may bring forth some fruit; at
all events, they have been repeatedly perused and
prayed over, and they shall ever be highly valued.   I
cannot say that I have made any sensible progress,

unless it be in the knowledge of sin. I sometimes imagine I see more than formerly of my own depravity. But I have latterly thought that one of the chief manifestations of sin within me has been a seeking for *comfort*, rather than a steady performance of *duty* even in the dark. I trust, by Divine grace, to address myself to the mending of this evil; to do somewhat of what my hand findeth, confessing all the while that any portion of peace or consolation is what I have no right to expect.

' And here the harvest truly is plenteous. Fourteen invalid strangers have already passed into eternity since the beginning of October; many more remain in a very precarious state, and among the residents there is scarcely a glimmering of religion. I have four invalid friends, whom I try to visit (as a professing Christian) once a-week, and one resident lady, who was, I hope, converted to God last year, with whom, on Monday mornings, I go through Ephesians. Langford labours among (I presume) a greater number; and B. has access to one or two sick-beds. L. visits a few, and offers them the sacrament most industriously; but he cannot preach to them *the Gospel*, for he is plainly ignorant of it himself. His chief subjects in the pulpit of late have been—against prayer-meetings as irregular; against the laity attempting to pray by the sick; against the Scotch meeting (of which more directly), and strong laudations of the Church and the Prayer-book.

' But I have not of late heard any of these lucubrations. For a good many Sabbaths after my attack I could not sit out a service; and for four Sabbaths past we have had a meeting for public worship in the Scotch form, Mr Barrie being the preacher. We met the first day in a merchant's house, and since that we have hired a large room in a boarding-house. Between 30 and 40 is the regular attendance, often more.

' Barrie and Kalley, who are both well, were anxious to have been engaged in a prayer-meeting of a public kind. But they could not have expected to get any hearers but a portion of those Scotch who hear the Gospel on Sabbath. Now, the persons we were most anxious to reach were the Anglicans, who hear *no* Gospel on Sabbath. . . . . So good Langford, although his health is worse, finding himself to stand between the Anglicans and want, agreed to *join me* in a meeting, lamenting that the prejudices of the people, which he could estimate much better than we, compelled him, *unwillingly*, to forego the aid of B., a Dissenter, —and K., a layman. Thus the thing lies on two broken reeds,—Lowe threatening, with regard to Langford, to apply to the Bishop of London for an interdict. Nathless, we mean, by God's help, to commence to-morrow. And I hope we shall have strength given us to go through with it, and grace to be found faithful.

' Literary labour has been out of the question. The tale of books read since July 17 is considerable—*forty* volumes; but many of them very small, and none heavy. Probably the most important has been " Newman on Romanism and Popular Protestantism," which I read twice, and wrote notes upon ; a very subtle attempt to demolish the general principle of Protestantism, beginning with the all-sufficiency of Scripture, and the right of private judgment, and to rear the *via media* on its ruins.—With unabated regard, yours,

' J. H.

' *Rev. W. Arnot.*'

Of seven Episcopal clergymen whose health admitted of exertion, only one would countenance and support the prayer-meeting. The opposition of the ministers of course considerably affected the attendance of the people. Thus checked in his efforts to reach the ears of those who most needed instruction,

Mr Halley was naturally led to examine the grounds on which the opposition rested. The result was, a little essay, entitled 'Vindication of Prayer-Meetings,' intended to be read at the first meeting in the beginning of January. As this paper, independently of its own intrinsic value, tends directly to throw light on the condition and character of the English population at Madeira, we shall give it a place in this volume.* It deserves to be recorded, both for its own sake as an argument on a most interesting subject, and for the sake of the light which it throws on the picture of Madeira life. We can learn much of the character of the persons addressed from the kind of arguments which an accurate observer felt it necessary to employ; and the grave use of arguments to prove what he himself must have considered self-evident, is an honourable testimony to the candour of the writer.

Still farther to show, what we in Scotland happily do not well understand, how strong a prejudice the Anglicans entertain against such meetings, it may be stated that this paper was never read. Gentle and charitable though it be, it was not deemed prudent to read it at the meeting, lest it should provoke a more active opposition. Of these labours we shall hear more in subsequent letters; and meantime, we extract from the diary a brief notice of what Mr Halley always accounted a most important event in his life.

' *Sabbath, 6th January* 1839.

' We have now, for some time, had the privilege of attending divine worship in our own Scotch form, under the ministry of Mr Barrie, a licentiate of the United Secession Church. . . . .

* Appendix, D.

'*Monday, 14th January* 1839.

'Having obtained help of God, I was enabled to preach yesterday from Rev. xxii. 5, first clause, in the Scotch meeting.   Was much encouraged by the attention of the people ; and feel unlimited cause for gratitude in no immediate mischief having resulted to myself.   And now,

'Father of mercies, I would humbly but earnestly entreat thee to give me some token for good in reference to this and my other labours.   Glorify thy Son by these poor ministrations; and lift on me, if it please thee, for his sake and for thy glory's sake, some such light of thy countenance as may encourage and uphold me in bearing testimony for Him.   Show me how much I can and ought to do ; and ever lead and guide me.   Amen.'

There is a more particular account of his feelings on that occasion in a subsequent letter, of date 26th April.   As might be expected from one who so much magnified the office, he experienced the most intense delight in being allowed for once to preach publicly the unsearchable riches of Christ.   The Spirit poured out on him, in some degree reached his audience. We have been told by a gentleman who visited the island soon after, that a great impression was produced, and a lively remembrance of it cherished long among the people.   It is worthy of remark that Mr Halley did not consider himself warranted, on ordinary occasions, to assume the functions of a preacher of the Gospel.   Even had his health admitted of it, he would not have felt himself at liberty to preach publicly without authority from the Church.   But on this occasion he yielded to what he considered his duty, on a sudden and unforeseen emergency.   Mr Barrie, who usually conducted the worship, was prevented from being present on that day, and Mr Halley determined to preach, as the only means of preserving the congregation who assembled from the other alternative—a silent Sabbath.

The substance of this discourse has been preserved. The text was Rev. xxii. 5—'There shall be no night there.' It is conceived in a strain of great tenderness, and eminently suited to the circumstances in which it was delivered. Elsewhere the reader will find a sermon more elaborately composed, at a time of greater vigour : from this we give only one brief quotation, as a specimen of its style. It is the last of six short heads intended to illustrate the doctrine of the text, and is followed by a lengthened application to the peculiar circumstances of the audience.

' 6. Finally, that night is the image of *death*. So Job speaks of the grave as a " land of darkness, as darkness itself ; and of the shadow of death, without any order, and where the light is as darkness." And as sleep has among all nations been called the brother of death, and night is the time of his dominion, it has become associated likewise with the thought of dissolution, so that he who speaks of the night of the grave, gives utterance to a language which is universally intelligible, as expressing the common feeling of humanity. And here, certainly, if any where, we dwell in the midst of this night,—in a land where death casts his longest and deepest shadow ; and wherever we move on earth, we find this darkness always before us, this night constantly impending. But there is *no night there*—no night of death ; and this it is which adds indefinitely to every joy of the Lord's redeemed, that they have come to a kingdom where all is immortal. Their cup of bliss will never have its sweetness impaired by the infusion of a single drop of

aught that is perishable; their inheritance is incorruptible and undefiled, and fadeth not away ; their felicity
shall be coeval with their being, and their being with
eternity.   Could the suspicion find a place, that even
after long ages this glory would terminate, the anxious
expectation of the end might mar the happiness of
heaven ; but the blessed assurance is vouchsafed that
these pleasures are for evermore,—that death, all-sub-
duing though he is to us below, shall be to the saints
in light a prostrate enemy, one over whom they have
achieved, through the might of Emmanuel, a final and
irreversible triumph.   And, oh ! what must be their
ecstasy, when they think that that spectre foe, from
whose onset, while on earth, in spite of the promises
of grace, nature would often shrink with an indescribable apprehension, shall never, never vex them more ;
when they know that that event to which, for a lifetime, they looked forward with solemnity, is buried
in the past, and never can befall them again ; when
they feel that they are grasping the palm of glory with
a hand that shall never more grow chill, and raising
the new song in a voice that shall never more grow
tremulous, and beholding the Divine glory with eyes
on which no shadow of death shall ever again descend,
and mingling with an assemblage for not one individual of which the grave shall ever again open.   This
will be the joy of their joy, the crowning element of
their transport ; and this, observe, will be the feeling
of every individual citizen of the New Jerusalem.
But suppose it to be diffused throughout a multitude
such as no man can number, and augmented by that
thrill of sympathy which the spirits of the just made
perfect *must* feel in each other's gladness, every bosom
swelling with the consciousness that the glory of all is
imperishable, and you will gain a new and loftier conception of what is intended when it is said, " There
shall be *no night there.*"

With reference to the same question—in what circumstances one is justified in preaching publicly, without express and formal authority from the Church—there is a very interesting note in the journal of a later date. To a mind constituted as his was, it was painful to be placed in the alternative of hearing the Gospel unfaithfully preached, or hearing it preached by one not set apart to the office of the ministry. In the choice there was no difficulty. His desires were all on the one side; but the want of 'all things in order' seems to have afforded him considerable uneasiness.

'*Sabbath,* 21*st February* 1839.

'To-day, Mr Barrie having suddenly left us, Dr Kalley conducted divine worship in a style of fervent piety and lofty spirituality. He spoke in the forenoon from Exodus xv. 11. I have been in much perplexity as to whether it is his line of duty to attempt the maintaining of these meetings. His own mind seems quite unembarrassed. The Lord confirm him, if he is right, and lead him to review his resolution, if he is wrong. And oh that He may give me light also, that I may be able either to attend him with a clear conscience, and in believing expectation of a blessing on the service; or, with a clear conscience, to adopt some other course. "Lord, send out thy light and truth."'

As the spring advanced, the question was raised again, whether he should spend the summer in Madeira or return home. A very minute statement of the case is given in a letter to J. C. Colquhoun, Esq., M.P., from which we shall present an extract.

'MADEIRA, 2*d April* 1839.

'My dear Sir,—If any thing could make you weary in well-doing, I think it would be having to do, in your present method and walk of benevolence, with

such a one as myself.   My hope is, however, that by
a good-natured blindness, you overlook these incon-
sistencies, which not unfrequently startle even myself.
At any rate, I feel that at one time I am apt to be so
brief as, to a less indulgent judge, would almost seem
disrespectful ; while at another—especially if any of
my own poor concerns require explanation——I am apt
to write at such length as to be absolutely tiresome.
Let your charity accept this excuse or palliation, that
bodily weakness, acting on a corrupt nature, has a sad
tendency to absorb every thought in itself, and that
invalids, by a kind of prescriptive right, are allowed
to be unreasonable. . . . .

‘ At the close of that letter, I said I thought it
would be my duty to return home in June, and let
our medical advisers there pronounce upon my state.
This was, of course, on the hypothesis that no peculiar
danger was to be apprehended from such a step.   Accordingly, to my friends here, of whom God has graciously given me not a few, I always spoke of my
return as a settled thing.   Some of them hinted an
opinion that I had better stay, but none so strongly
as to affect my purpose.   About six weeks ago, however, Dr Robert Kalley (my most endeared friend,
certainly, among this year's strangers—a medical man,
who had offered himself as a missionary for China,
but his wife's health having brought him here, is now
likely to labour among the Portuguese in Madeira),
having heard one of us mention this, said very decidedly, that, from what he had observed of my state,
he would consider such a step far from wise ; and
concluded by offering one or both of us a place in his
house (by way of farther reducing our expenditure),
if it should be thought fit that I should remain.   Some
time after, I got him to examine my chest ; and the
result, he said, was to confirm him in his view.   Still,
having spoken in such terms both to you and to my
father, I did not feel at liberty even then to consider

my return as an open question ; but waited anxiously
for last packet and Vernon (which arrived respectively
on the 21st and 22d of March), to discover the mind
of my friends in Britain.   However, my Glasgow letters contained no allusion to the subject ; and in consequence of my own inadvertency in not telling you
when the Vernon was to sail, I had none from you.
So I felt all I could do was to get Dr Renton to stetho-
scopize me anew, and then lay before my friends the
medical and other elements, so far as I know them, of
a judgment on the question. . . . He now detects one,
perhaps two *cavities*, in my right lung ; and the plain
inference is, that the disease has reached that stage at
which it is generally pronounced incurable.   Upon
being interrogated as to the propriety of returning, he
said that no one could calculate on the influence of
our native climate, even in summer, on a chest in such
a condition ; and although evidently unwilling to discourage me from returning, if my friends should desire
it, he intimated his opinion, that it would so greatly
accelerate the complaint, that if I lived to see the autumn, no question would ever be raised about another
removal.   In short, while he holds out no other hope
than that the disease will run its course, he thinks that
course will be more slowly accomplished here.

  ' Possibly, my dear Sir, it may seem strange that
such a judgment as this did not add strength to my
former resolution ; and that, as all the labour and usefulness for which I once wished to live is now for ever
hid from my eyes, no question need now be raised
about the duty of my going home, seeing my father
and dear friends in the flesh, and then resigning my
spirit to Him who gave it.   But you will not greatly
marvel at my mind being otherwise affected, when
you ponder how solemn a thing it is for a poor sinful
worm to have the near prospect of appearing as an
unclothed spirit before the King of kings.   Much of
the overwhelming sensation which this thought pro-

P

duces is doubtless the fruit of unbelief, and therefore
sinful ; but it is still here : and while I feel that the
very brief space to which care in this climate might
yet extend my days, is quite as nothing, with my impaired capacities, in regard to any of my cherished
plans of outward usefulness, it is no light thing as
regards the onward prospect into eternity.

' Such, then, I must own, in weakness of the flesh,
is the leading reason which called into doubt my former resolution of returning.   Farther consideration
has brought to light a few others, which I shall notice
as briefly as I may.   1. Probably, besides the mere
matter of a slightly lengthened span, my private religious advantages will be greater here. . . . . On the
other hand, at home, although I have many truly
Christian friends, I apprehend I should rather be
living in a crowd ; and many of those who are best
able to instruct me in spiritual matters, would (I am
afraid) as of old, renew the unhappy deference they
used to pay to my opinion in matters theological, and
the temptation might be too strong for me to talk of
books, and systems, and theories, instead of the one
thing needful for a dying man.   2. Although I can
now *do* much less good than formerly (for the swelling in my leg, which I probably mentioned in my
last, though kept down by no fewer than six bleed-
ings, has now for two months entirely prevented me
from riding, so that my visits are much reduced, and I
am only carried to the weekly prayer-meeting ; indeed,
I have just ordered a pair of crutches, to move about my
room) ; yet I have both the *call* and the *possibility* to
do *a little*—the *call*, for the invalids here are more
than one man can overtake, and the minister (though
he tried, which he does *not*, to overtake them), is so
far astray himself that he can teach them little good ;
and the *possibility*, for one or two come to me, and
in this climate I can safely get carried out to one
other.   Besides, speaking on human probabilities,

there is a chance that, remaining here, I may *subsist* till next winter in a state which will admit of my being present, and saying a few words quietly (we only sit and talk) at any prayer-meeting which may then be instituted. At home, still going on the same argument of probability, I should have neither the *call* nor the *power*,—not the call, for there I have many clerical friends on whom I could devolve such labour; nor the power, for probably I durst not go over my father's threshold. It deserves to be added also, in the estimate of the ways in which I could serve God while on earth, that there seems a bare *possibility* of my getting here a class of Portuguese padres, to teach them Greek (which not one of them knows)—a kind of usefulness, if attainable, which would a little ease my conscience in continuing to absorb funds, which, if not given to me, would no doubt find their way into the Redeemer's treasury. . . —Most affectionately yours, J. H.

' *J. C. Colquhoun, Esq.*'

The letter goes on to enumerate, with a similar minuteness, the reasons for returning, and concludes by asking to be directed by his benefactors as to the course he should take. The following short extract from a very long letter has reference to the same subject. It is addressed to his stepmother. His mother, whose memory he always affectionately cherished, died when he was about ten years of age.

' MADEIRA, 4th *April* 1839.

' My dear Mother,—I have often thought of it as one disadvantage of my situation here, that I am tempted not to correspond directly with those who ought to be dearest to me on earth. When there are so many others who have claims on me in the way of letter-writing, it is very natural to hand over our own family to Janet, who can write with propriety to you, while there are many to whom she cannot do so. But I now begin to feel that this was wrong; that nobody can have so good a right to get letters from my own hand as my own nearest friends; and that if my father and you have been so indulgent hitherto as not to complain of my silence, that is just the stronger a reason why I should be quickened in my sense of duty to you, and do all that I now can to show you how fully I retain all the feelings of a son to you both, only (I hope) increased and strengthened by the absence, and by this long season of retirement, in which God has been calling me to reflect on my manifold deficiencies in duty towards you in the years that are past. . . . .

' But in spite of all this present comfort, it would be very sad to deceive myself, and very wrong to deceive you and my dear father with any flattering hopes for the future. God has been pleased to mark all such as " vanity;" and we are bound to consider the operation of his hands. Now I feel it, in my own flesh, to be most certainly true, that I have lost much ground during the last five months,—so that Dr Kalley, with the affection and faithfulness of a Christian friend, told me that there is no hope of my getting better. And since this is the case, surely I am right in telling it to my dear parents, that they may be seeking to have their minds prepared, by the Holy Spirit, for what now seems inevitable. Returning to Britain would probably bring it to pass more rapidly; staying here may be a means, by the Divine blessing, of making it come more slowly; but the course of God's providence towards me all goes to show that it *is coming*,—that " I must soon put off this tabernacle."

' My dear mother, this is a very solemn thought,— a sinful creature feeling it likely that, before long, he must render his spirit back to God who gave it. The wonder is, when we *all* know that we must do this sooner or later, that we can think of any thing else in comparison. Pray much for me, both you and my father, that my sins may be blotted out in the blood of Christ; that, while I live, a large measure of the Holy Spirit may, for Christ's sake, be given me, so that I may enjoy the full consciousness, before I go hence, of being " accepted in the Beloved," " an heir of God, and a joint heir with Christ ;" that I may be strengthened for every suffering, and especially for the last of all ; and that " an entrance may be ministered to me abundantly into the everlasting kingdom of our Lord and Saviour." . . . .

‘ My dear mother, it is very possible we may never meet in this world ; if I remain here, it is most probable, nay almost certain, we never shall. Shall we all meet in a better ? Depending on the aids of God's Spirit, let us all pray and strive that it may be so, through Jesus Christ our Lord. Meantime, God bless you all.—Heb. xiii. 20, 21. So prays your affectionate son,   J. H.’

The following note is from the journal :—

‘ *Sabbath*, 21*st April* 1839.

‘ Two months of spiritual darkness, and trouble about many things. The Lord has dealt bountifully with me, in enabling me generally to hear Dr Kalley once a-day on Sabbath, and almost always to open my mouth for Him on Thursdays,—when, although my dulness and deadness of soul has prevented me from saying a word on the more spiritual subjects which came in our way, which I always handed over to my much more pious and experienced brother, Langford,—yet I have been enabled, I hope not without profit to some, to illustrate points of doctrine and the lower and plainer matters of duty.

‘ To-day, by God's good providence, as I doubt not, much of Dr K.'s forenoon discourse was wonderfully

applicable to my case. It was on Rev. iii. 1, 2.—
Lord, bless it permanently to my soul.'

Notwithstanding the painful sense of unfitness under which he laboured, his instructions were highly
valued by others. A letter written by Mr Halley to
a gentleman now resident in Edinburgh, who had
been in the habit of attending the prayer-meeting at
Madeira, furnishes indirect evidence of the estimation
in which his expositions of Scripture were held.

Saturday Evening, 20th April 1839.

' My dear Sir,—Your warm expression of brotherly
love so completely overcame me, that I fear I was
unable at the time to breathe out an assurance how
cordially it was reciprocated. Permit me now to
supply the lack, and to tell you how earnestly my best
affections will follow you as one of those whose presence and converse, so far as I have enjoyed them,
have always refreshed me in this land of our sojourn-
ing. And if surrounded (as you too probably were)
by some specimens of the ignorance of foolish man,
you have felt yourself strengthened in any measure
by the exercises of our meetings, you will join me in
rendering thanks to Him who is able " from the mouth
of babes and sucklings to perfect praise."

' I believe no higher character than the stammer-
ings of a babe is due to the most of what *I* at least
have uttered on these occasions. And I have been
repeatedly humbled by the thought (and never more
than when you so affectionately addressed me to-day),
that I have been professing to instruct some, at whose
feet, so far as the real inward heart work of religion
is concerned, it would have far better become me to
sit as a learner.

' But as God has ordained the bounds of our habitation differently, permit me to ask that you will confer on me another benefit, which no distance of place

can interrupt or hinder. I mean to bear me on your heart, when you attempt to " enter into the holiest by the blood of Jesus." My need of your continued intercessions is great and pressing, not only from the consideration that my time on earth seems likely to be short, but from this especially, that the natural bias of my mind unquestionably coincided too well with the peculiar *snare* of a professional education in theology, namely, the tendency to view Divine truth speculatively, and to attend to the furniture of the understanding vastly more than to the impression of the heart. Thus it is that what I know and am thoroughly convinced of, I scarcely ever adequately *feel;* and I crave your earnest supplications, that God would send me heat as well as light from above.

' You will not refuse the very trifling testimony of my endeared affection which accompanies this ; * it will show, if it does nothing else, that I would not willingly be forgotten. And perhaps its very smallness may procure it a look, when the means of more ample instruction are not at hand.

' And now, my dear Sir, what can I say more ?— " The Lord of all grace, who hath called us unto his eternal glory by Christ Jesus, after that you have suffered a while, make you perfect, stablish, strengthen, and settle you." So prays your friend and brother,

' J. H.

' *James Duncan, Esq., W.S.*'

The next letter, although almost wholly on the same subject, contains some new features, and exhibits some of the more tender traits of the writer's mind.

' MADEIRA, 26*th April* 1839.

' The melancholy news (although only on the *under* side) communicated in your last, I had, as you must know ere now, heard before. In February I re-

* A book entitled ' Shaw's Immanuel,' on which there is marked— ' From a companion in tribulation.'

quested Arnot to tell you that my first impulse, on
hearing of your affliction, was to write to you; but,
indeed, I felt myself quite incompetent, and I well
knew that, with your Bible and your father's writings,
you could not want for sources of consolation.   But
perhaps I was inexcusable in not performing such an
office of friendship, however feebly.   If so, try to forgive me on any score your kind ingenuity can invent.
And let me help you with this explanation among
others, that I verily believe I could not then have written of our dear Mary (permit the expression to stand,
for, being your brother, I was surely *hers*) without a
degree of emotion which would scarcely have been
safe for me; and that I really felt myself unable at
the time to grasp those strong comforts which I knew
belonged to the case.

   ' I have been amazed, my dear James, at the Divine
long-suffering, in sparing me so long amidst the re-
movals of many who seemed to bid far fairer for life.
Sir D. K. Sandford, poor Forsyth, Mr Wilkie, your
dear sister, and I presume I may by this time too
truly add, Mr Cadell, all gone down to the dust, and
I yet above it!   " It is marvellous in mine eyes."
Yet, strange to say, I can live on as if all this were a
matter of course; while, at the same time, in sober
thought, I know that " the graves are ready for me,"
and find daily more deeply written in my own constitution the " sentence of death."

   ' From Arnot, or Morrison, or Mackail, you will
surely have heard some of my downward history since
I wrote you.   Lest you should not, I must *sketch* it.
In the beginning of December, I was recruiting rather
from the effects of my hæmorrhage, got a pony, and
began to ride about a little, and visit a few sick folks,
and one inquirer after the way to Zion—a merchant's
wife, who (I have good confidence) is advancing *in*
the way.   By the by, on the 9th December, we began public worship in the Scotch form (as many by

his time felt they could not in conscience go to hear
opery preached), our minister being a Mr Barrie of
he Secession, who came out in charge of a sick youth,
and our church a hall. *Jan.* 3,—Langford and I
alone (about 15 English clergymen either opposing
or indifferent, Lowe preaching against it, and Langford himself so suspicious about exciting prejudice,
that he would not accept the aid either of Mr Barrie,
a Seceder, or Dr Kalley, an excellent layman, who is
likely to remain as a missionary among the Portuguese), commenced our weekly prayer-meeting. It
has been, blessed be God, better attended this year
than it was last,—our numbers, before the strangers
began to leave, being from 50 to 60. At present,
when more than half the visitors are gone, it averages
30. Our subject has been, the 1st Epistle of Peter
(preceded by one lecture on Peter's life and character),
Langford having Leighton, and I my Greek concordance and my memory, which last is really tolerably
fresh. We have got on slowly, but done our work
pretty thoroughly. I have acted the expositor; and
Langford, who is a fine, warm-hearted, assured Christian, and excels in appeal, has dealt with the more
spiritual and hortatory parts,—a sanctuary into which
I felt I durst not enter. Last Thursday we did the
first clause of the 17th verse, 1st chapter; and I presume the rest of that verse will give us work for next
Thursday. The point I mean to elaborate, God willing (for I want to let you see, as it were, how we do),
is, how God can be said to *judge all* according to
their works, when he *justifies the righteous* by faith.
The rest *leviter perstringam*, leaving them chiefly to
Langford. Some have said they have been refreshed
by the meetings; more have had their views on some
things cleared. Neither of us have suffered sensibly in
consequence of them; and we are thankful we began.
But I must back to my narrative. *Jan.* 13,—Barrie's
charge being just dying, he could not preach. In the

forenoon we made a prayer-meeting of it, Dr Kalley reading a chapter, and giving a running commentary; in the afternoon Kalley took both prayers, and *I preached (pace Presbyterii Edinensis*) on Rev. xxii. 5, first clause. The room was full, and a good many standing round the door; was much excited; but felt no harm. Felt it a *glorious thing* to preach, if one could but entirely forget one's self, and be absorbed in one's subject. And here I may let you into the secret of a little weakness I was guilty of. I knew very well I could *never* preach at home; but, having noticed one or two in tears, ελπις μ' εσηνε* for a short time, that I might *possibly* go home this summer, get licensed in Edinburgh, and do a little, in a regular way, in the work of the Lord here next winter. It was a very delightful dream; and even the ghost of it, though sadly attenuated, is fair. In the same month (the English clergy, in consequence of Mr Lowe's disapproving it, having resolved to have no *clerical* meeting like last year's one), Langford, Barrie, Kalley, and I formed ourselves into a little fellowship-meeting, which meets in my house, and to which a Mr Ware, a London attorney, and Mr Fullerton the publisher, have since been added. Barrie left in the end of February, and Mr Ware goes to-morrow; the rest continue to meet for a time.   J. H.

'*Rev. James Hamilton.*'

From the journal :——

'*Sabbath,* 19*th May* 1839.

'By the arrival of the packet, the letters are now in our hands which will determine our return home, or continued residence here. But I do not open them till to-morrow; desiring, by the help of the Holy Spirit, to devote this evening to such contemplations of the Divine dealings with me, and the grace of God in the Gospel, as may strengthen me to follow what-

---

* Hope stole in.

ever course the letters prescribe; or, if they settle nothing, may put my mind into such a calm state as will be most favourable for forming a judgment on a connected view of the whole of our present circumstances.'

Although they no longer cherished any expectation of his recovery, his friends at home consented that he should remain at Madeira during the summer. Indeed they did not think he could survive the voyage, and as he did not express any reluctance to stay, they were willing rather that he should die there in peace, than that he should attempt the voyage home with so little prospect of being able to accomplish it. The next letter, written after his stay had been determined on, is addressed to his father. We extract a portion of it, regarding the education of his younger brother.

' MADEIRA, 28th *May* 1839.

' My dear dear Father,—. . . . . . Especially would I wish to know how Patrick's mind opens, what questions he asks, and so on, on the subject of religion. I hope he grows in obedience as he grows in stature, and that his mother has been taking opportunities to impress it and other duties upon him from religious considerations.

' I am sorry that I feel myself unable to meet with any fulness your request about his education. And chiefly for this reason, that I do not know whether he has shown any wish for one occupation more than another in after-life. For my own part, unless some decided evidence appear that it has pleased God to change his heart and make him truly one of his own children, I have no wish that his education be conducted with any reference to the possibility of his entering the holy ministry; for I think there cannot be a more miserable being on earth than a man who

preaches the Gospel heartlessly and without feeling it.
With your limited means, therefore, unless some decided inclination towards the ministry (founded on
truly pious feelings) were to appear, or a strong wish
to enter the legal or medical profession, I do not see
that you are called upon to carry his classical education very far. But you must strenuously insist at
present on his giving real earnest attention to his own
language, to acquiring a good current hand, which
will be of use in any occupation, and to arithmetic
and book-keeping. And I should wish that he learn
no more dancing (it is but furnishing him with the
means of temptation), but that, as soon as possible,
he be put to learn French, which will be of greatly
more use to him. And whenever Mr Macnab thinks
he is master of arithmetic up to decimal fractions, I
would have you send him to Mr Connel in the High
School, or some other equally good teacher of mathematics, and let him learn plane and solid geometry,
algebra, and trigonometry; which, besides being an
excellent mental exercise in the meantime, would
give him the means of prosecuting any branch of
science he might care for; or, if he should think of
being a land-surveyor, or engineer, or any thing of
that sort, would be of the greatest use to him. But
I think all these acquirements quite secondary —
indeed as the small dust in the balance—compared
with bringing him up *for eternity* in the *knowledge,*
and, as far as precept, and prayers, and example will
go, in the *practice* of true religion. I know, by very
considerable experience, the evil of giving the mind
up entirely even to things that are accounted good
and praiseworthy among men, while "the good part
that shall never be taken away," was forgotten or
disregarded. And I would rather have my brother
the veriest dunce that ever was, "if so be the Spirit
of Christ dwelt" in him, than the most learned and
distinguished of men without it. Let it be your

endeavour, then, to urge him, that "with all his get-ting he get understanding,"—that he "seek *first* the kingdom of God and his righteousness," for then "all other things shall be added." It is quite wonderful how much better one's commonest pursuits will pros-per, how much more cheerfully and completely com-mon duties will be done, if they are done under the impression that "every one of us must give an account to God." If Patrick can be brought, by divine grace, to live and walk under the dominion of this feeling, and to know the love of Christ which passeth know-ledge, I am sure, that even though he should go on slowly in his learning for a while, all will come right in the end; while, if this be absent, he will, in in-creasing knowledge, be only "increasing sorrow." . . .

' My dear Father, I cannot say how greatly I long for the spiritual good of yourself and my mother. Janet will be able to tell you, if you ask her when you and she meet, about a letter she got from me about your birth-day in 1837; in which, being then under influenza, it was said, that supposing my own soul were thoroughly established in peace with God, I would willingly die on the morrow, if God would bless it to you.* In one sense it has pleased the Lord to take me at my word. He *is* removing me in the mid-time of my days. Oh! let us not want the bless-ing through the fault of not seeking it. "The Word of God and prayer" are the grand appointed means for sanctifying to us every dispensation. They are always at hand; and "the Spirit himself also helpeth our infirmities." To his blessed teaching and guid-ance, and abounding comforts, I desire to commit you all. Try to long for him, to depend on his aid, to feel his presence with you; ask him for a simple faith in Christ, for peace, and love, and hope, and joy; and who knows how abundant and refreshing the answer may be.—Eph. iii. 20, 21. . . . . .

* See p. 88.

' And now, my dear father, the very God of peace
sanctify you wholly, guide you by his counsel, and
afterward receive you to glory.   So prays your very
affectionate son,   J. H.

' *Mr Thomas Halley.*

' *P.S.*—When I next write home, it will be to
Patrick.'

The promise of a letter to his brother was very soon
fulfilled.   It is unique, and we present it almost entire.   It is an effort in a walk of very great difficulty
—a walk, too, in which he had not much experience,
and we believe our readers will account it eminently
successful.   We think it as good an evidence of the
versatility of his talent as any thing we have been
able to present.   It is known to his friends that he
considered himself very defective in the power of
speaking or writing in a style simple and attractive to
young persons.   His course of study and habits as a
scholar were not favourable to the cultivation of that
talent ; but genius sanctified enabled him to overcome
these difficulties, and to become all things unto all.

'MADEIRA, 12*th June* 1839.

' My dear Paty,—Our difference in age is so great,
and my time has always been so sadly taken up, that
I believe this is the very first whole letter you have
ever got from me.   And who knows whether it may
not be the will of God that it should be the *last.*
This, my dear boy, will probably go a good way in
making you attend to the little I may now be able to
say to you ; especially if you reflect how possible it is
that there may not be another little (big ?) boy in
Britain, who is hearing from an *only* brother, at such
a distance, and in circumstances so solemn.

' Now let me begin the few words I have to write,
by putting you in mind of what we were about when

we were last together. You remember what we did when I had some thoughts of going to Jersey, before Madeira had been much spoken of. We took the map of Great Britain and Ireland, and endeavoured to learn from it the roads and distances, that we might fix what would be the best route to get easily to Jersey. That was our object; and we were very willing to pay attention to any map or guide-book which might direct us in our journey to it. Now there is another *object* which all of us would like to get at; very few, at any rate, if you asked them, would *say* any thing else than that they would wish to reach it; that object is *heaven*. But if we would perform this great journey rightly, so as happily to reach its end, we must *very diligently search our guide-book.* You are already quite prepared to name that book,—it is the *Bible.* Now, my dear brother, what I would like you to ask yourself is—whether you have read the Bible for this purpose. We are very apt to read it as a lesson, or merely because we are bidden, or with the thought of getting some good which yet we cannot name or lay hold of. But our *duty* goes far beyond any such light and careless treatment of it; we ought to read it, as being, in very truth, " the words of eternal life," and as sent to us by God for the express purpose of helping to make us truly happy in the love, and favour, and service of God himself. And surely if we think nothing of the trouble of taking food three or four times a-day for the nourishment of our bodies, which must die after all our pains, we ought to be much more willing to take, at least as often, something of that food which God has provided in his Word for our souls—the nobler part of us—which can never die. Is it not a sad proof of our sinfulness, that we are so much less anxious about the latter kind of food than we are about the former? My dear brother, let me urge you to seek an appetite for this spiritual nourishment, from Him who can give it.

God might, without any one being able to blame him, have left us to starve in our own perversity; but in great mercy he has taken another course, and has told us that he will " give the Holy Spirit to them that ask him ;" and that good Spirit can create a new heart, and impart those desires (for the knowledge of God and for holiness) which we had not by nature. Blind, then, as we are, and foolish ; ready to turn away from the Word of life, and unable of ourselves to understand it rightly ; what can we do but go in humble prayer for the aid of Him who can give us clear light and eager desire ?——" For Christ's sake, O Lord, pour thou out upon my dear brother the gift of thy Holy Spirit, that he may long after the knowledge of thy will.   May his heart be softened, may he feel himself a lost sinner before thee, may he be taught aright by thy Word and Spirit about Christ as a Saviour, may he be led to trust and rely on him for salvation, may he be cleansed and sanctified, and enabled to walk with God while on earth, and at last may both of us meet together in heaven ! We are worthy only of thy wrath ; but give us all this for thine own Son's sake.   Amen."

' My dear brother, I am very earnest you should think on these things *now*.   I have seen a good deal during the few years I have lived, of many of those things which men think the best, and of the ways they try to make themselves happy ; and the more I think of them, I feel the more certain, that all must find themselves on a wrong course, who do not seek, as the *very first* element of their happiness, to be *reconciled to God through Jesus Christ*.   And, I am sure, that to delay a thorough turning to God, is just to delay being happy ; and to refuse it, is to refuse happiness.   I am very anxious that my dear brother should not have to look back upon so many years of distance from God as I have to look back upon ; and that, when you come to die, you may have this,

among other things, to mention as a subject of praise
and joy, that you began *early* to serve him, and (if it
be his will) continued long.   I often pray that you
may have this inexpressible comfort.

' The devout reading of the Holy Scriptures is the
chief thing I want at present to press upon you.
Some other very plain duties I would also barely mention : *obedience* to your parents, as in the fear of God,
that you may console them as much as possible for
the loss they must soon sustain ; *diligence* in your
learning, that you may be fit for the duties of life;
and cultivating a *quiet* and *gentle* temper, which will
not only gain you the favour of others, but add im-
mensely to your own peace and enjoyment.

' When you write next, let me know how you get
on, and what you are doing in the Sabbath school ;
and whether Mr Fowler or Mr Arnot has any class
for tall boys like you for religious instruction.   Ask
mother to buy you, *for my sake*, a nice little book,
entitled " Pike's Persuasions to Early Piety ;" read it
as soon as you can, and tell me what you think of
it. . . . .

' Tell father and mother that I always bear them on
my heart ; as also I do yourself.   And now, my dear
brother, *farewell !*   " May the God of peace, who
brought again from the dead our Lord Jesus, that
great Shepherd of the sheep, by the blood of the everlasting covenant, make you perfect," &c.—Heb. xiii.
21.   Ever your most affectionate brother,   J. H.

' *Patrick Halley.*'

The following notice of the conclusion, for the
season, of the weekly prayer-meeting, occurs in the
journal, of date June 6th

' *Thursday, 6th June* 1839.

' To-day, Langford and I, after five months of our
weekly labour, held our last meeting.   We took a
general review of the truths declared in the 1st chap.

Q

of 1st Peter, which we have gone over in course. I was in great darkness and confusion of spirit; and, though I felt this to be my *last public service*—the finishing of my active work for God, I was compelled to abstain from alluding to so instructive and affecting a topic. Through these meetings, 98 persons have heard more or less of the truth. Attendance never below 20; once 66.'

The next letter gives evidence of an activity and energy of mind altogether extraordinary in a consumptive patient. It contains also some valuable hints on the Oxford heresy.

'MADEIRA, 17th *June* 1839.

' My dear James,—It is now more than a year since I wrote you a letter, which reached Edinburgh when you were in London, disclosed certain hopes and wishes of a literary kind, and asked advice about employment for my pen, which (as is the fate of advice in general), when it came, I felt myself unable, some might say, unwilling—to take. That letter, if my memory serves me right, left this on the 11th June 1838. So more than a year has afforded tolerable room for trying, whether my brains, once prolific enough as regarded the quantity of their products, are now capable of yielding any thing to face that august tribunal—the public. The result, I lament to say, is nothing; partly for want of strength, partly for want of ammunition; partly from the feeling that subjects of Christian *experience*, on which some men could do much by simply digging inward, were not to be treated by one of such unclean lips; and partly from the obvious fact, that on matters of speculative theology, on some of which I could really have written with good will, one needs, in simple respect to his readers, to have a *corpus* of information by him to be able to state and discuss what others have thought; in short, to display a greater amount of " furniture" than is at

all compatible with one's opportunities in this distant
island of the sea. For some time, also, I had the
impression that it would not be my duty, as drawing
nigh another world, to devote the strength of my mind
to speculative points ; but if other things were favourable, and if it were not too late, I could now get over
this ; for I see, or I think I see, that if I were more
likely to be of some use, however trifling, in this
walk, it would not be right to decline it, because of
my want of qualification to enter on some of those
things which are higher and more spiritual. " To
every member his own office."

‘ My former letters will have informed you that
the Oxford Popery is one of those topics on which I
would have been most eager to let myself forth. As
a general corruption of Christianity, it would autho-
rise one to enter upon almost any field in the compass
of revelation. And my farther reading on it since my
last despatch to you, has only convinced me more
strongly of the truth of what I then said, that we of
the Church of Scotland have peculiar advantages in
entering upon such a controversy. An Anglican, however evangelical, as I have painfully seen, both in
reading and conversation, is sure always to have a
favour for some little corner or other in the system ;
and the very best of them are clogged and embarrassed by the worse than ambiguous expressions in their
formularies about baptism. And the able statement
made by Isaac Taylor, in his first pamphlet on " Ancient Christianity and the doctrines of the Oxford
Tracts," of the difficulties which beset various sections
of Christians in England in attacking the Oxford
men, makes it evident, by the points he condescends
on, that no such hindrances would attach to a Scottish
minister, who should give his strength to this great
argument. Besides Taylor's No. I., I have read
" Archdeacon Brown's Charge," and " Capes on
Church Authority, Tradition," &c.,—the former a very

fair exposé of some things ; the latter a remarkably
well arranged and closely reasoned work on the right
of private judgment, going to the very bottom of the
subject, and yet written with admirable clearness. It
is the most free of all the works I have met, of those
errors in *positive* theology, which, I think in my last,
I charged on some others who attack specific points
in the Oxford system ; yet, strange to say, he states
it as a matter of thankfulness that the formularies of
the Church of England admit of men being within
her pale who hold both views of tradition,—*i. e.*, the
right one, or equally with it, the one on which he has
thought it worth while to write an 8vo. volume, to
show that it is wrong. For my own part, I reckon
her fast and loose standards the very bane and reproach of the English Church. Possibly I told you,
that of single books on the Puseyite plan, so far as I
have seen them, " Newman's Justification " has the
" bad eminence " of being the most pestiferous. What
a shame to England that no detailed answer to it has
yet appeared ! The effrontery of some of the man's
misstatements is indeed so enormous, that readers of
any information will be led to suspect him ; but these
are a sad minority ; and there is an air of logic and
a tone of confidence about him that may deceive
many. I fully intended to have reviewed the work ;
but it was asked from me just as I was on the eve of
commencing ; and I found, on more reflection, that
the above mentioned want of ammunition was an
effectual bar. I wanted to have followed out his close
agreement with Bellarmine ; but Bellarmine I had
not. I wanted to have exposed his shameful artifice
in taking his statement of the Protestant view from
Luther and Melancthon, instead of the better digested
statements of Owen, Edwards, and O'Brien, none of
whom he ever quotes (he refers, indeed, to O'Brien,
and dismisses him by a side wind, in his preface ; but
you would never from his book suspect that the two

great Protestant writers on justification, Owen and
Edwards, had ever written on it); but Edwards was
the only one of them I had at hand.   I wanted to have
shown how nicely Downame, a bishop of his own
Church, upset long ago some parts of his theory; but
the Downame I consulted is snug under the wing of
our friend William Park.   Finally, I wanted to have
shown the futility of the common logical classification
of causes, as far as the including a " formal cause "
goes ; for it is on this distinction, shadowy at best—but
I should go farther, and call it wholly unsound—that
much of his treatise proceeds ; but I had no logical
work by me from which to give an authorised statement of the common doctrine of causes, and it was
possible I might not have given it rightly from memory.
These, my *desiderata*, I mention, not in the way of
complaint (for *surely* goodness and mercy have followed me), but to vindicate my silence on a subject
on which I might have been thought likely to write ;
and as hints of *loci*, to you or any other of my friends
who may care to review Newman, on which something might very well be said.

'But I think I hear you ask,—Granted your reasons
for not doing this or that are good, what have you
been doing (τί ποιεῖς ἔτεον;) all these twelvemonths ?
And I can almost fancy you conceiving with yourself
the pathetic answer : *Heu ! quantum mutatus ab illo
Hectore !*   This accounts, certainly, for very much of
the *infecta ;* but the *facta* remain to be told.

'*Resumed :* 22*d June* 1839.
'Well, then : I have dressed, eaten, ridden while
able, done my best to sleep ; visited occasionally, as a
professedly Christian friend, a few invalids ; aided at
a prayer-meeting on the Thursdays, from the beginning of January to the beginning of June ; and read
about 80 volumes, many of them, however, of rather
Lilliputian dimensions, 37 of them being works in
practical Christianity (inclusive of lives and the like),

and 14 or 15 being on that *vexata quæstio* already alluded to. If I have made progress in any thing, it is in the *knowledge* (I fear not in the *sense*) of the deep and inveterate corruption that reigns in me, and (I think a good deal) in observing the obstacles which withstand the reception of the Gospel, in the shape of prejudice, indifference, and other sinful states of mind. Were I ever to come into the ministry of the Word, this last part of my Madeira experience would not be quite useless. But of all such hopes we have long said, " *Vixere*." I have *written* nothing, save one sermon, a little Address in defence of Prayer-meetings, and long letters not a few. Various designs have indeed passed through my mind; but the difficulties always arose in the style of " Alps upon Alps," and I have no longer a " stout heart" to set to a " stey brae." The last and most cherished design, and the only one which I have now even a faint and glimmering hope of attempting, is a series of " Letters to Divinity Students and Licentiates, especially of the Scottish Church." I have had much experience, in my own person, of what a student should *not* do; and so, per contra, might be able to say what he *should* do. But no more of this castle-building; if any stones are really laid, you may hope to hear of them.

' Rursus : 1st July 1839.

'. . . I continue tolerably; my leg now a running sore; walk on crutches; very weak, but, by Divine mercy, very little pained. But sin abounds; pray that grace may much more. That the Lord himself may bless and keep you, and greatly honour and prosper you in your glorious office, give you the blessed experience of his presence, and at last take you to himself, is always the prayer of one who can never cease to love you,   J. H.

' *Rev. James Hamilton.*'

The possession of such a letter, while it shows the

writer's gifts, deepens our regret at the loss which the Church has sustained in his early removal. We would say, that at the present time there is peculiar need of talents such as his : but the Lord reigneth ; and He will provide his own instruments to defend his own cause.

The following short postscript in a letter to a young friend whose brother had lately entered the work of the ministry, refers to a subject which he never approached without strong emotion. It is dated 2d July 1839.

' . . . I cannot conclude without again begging, for myself, to be most affectionately, just as one who is in heart a brother ought to be, remembered to John. The Lord be with him in his glorious ministry ! I often think, as I lie here like a piece of driftwood on the waters, what a comely young minister John must make ; and I do not know what I would give to witness the expression of your mother's feelings, when she sees him, with all the authority of an ordained servant of Jesus Christ, beseeching and charging sinners to be reconciled to God.

' For myself, all thoughts of such an honour are long gone by. The will of the Lord be done ! Do you know, I sometimes find it harder to say this now, than I could at an earlier period of my illness. But, into whatever sin of unbelief or murmuring I may be tempted, I can still bear witness (if necessary, against myself), that the Lord is gracious, and that goodness and mercy have followed me. So, whatever may befall me, " Blessed are all they that put their trust in him."

' My dear friend, this world is all too little for the goodwill I bear you: it reaches out into eternity ; and contemplates nothing short of your being one of that multitude which no man can number, who have

washed their robes, and made them white in the blood
of the Lamb.   Amen and Amen.

' So ever prays your most affectionate friend,

'J. H.

' *Mr George Wright.*'

On the 10th of July another hæmorrhage occurred ;
but it was not nearly so severe as the former.   He
lost only about a breakfast cupfull of blood, and was
not more than a fortnight confined to the house.   Of
the reflections on this attack, entered in the journal
under seven distinct heads, the two last are as follows :

' (6.) Was a lesson to say, " If the Lord will ;"
which was needed ; for, when asked if we meant to
go on board the Dart, ere she sailed on the 11th, I
said, " Yes, if a boat is to be had."   There were plenty
of boats, yet I was not there.   (7.) A new and much
needed warning of dismissal.   The Lord be praised
for its reasonableness and gentleness.   It seemed just
an answering of my prayers " by terrible things in
righteousness."   Yet how long would it have been
ere I should have asked the bursting of an artery ?
How unsearchable are his judgments ! " Oh the depth
of the riches," &c.'

In the postscript, written August 5th, of a letter
begun on the 10th of July, occurs another of those
sad reminiscences which he liked so much to indulge.

' I take a pleasure in endeavouring to finish up this
letter to-day, in commemoration of the last picturesque
walk which you and I had together.   It took place
just this day two years (being a Saturday), and the
scene was from Tillicoultry to Castle Campbell.   I
have in my mind's eye at present the very paling on
which, after climbing up through that old gravel pit
above Dollar, I sat astride, watching your progress

through the intervening " *ley* " till you were lost in the Castle woods, or rather till a commencing shower compelled me to seek refuge in a house below. Full well, also, do I remember the kindness of the guid-wife of said house—a Mrs Wright—who would take no payment for her excellent warm milk; and, *jalous-ing* that I was a bookish lad, entertained me with many *spolia opima* which a son of hers had borne off from Dollar Academy,—in virtue of which (fortunate youth!) he was now promoted to be an usher in the said institution. Nor can I forget, as I was then beginning to guess at the real nature of my own disease, the melancholy thought that shot across my mind, that my father might soon be showing to some one certain spoils of literature in Great Hamilton Street, as the trophies of a son that *once* was his. I recollect also, that it was with a feeling akin to envy, that I saw you set off that afternoon, at such an easy swinging pace, with your vasculum surmounting that invisible green coat, which really seemed almost to bear a charmed life.'

About this period a number of Mr Halley's friends at Madeira employed an artist to take his portrait with the intention of presenting it to his father. To them, consequently, we are indebted for the power of presenting the print which accompanies this volume. The likeness is good. Although he was by that time much emaciated, it distinctly recalls his appearance to all who knew him. We find the following notice of it by himself in a second postscript to the letter last quoted.

' It will please you to be told, that nine gentlemen here, four of them being ministers of the Church of England,—viz., Langford, Shute, Freeman and Wall, took it into their heads to ask me to sit for my portrait, which they wished to present to my father as

an expression of sympathy with him under this trial.
It was executed in a small size in water colours, by a
Mr George, an exceedingly able artist, who has been
here in delicate health, and whose great personal kindness to me was shown in his stating to these gentlemen, that, had they not anticipated him, he had meant
himself to have asked me to sit.   It is in my father's
hands before now, having been put into them by one
of the donors, William Fullarton, Esq., of the publishing house of Arch. Fullarton & Co.'

The next letter is addressed to a relative in Glasgow,
about to commence the study of theology, with a view
to the ministry.   It is of great length, and contains
minute directions on every branch of theological study.
Looking to the number of books mentioned, with the
notices of their contents and estimate of their character, the letter, written so far from the means of con-
sulting authorities, is an amazing effort of memory.
Although strictly professional, it will be found by no
means unintelligible or uninteresting to the general
reader.   The introductory paragraphs in particular, are
very plain.   We give them in the hope, and with the
prayer, that those to whom they are specially addressed
may understand and apply the solemn instruction they
contain.   The known talents of the departed will give
his judgment weight with those who are following in
the same course.   It may do them good to read, in
language so tender and so scriptural, what was 'uppermost' in his esteem as a qualification for the Christian
ministry.

'MADEIRA, 12th August 1839.

' My dear Henry,— . . . . Be sure you refer my
silence to a want, not of affection, but of strength.
And that you may do so, let me tell you, that you have

now a double place in my daily prayers, not only as one of my dearest kindred in the flesh, but as having the near prospect of engaging in a systematic preparation for that glorious ministry, of which I have most righteously been deemed unworthy. . In connection with your entering on such a course, you will suffer me, in all humility and love, to tender you a few words of counsel and exhortation.   And, as I know I shall have a good deal to say, and reckon it highly improbable that I shall again be able to address you, I have taken one of the largest sheets in my possession, and have begun it with a density which will show you how much I wish to put into it all of my head and heart on this subject that it will hold, and how heartily any little strength that remains to me is at your service in such a cause.

' I mention first of all, because it is *really* uppermost, in my esteem, as a qualification for the ministry, that you be *personally reconciled* to God through the blood of his Son, and diligently strive after a comfortable *assurance* of being so.   On this I feel that it would be presumptuous in me to enlarge at any length, when I consider how much better fitted both by years and character, to enforce such an admonition, are your . . . . Yet I may be allowed just to say, that this is clearly the Gospel order—" *Lovest* thou me?   Feed my sheep."   "We also *believe*, and therefore speak." "God *hath reconciled* us to himself, and hath given to us the ministry of reconciliation."   " Take heed unto *yourselves*, and to all the flock."   " It pleased God, who *called* me by his grace, to reveal his Son in me, that I might preach him."   And it will take no great reflection to make it manifest, that, without a consciousness, and that tolerably clear and constant, of a personal union to Christ,—there cannot, if a man's conscience is at all awake, be much comfort or peace in preaching the Gospel.   One could not help feeling that, for aught he knew, he might be an Uzzah touch-

ing the ark.   And hence arises a peculiar and most
powerful call on every one who would be a Gospel
minister, not merely to be a believer, but to press after
assurance.   For, next to the misery of preaching what
one does not believe at all, must be the misery of
preaching truths, which, though fully received by the
understanding, one is not sure he has felt in their
power and influence on the heart.   May I mention
" Owen on the 130th Psalm," and " Guthrie's Christian's Great Interest," as books, from their plain, close,
and searching character, altogether invaluable in assisting one to conduct that process of sifting and self-
examination, without which (I believe I may say) it
is not usually God's method to lead any to a settled
and strong conviction of their personal interest in the
Redeemer.

' But, leaving this topic to your own meditation,
and to the farther light on it which others are so
much better qualified to give,—let me go on to speak
of that training and furniture in the way of *study*, of
which I may be supposed to be less unfit to give some
account, from the circumstance of having recently
passed through it, and having it fresher in my recollection than may be the case with older men.

' Your course begins with the Evidences; which,
of course, presupposes a general knowledge of *Natural Theology*.   On the *principles* of argumentation,
on which all natural theism rests, you will find no
book to compare with the first two volumes of
Chalmers' works.   The following out of these into
detail, will be so interesting a task, as almost to come
under *light* reading.   Such books as " Paley's Natural
Theology," the Bridgewater Treatises, and " Duncan's
Philosophy of the Seasons," will be your authorities.
And I have been told by a very competent judge,
that the three large volumes, by Dr M'Culloch the
Geologist, on Natural Theology, will amply repay a
very diligent perusal.

' On the *Evidences* themselves, permit me to mention the following books, which are in my small collection, as very much at your service,—Porteus' Outline, Paley's Evidences, Chalmers' Evidences, Grotius de Veritate Christianæ Religionis, Butler's Works, Campbell on Miracles, and his Sermon on the Propagation of the Gospel, Macknight's Truth of the Gospel History, Leland's Necessity of a Revelation, and Leland's View of the Deistical Writers.   (I regret that Hill's Lectures, and a small volume containing Watson, Jenyns, West, and Lyttelton's Tracts, which I have, are here with me; but you will easily get these.)   All these you should read.   Macknight, especially, you will find a magazine of information, although badly arranged, and frigidly written; and, if you master him thoroughly, you will not need to trouble yourself with a still more cumbrous work, " Lardner's Credibility."

' *August* 14.—Besides the works already named (of which, in case you should feel pressed for time, I may say I think Grotius, Porteus, and Chalmers, may be most easily *omitted* from your course of reading), I would strongly recommend you to peruse the Evidences, in two vols., by Daniel Wilson, now Bishop of Calcutta, the *best* work on the general subject that I know; Isaac Taylor's " Process of Historical Proof," and " Transmission of Ancient Books," which exhibit admirably the real logical power of the Christian argument, and in a page of one of which (by the by) you will find the whole elements of his book on " Fanaticism;" the portion of Hill's Lectures given to the Evidences, which is very able, and " Leslie's Short Method with the Deists."   These on the general subject.   For carrying the war into the enemy's territory, besides Leland above mentioned, you will find " Faber's Difficulties of Infidelity " very ingenious and pointed; " Halyburton on Deism" profound; and " Thomas Scott's Answer to Paine," " Watson's Apologies," " Andrew Thomson's Sermons on Infidelity," and Robert Hall's celebrated discourse on the same subject, well worth reading. Descending to individual topics, I would mention the Bishop of Chester's (J. B. Summer) book as incomparably the best on the *internal* evidence, of which, also, it may be worth your while to read the lively and graphic illustration in " Erskine's Remarks." Soame Jenyns was long reckoned a standard on this subject ; but his views of Christianity were defective ; and if you read him, you should read also " Maclaine's Animadversions " on him. On the place which internal evidence deserves to hold, you will find something very good in a small publication of Dr Mearns'. On the *experimental* evidence, I would name Mr Turner's admirable lecture in the Glasgow Series, and " Owen's Self-Evidencing Power of the Gospel ;" it is also frequently alluded to in " Newton's Cardiphonia," and you may glean much on it from Christian biography. Allied, in some respects, to both of these kinds of proof, and more nearly, perhaps, to that arising from the *visible* effects of Christianity, is the argument so admirably pursued by Lord Lyttelton in his " Observations on the Life and Apostleship of Paul." On *prophecy* (besides Keith, which you know), Bishop Newton should be read for facts ; and, on the principles of prophetic interpretation, " Hurd's Warburtonian Lectures," and a work by a Mr Davidson (which is said to be admirable), are the best books I know of. On the Evidences of Judaism (which I have not sooner named, because the divine authority of the Old Testament may be inferred from that of the New), the " Horæ Mosaicæ " of Faber, and the Lectures of Dr Graves on the Pentateuch, are all that could be desired. You may add, if you like, an ingenious little work by J. J. Blunt, on the undesigned coincidences in the Pentateuch ; as on the New Testament history, you will find some good matter of the same kind in the work of the same author on the Gospels, and more especially in Paley's "Horæ Paulinæ."

' On the subjects of the genuineness, authenticity, and credibility of Scripture, which come in very early in the study of the Evidences, there are matters of minute inquiry, which too many take on trust, but which, to be a well furnished divine, you must look into some time, and the sooner the better. (I may say, *en passant*, that the first volume of " Marsh's Divinity Lectures" gives the most clear-headed view I have any where seen of the natural succession of these kind of preliminary topics.   He is an admirable critic; but I must warn you, that, on doctrinal matters, he is far from a safe guide.)   These relate to the *text* of Scripture, and the *critical history* of the different books.   Respecting the text of the Old Testament, Dr Kennicott's two dissertations, and the Prolegomena prefixed to his Bible, are all you will need; only you must watch him on the subject of *conjectural emendations*, on which Griesbach's principle, " *Nihil mutetur e conjectura*," is the only true one.   On the *text* of the New, "Griesbach's Prolegomena" (my shelves contain a copy of him) will claim your first attention.   Whether his *principles* of fixing the text are right or wrong, his facts are most valuable.   But his general critical *theory* has been ably impugned in a dissertation by a Mr Nolan on the " Integrity of the Textus Receptus,"— so ably as to shake my belief in it; and I understand (for I have not had an opportunity of studying them) that the Prolegomena of Schöltz, a more recent editor, have, in the general opinion of German scholars, finally overthrown it.   When you buy a critical Testament, I would recommend you to get Schöltz, as all our libraries contain Griesbach already, and as the other will give both his views and their professed refutation.   On the *critical history* of the New Testament, the work I liked best is " Hug's Introduction," which

you will find in my library; it is free from the licen-
tious audacity of Michælis, and about as learned. On
the Old Testament, " Gray's Key;" or, if you have
time to go farther, and wish to keep up your French,
" Father Simon's Histoire critique du Vet. Test.,"
although 5 vols. 4to., is an interesting book.   On
all these topics, much good information, mixed with
a good deal of trash, in " Hartwell Horne's Introduction."   One thing, in connection with the *credibility* of the evangelists, may require more research
than usual : I mean the history of the resurrection.
On this West is well known.   And you will no
doubt consult the harmonists, Doddridge, Macknight,
Chemnitz, and (most recent) Greswell.   The most
satisfactory work I have seen on it is " Dr Townson's
Dissertations;" but, as you may not get these easily
(the only copy I have seen is my own, and it is here),
I may add, that a good abstact of his view is given in
" Mr Towsend's Harmony of the New Testament,"
which you will find in the Divinity Hall Library.

    ' *August* 16.—I find so many things remain, that
I must be very laconic on each.   One is apt to think,
that after having generally ascertained the divine origin of Christianity, the very next point is to fix the
precise *authority* due to the record in which it is embodied,—*i. e.*, to discuss the question of *inspiration.*
But we are not yet done with preliminaries.   For our
chief proofs of inspiration are from the testimony of
the inspired writers themselves, of whose *credibility*
we are previously satisfied, and of their *general* divine
commission.   Now this *testimony* we must be able to
interpret, ere we can make much use of it.   So that,
if we are to study the theory and rules of interpretation, they must clearly have a very early place.   I do
not myself put much value on this; a competent
knowledge of the original tongues, a clear head, an
honest heart, and the light of the Spirit, are the grand
necessaries.   But one may get good hints from some

books, as Pareau and Ernesti. Horne's part on Interpretation is a preposterous melange. A queer little impudent book by a man Carson, exposes many of the false principles of writers on "Hermeneutik." A knowledge of Jewish antiquities will be of great use; on which my library will furnish you with "Godwyn's Moses and Aaron," and "Jahn's Archæologia Biblica." "Calmet's Dictionary" is quite an indispensable book. I have just alluded to the original languages. On Greek I shall say no more, but that you should try to make yourself perfectly familiar with the Greek Testament, so as almost to be able to tell, without looking, what word is used here or there. This will be a work of time; but it is a knowledge which will grow on you as you use the Greek Testament. The Hebrew you ought decidedly to commence to study your first year of divinity. Besides the general desirableness of getting this past, as you know not but your third session may need to be irregular, there is this overpowering consideration, that in *doctrinal theology*, which I am supposing to be your chief study in your second and third years, not a step can be taken without Hebrew. Take the corner stone of Christianity for example, the doctrine of Christ's divinity,—you need Hebrew to fix the meaning of "the angel Jehovah," and of "the Father of eternity," in Isa. ix. 6,—to satisfy you that Micah v. 2, may be read interrogatively, "Art thou little?" (cf. 2 Sam. vii. 5; 1 Chron. xvii. 4;) so reconciling it with Matthew, &c., &c. There are two dictionaries on my shelves; but I say little about them, as you will need one of your own. You will, of course, buy Gesenius. I believe the small Leipsic Bible, edited by Hahn, is both cheaper and more accurate than our English edition of Vander Hooght. You will not, I dare say, care for *buying* any other grammar than the small outline by Brunton (borrowed from Wilson). But my bookcase will yield you Wilson, Jahn, and Moses

R

Stuart (if M. of R. has returned it; if not, ask it of him, telling him, with my kindest wishes, that, if he has not finished it ere now, he never will); of these I consider Jahn the best. In studying difficult passages in the Hebrew Bible, you will often find material help from "Michælis Supplementa ad Lexica Hebraica," which is in the Hall Library. Only he is very fanciful. As I have mentioned attendance on the *Hebrew class*, I may add, respecting the Church history (from which more good may be got than most of us obtained), that you can regulate your attendance on it according to your convenience and other engagements, but that, as to the *close* and *private study* of the subject, it ought to be pursued in company with *doctrinal theology*, on which it throws much light. Let me give an instance. One who should interpret the expression, "left to the freedom of his own will," in our Shorter Catechism, by the use of the phrase "free will," in Reid and Stewart, would blunder excessively. The peculiar aspect which that controversy took in their writings, and in those of Edwards, was yet in the womb of futurity when the Catechism was written. To understand the expression as used by the Westminster divines, we must ascend to the theological nomenclature of an earlier age. I am an *ignoramus*, rather, in Church history, never having read any one of the detailed histories of the Church right through. But, I believe, Fry is a good compendium. Some periods I have studied; and can recommend "Burton's Bampton Lectures," "Burton's History of the First Three Centuries," "Lord Hailes' Fragments," Mosheim's "De rebus Christianorum ante Constantinum."

'Pass we now to *inspiration*. All that can be said for those lower views of it, which make it apply chiefly to the thoughts, and scarcely at all to the words of Scripture, and which distinguish it into different degrees, will be found in " Wilson's Evidences " (above named), " Dr Dick's Essay and Lectures," " Dr Henderson's Congregational Lectures," and in some papers in the " Scottish Congregational Magazine," by Mr Lindsay Alexander of Edinburgh. A kind of medium view is taken by Dr Chalmers in vol. 4 of his works, and by Dr Woods of Andover. But the view in which alone my mind can acquiesce is the high one of *verbal* inspiration. It is very well set forth in Mr King's Glasgow Lecture; fully expounded in Robert Haldane's work on the subject, and in an essay of Dr Fraser's of Kennoway, in an excellent volume of a new family library (published by Affleck in Edinburgh, 1835), which contains also " Paley's Horæ Paulinæ," and Dr Alexander's (of Princeton) valuable work on the canon of Scripture ; and vindicated from objections with great versatility of talent, but consummate impudence, in two books of Carson's, one against Dick, Wilson, and Pye Smith, and the other against Henderson.

' The *inspiration* of Scripture being settled, its *sufficiency*, as a rule of faith, is the next subject of inquiry. This lands you in controversy with Rome and Oxford. But, although I feel that, had I lived and laboured as was once expected, it would have been my duty to go very deeply into this. I will not say, that, except on some very special call of Providence, it would be yours. I therefore name only one book against each class of adversaries ; " Chillingworth's Religion of Protestants," and " Capes on Church Authority, Tradition," &c.—both admirable.

' (*August* 16.) — Omitting many things of considerable importance, I hasten to say a little on one of the very highest. Fortunately I am in good time in mentioning it, before you have purchased experience at the expense of failure in various plans. Every man, such as a divine, who wishes to concentrate his energies on one subject, finds in almost

every book he reads—not to speak only of directly
professional ones—something he would like to preserve in connection with his main topic.   Hence the
use of common-place books.   Now I have tried many
schemes ; made innumerable blunders ; and expended
in such devices more time, thought, and ingenuity,
than on almost any other detail of study.   Some
plans utterly broke down ; some partially succeeded,
but were yet so cumbrous, that I could never have
made any thing of them, except for that somewhat
extraordinary memory which God had graciously given
me.   I should have liked to describe one or two, by
way of illustrating the superior simplicity of one which
only struck me when it was almost too late to use it.
But space forbids.   Of that I am about to mention, I
can only say, that, so far as I have tried it, I have
found it very manageable ; and you, by beginning on
it from the first, will find it more so.   Instead, then,
of setting up a great book, the very size of which
would discourage you, it would seem to fill so slowly,
get a common 2s. white paper book.   Mark it A ;
and when it is filled, your next will be B ; and so on.
Into this put, just as they meet you in your reading,
all matters you deem worthy of copying,—endeavouring so to *title* each extract, as that it shall either illustrate some *verse* of Scripture, or some *topic* in a system
of divinity.   By a little ingenuity, this will be possible
with almost every thing that will fall in with the scope
of professional study.   Now for the way to have all
this collection ready for use.   Get *one* good copy of
the Bible for your study-Bible, and use it throughout.
A reference one is best ; and I greatly prefer the ruby
8vo. or pearl 8vo. *Oxford* Bible to *Bagster's.*   Let
your copy have a good broad margin, even though it
should be a little dearer.   This, which will always be
in your hands, will be your index to all things in your
common-place book which illustrate *texts.*   *E. g.,* in
" Owen on the 130th Psalm," is a beautiful discrimi-

nating statement between laying the foundation, and building the superstructure.   You think it finely illustrates 1 Cor. iii. 11, &c.; and you write it out in p. 60 of your book.   Well, just put in the margin of your Bible, at 1 Cor. iii. 11, A 60; and, whenever you are going to write on that text, your mind will be turned to this illustration of it.   You find, in a missionary work, a graphic account of the unsatisfactoriness of idolatry: you engross it, say at p. 75; and opposite Isaiah xliv. 20, you write A 75.   For the *other* class of extracts, get some small Latin System of Theology: I would recommend " *Marckii Compendium*," chiefly because of De Moor's admirable expansion of it, which you can have from the Divinity Hall Library.   Interleave this; for it will not need, like the Bible, to be always in your pocket; and many short notes and references may be written on the white leaves.   But every thing *long* will go into the other book, and only a *reference* to it here.   *E. g.*, I shall suppose you to possess, or have easy access to, " Dr Erskine's Dissertations," in one of which he argues largely that faith is mere belief; you want to remember this, and you write on the white leaf, opposite the section on the nature of faith, " Intellectual view of faith : see Erskine's Dissertations."   But I shall again suppose you have only a reading of " Dr O'Brien on Justification;" you think his proof, that faith is *trust*, excellent; you copy it in p. 10 of your other book; and opposite the section you put "Faith—Trust: Ax" or Bx as it may be.

' I hope the above description is intelligible, but cannot enlarge : take its advantages on *faith* just now; I hope you will soon be able to add *experience*.

' I meant to have said a little on some things on which you may be furnishing yourself *incidentally as you go along;* but can only *name* them.   In going through the Catechism in your Sabbath school, you may be mastering, by the by, some system arranged as it is, as Boston or Vincent. Presbytery—be well grounded here—Anderson, Brown, Mason. Independence of the Church—Charles Brown's Glasgow Lecture. Natural History, especially Geology. Sermons —Bradley, John Venn, Howels, A. Thomson, Gordon, Welsh, " Jones' Baskets of Fragments." General powerful statements of truth—cannot go wrong in Howe, Bates, Owen, Hopkins, and Barrow (bating his Arminianism). Join the best Preaching Society. Cultivate (I value it *highly*) an acquaintance with *sacred poetry*—Cowper, Montgomery, Kirk White, Newton, Edmeston, Toplady, Wesley, Watts, Ragg, Pollok, Heber, Hemans, Milman, J. W. Cunningham, &c.

' I need not say with what pleasure I would have filled up this outline, and gone on to give an arrangement of topics, and list of my favourite authors in *doctrinal theology*, and in *practical piety*. But the Lord will raise you up better advisers. To his everlasting love and holy guidance I commend you, your father, your mother, your sisters, your uncle, and your aunts ; and am your affectionate cousin,   J. H.

' *Mr Henry Anderson.*'

Another letter—the substance of it written about the same time, though begun at an earlier date—gives similar counsels applicable to a prior stage of a student's progress. It is addressed to one of his former pupils, for whom he had contracted, and to the last retained, a very strong affection. We give the portion that relates to a course of reading in moral philosophy, not omitting the characteristic introduction.

' MADEIRA, 15*th July* 1839.

' My dear John,—Eben-ezer ! *Memoriæ causa*, I *date* this letter to-day, although, writing in bed, I shall be able to put down just now no more than a few lines.

Two years, my beloved friend, elapsed *yesterday*, since
you and I had our last lesson in Great King Street ;
and it is *two years to-day*, since, accompanied by my
faithful Arnot, I left Edinburgh for Forgandenny,—
having closed up my desk with a solemn presentiment
that I should never again, as a student, open it. It is
now *noon* here ; in Scotland about half-past one : at
which time, two years ago, having left the coach on
which I made my ineffectual attempt at κληγιφουια,
Arnot and I were trudging along from Bridge of Earn
to his father's, he generously bearing my knapsack,
and both of us making what speed we could to avoid
an impending thundershower. . . . . By the by, it
may interest you to know, that often, in the silent
watches, when I cannot sleep, and am equally unfit
to meditate, I have found a pleasing resource in turning hymns of Wesley, Watts, &c., into Greek,—the
kind of *memoria technica*, which, when one has got
a certain command of vocables, is all that needs to be
exercised, being to me a very light and interesting play
of the faculties. . . . . As to your reading in moral
philosophy, I may venture to give a hint or two.
The best systematic work on it I know, is, after all,
Principal Dewar's. His views are generally sound and
Christian, and clearly stated ; and he gives a fair catalogue *raisonée* of the leading ζητηματα. Dr Wardlaw's Christian Ethics is mainly borrowed, in thought,
from Dewar, but better clothed.   Dr Chalmers'
Moral Philosophy I have not read ; but I should
think it will be good, especially for one who wants to
make philosophy the handmaid of theology : and
" Butler's Sermons," which are his great *origo*, are
well worth reading—although certainly not *as* sermons, but as philosophical dissertations.   The best
and happiest application of the abstractions of moral
science to preaching that I have seen, is in Chalmers'
8th volume,—three sermons on the love of God ;—
but such a style of preaching, though interesting to

me as a *student*, is what I should never have chosen
to imitate.   It is our duty, however, to be *armed at
all points ;* and, although we may not use that knowledge in pulpit address, to *know* the exact *points of
contact* between human science and divine.   I need
not name Reid, Stewart, and Brown ; but on one important point you would be as well to accompany them
by reading " Edwards on Free Will," and perhaps
also Crybbace.   Drew's two volumes on the " Imma-
teriality and Immortality of the Soul," you ought to
master.   Of the older writers on immortality, the best
I remember is Dean Sherlock.   Cogan's Works on
the passions exhibit considerable power of arrangement; but I should think the author must have been
a Socinian, from his great indulgence to human nature.
Gisborne's book on Moral Philosophy (which, however, I have not read) bears a high character.   I may
add, that Blakey's History of Moral Science is very
poor, but may perhaps serve as a finger-post.   And,
to keep up your remembrance of classical lore, as well
as to bring you acquainted both with the strength and
with the weakness of unaided reason, you would do
well to read, thoughtfully, the Memorabilia of Xenophon, Plato's Republic, Aristotle's Ethics, Epictetus'
Enchiridion, and the Officia and Natura Deorum of
Cicero,—always allowing something for those shreds
and fragments of divine truth which unquestionably
got afloat among the heathen.   Natural Theology
is usually included, more or less, in a Moral Philosophy course.   On the *principles of argumentation* employed in this science, there is no book to
compare with Chalmers.   If you read Brougham,
read also " Turton's Reply" to him.   The following
out of details will come in, in great part, as *light* reading.   " Paley," the Bridgewater Treatises, " Duncan's Philosophy of the Seasons," &c., will be your
authors.   And, as I have mentioned *light* reading,
I may add, that, in my view, much of those ethics

which are most useful ultimately to the divine, is
to be found in works that may fairly come under
this character. I allude to works of descriptive moral-
ists,—delineations of character,—and so forth. The
" Rambler " (although you may laugh) is not a bad
instance. Several of Hannah More's Works are better specimens of the kind of thing I mean. And,
whatever knowledge of man and his motives one may
acquire in this way, can all be turned to the service of
the sanctuary, by coupling with it such a reading of
religious biographies, as will show the working of the
truth on minds of varied constitutions and tempera-
ments.

' You see, in all this, I am remembering the one
" but " in which your efforts are at last to find their
centre. I have no doubt you will steadily do the
same, and be blessed in the deed. The next summer
you will, of course, spend chiefly on the higher mathematics, in order to prepare for the natural philosophy.
Here I will not presume to advise. Mr Kelland will
be your best counsellor, or Professor Forbes. Only I
may mention, that the first book which gave me a taste
for analytical mathematics,—and these are now almost
exclusively used in physical research,—was " Hind's
Trigonometry." I swallowed it with absolute rapa-
city. And one principle I may name, more applicable
to the purely demonstrative than to any other kind of
study ;—" never pass any thing without being sure
you understand it." . . . .

' And may the God of peace be with you, and with
your very affectionate friend,　　　　　J. H.

' *Mr John Mackintosh.*'

The following is a very characteristic letter. There
are parts of it which we would have wished to withhold ; but to mutilate it would have been to destroy
its effect as an exhibition of the writer's character. It

contains some exquisite touches of pathos.   It is not
written for the purpose of producing emotion, yet it
will move : it is not written for the purpose of in-
structing, yet it will instruct.

'MADEIRA, 19th *September* 1839.

' My dear Arnot,—Since I cannot write you as I
ought and would, I must even write to you as I can.
I have deferred it long, in the hope that haply I might
be privileged to tell you a different tale from what my
former letters had borne—to say something about
being compassed about with songs of deliverance.
But I can see enough in myself to render it manifest
that God could not, in very faithfulness, bestow spiritual peace on one who deals so treacherously in his
covenant.   And so, with the strong feeling that the
expression of my love and obligations to you is at all
times a duty, be my own case what it may, and just
to give some vent to an affection which only grows
the more, the more I think of you,—I have resumed
my pen, really not knowing how I am to fill my paper.
' So you are again at your post—engaged in the
work of the Lord.   I need not say how much, in some
respects, I envy you your honourable post.   Yet I
have repeatedly been made also to feel that the hand,
which inhibited me from touching the ark, was one
of mercy.   I can hardly imagine a situation of more
fearful temptation and peril than would have been
mine, had I been allowed to enter the ministry, with
the flush of college successes fresh upon me, and (although I had met with *rubs,* and what the μαλαχοι
would call *hardships,* still), upon the whole, unsubdued by any affliction.   How probably would my
course have realized that which Paul ascribes to the
νεοφυτος ! *   Still, although reason and conscience most
fully adopt this view, nature *will* revolt at the evanish-

* Novice.

ing of all that one had hoped for; and surely He who knoweth our frame will pardon even a tear, when I learn of one and another, my juniors in study (yet, I confess, far my seniors in the faith), admitted to stations similar to that, to which, I may almost say without irreverence, the course of His providence seemed to point my aspirations. I do not know how it is; but, when I endeavour to pray for you all, my brethren in the ministry, and those preparing for it (and I have a goodly list of names, of whom I thus make mention), I feel a strange sort of swelling at the heart, —something which cannot better be described than by saying that " my spirit is overwhelmed." It finds its relief, however, in the contemplation of the dangers I have escaped, dear as the price of that escape has been, and in the certain conviction, that, if the great ends of the Christian ministry in Scotland would be in the least promoted by my sharing in it, I should not now be languishing in Madeira, and awaiting my dismissal. . . . .

' My dear Arnot, go on and prosper ; and the Lord himself be with you ! Think much of your office ; and the more, from the example that is now before you, that it is not to every one who seems to start fair that " this grace is given." And, under the guidance of the Chief Shepherd, may you be enabled to feed your flock with knowledge and understanding, and yourself to go in and out and find pasture.

' Morrison would surely tell you of me up to the date of my despatch to him. Since then my chest is very sensibly worse. The right lung, I am thankful to say, gives me little pain, and wastes away very gently ; still, for all useful purposes, the doctor said on 29th July, it is as bad as a lung can be—*no* respiration in it. But the left, since that time, has been much pained (I think I have needed four blisters during the last fifteen or sixteen days); and, if I may judge from my own feelings, the work of destruction goes on more rapidly in it than ever it did in the other. On one account, I have much reason to bless God. My leg, though the sore is still open, is now so easy, that I can ride daily ; and I do so for an hour—two hours being found to fever me.   This resumption of riding, and that too pretty pink complexion which I am beginning to assume, have deceived many of my friends here into congratulations ; but I know better.   It is a strange, an indescribable sensation, to feel the little breath that remains always getting shorter, and to be sensible (for I am a tolerably acute observer now) that the portion of the working lung which is doing duty is becoming steadily, though slowly less.   And it is fearful when even this " sentence of death in oneself" fails to arouse one, and the soul languidly allows itself to be carried down the stream, without any *certainty* of exchanging this fleshly tabernacle for " a house not made with hands, eternal in the heavens." My brother, pray for me.

' It would seem that our perverse nature clings to objects in proportion to their worthlessness.   What is life to me now, compared to what it once seemed likely to be ? And yet I appear to myself less willing to part with it.   Strange—to be in love with sorrows ! and yet not quite so strange, when the soul is bereft of the assurance that eternity will not disclose greater sorrows still.   In some points of view my present state seems far from attractive.   My whole body impregnated with disease ; lungs as above stated ; . . . . . the sore in my leg, and of course my eye.   Have lost sixteen pounds since this time twelvemonth. . . . . And, what is rather remarkable, as the inefficiency of my right lung, and the seton in my left side have long rendered it impossible to sleep on the left side, the solid framework is distorted, and the extreme bone of the pelvis on the right side is nearly an inch more prominent than the corresponding bone on the left.   Add to all, that, if peculiar mercy prevent not, the want of flesh

s likely soon to compel me to abandon riding. Does
his revolting detail disgust you? It well may, and I
ask your forgiveness for having inserted it. But I
hope to educe from it two lessons which may be of use
to you as an ambassador for Christ: that there is no
state so wretched that God cannot alleviate it; yea,
even with a preponderance of mercy; and none so
abject, that our corrupt hearts will not cling to parts
of it with something of a fond idolatry. The mercies
which contribute to uphold me are very many. I have,
now and then, letters from yourself and others, which
assure me of continued sympathy; and it is an unspeakable comfort to think that my friends are mostly
among those whose sympathy will always lead them
to a throne of grace. I have many kind friends here.
I have the remembrance of many signal mercies. I
am situated among much that is beautiful and grand
in nature; and my taste for such scenes, which you
know was never very dull, seems of late to have been
greatly quickened. Memory, too, seems to have experienced something of an invigoration; and all that
I ever knew of poetry, Greek, Latin, or English, seems
to be more in readiness to minister delight in association with the scenery, than it ever was. Only a few
days ago, going out a little earlier than usual, and
being fanned by a " gentle air," I felt as I never did
before, the truth and beauty of Gray's expression,
" The breezy call of incense breathing morn." In
fine, I have still my old, tried, dumb companions—
books, with whom I spend a large portion of every
day. These mercies surely demand the liveliest gratitude; but alas! my prevailing humour is that of
resting in them. I feel as one who would make them
κειμηλια, not χρηματα, something to be *laid up*,
guarded, and *retained*, not simply *used* as our brief
time proceeds, and then contentedly *parted with* for
ever. In this way Satan has got fearful advantage of
me; and, between books, scenes, and friends, I am

entangled in the meshes, now of one, now of another
idolatry, and sometimes seem quite ready to adopt the
desperate resolution, ὁποῖα κισσος δρυος, ὁπῶς τῆσδ'
ἰξομαι.* In this respect I have greatly retrograded
of late. Two years ago, I think I had really more of
a calm, sober, chastened willingness to die, than I have
now. My affections appear to be flowing backward—
ανω ποταμων ιερων χωροῦσι παγαι,—and, not content
with gratefully retracting, or (for even that might be
pardonable) mournfully revisiting bygone scenes, and
hopes, and companionships, would even sit down and
dwell among them. I well know that His power
alone, who stills the raging of the sea, can compose
this inquietude of the spirit. And my prayer would
be—and I know yours for me will be, that " as the
eyes of a servant look unto the hand of his master,"
so mine may be " upon the Lord our God, until that
He have mercy upon me."

' Thank you for your August letter, and for the very
interesting notice it contained of the Kilsyth work,
I shall be glad to hear farther particulars, as they
transpire.

' I finish this on the 24th. This day three years
you and I spent our last few hours at Easterhouse;
and on the 26th I left for Edinburgh. The consequences (partly) we now see, and yet I don't regret
that step so much as many others. " So days and
years, and ages past," &c. But the effects live, and
will live, after we are gone. Ever affectionately yours,

' J. H.

' *Rev. William Arnot.*'

Early in October of this year, the religious circle of
the place gained an accession of strength in the arrival
of one of the ministers of Glasgow, who was obliged,
for the sake of his family, to spend the winter in the

* As ivy clings to oak, so I will hold by this.

island. Mr Halley felt this a great refreshment. It was to him a spring opened in the desert. The following is his own account. Considerable exertion had been made, during the summer, to make provision for a resident Scotch minister in the island, but, from various causes, little progress had hitherto been made. After mentioning these difficulties, he proceeds,—

' But God has again renewed our hopes. Dr Henderson of St Enoch's is here with his invalid wife, and has begun to preach under very favourable auspices. L—— was simple enough to express a fear that Dr H. might alienate his people from *his* preaching. Dr H. will be here at least three months—probably more. But even on the supposition which makes his departure earliest, I think he will have laid an excellent foundation for a Scotch church. I trust he will dispense the Lord's Supper before he leaves, which will give a kind of consolidation to our meeting ; and I have good hope that we may send him home with a commission in his pocket to send out a man.'

The progress of this infant congregation is more fully detailed in the following extract from a letter, dated 4th December :—

' I have mentioned Dr Henderson as being here ; but he deserves more than to be merely named. I trust he has been sent here for good. . . . I had given up all hope of a permanent Scotch pastor here at present, and indeed felt that it lay with Providence whether we should have any public ordinances which I could conscientiously attend. It seemed like a meeting of our desires more than half way—a doing above what we had dared even to think, when Dr Henderson came—a man not only of high pulpit talents, but of the most amiable disposition, and admirably fitted, by his private intercourse, to conciliate respect and

affection. A single sermon of ———— satisfied him
that fatal error was taught in the English Church;
and he readily agreed to the request of myself and three
others, to preach to such of his countrymen as would
come to hear. Eight weeks he has done so, with
great earnestness and tenderness of spirit, and consummate ability. We have moved already from one
room to another larger; and it, I think, will soon
prove too strait for us. Very many of poor Lowe's
hearers have come from time to time, and heard the
truth as it is in Jesus. There has not, so far as I
know, been an objection breathed on the score of what
is preached, and all admire the way in which. Of
course, the high-church people object to it as schis-
matical. . . . . Meantime, I trust we who hear feel
some gratitude for such a privilege; and I both pray
and hope that good may come of it. To myself personally, Dr H.'s conduct, although I knew him but
little in Glasgow, has been more paternal than friendly.

'The little prayer-meeting, which was held last
year in my house, is revived: members—Dr Henderson, Dr Kalley, Mr Langford (who is too weak to
exert himself publicly this year), Mr Fullarton, Dr
John Russell, and myself.

'The public meeting for reading and prayer we
have not, Langford and I being *hors de combat*. But
instead, Dr Kalley has begun a meeting on Thursdays
for prayer in behalf of missions; at which, however,
I am sorry to say, the attendance has not been so
encouraging.

'I think I mentioned either to Mr C. or you, a
hope which I entertained early in spring, of getting
some of the Portuguese padres together to learn Greek
with me. This I hoped to accomplish by means of
a young man who has become very intimate with Dr
Kalley, and had begun his education for the priest-
hood. He has since found that it will be a much
pleasanter life to be a gentleman at large, and so has

abandoned his professional studies. However, he kindly made inquiries for me ; but the result showed I had miscalculated the movability of my materials— for the padres were unanimously like Oliver Goldsmith's Principal of Louvain—they had got on all their days without Greek, and didn't feel the want of it. So this door of usefulness was shut against me.

'But Dr Kalley, in his own province, is getting on well. Not only has he a class of boys and "hafflin" lads every evening, who learn English from the Testament, but he has commenced a Sabbath school, which about fifteen of these attend ; and, about ten days ago, three lads from the college came to him, asking to learn English at a separate hour, in the same way as the other class, and he having said that three were too few for him to give an hour to, they beat up for recruits, and he has now a dozen of *educated* lads (*i. e.*, as education goes here), coming to him three afternoons in the week. He is also going to try to get out from England a Christian teacher, to keep an evening school for teaching adults to read, and I think has every prospect of succeeding.

'*Mr John Wilson.*'

Mr Halley enjoyed intensely both the public ministrations and private visits of Dr Henderson. Besides the charm of hearing in that strange land a minister from his own native city, he valued very highly the character of the instructions delivered. He was in the habit of writing out on Monday a short abstract of the Sabbath's discourse.

On the eve of his departure an address was presented to the Rev. Doctor by those of his countrymen in the island who had attended his ministry : ninety-one signatures are attached to it. The address was drawn up by Mr Halley, with all his accustomed precision of thought and expression. Omitting the more personal compliments at the commencement, and the kind wishes at the close, we extract the following sentences, as not only creditable to the minister addressed, but highly characteristic of the writer.

' As it was the honourable boast of an apostle, that he " kept back nothing that was profitable, testifying repentance toward God, and faith toward our Lord Jesus Christ ;" so we are assured that we do not err in cordially bearing you witness, that the same conscientious rejoicing may most justly be yours.   And we reckon it no mean praise of your work among us, that, thus bestowing your chief regard on what Christians generally admit to be most essential, you have laboured, yourself to dwell, and to place your hearers, in a purer and higher region than that of doubtful disputation, and to preach the central truths of Christianity, " giving no offence in any thing, that the ministry be not blamed."'

His project for having a Presbyterian minister settled in Madeira has so far succeeded.   A minister was sent out by the Assembly's Colonial Committee, and has commenced his labours.   We regret to learn that his own feeble health has in a great degree retarded his operations.   Having been several times, since his arrival, laid aside from work by illness, he has at last been obliged to tender his resignation ; and arrangements are in progress for appointing a successor.

As we are anxious to preserve every record which the invalid has left, of his own state of mind when contemplating his approaching departure, we insert the following, although it is very similar to some that have preceded it.

' MADEIRA, 9th December 1839.

' My dear Sir,— . . . . On the whole, you observe

the disease has made very decided progress : at present
it does not seem in very virulent action ; but all my
medical friends have assured me, that, with so small
a part of only one lung working, the slightest cold
caught, or the least accession of febrile action, may
very possibly terminate life. And, although nothing
of the sort should occur—although it should even proceed at the gentlest rate that can be, still the day is
evidently, by many tokens, not far distant, when I
must put off this tabernacle. To contemplate this,
how solemn ! how much more solemn to find the
difficulty which the mind has in contemplating it as a
reality ! Strange as it may seem, I fear I must confess, that there is less vivid realization of my dying
state now, than there was in me two years ago, when
the thought of being mortally diseased was, comparatively, fresh and new. Yet I do trust there is, amid
much instability and perversity of mind, something
more of a sustained attempt to dwell, fiducially, on
the work of Him " who, through death, destroyed
him that had the power of death." But all that I
have of this I painfully feel to be far far short of what
it ought to be ; I feel as if there were *no* affection in
my religion ; I wonder, day by day, that I am not
more stirred with thoughts and circumstances so moving ; and, although I bless God that I have been preserved from vehement alarms and despairing thoughts
—so much so, indeed, that Renton said he believed my
equable temperament had been the means of length-
ening out my days,—yet I am bitterly conscious with
what truth this reproach might be taken up against
me,—Job iv. 4, 5.

' This great increase of disease has, I lament to say,
entirely prevented me from rendering myself useful
(since about June) in the ways I formerly mentioned,
or in others I had thought of. . . . . And partly from
physical inability to speak continuously ; partly, also,
from a sad barrenness of heart, which still more de-

cidedly unfitted me for the duty, I have done nothing among my "companions in tribulation." To one, indeed, a most interesting young *mater-familias* among the residents, I had the privilege of speaking a few words of comfort on the 27th September, but the next day I was myself laid up with a couple of blisters; and on the 30th she fell asleep, I trust in Jesus. This utter abandonment of any work that can be useful to others I feel as a sore trial, but I have no doubt it was greatly needed; for I have seen much reason to fear, that here, as at home, I was making outward usefulness a means of escaping from God, and had not learned the art of being willing to be absolutely nothing. O let your cry and prayer ascend, that this, and every grace proper to a suffering state, may be given me, as well as a quiet dismissal, and an abundant entrance.

'*Rev. James Gibson.*'

About this time Mr Halley seems to have thought his course was drawing near a close. His disease had begun to exhibit some new symptoms which he thought were the harbingers of death. He had no expectation then of surviving the winter. In the conclusion of the preceding letter, speaking of the several items of expenditure for which it was necessary to make provision, he enumerates among them ' those charges connected with the narrow house.' Again, in reference to the amount of remittance required, he says, ' It is considerably expensive (I do not know the exact sum) to get a burying-place from these sons of Heth.' In a similar strain, three days later, another change of residence is noted in the journal.

'*Thursday, 12th December.*

' Left Dr Kalley's, and entered again our little house in the Socorro. Most probably my next migration will be to a narrower house still. The Lord prepare me for awaking with him. Meantime, my soul would seek to magnify him for his long-suffering and forbearance, his preserving and sustaining mercy, the means of grace he gives me, and this hope, though faint and obscured by unbelief, of glory. The Lord perfect that which concerneth me, and make our residence here, whether long or short, a time of peculiar instruction, visitation, and refreshing, to my dear sister.'

This is the conclusion of the Madeira journal; and, so far as we know, the last secret record of his experience written by his own hand. Besides his increasing weakness, he was about this time disabled by a suppuration in the thumb of the right hand. From the middle of December 1839 to the beginning of June 1840, he was unable to write. This necessarily leaves a blank in his history; for we do not possess other materials from which to fill it up. This, however, is not much to be regretted; for there really was little variety in his mode of life, except that now he could do more, and now less, according as the symptoms of his disease were lightened or aggravated. During this winter he was weaker than he had been at any period of his residence in Madeira. If we had been enabled to present the history of that, as of the preceding period, in his own letters and journals, it might have been equally instructive; but when these materials are wanting, we think it neither necessary nor expedient to fill up the narrative from other sources. These five months were spent as others had been. As sickness increased, the field was narrowed; but the character of the work and the good-will of the labourer continued the same. Fewer opportunities of doing good were afforded to the invalid; but he continued to do good as he had opportunity. The talents once intrusted to him, had, by the Sovereign Disposer, been gradually resumed, till one only was left, but he did not bury that talent in the earth : he continued to ' trade' with it, that he might gain the ' true riches' for himself and all the needy near him.

Having, by the good hand of God upon him, survived another winter, he began again to entertain the thought of returning home. The proposal was weighed with all his characteristic coolness of deliberation. We fortunately possess a record of his decision, and the grounds of it, in the shape of a letter to his father. It is the first after the long interval in his correspondence caused by the ailment in his hand, and the last written from Madeira.

' SOCORRO, MADEIRA, 1st June 1840.

' My dear Father,—You will be both surprised and pleased to see my handwriting once more. . . . . Dr Renton examined me this day week : says the right lung (which formerly was hardened up) is now much wasted away, but that the disease has not made very rapid progress in the left : he thinks there is still about one-third of it working. But, as this is only the sixth part of a pair of lungs, you will not wonder that I am very short-winded. The only unpleasant symptoms I have had of late, are perspirations (which weaken me much), and, almost daily, severe gripings in the bowels. The perspirations, however, are not constant, and the gripings are not accompanied by diarrhœa. My pulse is always above 100, but seldom feverish.

' The reason of my getting Dr Renton to examine me is one which you will perhaps think strange. It was to learn whether he thought I had lung enough remaining to take me to Britain, and whether I could go to sea with a fair chance of reaching our own island in life. His answer was, that, if I had *other* good reasons for undertaking a voyage home, he thought there was nothing in the state of my lungs which rendered it unlikely that I should be able to accomplish it. The other reasons which have weighed with me (since I found myself so wonderfully preserved till the good weather; for, in winter, I did not think it *lawful* to dream of such a thing) I shall now mention. Some are not very strong of themselves; but they have all their weight when taken together.

'(1.) Patrick must have felt the want of Janet much, for she used to learn every thing with him; and I am very loath to deprive him of her longer, especially in such hopeless work as that of nursing me. (2.) If I remain here, and the hot weather does not give me diarrhœa, it seems not very unlikely, so far as my lungs are concerned, that I may live through the warm months, but in so feeble a state, that the first change of weather in October or November would be apt to take me off. In such a case, Janet could do nothing but go home in winter; which, I think, after three summers here, would be very dangerous for her health; and I do not think it right to endanger a good life, in trying to prolong a bad one. It is fair to say, that Janet does not think this a good reason, but it *is* good notwithstanding. (3.) It would be a pleasure to you to see us again in the flesh; although, no doubt, this would be much mixed with pain. (4.) Possibly, I might get more spiritual benefit from conversing, if I were once home, with such a dear and intimate friend as ———, than I could obtain from any one here. (5.) I reckon it a very strong reason that I really feel unable to ask the generous friends who support us, to provide us with funds to meet *probable events*. . . . . (6.) By coming home, we incur a *definite* expense. . . . By staying here, we commence another *indefinite* score. I have calculated the probable expense, if I hang on in life till the 20th October, and find it is between £30 and £40 more than what will be needed to bring us home. This reason is aggravated by the fact, that I cannot now render myself of any use. The only reason opposed to these, is, that I might live a short time longer here than in Scotland; but, as I am now totally shut out from all usefulness, I think the simple love of life ought not to overbalance such powerful reasons on the other side.

'So then, I mean, God willing, to attempt going home. But you must not be too sanguine in expecting us, there is so much between the cup and the lip. These gripings may turn to diarrhoea, or my disease may take some sudden bad turn, and stop us here; or, in spite of Dr Renton's hopes, it may please the Lord to remove me on ship-board; or I may be so ill when we get into the channel, as only to be able to land somewhere, and go to bed. So don't expect us too confidently.

'But our present purpose (if the Lord will) is to sail for London in the "Vernon," which is expected to leave this between the 20th and the end of June. Thus we are likely to catch all letters by the June packet; and this epistle will prevent you from writing by the July one. . . . .

'Miss Crawford is just dying—after a very rapid decline, in great peace and joy. Remember us to all friends, ... Your very affectionate son,
'J. H.'

We are inclined to set a very high value on this letter. It is full of instruction. It exhibits the scholar and the Christian united. The minuteness and logical precision of the reasoning may appear, in the circumstances, to be carried to an extreme; but that does not prove it to be wrong, it only indicates that it is rare. In itself and in any circumstances, it were an instructive example of method and accuracy in weighing the reasons on which a judgment is formed; but it is the Christianity of the letter that gives the charm to its logic. The affected coolness of a sceptic in the prospect of death, is repulsive to the observer. Not being natural, it does not sit easy; being put on with a view to reputation, it is generally overdone. It wants the peculiar charm of the coolness displayed here. In going about to set his house in order there is the most perfect calmness; but it is not the desperate determination of pride, nor the fruit of stoical indifference. It is a calmness chastened, not ruffled, by the fear of God; sweetened and hallowed by the hope of the Gospel.

Soon after the date of this letter he became much worse. For several weeks he was confined to bed. During the greater part of June he was in such a state that he could not have been removed. The hope of being able to return had almost failed. A slight improvement, however, took place a few days before the vessel sailed; and when the time came, he determined to adhere to his original purpose. Although he was very weak, and his lungs in such a state that the greatest danger was to be apprehended from the fatigue of the voyage, having, after full deliberation, definitely made up his mind, he resolutely carried his design into effect. On the 30th of June he was safely conveyed on board, and the packet sailed. Nothing remarkable occurred during the voyage. Beyond the inconvenience of close confinement, the invalid experienced no bad effects from exposure on the sea. He

maintained his usual cheerfulness, generally sat at
table in the cabin, and conversed freely with the passengers and crew. On this step of his life's journey,
as on all others, he felt that goodness and mercy followed him. Kept by the faithful Creator, on whom
he had cast his care, he was preserved from the dangers of the deep, and set down safe upon his native
land again. The vessel arrived in the Thames on the
19th, and the passengers landed at London on the
morning of the 20th of July. Feeling his strength
increased rather than diminished, Mr Halley remained
in London from Monday till Thursday, and even paid
visits to some companions in trouble, whose friendship he had acquired in Madeira. On Thursday he
was conveyed by Railway to Liverpool, where he
rested with a friend till the Monday following. On
that day he sailed in one of the Clyde steamers, and
arrived in Glasgow on Tuesday the 28th of July, after
an absence of two years and nine months.

'The works of the Lord are great, sought out of
all them that have pleasure therein.'——Psalm cxi. 2.
God's works are all great, however diminutive the
subject on which they are performed; his path is
always right, though his footsteps be often in the
deep; his purposes are wise, though they may be past
finding out. We have just been tracing the works of
the Lord in the life of one of his servants. In the
chapter of the history which we have just finished, the
Lord's way seems to lie in the deep. One who had
received many gifts, and whose gifts were cultivated
to the utmost, and whose powers, natural and acquired, were solemnly consecrated to the service of God
in the Gospel of his Son, is suddenly checked in his

course. A deadly disease has touched him, withering the beauty of youth—undermining the strength of manhood. When apparently near the period of his days, the prospect of a respite—even the hope of a restoration, is providentially opened up. By being transported to a more genial clime, the progress of his disease is checked, and several years added to his life. But his strength is not restored. He is allowed to linger on a few sickly years, but not allowed to be put in trust with the Gospel. He is allowed to live a while, but not to begin that work for which chiefly he desired to live. After this respite of nearly three years, he is restored to the place of his birth—to die. Here we have more to do than write or read the history. This is the work of the Lord; but it is not enough to 'remember' that work, it must be 'sought out.' Nor will the search be long or difficult. If the wisdom of that 'way' do not lie on the surface, neither is it deeply hid. If this work of the Lord do not force itself upon the observation of the careless passer-by, neither will it long elude the search of those 'that have pleasure therein.'

The reader of the preceding pages must have observed, that the desire which was uppermost in the mind of the exile while he sojourned in a strange land, was, that he might be allowed to preach the Gospel of the grace of God. His heart was full of this, and it was continually bursting out. It broke out in conversation with friends near, and in letters to friends far away. It broke out, too, in unwearied prayer to God. What then? Did God turn away that cry? He might have turned it away. Without giving any account of his doings, he may deny any request of his

servants, and in his own time make it clear that the
Judge of all the earth did right.   Or, he may grant
substantially the request, in a time, and way, and
manner, which we in the body can never find out.
In either case it is ours to ' be still and know that he
is God.'   But, in the present instance, it has pleased
God to give an answer to that prayer, in a form
which makes it evident that the answer has been
given.   God is not wont to leave without work and
hire, those who long to labour in his vineyard.   Mr
Halley had been filled with that desire, and enabled
to say, ' Here am I ; send me.'   God accepted his
offer, and sent him.   Work was appointed him to do,
and souls given him for his hire.

We have already laid before the reader a pretty full
history of the *means* employed ; the *effects* cannot be
recorded in these pages ; they will not be all known
till ' the day' reveal them.   Yet some of the blessed
effects of Mr Halley's labours are known.   Enough
is known to make manifest the design of God in
sending him to Madeira, and preserving him there.
His own conceptions of usefulness in the Church were
associated with the work of a parish minister in Scotland ; but that was not the place allotted him in the
design of God.   The King of Zion had chosen vessels
in a far off isle of the sea, and a chosen instrument
to employ in bringing them to himself.   This is explanation enough of the whole mystery.   The sovereign Lord might have appointed his servant a long
life of labour in the Church at home, with two or
three only as his crown of rejoicing—one here and
there, gleaned from the generation he had seen passing by.   The appointment was different, but not less

wise, and not less kind. The scene of labour was in a strange land ; but the stranger's help was present there. The labourer was sickly ; but the Holy Spirit makes his own word powerful, though it be spoken by trembling lips. The time was short ; but in it the work was done, and the servant was the sooner relieved from toil—the sooner admitted to the joy of his Lord.

A considerable number of instances have come to our knowledge, in which Mr Halley's labours in Madeira have been the blessed means of converting sinners, and of building up believers in their holy faith. Although in some of these cases the facts have been distinctly stated to us by the most competent witnesses—the relatives of the parties concerned—we do not feel at liberty to give the circumstances here in detail. Were we to attempt a narrative, we would be obliged, from various prudential reasons, to conceal so many of the features of it, that it would be no narrative at all. We shall content ourselves with bearing testimony to the fact, that there were such fruits of his ministry granted to him. In his own letters and journals there are some allusions to particular persons, which indicate his hope that a blessing from on high had rested upon his instructions. In one instance at least we find a distinct statement by himself that he had seen the work prospering in his hand to the saving of a soul. In one of his letters, speaking of two persons to whom he had often commended the word of eternal life, he says,—' One of them, I fondly trust, may have cause to bless my memory for ever.' The reader of his letters will not expect from him much of confident assertion regarding the success of

his labours.   He was not easily satisfied.   The most
distinguishing habit of his mind was, resolutely to
withhold his judgment until he found a sufficient
reason on which it might rest.   Reference is also
made, in his own letters, to a young married lady
among the residents whom he statedly instructed.   It
is understood that she was converted to Christ through
the word spoken by him.   She died before he left the
island.   Another of these cases on which we found
the statement that Mr Halley's teaching was blessed,
was that of a medical gentleman from Edinburgh, who
had also come to the island as an invalid.   Finding
himself becoming worse, he returned.   At the time he
left there was no prospect that Mr Halley would ever
be able to be removed.   When he had, with great
difficulty, reached home, he spoke of it as a mark of
distinguishing mercy to himself, that he should have
been brought home to die in the midst of his friends,
while the instructor who had taught him the hopes of
the Gospel, was left to close his days in a land of
strangers.   Another was a farmer from an agricul-
tural district in the west of Scotland, who, like his
instructor, after trying the climate of Madeira in vain
as the means of restoring his health, was enabled to
return in life.   On his deathbed, we have been informed, he continued to speak with gratitude of Mr
Halley, as the messenger who had spoken to him the
word of life.   These cases, even though noted in such
general terms, may suffice to show what is meant
when we say that this servant of the Lord was not
sent to Madeira in vain.   To show how widely the
influence of his instructions may have spread from
that centre to which so many invalids congregate,

and to show, at the same time, how very difficult it is to obtain detailed information regarding it, we may mention the following fact:—While these pages are passing through the press, inquiry has been made for this volume in the office of the publisher by some friend, on behalf of a gentleman in the south of England, who speaks of Mr Halley as his 'spiritual father.' This person is not known to the editors even by name.

But besides the instances of special good to individuals, whatever their number, Mr Halley was honoured to do a great work in Madeira, by his bold testimony for the truth, and the practical rebuke of ungodliness which he administered in a consistent conduct. In the opinion of a very competent judge, who spent a winter on the island—the last winter of Mr Halley's residence on it—the way in which he was enabled most extensively to serve the Lord there was, by diffusing the savour of a consistently religious life in a region pervaded by the spirit of worldliness. In this way, his learning—which we are apt to think was lost, after it had been acquired with so much labour—even his learning was made the direct instrument in advancing the kingdom of Christ. In a society where men of rank, and wealth, and learning from different parts of England were congregated, the thorough respect which his talents commanded, gained admission for his instruction and rebuke to circles from which they would otherwise have been wholly excluded. His learning, with all its acuteness, could make no wound on a hard heart; yet it was not useless there. It performed the part of pioneer in clearing the obstacles away, and giving the sword of the

Spirit an access to its object.   For example, religious
books were read with avidity on his recommendation,
by persons who would have paid no attention to the
judgment of a less gifted mind.

On the whole, looking to Mr Halley's mission to
Madeira in all its bearings as a work of the Lord, it
does not require much searching to discover in it both
wisdom and love.   That was not the field which he
would have selected—that was not the precise station
in his Master's service to which his desires and prayers
had tended; but surely He who chose for him the
lot of his inheritance as a son, had the best right to
choose the sphere of his labours as a servant.   He
who had appointed him a mansion in the Father's
house on high, had the best right to appoint the
bounds of his habitation on earth.   Christ, who redeemed him, gave him a work to do, and enabled him
to do it.   If the work was sooner done, the workman
was sooner admitted into rest.   The Master disposed
to the best advantage of his servant's talents.   The
servant knows that now.   It is good if we have a
desire to serve Christ; but we must leave the disposal
of ourselves and our services all to Him.   Let ministers and candidates for the ministry be bent on showing forth the Redeemer's glory, but not wedded to
their own method and their own means.   Their
'times' and places are in the Lord's hands; let them
lie there.   In asking for work, and offering their
services, why should they limit the Holy One?

CHAPTER IV.

IN continuing the narrative of Mr Halley's life beyond this period, we have no longer those rich materials which have hitherto supplied us with both facts
and commentary—his own letters. At home, and
enjoying the personal visits of his friends, he had no
longer the same motive which, during the last three
years, had drawn so many pledges of friendship from
his pen. Partly from the want of materials provided
by himself, and partly because he was now in a sphere
where persons and events are better known, we shall
contract, within a very limited space, the remaining
portion of the narrative.

On the day after his arrival he kept his bed, as the
best means of recovering from the fatigue of the journey. In the course of the day, two or three of his
friends were admitted to converse with him, and join
in his thanksgivings. His emotions on first meeting
them were strong, but he was in a cheerful frame, and
was soon able to converse freely. The wonder to
them was, that there was so little difference in his

T

appearance. After having long lost hope of seeing him in the body, it was with no slight emotion they looked on him again, still so like what he had been before. The lost was found. It was like a restoration from the dead. Paler indeed he was, and more emaciated ; but all the vigour of his mind survived, and all the warm affection of his heart was there. There was the same acuteness of judgment in reasoning with men, and the same fervency of spirit in serving the Lord.

After recovering from the effects of fatigue, he found that his health had been considerably improved by the voyage. During the remaining part of the summer, he was sensibly better than he had been for the last six months in Madeira. He sat up during the whole of the day, and though too weak for walking, accomplished, without injury, several journeys of considerable length. He paid two visits to Mr Colquhoun at Killermont—a distance of four miles from the city— going and returning on the same day, without being sensible of receiving any injury from the drive. The last occasion on which he was able to be out of doors was a visit to a minister in the city, who had been one of his most intimate college friends. He had often expressed a strong desire to see his class-fellows in their own pulpits declaring the unsearchable riches of Christ. This gratification he was not permitted to enjoy ; and it was as a kind of substitute for it, that he made an effort to visit at his own house the only one of them who was within reach. Although he was so weak that it was necessary to carry him up stairs, he conversed freely for several hours, and sat at dinner without evincing any symptoms of uneasiness.

Those who were present remember well the look of intense interest with which he regarded the books and loose papers that were lying about the room, indicating the ongoing of the work of the ministry. No mark of envy appeared on his countenance,—no word of discontent fell from his lips. His emotions were evidently the very reverse. The smile of a perfect resignation seemed now to have settled on his face. With regard to himself, the struggle was over; he was not only still under God's hand, but satisfied with his judgments. Having been by the Spirit brought at last into complete acquiescence in the decree which excluded himself from the ministry of the Gospel in the Church, it afforded him unmingled delight to see the friends of his youth actually engaged in the duties of their holy calling. This visit was on the 8th of October. The day was clear and mild. He was conveyed home in the evening, not injured by the exertion; but he was never able to go out again.

During the winter, he was able to receive, almost without limitation, the visits of his friends. We have seen him maintain a conversation with great liveliness for two or three hours together. The range of subjects was very wide. Some point of doctrine or of Christian experience; some event in the world or some question agitated in the Church, would afford the theme of a lengthened discussion, and then the whole concluded, at his request, with devotional reading of the Scriptures and prayer. Of the ministers of the city, Dr Muir, as the minister of the parish in which he resided, and Dr Henderson, on the ground of the friendship contracted in Madeira, were among his frequent visitors. He delighted much in these visits

from the more experienced ministers, and often spoke
of the benefits he derived from them.   Many of the
younger ministers, too, of the city and neighbourhood,
with whom he had formerly lived in terms of intimacy,
felt it a privilege to spend an hour in his sick-room.
They profited by his conversation at the time, and felt
his example an excitement to diligence afterwards.
Mr Stevenson has supplied a brief note of one of these
interviews, which may be given as a specimen.

' . . . It was on Monday, the 8th February.   He
gave me then a book, which he had marked out as a
LEGACY to me, with an affectionate note inclosed.
We conversed for a long time on our spiritual state,
read a passage of Scripture, and prayed.   He complained, with tears in his eyes, of his felt coldness and
wandering of heart in prayer.   He was in a very
tender, humble frame of spirit.   I requested him to
mention a passage of Scripture which he would leave
with me to be remembered.   He repeated 2 Cor. iv.
1—" Therefore, seeing we have this ministry, as we
have received mercy, we faint not."   I bade him a
long farewell, sorrowing most of all that I should see
his face no more.'

The following memorandum, by the Rev. Mr Lorimer, who frequently saw him at this period, will serve
as an example of the yet unwearied activity of his
mind, and the readiness with which he could still
apply the resources he had formerly acquired.

' I remember he was the first to inform me of the
appearance of universal redemption views among some
of the ministers of the United Secession Church.   He
seemed to be acquainted with the facts, and bore testimony to the faithfulness of the older ministers in
one of the inferior church courts.   He stated that he

had studied that controversy fully, and that there was only one passage which he regarded as a difficulty, viz., that in the 2d chapter of John, where Christ is said to be the propitiation for sin, and not for ours only, but also for the sins of the whole world. I suggested the usual explanation of the distinction between the Jews and the Gentiles. He said he was not satisfied with that; he did not see evidence that this distinction was intended. He still considered that passage a difficulty; all the others admitted of easy explanation. Of course he did not consider the doctrine doubtful, which is so clearly taught in Scripture, although a difficulty rested on the exposition of a single text. We concurred in thinking that the distinction of the old divines between Christ dying *sufficiently* for all, and *efficiently* for the elect, was the true key to most of the difficulties connected with the use of universal terms in this question.'

It may well be supposed that he regarded with the most lively interest the position and prospects of our own Church. He was thoroughly acquainted with the merits of the questions agitated, and his judgment had long ago been deliberately formed. His comments on events as they happened in the Church, in connection with the principles involved in the controversy, were most instructive to his friends. His evidence seemed to possess more weight now, than when the witness mingled in the strife. It was the testimony of one who felt that he had done with life, and was living under the power of a world to come. It was the testimony of one who was well qualified to decide in any circumstances, but was now removed from those disturbing forces which generally warp the judgment of men,—the testimony of one who considered the question in the calm which broods over

302 MEMOIR OF JAMES HALLEY.

the very entrance of the grave,—who examined all
its bearings in the light which a near eternity throws
across upon the confines of this present world. The
judgment of such a one, in such a position, necessarily
commanded respect. Nor was the sound uncertain.
His sympathies were as strong then as they had ever
been, in favour of the evangelical Church of Scotland,
and against those members of it who unnaturally rebel
against her authority, and press a policy which must
either degrade her as a Church of Christ, or destroy
her as a Church established. The solemnity of the
situation in which he was placed did not in the least
degree modify his opinion—did not affect at all the
substance of his judgment; it only had the effect of
increasing its force, by banishing all appearance of
passion from its form.

As his heart's desire and prayer for the country in
general was, that the Gospel of the grace of God
might be faithfully preached in all its parishes, so he
felt a peculiar interest in the state of the universities,
and the kind of training to which the future ministers
were subjected there. Of all the public questions of
the day, we do not remember any one in which he
felt more deeply concerned, than in the election of a
professor to the chair of theology in the university of
Glasgow. While the merits of the candidates were
undergoing discussion in the public press, and when
the time of the election was drawing near, we have
heard Mr Halley say with much solemnity of manner,
'I will not believe that the professors will reject Dr
Chalmers until they do it.' When the election was
over, and Dr Chalmers rejected, he did not often, so
far as we remember, recur to the subject. When the

deed was done, he thought of it more in sorrow than in anger. He was more occupied with grief for the injury sustained by the Church, than with resentment against the men who inflicted the blow. He left them to the distinction which they had earned for themselves before the country and the world.

While we thus record the unabated severity of his judgment against wrong principles and wrong practice, we owe it both to the cause of truth, and the memory of the departed, to record also that there appeared at this time a thorough charity, both in thought and ex - pression, toward the *persons* concerned. As an illustration of this, and at the same time to show the natural kindliness of his disposition, we shall insert here a note written about the middle of September, to a minister of the United Secession Church, who had been his class-fellow at the grammar school and at college. It is well known that Mr Halley felt keenly, and took a most active part in the Voluntary Controversy, that had agitated Scotland for several years; but he never allowed it to break up a private friendship, or diminish his estimation of personal worth.

' My dear John,—Not knowing how short my time might be on earth, I drew up, in Madeira, a little scheme of the way in which I wished my father to dispose of my books, marking some as *mementos* to different friends. The accompanying little volume I destined for you, deeming such a casuistical work peculiarly appropriate to one engaged, as you are, in the ministry of the Word.

' As my very dear friend J. H., whose parish is distant from you only a few miles, expressed a willingness to convey any thing I might have to send, I thought you might like as well to receive the book

from myself while yet a sojourner here, and was glad
to take the opportunity of saving my father from
future trouble in sending it, as well as of expressing
my unabated affection to you. H. will act the part of
Tychicus, and tell you "all my state and how I am,"
and so save me the effort of writing more.

'Be assured that I remember you most affectionately; and do not forget me when you get access into
the holiest by the blood of Jesus. The Lord bless you
and your ministry.—Ever yours sincerely, J. H.
'*Rev. John Paterson.*'

During the autumn and winter, Mr Halley wrote
several letters of great length to persons at a distance,
which we have not been able to recover. Two were
addressed to Mr Burn, the missionary sent out to
Madeira, containing a detailed account of the religious
condition of the island, and suggestions to aid him in
prosecuting his duties. The only letter of any considerable length that has fallen into our hands, is one
addressed to a former fellow-sufferer in Madeira. As
to the style, being written to a lady, it will probably
be felt to be deficient in the freedom which characterises most of his letters. Even in the matter, it does
not exhibit the vigour of his earlier efforts. We would
not have chosen it as a specimen of his epistolary
style, but the circumstances invest it with so much
interest, that we feel bound to preserve it entire.

'GLASGOW, 12*th October* 1840.

'My dear S———,—I sit down to write to you under
very considerable disadvantages. It was only this
morning that we received your sister's letter requesting me to send you a few lines; and I find the post-
office arrangements render it needful that my letter
should be despatched to-night, in order to be in time

for the packet. But a worse evil than the shortness of time is, my utter ignorance of the state in which you are, especially that part of it which is mental. That your *bodily* frame has been subjected to severe suffering, we know; but whether you have been enabled, in any good measure, to possess your *soul* in patience, has not been told us. And although there is too much reason to think, that still your weakness of body remains, perhaps to such an extent as to endanger life, it is my misfortune not to be sure whether you are " rejoicing in hope," and therefore " patient in tribulation," or " walking in darkness," and, to your own conception at least, " filled with the fury of the Lord, and with the rebuke of our God."

' Under this ignorance of your mental condition, it would be very discouraging, indeed it might seem altogether useless, to attempt to write to you, if one looks only at the human agent. It is our comfort and encouragement in such a case, to know that there is an all-wise Disposer of all things, who knows your condition although I know it not, and who can (as I earnestly beseech him to do) overrule my writing to you as the means either of establishing or of comforting you, as need may be. A bow drawn at a venture has been of use before now; and we do not know what blessing God may be pleased to send, even when we are working in the dark.

' Our great duty, and God's chief commandment, under the dispensation of Gospel light, is to believe on the name of his Son Jesus Christ. This faith, which is at all times our duty and happiness, has various exercises, united to the condition into which we may come. And one of its exercises, to which I would call your special attention now, is that of complete and unquestioning confidence in the wisdom and goodness of the Divine procedure; according to the hint given in the last verse of the 107th Psalm, it is often very profitable to review God's dealings with us

in a time of trial. All the illustrations which that
Psalm contains, are of dispensations of an *afflictive*
kind; and you observe that it is from these very *afflictions*, hard and severe as they might seem, that the
Psalmist says that a wise observer may learn the
loving-kindness of the Lord. In looking back on
what has befallen you, I doubt not you will be able to
trace the highest wisdom, directing all to a benevolent
end. Most people have some scheme or other of
earthly happiness on which their hearts are set; and
probably you have had yours. Of course I do not
know what it may have been. But this, I think, I
may venture to say, from all I have observed or been
told of the Divine procedure, that it is likely your
favourite plan or wish has been so thwarted, as to
make it manifest that the fulfilment of it could not
have brought that amount of happiness you expected
from it; or in such a way as to make you more sensible of your corruption of heart; or, finally, in such
a way as to strike at some of the sins to which you
felt yourself most liable. Such indications as these of
a kind purpose in smiting, you will easily find; and
I do not know an exercise more signally fitted to
tranquillize and soothe the mind, than thus to follow
out the course of Providence, till prayer and meditation
upon it are turned into thanksgiving.

' This meditation will, no doubt, be conducted with
the most abundant fruit and the greatest pleasure, by
a soul in the enjoyment of a conscious peace with
God, reconciled to him by faith in his Son, and ready,
in consequence, to see, with full and clear conviction,
that all things are working together for its good. If
you have attained to this happy state, I need not
speak to you in any other words than those of con-
gratulation; for nothing can be so blessed as to be
able to recognise God as our friend,—and to wander
up and down among his dealings towards us with the
confidence that all were dictated by kindness,—and

o be persuaded, that neither life nor death shall be
ble to separate us from his love in Christ Jesus our
.ord. But, lest you should not have attained to it,
ermit me to say, that (in subordination always to
God's blessing, which we must *ask*, that we may re-
eive it) the meditation on God's ways, which I have
lready recommended, is an excellent means of pre-
aring and disposing the soul towards the attainment
f that peace, and of all the felicity involved in it.
For that which chiefly obstructs faith, and so prevents
s from being at peace with God, is the distrust and
hrinking naturally engendered by a sense of guilt
which we are so perverse as sometimes to make a
merit of, by confounding it with humility). Now,
what can be better fitted to combat this distrust, than
o see, as we may, if we will attentively review the
matter, that, guilty as we are, God has manifestly
lealt kindly with us, even in those things which we
would have thought most severe? Such a view of
is providence, if His Spirit enable us to take it, must
wonderfully conduce to fill us with a general confi-
lence in him, and to give us that thorough belief in the
sincerity of his offers in the Gospel, without which
we cannot truly and effectually receive them.

' But this, as indeed every thing, must come from
Himself, and therefore must be sought from Himself.
Probably we, who are in such a state of weakness,
have been brought into it just for this very purpose,
that, disabled as we are from the use of other means,
we may be the more intent on prayer and supplication.
And if we have not enough of mental energy to follow
the train of reasoning in books,—or are unfit for conversing,—or have no Christian friends near, with whom
we may take sweet counsel,—we may still *pray* to
Him who is always near, and who will not despise the
prayer of the destitute. *This*, along with reading *the
Word*, is, I am persuaded, your great duty now. The
prayer may be short, it may be a mere ejaculation, yet

it may enter into the ears of the Lord of Sabaoth. And the passage read at any one time may, by reason of your weakness, be very brief; it may be but a single verse; yet it may be brought home, as God the Spirit has often already brought it, with his own demonstration and with power. The great thing to be aimed at in all, is an humble dependent frame of spirit; and if God give you this, he will, either in this world, or in the next, but certainly in due time, exalt you.

'I must now close, for the post hour passes. Janet desires me to send her love. We sympathize truly with you; but we would wish you a nearer acquaintance with One whose sympathies are infinitely valuable, that great High Priest, who is touched with a feeling of our infirmities.

'I have to beg you will pardon the defects of this hurried letter; and I pray that God also may pardon them, and may deign to use it as a messenger of some good to you. I do not ask you to answer it, but shall be glad that you mention that you have got it, in your first letter to your sisters after its arrival. With every good wish to your brother, and in the hope that this may find you partly restored; or, if this be not the will of God, rejoicing in his favour, and ready to depart,—I am very affectionately yours,   J. H.

'*P.S.*—I am a close prisoner, and very weak; but able to be up half the day, and not enduring much acute pain. Cough very heavy.   J. H.'

He sits down to write, he says, 'under considerable disadvantages,' not knowing the condition in which the person addressed might be when the counsel reached her. Alas, how true! She was dead before he sat down to write it. The dying, in ignorance, writing out consolation to—the dead! Such are the partings of those who meet in that little hospital isle! And that little isle set in the sea, is, in respect of brief meetings and sudden partings, a meet emblem of this wide world floating in the ocean of eternity.

As we are just taking note of incidents that may be characteristic of the deceased, or instructive to the reader, without making any pretension to a continuous narrative, we shall introduce here, in succession, extracts from four short letters—all written to early friends who had, in different places, entered on the work of the ministry.

'GLASGOW, 29th *October* 1840.

' . . . . *Hoc dimisso*, accept of my congratulations on your safe return to D——. How vastly I should like to see you going about in your parish! and how much more to look in at one of your little meetings, at which you are trying to follow your worthy bishop's advice and example, and crack to the people extempore! But these wishes are dreams, which can never become realities. Still, I can wish well to the work, and bid you God-speed, even from this my prison-house. . . . .

' My dear John,—I very much need your prayers, as a man of unclean lips, and laden with iniquity. Do not forget me when you endeavour to draw nigh to God.—Yours very affectionately, J. H.'

'GLASGOW, 17th *November* 1840.

' My dear James,—Before yours of the 7th reached me, I had been informed, through the "Guardian," of the intention of the trustees of —— Church to present you to it. I was just meditating a note to you, to state some reasons for which I thought you ought to accept, when your epistle arrived, and saved me the labour. Now that your decision is made, and partly executed, let me only say this,—that, however grievous, in respect to the people of A——, your removal may be, and however ominous the causes of it in

reference to any future appointment in that parish,—it
appears to me that Providence has now fixed, in great
wisdom and goodness, the bounds of your habitation.
Not to speak of the pleasure your mother will have in
your restoration (as it may almost be called) to her, and
of the advantage to the younger members of the family,
I would view your settlement in Edinburgh as of great
importance to your ultimate usefulness in a way in
which all your friends look for something from you.
No man could have been taken thither to whom it
will be more acceptable to be within reach of the
learned treasures of so many libraries ; and, while I
join heartily in your prayer that you may be kept from
the excessive and sinful love of distinction, I trust
that, in all humility and meekness, you may be induced, by your locality, to serve God and your generation as a writer on some subject of interest and
importance.   Meantime, you *must expect* great dis-
couragements in the attempt to rear a congregation ;
but such preaching as you spoke of, if the Lord enable
you faithfully to use it, will not return void, even in
the matter of attracting some ; and I doubt not, a
few years hence, you will be the minister, if spared, of
an intelligent and devout, if not an overflowing, congregation.   Andrew Fuller suggests it as a ground of
quiet acquiescence to ministers, when their visible
success is less than they would desire, that " better
breath than theirs was spent for nought and in vain."
Isa. xlix.   When I can pray at all, I shall not forget
to make mention of you in the way you desire. . . .

' Your friendly inquiry about the comment touches
me on rather a sore point.   Nothing has been done,
save, during the first few days after I saw you, the
collection of a few *notæ variorum*, and a cursory
glance over Locke (whom, by the way, I regard as a
very poor expositor.   I would give him up to the
Socinians, and let them make their best of him).   Perhaps about half the time since we met, I have been

physically disqualified, by the above named cold and languor, from doing any thing. But the worst and most constant disqualification is the moral and spiritual one, which has often before enervated me, and now, being forcibly brought to view by Paul's addressing his epistle to " saints," has stopped me altogether. I trust you cannot at all sympathize with the state of mind,—not even from recollection,—in which I write, when I say, that I have for a good while laboured under a strong impression that the conclusion of the 50th Psalm debars me from attempting to comment upon God's Word. It is a melancholy confession wherewith to afflict the mind of so dear a friend, who will be more impressed by its sadness than I am myself, having his spiritual senses far otherwise exercised than mine ; but it must be made ; that I have never yet known what it is to have a confidence of acceptance with God. A sort of quietness I have indeed had habitually ; but self-examination has always ended in a suspicion of its foundations ; and the fruits of faith, clear and unequivocal, I have never been able to see. In this case, I think, upon consideration, that I could not, without great hypocrisy, groping in the dark, and leading people to imagine me possessed of an experience which I have not, attempt to comment upon the Epistle to the Ephesians. Every other qualification I might possess for the task, would thus go to strengthen a practical fraud. And the sorest evil of all is, that I am not conscious of *feeling* this state of things as I ought, in its true character of a most sinful and miserable state. Only this I do in some measure see, that, if any thing could heighten the inherently infinite and inexpressible privilege of being in a state of conscious favour with the Almighty, it would be the enlargement of spirit which one could enjoy in expounding such a portion of the Word as the Ephesians. I do not say, my dear James, in what way your prayers for me should be directed in such a

case ; but you will be able to judge yourself, and I
doubt not you will not fail to ask for me, from the
Father of mercies, all needful good things. . . .

‘ That you may be strengthened with all might by
the Spirit in the inner man, so as to make full proof of
your ministry, and may know the blessedness of being
clothed with salvation to the eternal joy of many, is
the heart's desire and prayer of, your very affectionate,

‘ J. H.

‘ *Rev. James Hamilton.*’

‘ GLASGOW, *5th January* 1841.

‘ My dear John,—In ordinary circumstances I
might well be ashamed to see that your letter, which
refreshed and pleased me much, bears the date of 29th
October last.   But you know, and can appreciate, my
excuse.   I might, indeed, according to your suggestion, have used Patrick's hand ; but I felt quite confident that you would be hearing about me from. . .

‘ And now that I do write, I can manage nothing
more than literally a *line* to tell you how I do. Bodily,
I of course fail ; but not so fast as was to have been
expected.   For six weeks past, however, the descent
has been more marked, owing to a new form of illness
I have been visited with, namely, a total failure of
power in the stomach, frequent vomitings, and almost
constant nausea.   I feel, too, the steady diminution
of breathing power.   But I still get up about mid-day,
and spend till ten, P. M., in our parlour, mostly on
the sofa.   You will almost wonder to hear, that with
the power, I have nearly lost the inclination to read.
Sleep hardly any—a kind of disturbed dozing is the
utmost.   Spiritually, I have no good to say of myself.
I have, indeed, been mercifully preserved from dis-
tracting fears ; but I have never been able distinctly
to identify the kind of quietness I enjoy, with the solid
well-founded peace of a soul at one with its Maker.
I am aiming at this very elementary attainment, and

praying for it as I can; feeling, meantime, that my own impurity and backslidings render it inconsistent with God's usual administration in holiness and faithfulness, that I should be blest with the higher mercy of rejoicing in God through our Lord Jesus Christ. But whatever may be given, or whatever withheld, in the way of sensible comfort, I desire to be found making daily application at the Fountain opened for sin and for uncleanness, waiting upon God, confessing unworthiness of the least mercy, and bearing witness to the long-suffering and loving-kindness of the Lord.

' I rejoiced to hear of your settlement in a dwelling of your own, and hope it may be found a great accession to your comfort. Don't let the study contain too good an easy chair; for if it do, the sermons may suffer. How I should like to hear one of these said sermons! Indeed it is often a favourite dream with me, what delight I should have had, if it had pleased the Lord to continue a little more strength to me, in moving up and down the country, and hearing, on successive Sabbaths, those of my friends and brethren whom it has pleased the chief Shepherd to honour by calling them to the work of the ministry. But the event may be regarded as a proof that this dream is better not realized.

' 7th January 1841.

' These two days of intense cold have been very sore on me. I fear I can hardly expect again to write you, so little exertion is now fatiguing. But you will not be much at a loss with Mr J. for an occasional informant. If you ever favour me with another epistle, you must, in simple charity, not expect an answer.

' And now, my dear friend, farewell. Let me have the great favour of a constant interest in your prayers; and believe me to be, with every desire for your usefulness in the Lord's vineyard, affectionately yours,

' J. H.

' *Rev. John Wright.*'

U

'*22d February* 1841.

' My very dear Sir,—You will now see why I troubled you about Hume. " Being crafty, I have caught you," but not with guile. For I *indeed thought* you had a copy of his Essays, but that it was one of the old two vol. editions; and if this had been verified, I should still have sent the accompanying vols.—they are much more full. But if you had had this same edition, I should then have looked out some other book.

' Long ago, in Madeira, when many around me as well as myself thought that my pilgrimage would be shorter than it has pleased the Lord to make it, I thought it a duty to draw out a little scheme for the disposal of my books. My prizes, of course, as a thing they would much value, I desired to remain with my nearest relatives. But there was one friend, whose disinterested, laborious, kind, and persevering services seemed to me to give him a right to the only poor distinction I could confer—that, namely, of leaving him one of these same college rewards, and making him the only person beyond our own family to whom I did leave one. I need not say you were that friend.

' In looking over the list of them for one not unsuitable to a divine's library, and of such value as to be something like an expression of my feelings—this book struck me as the most appropriate; and I was aided, probably, by the consideration, that it was sending Hume where he could do no harm. I am glad now to find you have none of him, as it makes it more appropriate still.

' Although it comes prematurely, I would have you consider it as a *legacy*. . . . .

' Praying that your kindness to me may be amply repaid into your own bosom, and that the Lord may richly bless you in all your ways,—I am most gratefully yours,   J. H.'

' *Rev. James Gibson.*'

And now we have done with the letters. Beyond this date we have no materials supplied by himself.* Hitherto we have extracted his history almost exclusively from his own writings. These have failed us now ; but not until the tale has been nearly told. The date of the last is only twenty-four days before his death. Though, from the change of circumstances, his letters written at Glasgow never go so fully into a statement of his hopes and prospects as those which were written at Madeira, the tone of them is still the same. Though they are but notes written to persons near on some subjects of private interest, they are all characteristic of the man. They afford a better evidence of the state of the writer's mind, than if they had been more laboured and professedly on religious subjects. We have given his latest letters on common subjects, just to let the reader see that his latter days were very like what the tenor of his life had been during the preceding four years. There was the same calm victory over the world and the fear of death— the same humble estimate of his own spiritual attainments—the same unshaken faith in the truth of the Gospel—and the same ardent longing to be satisfied with the mercy of God. Having told so fully what his life had been, we have little more to do now ; we have only to say that his death was like it.

One thing that attracted the attention of all his

* Since this was written, a letter has been put into our hands dictated by Mr Halley, but not written by his own hand, bearing date the 8th of March 1841, just eight days before his death. It is addressed to one of his former pupils, and wholly occupied with a description of manuscript books on subjects connected with Greek literature. Having no more use for the notes which he had taken in the earlier period of his studies, he was unwilling that they should be lost, and took care to have them conveyed to one who would profit by them. The chief interest of the letter is the evi-

friends towards the close of his life, was the perfect
coolness with which he spoke of his own death.   We
have seen some, and heard of more, who, in the confidence of hope, could speak on their death-bed with
something like ecstasy of coming glory.   In him we
saw an example more rare, and perhaps equally instructive—a believer who would not assume the attitude of victor, and never dared to adopt the language
of triumph, yet, through the Saviour, actually overcoming death and him who hath its power.   While
he refused to display the form, he manifestly possessed the substance of a triumph. · It pleased God to
withhold from him to the last that amount of joy for
which he had long been striving ; and besides observ▾
ing the fact, perhaps those friends who best knew the
constitution of his mind, may be able also to perceive
the reason of it.   Considering the peculiarities of his
character and talents, they may be able to perceive
that the path by which he was led, was the very path
on which he was best fitted to glorify God.   Some are
enabled to glorify their Saviour by being ' compassed
about with songs of deliverance ;' he was enabled to
do the same thing by ' hoping against hope.'   The
form which his faith assumed was, ' though he slay
me, yet will I trust in him ; ' and faith given in this
form, honours Him who gave it.

During the two or three last weeks of his life, when
now very weak and nearly altogether confined to bed,
Mr Halley made the arrangements for ' setting his
house in order ' with all his characteristic deliberation,

dence it gives of the continued perfection of all his faculties, when so near
the period of dissolution.   Having been dictated to another person, it
bears the marks of constraint, and contains none of those outpourings of
his heart on religious subjects which abound in his other communications.

and with even more than his usual precision in the details. He prepared a catalogue of his books, pointing out the characteristics of all the more valuable works, and gave directions for their sale about a fortnight before his death. Those friends who had access to him accounted this an error, but unwilling to press upon him those considerations that might have induced him to desist, they received his instructions in silence, and executed his commands.

In making out his Will, a difficulty occurred in regard to the expenses of the funeral. To leave the sum contingent, and to throw an uncertainty over all his other calculations, was altogether alien to the habit of his mind. He could not leave any thing uncertain, while the means of ascertaining it were within his reach. Accordingly, two of his friends having called while the matter was under consideration, he laid his commands on them to make the necessary inquiries, specifying minutely the various items, and carefully limiting the style to what he considered his own rank, that no unnecessary expense might be incurred. His friends received and executed the melancholy commission. A note was handed to him of the estimated expense of the funeral, by aid of which he was enabled to substitute a definite for an indefinite expression in the settlement of his worldly affairs.

We feel it to be wholly unnecessary now to detail the events of each successive day. Alas, who of our readers cannot call up from the records of their own observation, a more vivid picture than we could hope to present, of a lingering consumption drawing near its close? And as we have done with the events of his life, so but little of his spiritual history remains to be told.   If any of our readers have been hastening through the substantial instructions which his life conveys, expecting something brilliant and exciting in his death, they will assuredly be disappointed.   We shall note, in the simplest possible form, gathered chiefly from the members of his own family, some of the incidents and expressions that tend to show the state of his mind in the immediate prospect of departure.

About ten days before his death he said to one of his friends on entering the room,—'The dark valley is drawing very near now.'   The reply made was partly in the form of a hope expressed, and partly in the form of a question put to ascertain if the dark valley appeared more dreadful as it approached.   After a pause, gathering up his thoughts, and considering the grounds of his judgment, he said slowly and firmly, —' No ; it does not appear more dreadful as it approaches.'   It is impossible to give in words an idea of the satisfaction which such an expression from him was calculated to convey to his friends.   Such a cautious and measured statement in his lips, was equivalent to a confident affirmation from a mind differently constituted.

About that time, as the spring advanced, the children from the neighbourhood began to assemble in the evenings to play in a court immediately beneath his window.   When a fear was expressed that the noise would disturb him ; he said, ' No ; it gives me pleasure to think that others have animal enjoyment yet, though I have none.'   And when the children's loud shout of mirth first reached his ear in the evening, he would smile and say, ' There is the physical enjoyment beginning.'

On Wednesday, six days before his death, in a time of severe suffering, an expression of great impatience escaped him. When relieved, he remembered it and mourned over it much, saying, 'How the flesh lusteth against the spirit!' and asking his sister, when she left him at night, to pray for pardon of this sin. On the day following, he said, 'I am not able now, and I don't perplex myself with any laborious attempt to settle or ascertain my state. I simply look to Jesus.' Seeing his sister in tears, he said, 'My dear, you mourn sore like a dove; what's wrong now?' She said, 'Just a rebellious heart; I cannot part with you.' 'Ah, you must,' he replied; 'my heart was long rebellious, but I trust it is not so now—oh I *trust* it is not so. "Be still, and know that I am God." It was long ere I could be *still*; but since I attained it, I have never been shaken from it.'

The paper in the form of a Will, which he dictated to his brother, sets out with a declaration that he is of sound mind. It was drawn up towards the end of the week. On Sabbath evening, on one occasion, his memory faltered a little. He detected it, and inwardly reflecting on the expression in the Will, said to his sister, 'Is that true?' Perceiving that she did not understand to what he referred, he said, 'Am I yet of sound mind?' She answered she had no doubt of it. 'Because,' said he, 'I would not like to put my name to a document containing such an assertion unless I were sure of its truth.'

On the same evening, when he complained that he looked but feebly to the cross of Christ, his sister repeated a verse of an Olney hymn, ending, 'For never needy sinner perished there;' he said, in a tone of calm satisfaction, ' Oh yes, and we have his own words : " *Whosoever* cometh unto me, I will *in no wise* cast out."'   Observing his own weakness when some little office of kindness was done for him, he said, " Is not that the grasshopper being a burden ? Truly desire *has* failed ; what could I desire now ?" Then, in a tone of great tenderness, added, " I am like a broken vessel ; I am a wonder unto many, and to myself also ; I am feeble and sore broken." His sister took the opportunity of reminding him, as an evidence of mercy in the midst of judgment, that his heart was not disquieted within him as the hour of departure approached.   To this he assented, saying, with a deliberate and solemn voice, " a *great* mercy indeed."

On Monday morning, a member of the family told him the report (which had just reached this country, and was at first believed) about the rocks at the Falls of Niagara being carried away, adding, ' the mountains shall depart and the hills be removed.' He took up the verse eagerly, and finished it, dwelling with much emphasis on ' the covenant of *my* peace '—repeating over and over, ' *my* covenant.'

On Monday night his mind wandered a little. Observing it and checking himself, he said to the members of the family near, ' Why did you not tell me I was raving ? It would have been kind to have said so, and stopped me at once.' Seeing them look sorrowful, he said, with the cheerful tone of one who would encourage and console, ' You know, at the close of life, such things must be.'

On Tuesday he spoke little.   About eight o'clock in the morning he intimated, with some difficulty, that he wished pen and ink. This was to write an inscription on a book to be presented to a friend who, having come from a distance to see him, had called unexpectedly on the preceding evening. Being supported in his bed, he wrote, in fair characters, on the blank leaf of a small Greek Concordance, the following inscription :—

JOANNI W. WRIGHT,
V. D. M., A. M.,
Amico Dilecto,
Hunc Libellum,
Plurim. in insula Madeira
usitatum
(modo G. T. excipias),
D. D. D.
JAC. HALLEY.*

This was about eleven hours before his death. It is with no common measure of delight that we present this inscription to our readers. It is evidence providentially afforded, and most satisfactory in its nature, that it had pleased God to continue to the last the full exercise of his mental powers. The clearness of intellect, and tenderness of heart, which distinguished him through life, appear unimpaired in the hour of departure. Besides the accuracy of the inscription as a whole, there is a very striking incidental proof that memory was at the time in a state of the most perfect activity. It is said, this book was most used in Madeira, ' if you except the Greek Testament.' Now, about two days before, he had dictated the following

* To JOHN W. WRIGHT,
Minister of the Word of God, A.M.,
a beloved friend,
This little book,
most used in the island of Madeira
(if you except the Greek Testament),
is presented by
JAMES HALLEY.

sentence in his Will :—' To the Rev. W—— A——, my Greek Testament, the book which, beyond all question, I have handled most during the last three and a-half years.'   This fact had been distinctly before his mind when he wrote the inscription.

The day of a believer's death is a ' great day.'   It is much to be remembered.   It is the final application to its needy object of the ransom which Emmanuel paid.   It is deliverance to the captive.   It is joy in heaven.   It is glory to God.   We stand still, and look with awe on the departure of a redeemed soul. Surely the Lord is in this place.   The death of a believer is a great thing ; but its greatness is one of the things that ' are not seen.'   Not seen, it cannot be described.   We do not try to describe it.   We leave it to ' the day' to reveal how much glory the Redeemer hath gotten, each time a saved soul has departed from a body of sin and death.   Knowing that the grandeur lies all on the other side looking into eternity, we make no attempt to decorate this side that looks into time.   We present unaltered the notes which his sister has supplied.

' He was much distressed that day.   About three, Mr Gibson called and prayed.   When I asked if he had heard, he said distinctly, " Yes, every word," and thanked him.   About five, Mr J. Smith called and prayed shortly with him.   He said, " My friend, we have been commending you to God." . James answered, " I too endeavour to pray through the one Mediator," and then added with much difficulty, " the spirit is willing but the flesh is very weak."   In an hour, perhaps, afterwards, in a paroxysm of pain and restlessness, he tossed the clothes off him, and would be up.   He said something very indistinctly : I only

caught the word *Emmanuel*, and said, " God with us."
He replied, emphatically, "Yes, *with us ;*" and, so far
as I recollect, these were the last words he uttered.
Yet I believe he was conscious to the very last.   A
minute or two before his departure, he raised his dear
hand, and passed it slowly all over his face.   It was
the cold dew of death stealing over him that he felt.
He seemed satisfied when he ascertained this; and,
replacing his hand on his bosom, almost immediately
expired.'

It was on the evening of Tuesday the 16th March,
1841.   He had entered on the 28th year of his age.

Over the grave where his body rests, a small marble
tablet has been inserted in the wall, charged with the
lesson which his life proclaimed,—

' *Seekest thou great things for thyself? seek them
not.'*

' *One thing is needful.'*

If the moral portraiture of Mr Halley, drawn on the
preceding pages almost wholly by himself, fail to convey to the reader's mind an adequate conception of
the original, we need not expect to make up the deficiency by any additional touches of ours, now that the
artist's own hand is cold.   And yet we feel that something may—that something ought to be done.   In
the intercourse of a long, unbroken, endeared friendship, we enjoyed opportunities of observing and ap-
preciating the character of the departed, of which our
readers, generally speaking, have no experience.   In
these circumstances, if we have marked some features
that are not exhibited in the correspondence, or that
being embodied there might not attract the notice of

a stranger, it seems our duty, as it will be our pleasure, to point them out. From our recollection of his habits, and from his own manuscripts now before us, we possess an abundance of materials to illustrate any faculty of his mind, or aspect of his character, which it may be necessary to recall.

:" In looking to the faculties of mind as they are developed in active life, it is impossible to distinguish with precision, between what is natural and what has been acquired. They are so interwoven with each other in their exercise, that an exact division cannot be made ; nor, though made, would it serve any good end. It may, however, in the present instance, be of use to keep the distinction in view, as affording an intelligible principle to regulate the succession of subjects. There are certain dispositions of mind and features of character which are generally accounted constitutional, which may be modified by circumstances, but cannot be made. Then there are certain other dispositions, and powers, and habits, which are generally spoken of as acquired, which depend on circumstances for their form or their existence. These, according to their objects, may be divided into the merely intellectual, and the directly religious. According to this method, and we care not to defend the logic of the division, the brief illustrations of Mr Halley's character which we propose to submit, would arrange themselves under three distinct heads ; and, if it were necessary to represent each by a single general term, they might be —*his genius, his learning, his faith.* This order, accordingly, will be adopted in the notices that follow. We shall take care, however, when the alternative is presented, rather to break the laws of logic by minging the subjects, than offend against a higher rule by artificially separating things that nature has indissolubly joined.

1. In the department of natural genius—belonging to what is generally accounted constitutional, there were several prominent and strongly marked features.

One characteristic, strengthened doubtless by habit, but certainly inherent in his constitution, was a scrupulous accuracy, amounting sometimes to an extreme fastidiousness,—carried into every thing he undertook, small and great alike. This, we have no doubt, was the foundation of much of his intellectual greatness. Not that this alone was the germ of the abundant fruit that followed. We have often seen an equal appetite for accuracy associated with littleness of mind. Perhaps this conjunction is of more frequent occurrence than the opposite ; and hence many have fallen into the pernicious error of supposing that a certain eccentric disregard of order is an element of mental greatness. It may be true, that the strong developement of the faculty of order has, in many instances, proved abortive, or even appeared ludicrous, where there was not a corresponding solidity of judgment ; but that is no disparagement to the faculty itself. It is essential to the profitable employment of a vigorous understanding where that has been imparted. For want of it, the best gifts of God have often been squandered. Without it the richest talents, ill laid out, yield no adequate return. True, this alone will not constitute or produce greatness of mind ; but it is an efficient element of mental greatness notwithstanding. It is scarcely necessary here to do more than mention this feature of Mr Halley's character. The reader of the Memoir has seen it exemplified in almost every page. In his letters many instances occur of his method of balancing the reasons on both sides of a question. His judgment was always formed upon a careful examination of evidence ; when formed, it was firmly adhered to, and vigorously carried out. Even in familiar intercourse with his friends this habit held its sway, often to their annoyance indeed, but not less for their profit. Every attempt to huddle up things in the easiest way—every effort of indolence to do a thing by guess, which might be done by demonstration,—every indication of a wish to leave a thing half done, when it should be finished, was sure to meet with an instant reproof. There seemed to be a something in his nature,—a string set deep in his constitution, on which every kind of slovenliness and inaccuracy jarred painfully. He could have no sympathy with the disposition to take a thing for granted, and have done with it. He refused to wink at it when it appeared in his friends. Much to their profit he often met it with a stern rebuke.

His memory was extraordinary. He was himself conscious of its strength, and took great delight in exercising it. Several instances of it have been given in the letters written from Madeira. This faculty, too, has sometimes been foolishly underrated. The power of remembering accurately dates, and events, and places, has sometimes appeared dissociated from the power of generalizing facts, and so turning to good account the things stored up in the memory. Observing this, some who would take the easy way of being great, have forthwith set themselves to undervalue a retentive memory. This is a grievous blunder. A etentive memory may have been conjoined in certain cases with a weak understanding; but there is no necessary connection between them. Like the accuracy mentioned before, it is a most powerful instrument of good,—in so far as it is a gift, devoutly to be desired, —in so far as it is a habit, diligently to be cultivated. Mr Halley set a high value on his gift of memory. He knew the use of it, and turned it to good account. With him it was a vast storehouse of facts on which his judgment was continually operating—classifying the materials, drawing general conclusions, and reducing to practice the results.

As might be expected from the manner in which his opinions were formed, they were firmly held. In the *process* of reasoning, he was any thing but dogmatical. He listened with attention to every one's suggestion. He carefully weighed the opinion of the weakest. The argument put forward by himself, he was willing to abandon when another pointed out a defect in it. But when he had in this way deliberately arrived at a conclusion, he was inflexible in maintaining and acting upon it. We have seen him in his earlier days, in one or two cases of very trivial import, adhere to his point with an obstinacy which offended his friends and discomposed himself. This, however, was rare, even in these days, and latterly we did not detect it at all. There was always a firm adherence to his judgment, and often, when occasion required, much severity of expression in announcing it; but this was a thing altogether distinct from obstinacy. It was not clinging to an opinion because it was his own—it was a refusing to surrender it, because, on a careful investigation, he was convinced it was right.

It is very remarkable, that with these sterner qualities, which he never checked, he was yet so much loved in every circle that he entered. There was some appearance of intellectual arrogance in his bearing, and even something that looked like petulance in his manner,— so much of this there was, that it may even have repelled some in the first steps of advance to his friendship ; and yet we never knew any one of his age who *loved* so many, and was *loved* by so many again. He possessed in a very high degree the power of winning the affections of others. The exercise of the benevolent affections afforded him great delight. Any one who reads his letters will perceive that his affections were ardent and lasting. But it is a fact equally necessary to illustrate his character, and not, of course, so directly exhibited in the letters, that the affection of his numerous friends for him was similar in its strength and duration. Even those who have most smarted under his rebuke, loved him to the last. There was something attractive in his tone and manner when application was made to him for advice. No matter who applied. He interested himself in every body's case. It was no fair speaking merely ; it was an evident, and always really efficient concern. His willingness to help, and the frankness with which he did it, conciliated the good-will of almost all who came into contact with him. But while there were many amiable points of his character, even as a scholar, those who knew him as a Christian loved him most. Those who were admitted to unreserved communion with him on spiritual things, were drawn to him by a bond whose strength and sweetness they cannot describe. The humility of the believer possessed a charm over the hearts of his friends, which the brilliant career of the scholar could never exert.

It seems scarcely necessary to allude here to the style of his composition. In the letters the reader will observe the form which his more familiar effusions assumed; and at least one example—the sermon —of his more finished compositions will be found in this volume. We refer to it at present, chiefly to say that Mr Halley's style suffers much by being transferred to paper and read by another. We feel assured that had he lived to see many of his compositions in print, he would have altered and improved it. It is difficult to condescend on the peculiarities we have in view; but one of the most obvious, is the length of the sentences. As spoken or read by himself, with the aid of tone, and pause, and emphasis, which he knew so well how to employ, it was not felt a disadvantage; but to readers generally, his more laboured compositions may appear in some degree defective on this point. If there be in any instance something approaching to heaviness in the structure of the sentence, it is never indistinct—never inelegant. Moreover, the very thing which, on paper, may appear a defect, was in the living voice a positive excellence. Those who were in the habit of hearing him speak, remember that very much of his power lay in the peculiar modulations of his voice. The charm seemed to lie chiefly in laying emphasis on particular words. In his speaking, a very great part of the meaning was conveyed by the skilful management of the emphatic tones, and the form of the sentences afforded scope for the exercise of this talent. In writing letters, he always attempted to represent these tones by marks

x

of emphasis under the words.   Those who had heard
him speak, and were accustomed to his style, could,
in some measure, recall the tones, and the shades of
meaning which the marks were intended to express;
but others could not possibly appreciate them.   In
printing the letters, accordingly, we have suppressed
the greater part of them.   We know he would have
done so himself; for they do not appear in those
manuscripts which he prepared for the press with
his own hand.   To have retained them all, would, in
many cases, have presented the appearance of a page
spotted over with italics, without any corresponding
advantage.   This peculiarity of his eloquence found
freest scope in an address strictly religious.   On any
subject, his spoken language was eminently transpa-
rent ; but on a religious topic, besides the intellectual
precision which convinced the understanding, there
was a glow of fervency which commanded the emotions
of the audience.

The deep humility of his spirit—the overpowering
sense of unworthiness that pressed upon him when he
drew near to God, imparted an indescribable tenderness
to his tones—gave a charm to his eloquence, which
the captivated listener felt, but of which the speaker
was wholly unconscious. The talent of which we speak
might have been a mighty instrument in the preaching
of the Gospel, but it has not pleased God to employ it.
He who possessed it was enabled to ' be still' when
he saw it taken away, and why should we repine ?

Mr Halley had not naturally much of what is called
imagination.   He was sensible of the deficiency, and
latterly exerted himself to have it remedied.   He considered it a talent that might be employed to good

ffect in preaching, and accordingly endeavoured to acquire it. In his discourses he often introduced llustrations from natural objects, which his friends considered just and appropriate, but he always spoke of them as the efforts of a learner. On this point he had no confidence in himself, and would have yielded at once to the judgment of one far his inferior in other things. With the view of cultivating and exercising a sanctified imagination, he was much occupied, during the few last years of his life, in reading sacred poetry. During his residence in Madeira he procured and read almost every collection in the language, tran- scribing with his own hand, in a book, all that par- icularly pleased him. It is remarkable that only once in his life was he ever known to make any attempt to write verses in English. The solitary speci- men has been preserved, and we gladly insert it here. Considered as a first effort, it will certainly prove, that if Mr Halley had not naturally a poetic imagina- tion, his efforts to acquire it had not been made in vain. As he borrowed hymn-books from all who had them, some person lent him one entitled *The Ever- green*. This suggested the subject of the poem. The plan of it—the thought that runs through it, we think is exquisite. Some of the lines towards the be- ginning are not so full of the graces of poetry ; but, so far as our judgment goes, the greater portion of them may challenge a comparison, with regard to the beauty of the conception and the smooth flow of the numbers, with any verses in the language. At all events, whether the reader agree with us as to the merit of the poetry or not, we are sure he may derive benefit from the instruction it conveys :—

' THE EVERGREEN.

' Of plants, that verdant still throughout the changing year are seen,
Come tell me which I most may prize, as —— ——'s evergreen.
The laurel?   No; it twines around the blood-stain'd victor's brow,
And binds the poet's fever'd head in fancy's wildest glow ;
But milder triumphs—o'er myself—are all that I desire ;
And calmer joys, whose kindling spark is drawn from holier fire.
The pine?   It seeks the mountain top and glories in the gale ;
Be't mine, with meek humility to haunt the peaceful vale.
The myrtle?   No; 'twas Venus' flower—the type of earthly love ;
But perish all that does not own the smile of One above.
The ivy leaf?   Ah no ! it speaks of ruin and decline :´
Deceitful is its best embrace ; it clasps to undermine.
The cypress ?   'Twould but teach the heart to dwell in needless gloom ;
Dark guardian of death's victories ! stern watcher o'er the tomb !
The palm ?   Oh yes ! 'tis this I love—type of the single eye ;
Which, bend it as you may, still shoots right upward to the sky.
'Twas borne, to swell the harvest joy, at that glad festival,
By which the prophet has foretold the distant Gentiles' call ;
And when the Son of David once in lowly triumph rode,
Its graceful wavings welcomed him to Salem's loved abode.
It marks, in sacred song, the growth of holy souls, while here,—
And shadows forth their ecstasies, beyond this mortal sphere.
When myrtles cease to speak of love, and ivy of decay ;
When pines no longer clothe the hills, nor warriors snatch the bay ;
When cypress needs no more around the narrow house to wave,
Because the voice of Christ hath called the slumb'rers from the grave ;
Still, still remains the rest above, the deep celestial calm,
The joy of harvest in the heavens—the bright unfading *palm*.

' Lev. xxiii. 40 ; Zech. xiv. 16-20 ; John xii. 13 ; Psal. xcii. 12 ; Rev. vii. 9.'

His natural temperament was sanguine and sprightly.
Even though he had never been actuated by a holier
principle, he possessed enough of constitutional enterprise to undertake any task which perseverance and
desperate exertion could accomplish.   In consciousness
of strength, he sometimes allowed the latest possible
moment to arrive before he commenced his preparations.   When competing for the Lansdowne prize, as
the examination drew near, and great part of each day
was necessarily consumed in classes and private teaching, he had no alternative but to borrow from the
night.   During the last fortnight, except on Saturday

and Sabbath, he sat up till four in the morning, and was called again at six.   When out of bed, he did not consider himself fully awake till the affusion of cold water on his head had completely aroused him.   The excitement of study then kept him alert till the next morning.   His sprightliness was one reason why his strength lasted so long.   It acted like sinovia on the joints of his body.   It was the elastic medium which deadened for a time the shocks given by an over-active mind to the material framework.   And, we doubt not, when that framework was so shattered that nothing but the direct interposition of the Almighty Builder could rear it again, this buoyancy of spirit was one reason why life lingered so long.   Though the sprightliness of his latter days was often the result of benevolence—an effort of kindness to lighten the grief of those whom he tenderly loved.—yet it was usually spontaneous.   Amongst many things calculated to depress his spirits—the crushing of his fondest hopes—the suspension of his studies—the conviction that a malady, for which man knows no cure, was his disease—the likelihood that it would land him in the ' place where they bury strangers,' in a land that had no endearments to him—and, deeper than all, the prevailing dissatisfaction with which he regarded his own spiritual state—amidst all these causes of depression, it was wonderful how the playfulness of his mind would glance out in a letter to a familiar friend, and how his countenance would brighten when an acquaintance stepped into the room.   Like asphaltus in eastern lakes, this gaiety was deep in his nature, and portions of it always floated on the surface, however dark and bitter the depths below.

2. Proceeding now to notice his acquirements, we feel that this is not the place to enlarge on his *learning*, properly so called. To give evidence and illustration of it to any great extent, would not suit the plan of this volume ; and to make many assertions regarding it, would not be profitable. At college he was looked upon as a prodigy throughout. In extreme youth, he was exposed to all the temptations incident to one who is the ' admired of all observers.' By the special mercy of God, he was kept from falling. The learning he acquired at college, he always kept in its proper place. He never considered it as an end. He laboured to acquire it, in order that he might employ it as an instrument. When his views were intelligently and devoutly directed toward the ministry of the Gospel, he employed his previously acquired knowledge with extraordinary zeal and success, in prosecuting the studies that are more immediately connected with his destined office. His progress in this department was less generally known, but not less wonderful than his earlier efforts had been. Indeed, we think his learning was as far above a medium in theology as in the classics. The former accomplishment was matter of greater surprise to those who knew it than the latter. It is comparatively common to find a stripling skilled in the languages ; it is rare to find such a one a sound and deeply-read divine. His reading was immense ; and he was able from memory to give an intelligent account of any book he had ever read. His vast stores of knowledge were always ready to be turned to account. No one could be long near him without discovering that he was an extraordinary person ; and he certainly was not guilty of making an ostentatious

display. The natural kindness of his disposition was a great means of bringing out his learning. He was ready to assist every one. He took an evident pleasure in turning his information to account for the benefit of another. Yet he did not in such a case assume the air of a superior. In whatever form the sin of pride may have beset him, there was certainly no manifestation of it here. Of all that he ever assisted, we never knew or heard of him giving offence by his manner of doing it.

Instead of making any attempt to enumerate the branches, and estimate the amount of Mr Halley's learning, we shall venture to insert here another specimen of his Greek versification. We give it, not so much from any judgment we have formed of its absolute merits, as from the circumstances in which it was written. We do not present it to challenge the inspection of critics, on the ground that we have examined it and found no fault ; yet we believe hostile criticism cannot touch it, because it is the product of Mr Halley's pen. It was written in a time of sickness, at Madeira, where he had no critical apparatus, and so far as we know, not a single classical book. We repeat, that the object we have in view is quite independent of the absolute excellence of the version. Whatever opinion may be formed of its character, its existence in these circumstances is evidence of a very retentive memory, and an uncommon familiarity with the vocables of the language. Though a scholar should say (which we do not anticipate) that it is not well done, he will still be left to wonder how, in these circumstances, it was done at all. The subject—the

third chapter of the book of Job—accords, alas! too
well with the situation in which he was placed.

Job, chap. iii. ver. 3–26. ·

Ολοιτο γ᾿ ἦμαρ, ᾧ το φῶς ειδον ταλας·
νυξ, εὖτ᾿ εχλειον γενεσιν αρσενος τοκου.
σκοτος γενοιτο· μηδ᾿ ανωθεν ευμενῶς
Θεος σφε λευσσοι, μηδ᾿ ετ᾿ επιλαμποι φαος.
σκια θανασιμος κεῖνο, και σκοτος, χρανοι·
νεφος καλυπτοι, χἠμερας φοϨοῖ ζοφος.
την νυκτ᾿ εκεινην παντελῶς σκοτος λαϨοι·
μη προστεθειη ταισιν ἡμεραις ετους,
μητ᾿ εις αριθμον εισιοι μην·ων ποτε.
ιδου! μονη λειποιτο νυξ κεινη· χαρας
φωνημ᾿ εσελθοι μηδεν· αλλ᾿ αραις πικραις
βαλλοιεν, οἱ, φῶς ἡμερας κακῶς λεγειν
αει προχειροι. στονοεν ιειῖσιν μελος.
ταυτην επεισφροντ᾿ αστρα κρυφθειη σκοτῳ·
ζητοῖ ματην φῶς, μηδ᾿ εῶ πρωτην ιδω.
ἐθ᾿ οὑνεχ᾿ ουκ εχλεισε νηδυος θυρας,
ευδ᾿ αχος εκρυψεν ομματων εμων απο.
τί δ᾿ ουκ εθνησκον ευθυ προσϨλεψας φαος;
τί πνεῦμ᾿ εμεινε; τί δε μ᾿ εσωσε γουνατα;
τί μ᾿ ελαϨε κολπος; η τροφην εδω γαλα;
εὑτω γαρ ὑπνον ἦγον αν προκειμενος,
αμπαυμα τ᾿ ειῖχον ἡδυ, των πονων διχα,
ξυν τοις τυραννοις, τοις τε βουλευταις χθονος,
μεσση ᾿ν ερηᾳω δωμαθ᾿ οἱ σφιν εκτισαν,——
η κοιρανοις, πλησασιν αργυρου δομους·
η, κρυφιον ὡς γεννημα, μη ᾿Ϩλεπον φαος.
Εκεῖ ταρασσους᾿ ουκεθ᾿ οἱ κακοι χθονα,
εκεῖ δε τοις καμουσιν αναπαυσις πελει.
αμπαυμα κοινον εστι δεσμωταις εκεῖ,
βιας ἱν᾿ ουπορ᾿ οψ διερχεται πικρα.
οἱ καρτεροι κευθουσιν, οἱ μικροι θ᾿ ὁμοῦ·

κεῖται δ' ὁ δοῦλος, δεσποτῶν ελευθερος.
τί δυστυχεῖ φῶς, δυσκολῳ ζωη μενει ;
τον ὀην αποντα θανατον ὁς μολεῖν καλεῖ,
ζητεῖ δ', ὀπως τις αργυρον θηρωμενος,—
τυμϐον δ' αν εύρων, χαρμονης τεινει βοην ;
ὀτῳ κελευθος κρυπτεται, Θεος δε νιν
παντη καθειρξε ; πριν φαγεῖν γαρ ερχεται
εμοι στεναγμος· ῥεῖ δ', ὑδωρ ὁπως, βοη.
ὃ γαρ μαλιστ' εδεισα, τοῦθ' ἠκει σθενει·
εληλυθεν τε δεινος εξαιφνης φοϐος.
ου γαρ μ' εθελγε θυμος ελπισιν κεναις,
ουτ' εσχολαζον· αλλ' επεσκηψεν κακον.

J. H.

MADEIRA, 13th December 1839.

3. Having enumerated some of Mr Halley's *gifts* and *acquirements*, it remains that we notice also his *graces*. Having seen what Nature did for him, and what Art, it remains that we take some account of that was wrought by the Spirit of God. We would like to bring before the reader again, in a few words, some of the more prominent traits of his religious character. We do not attempt to draw a finished portrait; we merely propose to direct attention to some of the more strongly marked peculiarities.

We proceed upon the assumption, that the reader has seen in the preceding Memoir, evidence that Mr Halley was sound in the faith—that he believed in Christ to the saving of the soul. On this supposition we go on with our notices. We do not wait either to show what a sound faith is, or to show that he possessed it; we proceed at once to mention some of the special characteristics of his faith.

One thing very evident from his history is, there

was much of *humility* in his religion. Besides the
orthodox belief, that by the works of the law no flesh
living shall be justified, he felt deeply his own worthlessness in the sight of God. The strong expressions
that frequently occur regarding his own unworthiness
are certainly not words of course in his lips. Like
others to whom God has given the grace of repentance, he knew sin best as it existed in himself, and
therefore he accounted himself the chief of sinners.
He accounted others better than himself. This grace
was peculiarly beautiful in him, where it was joined
with so much of intellectual superiority. The bril-
liancy of his natural genius served to set off to advantage the childlike humility which the Divine Spirit had
wrought in his soul. It was this, we think chiefly,
that gave the peculiar charm to his prayers. Along
with the clearness of conception, and felicity of expression, which were to be expected from the character
of his mind, there was a depth and tenderness of tone
—the product of a pervading spiritual humility—that
solemnized and captivated the listener. As a consequence of this judgment against himself, he was kept
at the remotest possible distance from that presumptuous sin—arrogance of language or manner in a
creature's prayer to God. Like Nehemiah, he was
accustomed to fear God as the 'Great and terrible,'
even 'in keeping covenant and mercy.'

His *belief in the Scriptures*, as the revealed will of
God, seems never to have wavered. No doubts beset
him. In this case, as in others of minor import, his
belief was based on a most searching examination of
evidence. It was the character of his mind to do this.
He could not with ease retain any opinion, while the

east uncertainty attached to the grounds of it. The craving for evidence and accuracy seemed to be an instinct of his nature. Whatever difficulties he felt in matters of faith, they all related to his own experience. In all his fears, he was ever ready to acknowledge that 'God is true.' His reception of the Christian revelation was pre-eminently a *reasonable* service. There was certainly as much of the *rational* in his religion as any sceptic could desire; and yet the effect of all his reasonings was only to stablish more securely the foundations of his faith. It was most refreshing to converse with him on the evidences of Christianity. He was thoroughly acquainted with every department of the subject; and so perfect was his own conviction of the truth, that he habitually regarded infidelity, apart altogether from its sinfulness, as the very extreme of intellectual perversion and blindness. It is a remarkable fact, illustrating the strength of his own confidence in the ' reason ' of his faith, that he wrote out and read a complete course on the Evidences to scholars in his Sabbath class.*

Another feature of Mr Halley's religious character, which must have pressed itself on the notice of the reader throughout the Memoir, is his *love of the Scriptures.* In his study of the Scriptures there is a beautiful union of the scholar and the Christian. His search into the Bible was at once critical, as became a student,—and devotional, as became a sinner seeking there the words of eternal life. While, from a sense of duty, he applied his mind to the understanding of its doctrines and the solution of its difficulties, he was drawn to it by a desire which nothing else could satisfy

* At a separate meeting on Saturday evening.

—a hungering for the bread of life. His Bible is now lying before us, and reminds us how richly the Word of God dwelt in him.   We find a pleasure in exploring the Bible that has belonged to a devoted Scripture student.   It is not merely because it has been the chosen companion of a saint now at rest with God; but because it has many traits of character and little incidents of history to tell.   There is a sort of oryctology connected with it—organic remains, which, like the fossils on a larger scale, tell more than meets the eye at first.   Turning over the leaves of an old Bible, we have tried to draw inferences from the sprig of thyme, or the hawthorn blossom, or the May-flies entombed between its leaves.   We have formed conjectures of the season of the year, and the likely place where that Bible has been read ; and have found our way back to summer evenings, and sequestered spots consecrated by meditation on the Word of God.   Mr Halley's Bible is a common school copy, and the state in which he has left it, after manifold perusal, gives incidental illustration of some minor points of his character.   Though it had been the most costly edition, greater care could not have been taken to preserve the pages smooth and unsullied.   There is not a single corner folded or dog-eared.   But almost every page is studded with delicate markings of the pencil or the pen, with frequent annotations in a very small but legible handwriting.   In studying the Scriptures, his object was to master the meaning of every sentence, and the coherence of every paragraph.   Accordingly, the page is frequently interlined with more exact renderings of the original, and brief explanatory glosses. He sought to be so mighty in the Scriptures, that no gainsayer or heretic should ever disturb him; and that no inquirer should leave him with his difficulties unresolved. At the same time, he searched the Scriptures to find food for his own soul, and every passage is marked which, in the perusal, had brought him clearer light, or ministered consolation. A favourite exercise, and one for which his tenacious memory gave him singular advantages, was to search out the texts that bear on some given doctrine or duty. In this pursuit, he refused the aid of Concordances and marginal references—the passages collected and written down being all the result of his own industry. Perhaps to this employment he was partly stimulated by the well-known pleasure which men find in exercising a faculty strongly developed. Doubtless he found a gratification in feats of memory; but the field for its exertion was chosen by the controlling presence of that new taste, which neither flesh nor blood had given him, but his Father in heaven. The simple Word of Truth was sweet, and he found satisfaction in amassing stores of it.

Several of these accumulations of texts on particular subjects have been preserved. Some of them are in a very exact logical order; others are left in the process of collection under a few general heads. We shall give some account of one of these, drawn up at Madeira, and extending to a considerable length. The subject is *affliction*. It is introduced by a short preface written in Greek, and dated Funchal, December 1, 1837. The substance of the preface is an acknowledgment of distinguishing mercies to himself, a dedication of all to the service of God in the Gospel, and a prayer. The titles of the several divisions are written very happily in Greek, and the texts marked below—a few of the first words of each being written out to indicate its import. The texts are numerous, some of the heads occupying several pages. We shall give the titles (subjoining a literal translation), with the first two texts under each. A few of them have English mottoes. He does not seem to have determined the order, as no numerals are attached. We present them as they are found in the book.

1. A Christian without affliction is only like a soldier on parade.—FELIX NEFF.

'Η θλιψις—ὁτι ουκ αποφυγητον.
. (Affliction—that it cannot be avoided.)
Gen. iii. 17.—In sorrow shalt thou eat.
Job v. 6, 7.—Although affliction, &c.

2. Της θλιψεως—αιτια, και εργατης.
　　(Of affliction—the cause, an worker.)
Rom. vi. 23.—The wages of sin is death.
Psal. lxvi. 10, 11.—*Thou* oh God hast proved us.

3. Της θλιψεως—τελος (εν τῳ Θεου νοηματι).
　(Of affliction—the end (in the intention of God.))
Psal. xciv. 12, 13.—Blessed is the man whom thou chastenest, &c.
1 Cor. xi. 32.—But when we are judged we are chastened, &c.

4. Της θλιψεως—καρπος (εν αγιοις φερομενος).
　　(Of affliction—the fruit (in saints produced.))
Psal. cxix. 67.—Before I was afflicted, &c.
Psal. cxix. 71.—It is good for me that I have been, &c.

5. Εν θλιψει—εις οντινα ιδειν οφειλομεν.
　　(In affliction—to whom we must look.)
Psal. xlvi. 1.—God is our refuge and strength, &c.
Psal. lvii. 1.—In the shadow of thy wings will I make my refuge, &c.

6. Why should a living man complain ! A sinner has no *right*; a saint no *reason*.—JOHN NEWTON.

Την θλιψιν—όπως φερειν δει.
(Affliction—how it is necessary to bear it.)
Heb. xii. 5, 6.—My son despise not, &c.,—nor faint.
Prov. iii. 11, 12.—My son despise not—neither be weary.

7. Εκ της θλιψεως—αποφυγαι.
(Out of affliction—escapes.)
Psal. xviii. 16.—*He* sent from above and took me, &c.
Psal. xxx. 2.—Oh Lord my God, I cried unto thee, and
thou hast, &c.

8. Την θλιψιν—εκφυγοντα, ὁ,τι δει ποιειν.
(Affliction—having escaped from it, what you must do.)
Psal. lxvi. 13.—I will pay my vows, which my lips, &c.
Psal. xxii. 22-25.—I will declare thy name, &c.

9. Εν τη θλιψει—ευχαι αγιων.
(In affliction—prayers of saints.)
Psal. cii. 24.—I said, O my God, take me not, &c.
Psal. xxii. 11.—Be not far off, for trouble is near, &c.

10. Τοις θλιβομενοις—επαγγελιαι.
(To the afflicted—promises.)
Psal. xxviii. 14.—Wait on the Lord, be of good, &c.
Isa. xxvi. 3, 4.—Thou wilt keep—trust ye, &c.

11. Ἡ θλιψις—ʼως ολιγοχρονιον.
(Affliction—that it is of short duration.)
Psal. xxx. 5.—His anger endureth, &c. : weeping may
endure, &c.
Isa. liv. 7.—For a small moment have I forsaken thee.

12. Ακεσματα τῳ φοβῳ του θανατου.
(Cures for the fear of death.)
Isa. xxv. 8.—He will swallow up death in victory.
Isa. xxvi. 19.—Thy dead men—awake and sing.

13. The Lord save us from the greatest of all afflictions—an affliction lost.—BRIDGES.

Θλιψις—ακαρπος.
(Affliction—unfruitful.)
Jer. ii. 30.—In vain have I smitten your children, &c.
Isa. xxvi. 11.—Lord, when thy hand is lifted up, they
will not see.

The Bible to which we have referred, bears testi-

mony to another and an earlier taste.   It contains
many illustrations and parallel expressions from the
classics.   He had purposely left behind him, when
he went to Madeira, all his Greek and Latin books;
but the treasures of their language were laid up in his
memory, and ready on every occasion to be applied.
In his devotional, as well as critical reading of the
New Testament, he preferred the original.   In the
Old Testament, when not engaged in critical inquiry,
he employed the translation.

We conclude the notice of his scriptural studies,
with the motto inscribed on the fly-leaf of his English
Bible.   ' With what a mixture of fear, reverence, and
holy joy should we open the Bible ! the book of truth
and happiness ! God's heart opened to man ; and yet
the whole, and every part of it secreted from him, and
hid under an impenetrable veil, till he opens his heart
to God !   THO. ADAM.'

Mr Halley was eminently a man of *prayer*. What
we speak of is not merely that he possessed in a high
degree the gift of prayer, and that, in point of fact,
he very frequently exercised it.   We would have the
reader to observe that prayer with him was a *real*
asking of things that he needed, in the belief that in
this way they would be obtained.   He prayed much
—very much ; but it was not because he spurred
himself up to his duty ; it was a yielding to an irre-
pressible desire.   It was not the calculation of a dictated orthodoxy, ' I must pray;' it was the simple
filial trust imparted by the Spirit in his regenerating
work, ' I am in need—God is in Christ the hearer of
prayer, I will cry to him.'   As an evidence of his
belief in the efficacy of prayer, the reader will remem-

ber how frequently and how eagerly he applied for a place in the prayers of others. The desire pervaded his mind; he did not need to call it to remembrance. It was habitually present; and it comes out wherever an occasion is offered, in something equivalent to the apostle's fervent appeal, ' Brethren, pray for us.' Looking to the number and the form of these requests, and the manner in which they protrude themselves in his letters, whatever the subject be, we think they give indication that they proceed from one who really has an 'expectation from the Lord.' We have before us now a very remarkable manuscript, which throws much light on his devotional habits. We are informed, that during his residence in Madeira, he kept it always in his Bible. It seems to have been his manual of devotion; and a very unique prayer-book it is. It consists of four octavo pages, closely written over in Greek. The characters are very minute, and it contains a great amount of matter. By employing the Greek he contrives to put many things in a very short space, and also to throw a veil of secrecy over the sanctuary of his devotions. After his death, when his sister got possession of the document, she presented it to one of his friends, eagerly asking ' What is that?' adding, ' he had it always in his hands.' It contains an immense accumulation of topics, set down evidently for the purpose of aiding his memory in prayer. They are arranged under four heads, with the following titles :—

1. Αἱ ἐμαὶ ἁμαρτίαι—κατα τας εντολας τεταγμεναι.
(My sins—set in order against the commandments.)

2. Αἱ ευεργεσιαι Θεου προς εμε τον ἁμαρτωλον· πλειους η κατ' ανθρωπον αριθμεῖν.
(The mercies of God to me the sinner; more than can be numbered in the language of men.)

Y

3. Τα το βαρος των αμαρτιων αυξανοντα.
(Things that add to the weight of my sins.)

4. Τα προσευχων πλειστων δεομενα.
(Things that demand the most of my prayers.)

Under the *first* head there are ten separate lists of sins, arranged according to the order of the commandments. Many of the things noted give evidence of great tenderness of conscience, and· a very enlightened view of the depth and spirituality of the law of God. We can recognise allusions to several events of his life, which came under our notice at the time. We have found it very instructive to observe from this paper what view he took of them in his nearest approaches to God, and in prospect of eternity. For example, certain quarrels which we remember well, arising out of disputed questions at college, are set down as sins to be confessed. The thing noted, is the anger into which on these occasions he was betrayed. They are placed under the sixth commandment. In some cases the names of the parties are written in full ; in others, only the initials. The *second* head, beginning, Βρεταννος γενεα, και Βρεταννων Σκωτος κ. τ. λ. contains the materials of thanksgiving. The enumeration of blessings is very full. The expressions are always brief ; sometimes elegant. It includes a very long catalogue of the names of his friends ; generally specifying some characteristic of each, which was beneficial to him. The *third* is a list of peculiar aggravations. The *fourth* specifies things to be most frequently asked for in prayer. The first part of it is occupied with wants that more immediately concern himself, such as, ' To possess my soul in patience—to know my adoption—a peaceful departure.' The latter portion contains another list of his friends, for whom he was in the habit of praying by name.

' Behold he prays.' This mark of the new creature certainly appeared conspicuous in Mr Halley, from the time that he was first brought to a knowledge of the truth.

Another thing which the reader must have marked as a prominent feature of his religious character, is a frequent self-examination carried to an extraordinary degree of minuteness—a consequent despondency as to his spiritual state—and a writing of bitter things against himself. Closely connected with this, was his practice of binding himself by solemn resolutions, consecrated by prayer, to a certain line of conduct—and then making bitter reflections on discovering his shortcomings. In these points we humbly think he fell into error; but on examining his manuscripts, we find it would be very difficult to point out where the error lay. We do not find, from any of the lengthened records of his self-examination, that he was theologically wrong. Throughout them all his mind is clear on the doctrine of justification by the free grace of God. Always when he is seeking into his own heart, he has a correct and distinct conception of what should be sought there. He never loses sight of the truth, that a sinner must look to Christ for *all* his salvation. We cannot detect error in any of his examinations or covenants. On the contrary, a remarkably clear conception of the covenant of grace runs through them all. We apprehend the difficulty must be solved in this way. It had been given him to know the Gospel—to receive Christ his Saviour. By the teaching and power of the Holy Spirit, he had been delivered from seeking justification by the works of the law, and made willing to submit to the righteousness of faith. Having learned the truth, and received it, he was kept from falling. He held fast the beginning of his confidence firm unto the end. But he did not live up to his privileges ; he did not walk wisely for his own comfort. Practically, too much of his time and energy was given to looking in upon his own heart, and too little to looking out unto Jesus. It is not that he was wrong, either when he looked inward upon himself, or when he looked outward upon the Saviour. He was right in both. When he looked to himself, he sought only for what should be found there,—evidence of his own sinfulness, and the marks of a living faith. When he looked to the Saviour, he gave Him the honour due—he looked to Christ as all his salvation. The error lay not in this exercise, or in that ; but in a wrong apportioning of the two. He did not search his own heart for what was not to be found there ; but searched it comparatively *too much*. He did not look unto Jesus with a wrong conception of his person and office ; but looked to Him comparatively *not enough*. We are willing to confess that he ensnared himself in these examinations ; but we are anxious to show that not one of these was in itself wrong. We can see a want of wisdom in his practice, which actually diminished his peace ; but no error in his faith that could endanger his safety.

One other peculiarity of Mr Halley's faith we recall to the reader's remembrance—his habitual strong desire for assurance of his own peace with God. On this subject we do not venture to enlarge. We have done our duty, however, in placing upon record, again and again, Mr Halley's views and desires in regard to it. From the period of his residence in Edinburgh, his friends observed that this desire had been formed, and had taken firm possession of his mind. It is first developed in a letter written in the summer of 1837.* From that time forward it occupied much of his thoughts. It was always in his own prayer; and always formed part of instructions to friends, when he condescended on particulars in asking theirs. Latterly, without at all losing the desire, or checking the prayer, he began to fear that he had sinned in seeking too eagerly his own peace, instead of simply looking to Jesus, and waiting upon the Lord. To the last he never would say in so many words that he had attained the object of his desire; but on several occasions he said or wrote what was equivalent. On the occasion of the bursting of a blood-vessel in his lungs, when he thought his departure was near, he records it thankfully, that he trusted in Christ, and 'felt no fear.' In the list of blessings which constituted the materials of his song of praise, one is ' ολιγη ουρανου ἐλπις'—'some hope of heaven.' Towards the close of his days there were many expressions which, taking into account his extreme caution on these subjects, his friends accounted equivalent to a good hope through grace—a hope that his life was hid with Christ in God. One thing is certain, his faith failed not. He who in sovereignty saw meet to keep a cloud between his own countenance and the uplifted eye of his servant, graciously preserved from fainting that servant's soul, and so strengthened his faith, that it held by the Saviour to the last without the aid of joyous emotion.

* Page 107.

The word that lingered latest on his dying lips was,
'God with us.' The change came, and he was with
God.

And now that we have endeavoured to mark some
of the graces that appeared in a believer's life, let no
one mistake our meaning, or misrepresent our design.
We have not tried to make a man righteous. We
have not tried to present a portrait of unsullied virtue.
We have begun and carried on our delineations on the
assumption that the subject of them was originally
and practically deformed by sin; and we have been
pointing to the work of the Lord in subduing the
power of evil, and imparting here and there features
of life to one who had been dead. We have not been
depicting his sins so minutely as his graces. But
our design in this was not to represent him faultless.
Our object was neither to magnify his good nor his
evil; but to show the 'work of the Lord' in making
many things beauteous where all had been deformity
—in causing trees of righteousness to grow and flourish
in a barren land. So far from denying that there was
evil in the soul of our departed friend, we confess, as
he did, that all was evil. In him dwelt no good thing.
We have shown that some good things were put in—
and shown, too, that the good things were 'the planting of the Lord, that He may be glorified.'

APPENDIX.

A—*Page* 33.

EXTRACT FROM REVIEW OF 'MITCHELL'S ACHARNENSES OF ARISTOPHANES.'

. . . .
WE have already intimated our conviction that the editor's
admiration of the Spartan character and institutions is
extravagantly great, and we find this error to be completely pervasive of the notes of his present performance.
If he is indeed an adopted son of Athens, he seems to be
an ungrateful offspring of so venerable a parent ; and although he is well acquainted with her ancient progeny
who sang her praise—although he has drawn much delight
from the fresh fountains of her immortal literature, he
loses no opportunity of expressing his dislike of her institutions and inhabitants. Yet, so far as this kind of poeti-
cal ingratitude is concerned, we could easily forgive the
crime ; but we cannot so easily understand the force of
prejudice, or the obliquity of intellectual vision on this one
subject, which has led so accomplished a scholar to evince
such a thorough-going preference of Sparta to Athens.

Mr Mitford has been termed, with equal point and justice, by Mr Patterson, in his Essay on the Character of the
Athenians (p. 177), a Philippizing historian : Mr Mitchell
certainly merits the analogous title of a *Laconizing* critic.
In his introduction, in particular, he presses to a preposterous length his notions of Lacedæmonian superiority. It
were but little to assign to the Dorians the palm of ancient
descent and traditionary fame, or to denominate the Spartans a nation of gentlemen ; it were well even to give a
temperate and restricted preference to their form of government ; but it is too much to make their policy the
subject of such unqualified praise, to sanction—by an ex-
pressive silence—the ideas (we had almost said the whims)
of Müller on the subject of the Spartan literature, and to

leave nearly unnoticed the claims which Athens had on the gratitude of Greece, and on the admiring remembrance of all posterity. We do not mean to deny that there were points in the Spartan character, which tended greatly to insure the stability of Lacedæmon's government, and the extension of her empire ; there were certainly a decision in fixing on measures, and an indomitable perseverance in pursuing them, which, as opposed to the fickleness and nameless inconsistency of the Athenians, proved the very pillars of Spartan pre-eminence. But what else was there which could make the Lacedæmonians proper subjects of such lofty eulogium ? Was it the cultivation of the arts of civil and domestic comfort ? In these the Athenians are acknowledged, by the unanimous voice of a not too indulgent antiquity, to have taken precedence of all other European nations. Was it the uniform direction towards war, which was given to all the energies of Spartan citizens ? This is certainly, in many—and these the highest —points of view, a very questionable excellence ; nor will the restless ambition of Attica, to which the historian must refer her downfall, and which the philanthropist must bewail as having proved for many years the scourge of Greece, form any apology for the cold-blooded and hard-hearted ferocity which too often marked the Lacedæmonian warfare. And where, after all, is the boasted superiority of the Dorians in the art of war ? Few indeed were the great captains that arose among them,—not one for ten who shine in the annals of Athens ; their best generals were often mere pigmies, when compared with those men of genius and renown who led her armies to victory ; the crafty Pausanius, and the cunning Lysander, perhaps even the chivalrous Brasidas, the heroic Agesilaus, and the devoted Leonidas, make but a tiny figure in the page of history, beside the bold Miltiades and the subtle Themistocles, the versatile Alcibiades, the patriotic Thrasybulus, and the philosophic Xenophon.

But will it be urged that there was something in the constitution of Lacedæmon, and in the habits of the people, which produced among them a more sterling morality, and gave assurance to the other states, that by them ' they might reasonably expect to be left masters of their own, and to be treated on general occasions with courtesy and kindness ?' (*Introd.*, p. 9.) It will be hard, at least, to draw this inference from Grecian history. From the great historian of the Peloponnesian war, spoken of by Mitford

Hist., vol. iii. p. 9), whom Mr Mitchell will consider a most competent authority, as possessed 'of uncommon abilities, and still more uncommon impartiality,' we could only deduce, regarding the character of the Spartans, that it was one of almost unredeemed selfishness,—cool, calculating, grasping, revengeful. It is absolutely laughable to find Mr Mitchell ranking among the virtues which prevailed in Sparta, 'a sense of what belonged to others,' when we reflect, that stealing was there a polite accomplishment, sanctioned by the state, and most sedulously and conscientiously cultivated by the subjects. And nearly as great was our amusement, when we read his glowing invectives against the oppression which Athens practised upon her foreign dependencies and tributary states, and reflected, at the same time, that his much-loved and much-praised Lacedæmon, was not less arbitrary and severe towards her *Periœci*, whom she uniformly treated with as much haughtiness as ever William the Conqueror and his Norman aristocracy displayed towards the Saxon serfs, on whom they trampled. The land which the members of this degraded caste held, was taxed by the state (*i. e.*, the Spartan chiefs), and thus applied to confirm the dominion of their masters ; they were bereft of all the rights of citizenship ; they had no vote in the legislative assembly ; and intermarriage between them and the Dorian conquerors of Laconia was a thing unlawful and unknown. The state of society, therefore, resembled that which pervaded Europe during the middle ages,—a feudal aristocracy ruling proudly over the subject tillers of the soil, and concerting all their measures for the secure maintenance of a jealous and insolent domination.' It is hardly necessary to add, that, if the Spartans treated the Periœci ill, much more harsh was their treatment of the Helots. The common story about their exhibition of the intoxicated Helot, as a warning to their children, while it does honour to their temperance, affixes an indelible blot on their humanity. So cruelly and tyrannically was their power in general employed, that the Helots were always on the watch for the misfortunes of their lords ; and such, accordingly, was the danger which naturally and most deservedly ensued to the Spartans themselves, that, when an alliance was made with Athens, after the battles of Delium and Amphipolis, one express condition was, that the Athenians should assist them in the event of a revolt of their slaves (*Thucyd.*, v. 23), a condition which, in consequence of the

unusually mild slave-system of Athens, needed not to be
made reciprocal.

Athens has been often upbraided on account of her
cruelty in war ; and these upbraidings she certainly did
much to deserve.   But the fault was one rather of the age
than of the individual nation ; the spirit of the times was
prone to military severity ; and the blame, in the cases
where Athens erred, is by no means imputable to her form
of government ; for the stern oligarchy of Lacedæmon was
not guiltless of similar enormities.   Witness the gratui-
tous and wanton punishment inflicted on those brave but
unfortunate men, who had been compelled, by the vicissi-
tudes of warfare, to lay down their arms, and who, after
languishing long in the prisons of Attica, had returned,
full of new hopes and aspirations, to the land of their
fathers.   That land received them ; but it was only to
blast their hopes, by decreeing, on the much-abused plan
of state necessity, that they should be degraded from the
rank—in many cases of high eminence—which they had
formerly held, rendered incapable of office in the Lacedæmonian government, and deprived of the right of traffic,—
a right which was not denied even to the despised Periœci.
(*Thucyd.*, v. 34.)   And witness also, in still more melancholy confirmation of the truth of our remark, the conduct
of the Spartans, when Brasidas required an addition to
his forces, in order to foment and strengthen rebellion
among the Thracian dependencies of Athens.   Afraid to
weaken their internal defences, and unwilling to abandon
a design which the bravery and address of Brasidas might
be expected admirably to accomplish, they fell upon an
expedient of state policy, for the atrocity of its deceit perhaps unmatched in history.   They proclaimed to the
Helots, that as many of them as thought themselves able
for the duties, and worthy of the dignity of Spartan citizens, should come forward, and submit themselves to a
trial for this proud distinction.   Two thousand being selected, they were adorned with chaplets, and went round
the temples, in solemn procession, in the guise of freemen.
But their imaginary freedom was of short duration.   It
was from men of courage and enterprise that danger was
apprehended ; to find out the most elastic and aspiring
minds among the Helots the lying proclamation had been
made ; and very speedily, therefore, the chosen two thousand mysteriously disappeared.   (*Thucyd.*, iv. 80.)

The greatest reproach of Athens unquestionably is—

hat, while she was the most wealthy and powerful, she
was also the most dissolute of Grecian cities ; and much,
on the other hand, has been said of Lacedæmonian virtue.
What the public virtue of the Spartans sometimes was, we
have already partially shown. Of their private life less
by far is known than of that of the Athenians ; and perhaps to this, if we may draw any inference from the disclosures which are made with regard to other nations, by
unrolling the records of domestic life, they may be indebted for their escape from similar—although, we doubt not,
gentler—censure. Enough, however, appears in the scattered hints of ancient history to assure us, that, about the
close of the Peloponnesian war, the austerity of Spartan
morals suffered a grievous declension, insomuch that Xenophon, or the anonymous author of the treatise on the
Laconian constitution (cap. xiv. § 3), declares, that those
who had formerly feared to be seen with money in their
possession, now openly plumed themselves on their riches
and grandeur. Wealth attended upon conquest ; luxury
and still increasing avarice grew with the growth of their
resources ; and these, superinduced upon the hard and
griping selfishness of Sparta, formed a character scarcely
less unlovely than that of the now degenerate Athenians.
And what must have been the state of morality in Lacedæmon, when (almost as the direct consequence of those
laws of feudal heritage, which made the Doric lords of the
soil 'a nation of gentlemen') we find it recorded by Poly-
bius as an ancient and prevailing practice, for two or three
brothers to marry one wife, and to rear her offspring as
their common family !

But, although the Spartans seem not greatly to have
excelled the Athenians in morals, perhaps their religion
may have been less exceptionable. So at least thinks Mr
Mitchell, and edifies his readers with a long discussion of
the simplicity and purity of Lacedæmonian idolatry. Indeed, were it not for the uniform and strongly marked
veneration which he evinces for the Scriptures, whenever
he has occasion to mention them, his introduction would
almost have led us to suspect, that, in reference at least
to the worship of that Apollo, whose companions were the
graces, he could sympathize with Mr Gibbon's encomiums
on the 'elegant mythology' of the ancients. But, while
we are bound completely to exonerate him from the suspicion of any such perverse sympathy, we cannot but express our wonder at even the *comparative* praises which he

lavishes on the religion of Lacedæmon. Wherein consisted the superiority of that superstition which revered Jupiter Hellanius, or him who was the coryphæus of the muses, to that which bowed before the bounteous Ceres, or Jove's quick-eyed daughter, the guardian power of Athens? Was it in its deeper solemnity? Let this be proved, otherwise than by an apocryphal response of the Ammonian Jupiter. Was it in the more frequent celebration of its rites? Let Xenophon bear witness, that Athens surpassed every other Grecian city in the number of her religious festivals. Was it in the amount of instruction which was communicated to its votaries? Listen to the solemn disclosures of Eleusis, so far as they have escaped the safeguard of the golden key, and you will find every reason to believe that they consisted of a dark embodying of the doctrine of a future retribution, which is indeed the sum of Nature's religion. Was it in the supposed attributes and excellencies of the imaginary beings who were the objects of such deluded adoration? If so, let us be told where lies, and whence is drawn, the difference between the moral effects—produced on the one hand, by worshipping a personification of brightness, and healing, and defence, and avenging justice, such as was the god of the silver bow,—and, on the other, by paying religious veneration to a character, comprising those notions of virgin purity, and wisdom, and strength, and sure deliverance, which entered into the idea of the Panathenaic goddess. Surely the one series of qualities does not greatly excel the other ; and hence, if it be remembered, that the same inadequacy of conception adheres to both these ideal divinities, that Apollo is no more a perfect impersonation of the one aggregate abstraction than Minerva of the other, —the difficulty of making out in this way a feasible vindication of Mr Mitchell's expressed preference, will appear sufficiently manifest. In truth, while we would wish to steer clear of the unphilosophic error of contenting ourselves with including all the superstitions of antiquity under the vague generality of polytheistic systems, of imagining that the results of all of them must be precisely identical, and of neglecting to inquire into the specific traits which distinguish the opinions of different tribes,— and while we not only admit, but strenuously assert, the important influence which their respective sentiments in regard to the nature of higher power, and of man's connection with another world, must of necessity have exerted n moulding their national dispositions,—we yet very much fear that too little is known of the interior mechanism of their religious mysteries, to enable us to form a comparative estimate of their demerits, with any rational hope of arriving at a definite and well-ascertained conclusion. Ruinous and debasing as all idolatry must ever be, we do not think that there is enough of evidence to justify the affirmation, that the form of it which prevailed at Athens was more potent than that which the Spartans most approved, in putting forth its poisonous energies.

Need we prosecute this inquiry farther, and contrast the literature of Athens, which has enshrined her name in the grateful affection of all posterity, with that ' *vox et prætarea nihil,*' which proceeds from Müller, and is re-echoed by Mr Mitchell, on the subject of the Spartan ' intelligence ?' That, ' up to the Persian war, mental excellence existed in Sparta *in the utmost perfection*' (*Introd.,* p. viii.), is the bold and novel asseveration which the one of these writers conceives to be fully borne out by the proofs adduced in the work of the other. But to pass over the fact, that in scarcely any instance is more known than the names of these heroes of Spartan literature, and that a thoughtless and ungrateful posterity has unaccountably neglected to preserve their works as an imperishable monument of their fame,—may we be permitted to ask how the total eclipse of the intellect of Sparta came to be so precisely coincident with her arrival at her loftiest eminence among the states of Greece ? Such is not at least a common phenomenon in the history of nations. The literature of Rome reached its highest pitch of refinement, when, under the sway of Augustus, her brick houses were exchanged for palaces of marble ; that of Athens attained its acmè, when Pericles ruled and aggrandized and adorned his country ; —what, then, became of the historians and poets of Lacedæmon, when, after a protracted struggle, she took political precedence of Attica ? What shall we think of its former perfection, when, at the time of her greatest glory—a time which, in other nations, has been marked by the most vigorous developement of mind—it was so sickly, that scarce a name remains to rescue it from the charge of utter extinction ? What must we infer regarding the previous luxuriance of this tender plant, when we find it all leafless and withered, at the very time when it might have been expected to bud and blossom most brightly ?

It is singular enough, that almost every thing we know

of the institutions, and the policy, and even the literature
of Sparta, we learn from the writings of that remarkable
people, between whose literature and that of their political
rivals, we are so much surprised at meeting with even an
insinuated comparison. But the fact is, that the Lacedæmonians, a nation of warriors, for the most part ' regarded
literature as unmanly ;' their whole system of life and
government was rigid, monotonous, unexpansive, and inherently adverse to mental developement. They thus
voluntarily abandoned man's noblest distinction ; and in
the comparative neglect with which posterity has treated
them, they have reaped a just reward. Athenian manners
and policy, on the other hand, were so framed as to encourage and foster the bold and uncramped evolution of
intellectual power. Their cultivation of feeling and im-
pressibility was sometimes, indeed, carried so far, as to
terminate in a captious and nervous feverishness of taste ;
but this was only the abuse of the system by which their
literary character was trained ; and its general results may
be seen in the admiration which they earned from all the
states of Greece, and the renown which in more modern
times has been felt to be the rightful prerogative of Athens.
The single example of the works of that author, on whom
Mr Mitchell has so happily bestowed his labours, will show
the remarkable pitch of mental cultivation to which
Athens had attained. When we reflect, that, in those stu-
pendous structures, where *all* the free-born males of Attica
met from time to time in festive convocation to decide the
palm of comic rivalry, the poet could, with a reasonable
hope of being generally understood and appreciated (and
such *must* have been his hope, if he wished to strike the
fancy and elicit the acclamations of his audience), parody
the strains of Æschylus and Pindar, Sophocles and Euri-
pides ; and when we consider how few auditors in a British theatre could possibly recognise or value a burlesque
of Shakspeare or Collins, Home or Addison, we have matter enough for amazement in the acute perception and
correct knowledge on literary subjects which must have
pervaded Athenian society to its very basis ; and we may
well believe that the archives of the Doric tribes will need
to be more carefully examined than they have yet been,
ere they can afford to this exhibition of intellect, so frequent at the Athenian Dionysia, even the faintest sem-
blance of a parallel.

B—*Page* 92.

EXTRACTS FROM ESSAY ON MISSIONS.

CONNECTION BETWEEN THE HOME AND FOREIGN WORK.

THE cause of extending the blessings of Christian instruction to the whole of our people at home, and that of sending the Gospel to the heathen abroad, are, each of them, so obviously deducible, in their great principles, from the Divine Word, and so certainly the objects of a common interest in heaven,—and so very plain is the maxim, that the performance of one duty can never vindicate the neglect of another, that it might at first be a matter of wonder that such a subject as that now read in your hearing, has come to be discussed at all. But the truth is, that distance, although in other cases it may lend enchantment, is often, in regard to the efforts of benevolence, the ground of unreasonable prejudice, or the last entrenchment behind which an indifference to the whole matter is apt to find or make for itself a shelter. And hence, instead of supporting home and foreign missions, as essentially one and the same cause, by one and the same line of argument, we are compelled to treat them as if they were different, and, for a little, to keep them asunder, in order that, by God's help, we may at last the more effectually join them.

Our general subject comprehends two specific inquiries, —the one relating to a point of duty—the other to a point of fact. It may be asked, *first*, whether the call to diffuse religion at home, affords a *valid* reason for giving less heed to the work of sending it abroad ; and then, whether it affords an excuse, which, be it valid or the contrary, many will be disposed to employ. In other words, our double inquiry is, *Ought* the home work to cause any suspension of our labours in promoting the foreign ? and then, *will* it tend to interrupt or diminish them ?

Now, to the first of these, the answer, we apprehend, is so evident, that little time need be spent either in proving or in expounding it. We assume that, as God has made of *one* blood all nations to dwell upon the face of the earth, —so, to their common misery, he has adapted *one* scheme of salvation. The disease is co-extensive with the human family ; and the remedy provided by Divine wisdom,— like some of those simples which Nature's pharmacy commends to every tribe alike,—is of such a kind that no one

360

member of that family can ever truly deny its fitness and sufficiency for him. . Nor is this all. As the Gospel is suited to the universal want, so it is made over to all in a deed of universal donation. ' I will give thee for a light to the Gentiles, that thou mayest be my salvation unto the end of the earth.' Hence, no sooner does one sinner receive this Gospel for himself ; no sooner, as a *joyful* sound, does it obtain a lodgment in his ear and heart, than he is bound to let others hear it, and to make them (if possible) partakers of his own gladness. He dares not attempt to retain it for himself alone ; the word of God is not *so* to be bound ; the command is imperative, to be, not a grasping miser, but, a *good steward*, of the manifold grace of God. So that every member of our race, to whom the word of this salvation is sent, is just in the same position with the man who, in a country distracted by the alarm of hostile invasion, is keeping watch on the top of some conspicuous hill. When he sees, afar, the gleam of that friendly light which warns him of the coming danger, his duty is, not merely to consult for the preservation of his own possession, but to kindle another blazing messenger, which may send the warning across another province, and so to make the sharers of his peril sharers also of his means of safety.

Let it be particularly observed, that the formal and explicit ground on which Christians are under obligation to diffuse the blessings of the Gospel, is totally independent of proximity of place,—has no concern with the geographical position of those for whose good they are charged to labour. The duty on man's part is measured by the grant on God's. And if 'salvation unto the end of the earth ' is the Redeemer's glorious title, we are not at liberty to confine our aspirations and exertions within narrower limits than the circumference of the globe. We owe this debt of pious effort—not to *neighbours*—but to *men*. A common nature—a common need—a common misery—is the bond of union ; and that bond is wide enough to embrace all nations, and kindreds, and people, and tongues. We may, indeed, be better able to transmit the truth to one people than to another ; and on the scene of the greatest probable utility, a Christian prudence would lead us to expend our contributions and endeavours. But, viewing the subject in its general aspect,—as it is presented in the injunction, ' Go ye and teach all nations,'—it makes a claim upon us for the widest sympathy—the most diffusive kindness ; it calls upon us, in sending forth the message of life, to ask

— not, ' Who is nearest,' but — ' Who is most necessious?

But some, perhaps, will be ready to answer all that may thus be reasoned respecting the abstract and general claims of the *world*, by a reference to the fact, that multitudes within our own borders are yet in the gall of bitterness and in the bond of iniquity. We admit the fact ; we trust we are not insensible to its mournfulness; and he who deplores it, will find, we are sure, in every true advocate of foreign missions, a sincere partaker of his sorrow. But we cannot see its weight as a reason for suspending our efforts in behalf of the distant heathen. True, those who are perishing at home are our brethren, our kinsmen according to the flesh ; and their case demands and deserves much of our solicitude. But, because the churches have been faithless stewards in regard to them, are we, therefore, to rob of their patrimony those remote nations of idolaters, whose cry, wafted across intervening oceans, falls more faintly on our ear ? Because our care for the heathen among our own countrymen is to be *earnest*, must it therefore be *exclusive*? Surely not. If a balance *must* be struck between the two cases, we have little hesitation in saying, that, on the side of the destitute in other lands, is found the pressure of heaviest wretchedness. If many at home are sinking under the faintness which is caused by a famine of the word, they are at least not far from a plenteous supply ; if over the greater portion of our country, there rests the gloom of spiritual darkness, yet does it also contain a Goshen—where all is light. It is not so with other climes. *There* is famine, unmitigated by a single fragment of the bread of life ; *there* is an horror of great darkness, pierced by scarce a single ray of the beam that shines from Zion. If, then, the lesser evil calls forth your pity, with what intensity of compassion should you contemplate the greater ? If you *seek* the good of the perishing *thousands* at home, what *striving* is required to meet the urgent necessities of the perishing *millions* abroad?

The utter vanity of the imagination—that the diffusion of divine truth at home can ever in the least relax the obligation to send it abroad—may obtain from an analogous case a very plain illustration. It will at once be conceded, that if the wants of our own land may lawfully absorb that regard which has hitherto been bestowed, in too small and stinted a measure, on those of the world,—so, by parity of reasoning, we are at liberty to look exclusively homewards

z

in the matter of our own personal salvation, and to let our neighbours shift for themselves, while we are giving all diligence to make our own calling and election sure. Yet who would maintain this selfish paradox in reference to individual Christians ? Who would say that it is no man's bounden duty to labour in bringing others unto Jesus, until he has cleansed *himself* from all filthiness of the flesh and spirit,—until every fall has been retrieved, and every obstacle surmounted, and every lust mortified, and every temptation vanquished, and every grace matured ? A moment's thought is enough to satisfy us, that, if the work of endeavouring to promote the conversion of others were suspended, or interrupted, or pursued with feeble and divided aim, till all *this* were done, the period of cordial and vigorous exertion would come just a lifetime too late —would arrive when he who should have so exerted himself, has taken his departure for a better world. Every one sees, that, if the Christian must wait for perfection ere he invites others to lay hold on that blessed hope which is the anchor of his own soul, he will just wait till the earthly house of his tabernacle is dissolved.

But the line of conduct which would be thus preposterous in a Christian man, is not rendered a whit more rational by its transference to a Christian community. It is granted, that every man's first concern is the salvation of his own soul ; and it is granted, in like manner, that the spiritual wellbeing of those who are our brethren (as being the children of the same soil), has the *foremost* claim on our compassionate regard. But it is contended, that as, in the *first* case, we are not to suspend, or languidly to prosecute, our labours in behalf of others, till we ourselves are perfect,—so, in the *second*, we may not defer the season of energetic action in behalf of the distant heathen, till our own country has attained the measure of Christian fulness. The man who is most deeply sensible of the claims of the spiritually destitute of Britain, and who is most thoroughly under the dominion of that selfishness (so often mistaken for patriotism) of which we have spoken, will freely admit, that, *at some time or other*, the forlorn dwellers in heathen darkness are to become the subjects of our most fervent sympathies. Yet, if his principle is good, we may put the question, *When* are they to become so ? If the existence of unreclaimed wastes at home is a good reason *now* for giving a measured and half-reluctant aid to foreign missions, it is likely to hold as good *for ever*. It were, indeed, a glorious consummation—and one for which we would both hope and patiently wait—that, in our own beloved country, the people should be all righteous,—that, from ' each old poetic mountain ' of our fatherland, there should breathe the strains of a higher ' inspiration ' than ever mingled with the poet's raptures. But we dare not conceal from ourselves the fact, that, if we are to lend but a faint and irresolute hand to the foreign work till this consummation arrives, we shall be found hesitating, and calculating, and expecting, and deluding ourselves with vain excuses, when the Son of man comes in the clouds of heaven. The fountain of human depravity is ever sending forth its bitter waters ; and never, in this world of sin, shall a single channel of its thousand streams be left entirely dry. In pausing till our own land is all reclaimed, we are just planting ourselves on the bank of one of these ceaseless currents ; and if we are to go no farther till its waters fail, *we shall stand still for ever.*

> ' Rusticus expectat dum defluat amnis ; at ille
> Labitur, et labetur, in omne volubilis ævum.'

. . . .

But, bad as our nature is, we trust these are but a small minority among the number of givers ; we trust it is seldom that these motives operate alone. Even in those who are much under their dominion, there is still an intermixture of something less degrading ; and we hope we are taking up by far the most common case, when we turn to that of a man, whose liberality is the product, either entirely or in part, of higher considerations. Now, there is not one consideration of this order in favour of the home missionary enterprise, which may not be urged, with still augmented power, in favour of the foreign ; or which, if faithfully represented, will not appear to have gained an accession of cogency.

Is, for example, our supposed contributor to domestic objects influenced chiefly by a view of the misery of those around him who are still sitting in darkness and in the shadow of death ? But what, I beseech you, in comparison with the state of the far-off heathen, is all *their* misery ? *Around these,* if not *upon* them, the true light now shineth ; *those* are enwrapt in the sevenfold gloom of what seems to be helpless—hopeless ignorance. *These* are subject to laws, and are encompassed on every side by the restraints of a morality, founded mainly on the Bible ; *those* either have no law but violence, no restraint save feeble, groping, undecided conscience,—or yield too ready an obedience to statutes, under which the wicked triumph, and the workers of iniquity boast themselves. *These* are occasionally warned by the godly walk of some around them, for few recesses, even of our cities, are so abandoned, that no solitary member of the little flock is found to tenant them ; *those* are unvisited by so much as the silent admonition of a single holy life. *These*, at the very worst, cannot escape the solemn invitation of the Sabbath-bell, calling the weary and heavy-laden to forget their sorrows in the peaceful house of prayer ; on *those*, although all creation around them seems to enjoy its Sabbath, there lights no such melody of rejoicing and salvation,—there is one deep gladness of which they *cannot* taste—for it is never said unto them, 'Let us go unto the house of the Lord.' Surely, then, the man who glows with desire for the diffusion of the truth among the one class, will, if their relative situations are fairly depicted to him, burn with enthusiasm for its transmission to the other.

. . . .

From these specimens it is apparent, that if the friends of missions are but true to their own cause, and apply, with all the enhancement that the subject gives them, those very motives on which the supporters of Christian exertions at home have already acted, contributors will not be wanting. If any other consideration were necessary to evince the natural harmony of the two classes of objects, it would be found in the fact, that benevolence is a progressive thing. It increases by exercise. ' *Mobilitate riget, viresque acquirit eundo.*' It spreads like a conflagration, involving first one object and then another, till it has laid hold on every thing by which mankind may be benefited. The luxury of doing good once enjoyed in one of its departments, he who has tasted it will recur gladly to what was found so delicious. He comes, moreover, to experience that, the more he gives away of the word of life, the more of its excellence does he himself know and feel. You can imagine that scene of wonder, to which, in the days of the Redeemer's sojourn upon earth, the wilderness of Bethsaida was witness. You can mark that one man —although ' a man of sorrows, and in the form of a servant,'—standing in the midst of perishing thousands, and, with his single hand, satisfying the hunger of them all. He has already distributed a supply far exceeding the five loaves with which he was at first furnished, but still the work of this mysterious provider goes on. You marvel whence arose the materials of so copious a feast ; but astonishment gives place to adoration, when you recognise a present deity, and see that the food multiplies as it passes through his hands. In spiritual things, although there we do not so well appreciate it, the same wonder is daily wrought. He that begins by contributing to the cause of Christianity at home, will soon know, that our Saviour's mode of supplying the multitudes is but an image of the way in which the bread of life increases. He will find that, by communicating of it to others, his own stores are nowise impoverished ; that, in truth, it grows in his hands ; that he grasps the more of it—and that the more firmly—the more he gives away. Hence he will go on more largely to dispense it ; and ever as he proceeds, his own portion will multiply. He will drink more deeply into its spirit, and be more conformed to its standard ; his benevolence will take a wider range ; in the arms of a Christian and comprehensive charity, he will embrace the world.

If all the considerations, to which we have now briefly endeavoured to advert, be put together, we are assured that it will appear indisputable that the foreign labour will go hand in hand with that at home—nay, that by spreading the Gospel among ourselves, we are providing most effectually for its triumphs abroad. The apostles never dreamed of such a question as that which we are now discussing ; they assumed as certain the perfect consistency of the two departments of Christian effort. More than this, they steadily acted upon it ; so that at once, ' from Jerusalem, and round about unto Illyricum,' they ' fully preached the Gospel of Christ.' All experience tends the same way. A Simeon and a Chalmers, the most zealous in striving for the regeneration of our own land, have enkindled or fanned the missionary flame in the breasts of the most potent assailants of the kingdom of darkness in its distant strongholds—in the breasts of a Martyn and a Duff. In fact, the work is one in essence, though in place divided. The churches at home constitute the grand reservoir whence the waters of the sanctuary are to flow forth for the fertilizing of the dry and parched soil of heathenism. Fill, then, the reservoir to overflowing ; and, in doing so, you will irrigate the desert. It is one and the same plant of renown, of which the churches in Britain and the infant assemblies of believers

in heathen lands are branches : and if but a drop of the
grateful dew be made to fall on one leaf, it will instantly
be absorbed, and will circulate refreshment through its
whole organization.   Let not, then, the labourers who are
ministering a sap to one of its spreading boughs, look with
jealousy on those who are watering another.   They are
brethren in the service of the same Divine Husbandman.
They are both, in their own way, performing his work—
speeding the time when Zion, in joyful amazement at the
multitude of her thronging children, shall ask, 'Who hath
begotten these ! and who hath brought up these ! Behold !
I was left alone : these, where had they been !'—hastening the dawn of that morn of ecstasy, on which, framed
and fashioned anew, this long-disordered world shall be
clothed with the moral beauty that shone in it at first,
when the face of Deity smiled on a young creation bright
with the reflection of his own transcendent excellencies.

C—*Page* 92.

SERMON.

' And hath given him authority to execute judgment also, because he is
the Son of man.'—JOHN v. 27.

IF our text affirmed that Jesus Christ was ordained the
Judge of all, because he is the *Son of God*, it were a matter of no great difficulty to discover some of the reasons
of such an appointment.   The necessary preparations, the
act itself of deciding the eternal state of all, and the giving
effect to this final award,—all demand and proclaim that
none other than a Divine Person may sit on that tribunal.
The parties, whose actions the great day is to review, must
be summoned from their repose of years, or centuries, or
millenniums, by a voice not inferior in majesty to that
which shakes the wilderness.   The Judge must possess an
arm, strong enough to drag reluctant generations before
his bar, so that none,—no, not the mighty monarchs of the
earth,—shall be able to offer effectual resistance.   He
must have an eye so piercing, that no shadow of death can
hide a single trembling criminal,—and that, of the inconceivable multitude that shall stand before him, not one
individual shall be able to elude its glance, or pass undis-
tinguished in the throng.   He must have an understanding

omprehensive enough to grasp all the deeds of all the
nen on whom the sun ever shone, to fathom their motives,
o estimate their character, to pronounce their doom.
And, after the first grand object, for which the vast as-
embly was convened, has been accomplished,—after mankind have been judged out of the things written in the
books, it remains that, if he would not hold up his autho-
ity to the scorn of his subjects, he should make infallible
provision for carrying his allotments into full effect ; so
hat, as no reluctancy could exempt from appearing at his
ear, so not the fiercest struggles of despair shall stop the
execution of his sentence. In short, his arm must be
omnipotence ; his eye, omniscience ; his word, the universal law. It is God that must be the Judge of all ; and,
were the Redeemer no more than man,—nay, were he the
most honoured and most scrutinizing spirit that ever re-
oiced in heaven,—were he other than the mighty God and
he everlasting Father, he were unequal to the burden of
so weighty a judicature.

But it would seem from the words of our text, that from
is manhood, as well as from his Godhead, he derives a
itness for presiding in this ultimate assize. It would
seem, that, though there may be other reasons—hidden
among those profundities of the Divine nature and coun-
els which the line of our reason is too short to sound—
why the second Person of the Eternal Three, rather than
he Father or the Spirit, should adjudge to every man his
final destiny,—yet this is certainly one most sufficient reason, that the Word was made flesh, and still continues
incarnate. It would seem, that, in addition to those *general*
qualifications for this office of loftiest dignity, which are
his in virtue of his Divinity, he possesses others of a special
and peculiar kind in virtue of his being clothed with the
nature of man. Now, a connection between his humanity
and his function of judgment, thus explicitly asserted for
our learning, cannot but afford the materials of profitable,
if modest and reverent, meditation ; and we only strive to
be wise up to what is written, when we would search the
Scriptures for the reasons and constituents of this connection. Great, indeed, above measure, are the works of the
Lord ; and, certainly, this work of judgment holds no
mean place among them : yet are they sought out of all
them that have pleasure therein. Remembering, then,
that the ground whereon we stand is pre-eminently holy,
and imploring the guidance of that Spirit who searcheth

all things, let us address ourselves to this high contemplation, and learn, if we may, *how* it is that the Father hath
given the Son authority to execute judgment, because his
name is *Emmanuel.*   And,

1. Christ's investiture with this authority seems to be
necessary to the completeness of his kingly office.

We need not detain you by showing at length, that the
kingdom which our Lord administers is a *mediatorial* kingdom, and that it is in his *human* nature that he is set at
God's right hand in the heavenly places, far above all
principality and power.   That he rules *as* he is, and *because* he is the *incarnate* God,—that there is some connection, which we stop not now to investigate, between his
manhood and his peculiar sovereignty,—is implied in the
tenor of all those Scriptures that make mention of his
reign.   If he is *exalted* to be a Prince as well as a Saviour,
—if he is *given* to be the Head over all things to the
Church,—if his Father hath *appointed* him a kingdom,—
it is obvious that all this can be said of him, only as he is
a partaker of flesh and blood, in which capacity alone it
was possible for him to *receive* a dominion.   In his original and ineffable majesty, he was, by a glorious necessity of nature, the upholder of all things by the word of
his power, and the object of all creation's worship ; inasmuch that, before the foundations of the earth were laid,
he could have been hailed with the adoring exclamation,
' Thy throne, O God, is for ever and ever !'   Such is the
native and independent royalty, essentially annexed to his
Godhead,—an empire so vast, that it has no limit save
what his own will may set to the forthgoings of his creative energy,—a dynasty so ancient, that in the abyss of
the past eternity, you will search in vain for the traces of
its origin.   Had he borne, therefore, no other nature than
the Divine, it were impossible that he should have *received*
a kingdom by dispensation of his Father.   Yet, that he
did so, the whole scheme of salvation emphatically pro-
claims.   It remains, then, that this reception of a kingdom
is among those actions that belong more peculiarly to his
humanity ; that, when he is *exalted,* it is as one chosen *out
of the people ;* and that, since, as the *Son of God,* he was
from everlasting the sharer of his Father's throne,—when
all power is *given* him in heaven and in earth, it must have
been given *because he is the Son of Man.*

The sway thus conferred for his Church's benefit, as
every consideration of the Divine wisdom must assure us,

comprehends all the principles, and elements of a *perfect dominion*,—every thing that can contribute to insure stability, or to encircle the throne with a fitting dignity and lustre. It was typified by the kingdom of Solomon, in the earlier and more prosperous periods of his reign, when a power, which no enemy had the daring to oppose, walked hand in hand with a consummate and heaven-born prudence,—and when all the glories of a dominion, extending from sea to sea, and reposing in the abundance of peace, were enhanced—if indeed they were not eclipsed—by the more excellent glory of a monarch who possessed an understanding heart to *judge* his people. Now, in accordance, both with our most accurate and elevated conceptions of the regal office, and with what is required to answer the type in the fulness of its meaning, it is fit and suitable that the throne of eternal judgment should be occupied by him who has in all things the pre-eminence. It belongs to a king to be the fountain of justice, and shall he have no control over its streams? From him the laws are primarily to emanate; and would there be harmony or consistency in a scheme of administration, which should prevent him from seeing that they are executed; and, while it placed him in the seat of legislation, should sternly exclude him from the seat of judgment? Where were the respect due to majesty, if it could only frame the statute, and perhaps wield the sword, but durst take no concern in holding the impartial scales? And where the completeness of royal authority, if, after subduing his people's enemies, the triumphant monarch must transfer the adjudication of their punishment to other hands, and thus be robbed of half the fruit and honour of his victory? Our Saviour is invested with no such modified and measured sovereignty. His is the honour of a royalty, perfect and unbroken in all its parts and prerogatives. His wisdom devised the statutes of his kingdom,—he gave Jacob a testimony, and Israel a law; his power is armed against those who transgress them; and, in order to make his sway complete, it belongs to his justice to summon all his subjects to one vast assembly, that he who enacted the ordinance may execute the judgment. His government is not stricken with such imbecility of counsel, or his mind so distracted with the multiplicity of cares, that he must leave to others the crowning act of his monarchy,—that act in which his infinite understanding, as it would be most needed, would most conspicuously shine. Hence the Scripture tells us that he shall *judge* the quick and the dead at his appearing and his *kingdom* ; represents him not only as making war, but as judging in righteousness ; and seems not obscurely to specify two of the most important functions that enter into our idea of a perfect royalty, when it announces that the Lord is our *judge*, the Lord is our *lawgiver*, the Lord is our king. Were it otherwise, might we not ask, although with fearful and reverent amazement,—' Is Christ divided? Is that changeless one, who is the same yesterday, to-day, and for ever,—to be putting forth, at one time, what some might deem a royal power, in legislating for the universe, —and, at another, to be stripped of sovereignty, in being debarred from judgment ? Is the everlasting dominion, after all, imperfect, since there is one province of government into which it makes no entrance ? Or, is the kingdom, of which Daniel prophesied that it should *never be destroyed*, to be *suspended or interrupted*, that another than he to whom the Ancient of days gave it, may administer its laws on one grand day of reckoning !' But the inquiry is needless ; our solicitude is spared. *He* wears not the robes of an imperfect royalty. If the Almighty Father announces that he has set his *King* upon his holy hill of Zion,—he assures us also, that *there*—on the sacred mount where Jesus reigns—he has set the *thrones of judgment.*

Observe, now, what we have gained in explanation of our text. We have shown you, briefly, that the kingdom which our Lord administers is the result of a peculiar economy—an economy which turns wholly on the cardinal fact of his incarnation ; insomuch that he is invested with the peculiar regal honours which he now bears, mainly in consequence of being the Son of man. But the kingly office, thus dependent on his humanity, were shorn of half its splendour, and his supreme wisdom were shut out from a field of most appropriate and most needful exercise, if he were not constituted the Judge of all. And hence, if his kingly office depends on his humanity, and includes in it that declaration of doom which the last day shall witness, —if he reigns because he shares our nature, and, because he reigns, must hold the seat of a universal judicature,— if that economy, by which his manhood is a main reason of his rule, is combined with another economy, by which he who rules must judge ; we are furnished with one sense, and that neither unimportant nor obscure, in which it is true, that the Father hath given him authority to execute judgment *because* he is the *Son of man.*

2dly, We observe that Christ is invested with a judicial authority, as a part of the *reward of his humiliation.* This, we would have you remark, is something quite distinct from that completeness of regal dignity of which we have already spoken. That dignity of the Saviour is, indeed, in part, the joy set before him—the requital of his descent to so low an abasement ; but it is chiefly to be viewed as one of those *offices* which were necessarily involved in his great work of mediation. He might have possessed a kingdom, independently of every idea of recompense, in virtue merely of his sustaining the part of a Redeemer ; and, in consequence of this possession, we have seen that the seat of judgment is his due. But let us superadd to this the conception—unquestionably both reasonable and scriptural—of his exaltation being awarded him, because he abhorred not the Virgin's womb, and bowed his head to the stroke of a death by himself unmerited,—let us add this conception, and we double our argument for the suitableness of his obtaining authority to execute judgment. We are, indeed, still looking at the same Jesus,—and beholding him still, as Stephen did, on the right hand of God ; but, while the object is the same, our point of view is different : instead of drawing our inference now from the entireness of his kingly state, we are to make it good from a consideration of the fitness of his reward ; and, instead of regarding the crown of royalty and the robes of judgment only as the insignia of his office, we shall endeavour to contemplate them as the ornaments of his triumph.

To apprehend this argument, conceive, first, how mighty was the downward step, to which the eternal Word condescended, when he became a dweller in a tabernacle of clay ; or rather, admire and adore a mystery, on which the most soaring of created intellects must ever exert itself in vain. That he, who was above the law, should be made under the law ; that he, who was the essential image of the invisible God, should be shrouded in a vesture of earthliness ; that he, who had reigned embosomed in uncreated glory, should make his visible entrance into his own world in the likeness of a nature which sin had marred and deformed ; that he, in whom dwelt everlasting strength, should appear in the form of a weak and weeping infant ;—this presents to us the overpassing of an infinite interval with so vast a condescension, that we can no more conceive of it aright, than scale the heavens, or measure that shoreless sea of space which on every side

surrounds us.   But scarcely have our minds had time to
recoil upon themselves, baffled and amazed at this infini-
tude, ere another step of abasement, too great for their
comprehension, challenges them to a new defeat.   The
Messiah assumes not the temporal throne of his father
David,—he appears not as one of earth's noblest and most
honoured sons (although even this had been marvellous in
him who humbleth himself to behold the things that are
in heaven) ; but he is born in the mean chamber to which
overbearing wealth had driven his mother's unpretending
poverty ; the only member of the human race, of whom it
could be said that he deserved *no* suffering, he yet meekly
stooped to the endurance of all ; not shining forth as the
bright centre of heaven's attraction, he lived in obscurity ;
receiving not the homage which all creation owed him, he
was subject to those whom his own hands had made ;
instead of the praises of eternity, he was encompassed by
revilings,—instead of angelic attendants, by the fishermen
of Galilee, or the rude soldiers of Rome ;—worst of all,
instead of enjoying the light of his Father's countenance,
he was visited with the intolerable sense of desertion and
wrath, settling down like the shadow of death upon his
spirit.   To consummate his abasement, the Prince of life
yielded to death a temporary triumph ; and, instead of
leaving this world in that perfect peace which his grace
has shed around so many expiring sufferers, he gave up
the ghost in unparalleled ignominy and anguish.   Herein
indeed is love ; here is condescension unutterable ; a descent, first from heaven to earth, and then, from the deserts
of a stainless purity, to the worst punishment that could
have been dealt out to the very chief of sinners.   If any
honour could be added to that spotless humanity which
the eternal Word had assumed into personal union with
himself, surely it was nobly and dearly won, and would
never be withheld by the Father, who set him apart for
such a career of mercy and of suffering.
    Accordingly we learn, that, *because* he made himself of
no reputation, and took upon him the form of a servant,
and was made in the likeness of man ; because, being found
in fashion as a man, he humbled himself still farther, and
became obedient to death, even the death of the cross ;
therefore, God also hath highly exalted him, and given him
a name which is above every name ; that at the name of
Jesus every knee should bow, of things in heaven, and
things in earth, and things under the earth ; and that

very tongue should confess that Jesus Christ is Lord, to
he glory of God the Father.   It is then the will of Him
whose counsel *shall* stand, that, as the fruit of his toils and
sorrows, there shall one day resound, from the whole crea-
ion, the confession that Jesus Christ is the Lord supreme.
But *when* shall that welcome sound be heard?   Never, we
believe, till the time of the end, when he, who was once
smitten with a rod upon the cheek, shall appear as the
Judge of Israel,—when all his enemies shall have been put
under his feet, and all his saints gathered together around
him.   So long as a foe is unsubdued, or a remnant of unbelief and unholiness resides in any of his people,—so
long will there be something to hinder the utterance of
that confession in its fullest and largest compass.   But,
when all nations are gathered before him, his people joy-
fully acknowledging that power which has preserved them,
and his enemies constrainedly, and from bitter experience,
admitting his resistless might, then will that saying of the
apostle obtain its complete fulfilment.   So that, if that
confession shall only then be fully made, when he comes
to judge the world ; if the confession itself is an important
element in the reward of his humiliation ; if no small part
of his humiliation consisted in his assumption of manhood ;
it seems clear, that his assumption of manhood contains a
reason for his pronouncing the ultimate award,—that the
Father hath given him authority to execute judgment,
because he is the Son of man.

If you consider, also, the steps of his exaltation, you
will see that they are in general correlative to those of
his abasement.   Was his birth mean and companionless?
His second birth—his resurrection from the dead, was
clothed with a majesty worthy of his nature, when the
rocks were rent, and many bodies of the saints started
from the sleep of ages, to do homage to their king!   Was
his visage marred more than any man's, and his form more
than the sons of men?   That body now shines in an excellent glory, of which his glistering raiment on Tabor was
but the distant reflection.   Did he make supplication, with
strong crying and tears, to him that was able to deliver?
He is now the object of the prayers of all believers ; the
constituted way, by whom alone it is that any man cometh
into the Father.   Did he grieve under the hidings of that
face, which had beamed on him from everlasting, with an
inexpressible divine complacency?   Yes, but now is that
prophecy accomplished, ' Thou hast made known to me

the ways of life ; thou shalt make me full of joy with thy countenance.' And, finding an analogy in so many particulars, to which as many more might easily be added, may we not infer that that correspondence of his reward to his humiliation pervades the whole of his history and state ; and that, because he stood (we will not say ' *trembled,*' for he was tranquil and unmoved as innocence ; but, because he *stood*) before Pilate's tribunal, there shall be enacted, to match this degradation, a great scene of assize at which all the kindreds of the world shall await his disposal ? Then shall come the time of peculiar honour to the crucified Jesus ; the purchase of his pain ; the very triumph of his victory. Then shall the Sun of righteousness, who appeared beforetime in dim and disastrous eclipse, break forth in all his native splendour ; and he, who once seemed but a root out of a dry ground, shall be admired as the rose of Sharon in full-blown loveliness. The hands, once nailed to the cross, shall bear the sceptre ; the lips, once smitten, shall announce the destinies of eternity ; the head, once crowned with thorns, in cruel mockery, shall sparkle with many diadems, studded with countless jewels—the spirits whom he saved ; the soul, that was once exceeding sorrowful even unto death, shall thrill with a satisfaction, deep, glorious, divine. Then shall all confess that he is Lord,—the wicked in abject terror, and the righteous in joy unspeakable. Then his saints, when they see him raised so high because he stooped so low, shall gladly read the full meaning of his saying, that this authority was given him *because* he is the Son of man ; and, as they proceed, exulting, across the everlasting hills of heaven to their final habitation, the burden of their song shall be, that all this gladness and all this glory have issued from that fountain which was opened by the soldier's spear.

3. We remark that Christ is constituted the Judge of all, in order that there might be a *visible* Judge.

' No man hath seen God at any time ; the only begotten Son, who is in the bosom of the Father, he hath declared him.' In the divine communications with our race, the Incarnate One has ever been the great medium of intercourse. Like speech, which embodies the impalpable and ætherial something that men call thought, the Word has graciously brought nigh unto us the Father, who dwelleth afar in the light that is inaccessible. In the days of patriarchs and prophets, he gave such disclosures of himself as formed a sure presage of another and a

clearer advent ; he announced himself to Abraham as his
shield and exceeding great reward ; he was the Angel
who redeemed Jacob from all evil ; it was he that spake
with Moses, as a man with his friend ; and it was he whom
Isaiah beheld on a throne high and lifted up, and of whose
glory he revealed as much as it was befitting for unclean
lips to utter. In due season, these mysterious omens obtained their accomplishment ; he assumed a true and permanent humanity ; and, filling up the shadowy outline
which he had traced as the Messenger of the Covenant, he
gave a more explicit revelation of the Father. And now,
as the glorified Son of man, he abideth ever—the visible
representative of an unseen Godhead—the Shechinah of
the heavenly temple. But another grand exhibition of
the Divine character and counsels is yet to come ; when,
before the myriads of men and angels assembled, he will
bring to light the hidden things of darkness, and judge
the secrets of every heart. Can it be, that the function of
declaring the Father shall have expired before that day of
disclosure comes ? or rather, is there not a fitness in the
arrangement, whereby he, who has been the medium of
Divine manifestation hitherto, should be the *visible* medium
of Divine manifestation then ?

Consider the nature of those who shall stand before that
dread tribunal. It shall be no company of unembodied
spirits ; but the souls of mankind, inhabiting the same
tabernacles which here encased them,—only no more to
see corruption. Now, we all know the power of the eye
and ear, those great avenues of feeling, in the production
either of terror or of joy ; and how vastly the hearing of
the ear rises in impressiveness, when it is aided by the
faithful painting of the eye. A voice might have come
from heaven to Ahab, as he walked, in guilty satisfaction,
through the rows of Naboth's well-trained and fruitful
vines ; and he, who had so oft resisted the still small voice
within, might have passed off *this* sound lightly, as proceeding from some lurking malcontent or ambushed foe ;
but when, like a statue, cold and still, unchanged in feature, unabashed by the presence of royalty, the figure of
Elijah stood before him,—that marble visitant shot a chill-
ness into his very soul ; the king quailed before the prophet, and faltered out his fear in the tremulous inquiry,
' Hast thou found me, O mine enemy ?' A voice from
heaven *did* come, when our Saviour was baptized in Jordan, proclaiming him the well-beloved of the Father ; but

think you that that sound, strange and solemn as it was, sunk so deeply into the hearts of those who heard it, as the same words into the hearts of the three disciples on an after day, when there burst forth on Tabor a single beam of that glory which is yet to be revealed on the heavenly Zion !

Since, then, the ear, and especially the eye, forms the main entrance of whatever is to affect the mind ; since our Maker knoweth our frame, and treats his creatures, in his wisdom, according to the constitution he has given them, is there not an obvious fitness in supplying the closing scene of this world's history with all that is calculated to keep the eye vigilant, as well as the ear attentive,—in providing not only that mysterious trumpet to awaken the sleeping generations, but also a *visible* Judge to fix, in awful reverence, the gaze of the unnumbered multitude !

Not certainly, that such an element of augustness is needed to throw around the Godhead an additional majesty (the thought were blasphemous), but that it is needed to carry some rays of that majesty to the minds of those who are not bodiless and aerial spirits, but the tenants of a structure, which, refined and immortalised though it be, is still material. To such a nature, when deeds done in the body are to be quoted as the measure of the ultimate doom —the appointment of a visible Judge contains, palpably, a most wise adaptation ; and the consideration of the fact, that such a nature is ours, may serve to heighten the emphasis of Isaiah's declaration, that " the Lord shall cause his glorious voice to be *heard*, and shall *show* the lighting down of his arm ;" to disclose the ground of Job's rejoicing, because in his flesh he should *see* God ; and to suggest a most valid reason for the statement of our text, that ' the Father hath given the Son authority to execute judgment, *because* he is the Son of man.'

But we stop not here in our argument for the desirableness of letting those who are to receive the sentence *behold* Him who is to pronounce it. We argue, also, that the honour and equity of Heaven's high jurisdiction must be preserved unimpeached and unimpeachable. Now, were the Judge *unseen*, there might remain (we say not with the shadow of justice, but still there *might* remain) to the wicked the materials of murmuring and complaint. They might say that they had been sacrificed to a dark and dismal inquisition ; abandoned to a doom over which hung the cloud of an impenetrable mystery ; hurried from a dead unbroken silence, with no crime alleged, and no liberty of defence accorded, to their prison of eternal wailing ; the victims of a sentence, proceeding they knew not whence, and passed they knew not why, and executed they knew not how, save that all was done with a fearful and despotic rapidity. This utmost refuge of cavilling shall not be given. The Son of *man* is Judge, that every eye may see him. All will be done ' in open court ; in the face and audience of the universe.' * The criminals shall be confronted with their Judge. And as we learn from our Lord himself, if any one dares to mutter dissent from his equal allotments, the miserable plea shall be heard, and weighed in the balances, and found wanting : ' When saw we *thee* an hungered, or athirst, or a stranger, or naked, or sick, or in prison, and did not minister unto thee ?' ' Inasmuch as ye did it not to one of the least of these, ye did it not to *me.*' Thus unchallenged, or, if challenged, triumphantly vindicated, eternal justice shall hold on her course ; and thus, that every mouth may be stopped, hath Jesus obtained ' authority to execute judgment, *because he is the Son of man.*'

It is now time to add,

4thly, That the humanity of Christ qualifies him for being a *sympathizing* judge. In the words of the prophet, ' Therefore shall the Lord be exalted, that he may have mercy.'

It may seem strange to you, on a first announcement, that we should speak of *sympathy* as a quality which is desirable in a judge. You have been wont, probably, to conceive of one who is placed on a tribunal, as occupying a majestic elevation, where any such feeling, even though entertained, ought never to be shown ; to invest justice with every attribute of hard constraint and immitigable sternness ; to paint her as ruling with a rod of iron, bearing the sceptre of an adamantine sway. And no doubt, in the case of fallible men, in whom, if mingled at all with milder ingredients, she is either enervated by irresolution or corrupted by partiality, there may be some cause for endeavouring to abstract her from softer feelings, and some temptation to view her as most perfect when she is most austere. But, in the Divine mind, we may not look upon the attribute as thus naked and unrelieved. The light and the love of that glorious character, we cannot—we would not separate. *There*, justice is never for a moment disjoined from gentleness ; mercy and truth are met in indis-

* Quoted, it is believed, from *Barrow ;* but only *memoriter.*

A a

soluble companionship ; righteousness and peace are locked
in one eternal embrace ; the awards of equity are tempered
by so tender an affection, that even when he sharply re-
bukes, his repentings are kindled together ; the soft and
the severe melt into each other, like the brighter and
darker hues in that glorious bow which is the emblem of
His covenant of peace.

Now, in the final reckoning, the Lord would manifest
this blessed peculiarity of his government. He would allay
to us the terrors of Deity ; and in his own unerring wisdom,
he attains his end, by raising Jesus to the throne of judgment, *because he is the Son of man*. In him we recognise a
Judge who is touched with a feeling of our infirmities.
Were we to be arraigned before a God, of whose throne
justice and judgment—unmitigated—were the habitation,
our sole feeling would be that of the affrighted Israelites,
—' Let not God speak with us, lest we die.' But goodness
is co-ordinate with justice on that tribunal ; and the way
which Infinite Wisdom has adopted, to mark this character of its ultimate decisions, is to put the authority of executing judgment into the hands of him who is bone of our
bone, and who, as a high-priest over the house of God, has
already proved himself to be *merciful* as well as *faithful*.

It would seem, moreover, that the appointment to this
high jurisdiction, of one who can sympathize with the
trembling multitudes at his bar, is desirable (we will not
say ' necessary ') for precluding any one from reclaiming
against his sentence. We are far from thinking that the
Monarch of the universe was *bound* to adopt such a measure for securing a full and unanimous acquiescence in the
proceedings of the great day ; but the measure once
adopted, and the *man* Christ Jesus once ordained to be the
Judge, we can easily see how completely the end is thereby
attained of stopping or shaming every murmur against his
awards. Were an angelic nature elevated to the seat of
judgment, we can understand how the finally rejected,
grasping eagerly at any poor alleviation which an impeach-
ment of the equity of their sentence might be thought to
yield, would argue that such a one, moving in a higher
sphere, inhaling (as it were) a purer æther, unconscious of
that gravitation whereby the souls of men are made to
cleave unto the dust, and, therefore, void of any thing like
sympathy with the subjects of his jurisdiction,—could make
no proper account of the difficulties and temptations which
palliated their offences, and thus, from the want of such an

ssential element of computation, could not strike a fair
nd equitable balance between their virtues and their
rimes : and we can even imagine some lost spirit, in the
udacity ministered by desperation, uttering the like com-
laint against him who is the Lord of angels. The human
ature of our Judge is the ground of an easy reply. To
uch a plea, if urged in arrest of judgment, it might be said,
—Look again to the midst of the throne, and see whether the
dispenser of doom is not one like unto the Son of *man*. Yes !
hou that repliest against God, it is no enemy that judges
hee ; no, nor one indifferent ; but a friend ; one whose
delights have long been with the sons of men ; who was
tempted in all points like thyself ; who is still of the same
mind as when he prayed for his murderers ; who is not
raised to a cold and haughty elevation, but qualifies the
awfulness of Deity with the warm and overflowing tenderness of a most perfect manhood. If he condemns, where
in the universe is there a holy being who would absolve ?
If mercy itself denounces wrath, where will one be found
to gainsay the sentence ? Cease, then, to quarrel with
divine justice, as something harsh and severe ; it is compassion that holds the scales ; the judgment of the great
day will involve nothing inconsistent with the softest sympathy, for he who presides in it is the Son of *man ;* and
when *he* speaks, the heavens themselves shall declare his
righteousness.

But we have not forgotten, that besides those who might
be disposed to cavil at the allotments of that assize,
another class remains, whose case can be met only by the
appointment of a sympathizing Judge. There are many—
perhaps a majority—of his own people, whose spirits would
fail within them at thought of meeting an *absolute* Deity ;
and whose feelings, in such a prospect, these words of
David would best express,—' My flesh trembleth for fear
of thee, and I am afraid of thy judgments.' For their re-
assurance, it is wisely and well ordered that he who is to
execute judgment is the Son of *man*. Let them but be
reminded that the occupant of the throne is not ashamed
to call them brethren ; that he loved them more than his
own life ; that on the mystic vesture in which he is robed
above, his people's names are inscribed for an everlasting
memorial ; and faith may again be able to assert her
empire. Their Advocate is their Judge ; and who is he
that condemneth ? A fearful tempest, indeed, awaits the
world at the great and dreadful day ; but their Lord and

Master—his human sympathies unimpaired by his glorious elevation—shall walk the angry waves, and rule in the midst of their fiercest commotion ; and they shall hear, from his voice of placid majesty, the words of encouragement,—' It is I, be not afraid.' In a word, a constant operative conviction of the truth that their Judge is susceptible of that nameless feeling of fellowship which springs from the possession of a common nature—that He is, in very deed, the Son of *man*—is one most valuable mean of promoting their comfort and establishment. By meditating on this truth, they are brought to *love* his appearing,—to think of his coming as the signal for their return to Zion with songs and everlasting joy,—to feel that the pale horse will but bear them to Emmanuel's land,—to look forward to the tramp of God as that silver trumpet whose welcome note shall sound their invitation to an endless jubilee.

And now, brethren, what shall we say to these things ! It is truly an impressive, an overpowering thought, that *our eyes shall behold* the Lord when he comes forth to judgment. Has it obtained that deep seat in our convictions, that constraining power over our conduct, which it may most rightfully challenge ? Not more surely do we see each other now, than on that great day which is so swiftly approaching, they shall see the Son of man coming in the clouds of heaven, with power and great glory. Has this amazing certainty ever impelled us solemnly to put the question, how we shall stand when he appeareth ? If so, what is the tenor of the answer which conscience has returned ?

Are there here any who can say, humbly yet hopefully, that they have fled from themselves to him ; that in him their confidence against that day is all reposed ; that in his righteousness alone they would wish to be exalted ! Brethren, do your hearts misgive you, when you contemplate, from afar, the great white throne ! Why should this be ! Your Brother sits on it ; he whose name has been to you as ointment poured forth—who is all your salvation and all your desire. Lift up your heads, then ; grasp your privilege of a good hope through grace, of a holy confiding joy. Call him no longer Baali, but Ishi,— your Master no longer, but your Husband ; for lo ! he declares that he appoints you a kingdom, even as his Father hath appointed him. And whenever Satan would attempt to subject you to bondage through the fear of death and of a subsequent judgment, remember that he who is to execute that judgment is the Son of *man*, whom, having not seen, ye love, and for whose glorious appearing it is your duty and privilege to wait with a calm unruffled expectation.

On the other hand, are there any who feel that they have never unfeignedly submitted to the righteousness of Christ, or who are in a doubt about their condition, as painful and (if rested in) as dangerous, as the most dreadful certainty ? We would warn you that he cometh quickly —that Saviour whom you have wronged, dishonoured, and disclaimed,—that he cometh with clouds, and *every eye shall see him*, and they also which pierced him. How, if you continue impenitent to the end, will you endure the sight ? How will you bear the lightning of his eye ? How will you stand in his presence, before whose face the heaven and the earth shall flee away ? Can you think without a shudder, of taking your dreary place among those kindreds of the earth which shall wail because of him ? The rapid approach of those scenes of astonishment, at which all faces, that are not lightened by *Him*, shall gather blackness, is no dream—no sickly and unfounded fancy ; ere long, they shall pass in startling succession before our eyes. ' The hour is coming, *and now is*, in which all that are in their graves shall hear his voice,' evoking them from their long unbroken slumber. And if there is one ingredient in the cup of trembling, which, above all others, renders it a cup of insupportable woe,—it is the thought of being condemned by a Judge so full of sympathy—of incurring the wrath of the Lamb.

If these his terrors will not persuade you, perhaps you will be drawn by the sweet constraint of his mercy. We preach him, not merely as a *Prince*, but as a *Saviour*. We implore you, in fleeing from his anger, to make trial of the tenderness of his compassion. The door is open, and the feast is spread ; the guests are thronging in, but still there is room ; the Master waits ; rejected, scorned, contemned so long, he invites you still ;—come, and he will rejoice over you in his love, and forgetting all your folly and perversity, he will yet cause you to be glad in his occupancy of the throne of judgment, and to account his exaltation to so high an authority, the very pledge and security of your happiness.

Feb. 27, 1837.

D—*Page* 227.

VINDICATION OF PRAYER-MEETINGS.

I FEEL, my friends, that I owe you some explanation for troubling you with the formality of a written document, instead of that more easy address, to which you are probably accustomed on occasions like the present. But the reason is one which, I hope, will commend itself to your judgments. Having been informed that some of our countrymen here were not sufficiently aware of the precise nature of our object in holding such a meeting, and that certain misapprehensions respecting it had probably obtained a lodgment in the minds of a few, I deemed it desirable to meet these in such a form as might be supposed to give a more deliberate and condensed view of the principles on which we wish to act, and the ends at which we wish to aim, than it would have been easy to afford in an extemporaneous exposition of them. It is of the first importance, that you in hearing, and we in speaking, should be fully persuaded that we are doing what is right; we cannot *confidently* expect a blessing on what is undertaken with an *embarrassed conscience*; and I feel, therefore, that I can fairly solicit, for a few moments, your best attention, while I attempt to show you on what firm foundations of scriptural truth we lean, in endeavouring, even here, to hold forth the word of life.

Let me request you to turn, for a motto to our observations, to Malachi iii. 16, 17. In that chapter, from the 7th verse downwards, the prophet is obviously indignantly rebuking a great religious degeneracy which had come over the Jewish people; and which was exhibited, first, in withholding those offerings which He who gave them all their substance had claimed as his own, and afterwards, with still greater hardihood, in setting their mouth against the heavens, and declaring God's service a weariness and a loss. But, in the midst of this worse than barrenness which overspread the nation, there was a remnant, who, planted in the house of God, flourished, and brought forth fruit to his glory. There was a spot on which the weary eye of the prophet could rest with pleasure; where a few, in the midst of prevailing iniquity, assembled to converse on the things pertaining to the kingdom. ' Then they that feared the Lord spake often one to another;' and, from the mention of their character, you may infer the themes on which they held converse. But, if you would have these more fully indicated, let us take them in the words of David : ' All thy works praise thee, O Lord ; and thy saints shall bless thee. They shall speak of the glory of thy kingdom, and talk of thy power : to make known to the sons of men his mighty acts, and the glorious majesty of his kingdom.'* We speak not now of the blessedness that accompanied and followed their attempts to edify one another ; of the Lord bending his ear, and that book of life in which their names were written, and that glorious acknowledgment which will be made of them as his most precious treasure ; but we wish to fix your minds on the fact, that it is *their very exercise* which we seek to make *our own.* Our humble desire is to bear in mind the precept to ' do good unto all men as we have opportunity ;' † and our humble hope rests upon the promise, which can never be shaken, that in all such attempts to make disciples to his faith, Jesus will be with his people alway, even unto the end of the world.‡ He has given all his servants various talents, and commanded them to occupy till he comes ; and it is an obvious enough thought, that the peculiar talent committed to our keeping is that knowledge of his Word, be it great or small, which the advantages of a professional education have imparted. This talent, had it been His will, it would have been our rejoicing and our delight, to have laid out to more abundant interest at home ; declaring, had he permitted us, each in his own appointed sphere of labour, the unsearchable riches of Christ. And now, since he has yet left us a little strength, we do not feel at liberty to wrap it up, and leave it unemployed. We cannot resist the conviction, that, among our exiled brethren, the harvest truly is plenteous. Every time we go forth we see a multitude in similar circumstances to our own, whom the heavy hand of the Almighty, laid on themselves or their relatives, has brought to this island of the sea ; who have such abundant leisure, that our brief assemblies will scarcely be felt as an incision on their time ; at whose hearts, it may be presumed, the Redeemer has been knocking, when they are thus called out from the bustle of the world ; and who thus offer the fairest opportunity to any who might seek their everlasting good : and we should feel ourselves traitors to His cause if, with all this before us, we did not

* Ps. cxlv. 10-12. † Gal. vi. 10. ‡ Matt. xxviii. 20.

beseech the Lord of the harvest to send us out as labourers.
And then, among those who are in different circumstances
—among those regular dwellers here whose kindness we
have experienced in a land of strangers, we would fain
have some to join themselves with us in holier bonds, and,
in company with us, to seek the rich and peculiar blessing
that rests upon them who fear the Lord, when they speak
often one to another of his saving grace and power.

Such, brethren, is, simply and broadly, the *end* we have
in view. And the *means* by which we propose to attain it
are those which God himself has sanctioned ; to praise his
name—for praise is comely ; to pour out our hearts before
him—for he is the hearer of prayer ; to read his Word—
for it is able to make you wise unto salvation ; and to ex-
pound and enforce it, and carry its message of reconciliation round you all ; for we are commanded to edify and
exhort one another, and it pleaseth God, by the foolish-
ness of preaching, to save them that believe.* We know
that a pearl of great price is hid in the field of the Gospel ;
and we wish to tell you where and how you will find it.
We know that in Christ are hid all the treasures of wisdom and knowledge ; and if, by any exhortation of ours, so
much as a single soul should be led to sue for a participa-
tion in these riches, we have our reward.

Against such an end, pursued by means which we humbly think are simple, suitable, and scriptural, it is hard to
think what objections can be urged. Yet that some doubt
or hesitation regarding it exists in the minds of not a few,
we have been so frequently told, that we cannot help
believing it. But we are willing to think that such a
feeling could originate only in not perceiving the *aim* of
our enterprise in this its naked simplicity,—in fixing the
attention on some of the details on which possibly conscientious difficulties might arise, and so forgetting, for a
time, the great and overwhelming object we contemplate,
namely, the directing our fellow-sinners and fellow-suffer-
ers to what we *know* and *are persuaded* are the only pure
and exhaustless fountains of comfort and joy.

Permit me briefly to examine, in the clear light of Holy
Scripture, a few of those special difficulties which some
may feel, when asked to give their attendance at such an
assemblage as ours.

1. And, *first*, it is possible that a feeling of hesitation
may arise in the minds of some, from the fact that our

* 1 Cor. i. 21.

meetings are held in an *unconsecrated place*. And here I would wish to treat with all respect the minutest scruples and hereditary feelings of Christians who are members of those churches, in which a peculiar importance and sanctity is attached to the edifices that are set apart for the worship of God. But I would call upon them to reflect on this very plain distinction, that it is one thing to view these with veneration as being *restricted* to the service of our Maker,—and quite another thing to imagine that, in any form, whether public or private, the service of our Maker is to be *restricted to them*. These two things must not be confounded ; and yet it is only by confounding them that any reason can be given for objecting to the social worship of God in any place whatever. What the Apostle Paul says of meats may, with perfect fairness, and on the self-same principle, be applied to places, when used as we propose. ' Every creature of God,' he says, ' is good, if it be received with thanksgiving : for it is sanctified by the word of God and prayer.' * And tell me, where is the place which these same means will not sanctify ! or, where are we informed that our conjoint prayers will be unheard, or the word of exhortation ineffectual, simply because the prayers ascend and the word is uttered in a building not formally consecrated to sacred objects ?

But let us look a little more narrowly at the evidence of Scripture on this subject. Let us go back, for instance, to that ancient dispensation, in which there was more of the embodying of sacred truth in outward forms, than any one pretends we now have under the Gospel ; and there we shall find, in the wanderings of Israel, that it was not so much the place that consecrated the worship, as the worship that ennobled and dignified the place. God's own promise is indiscriminate : ' In all places where I record my name, I will come unto thee, and I will bless thee.' † And equally unconfined was its performance, insomuch that, whether they encamped by the palm-trees of Elim, or the waters of Meribah, or the coast of Edom, or the plains of Moab,—in all alike did he remember their offerings, and accept their burnt sacrifice. ‡ But, coming at once to the New Testament economy, our Saviour repeats, almost in the same terms, that precious promise of the Old,—' Wherever two or three are met together in my name, there am I in the midst of them, to bless them and to do them good.'§ And lest we should mistake the nature

* 1 Tim. iv. 4, 5.   † Exod. xx. 24.   ‡ Psalm xx.   § Matt. xviii. 20.

of his kingdom, he points out plainly to the woman of
Samaria the spiritual character of the worship he demands.*
Anxious, like all of us, when the truth begins to sting our
consciences, to avoid the personal question, she tries to
bring him to settle for her a point of speculative controversy, whether Mount Zion or Mount Gerizim 'is the place
where men ought to worship ?' In reply, he tells her,
that ' the hour cometh when they should neither in that
mountain, nor yet at Jerusalem, worship the Father,'—
intimating most plainly, that *places*, thenceforth, would be
comparatively unimportant ; but that a *spiritual* worship,
wherever rendered, would be acceptable and well-pleasing.
Nor need we go farther than his own example for an illustration of what he means ; for he made the mountain and
the shore the scenes of his preaching, and, in an upper
room, instituted that ordinance in which his people are to
show forth his death till he come. And, in this particular,
the apostles were not greater than their Lord. Peter,
when the angel delivered him from the prison, ' came to
the house of Mary, the mother of Mark ; where *many were
gathered together praying ;'†* and to this primitive prayer-
meeting he declared his great deliverance. And to Paul,
when he had his Master's work in hand, it was all one
whether he preached in the jail at Philippi,‡ or on Mars
Hill at Athens, § or in an upper chamber at Troas, ‖ or at
Tyre kneeled down on the sea-shore and prayed, ¶ or at
Rome, ' in his *own hired house*, for two whole years, taught
those things which concern the Lord Jesus Christ, with all
confidence, no man forbidding him.'** In all these ways
he gave ample illustration of his own saying, that ' God
dwelleth not in temples made with hands.'†† And if it
were lawful, in pursuing such an argument, to refer to the
practice of any of God's people in more modern times, it
would be pleasant to speak of those of whom the world
was not worthy—the

> ' Slaughtered saints, whose bones
> Lie scattered on the Alpine mountains cold,'—

and who worshipped the God of their fathers amid those
scenes which are still fragrant with their memory. But
enough surely has been said to show that ' the word of
God is *not bound*' ‡‡ within such narrow limits as some
might fancy ; that we may have a blessing even here, like

*John iv. 20, 21.   † Acts xii. 12.   ‡ Ib. xvi. 32.   § Ib. xvii. 22.   ‖ Ib. xx. 8.
  ¶ Acts xxi. 5.   ** Ib. xxviii. ult.   †† Ib. xvii. 24.   ‡‡ 2 Tim. ii. 9.

Paul, when ' many came to him in his lodging ;' * and that, as it is said in Scripture of believers, ' Ye are the temple of God ; ye are God's building,' †—so, *wherever* a *true* worshipper is found, *there* is a lawful and a holy temple.

2. But I go on to notice, *secondly*, an objection which some may feel in reference to the *persons* who may be engaged in conducting these meetings : that some of them have never been specifically *ordained* to the care of congregations or parishes at home. I shall not here insist on the fact, that want of health was the sole impediment, but present such views of Christian duty as perfectly satisfy my own mind, and I trust will satisfy yours, that, matters being as they are, we are bound not to keep silence, but to do what we can in the way of edifying our brethren. Now, surely, you will not suspect my rev. friend ‡ and myself of any wish to bring down the honour, or invade the privileges of the Christian ministry, as an ordinance of God. Nay, rather, like the great apostle of the Gentiles, we magnify our office ; yet we dare not magnify it at the expense of the cause of Him whom we call our Master. We regard it, certainly, as one of the great appointed means of establishing and extending his kingdom among men, and we feel that the triumphs of his cross are connected, in a good measure, with the efforts of those appointed leaders whom his providence has placed in the front of the battle against unbelief and sin ; but we dare not forget, that the same Holy Volume which commands them to ' preach the word '—to be ' instant in season and out of season '—to ' be examples of the believers '—to ' give attendance to reading, to exhortation, to doctrine '— and to ' give themselves *wholly* to these things, that their profiting may appear to all,' §—enjoins it as strongly upon every Christian to ' hold forth the word of life,' ‖ and to ' seek that he may excel to the edifying of the Church.' ¶ In very many passages of sacred writ, this mutual duty of instruction and exhortation is manifestly implied. Thus, Jeremiah, in prophesying of a day of glory, which has certainly not yet dawned in its full brightness on our dark and bewildered world, mentions this as one of its blessed peculiarities, that ' they shall teach no more every man his neighbour, and every man his brother, saying, Know the Lord,' manifestly implying, that, till then, the duty of

* Acts xxviii. 23. † 1 Cor. iii.; xvi. 9.
‡ Rev. Mr Langford ; he survived Mr Halley only two days.
§ 1 and 2 Tim. ‖ Philip. ii. 16. ¶ 1 Cor. xiv. 12.

mutual instruction would be in full force and operation.
Paul, too, enjoins it on the Thessalonians to ' edify one
another,' * and on the Hebrews to ' exhort one another.' †
And if example be wanted, we find David, who was neither a priest nor a Levite, vowing that he would ' teach
transgressors God's ways ;' ‡ and, at the great persecution,
after the death of Stephen, the members of the Church
' scattered abroad every where, preaching the word,' §
while the apostles alone remained at Jerusalem ; and, in
fine, Aquila and Priscilla, a Jewish tentmaker and his
wife, expounding the way of God more perfectly to Apollos,
who, although an eloquent man, and mighty in the Scriptures, did not disdain to sit at the feet of these humble
disciples of Jesus. ‖ These principles and examples from
the Word of God, are a warrant for our humble efforts, on
which, as on a rock, we can take our stand. We claim no
authority over conscience, derived from any *official station*,
but only such as our *message* may give us ; we seek not to
' have dominion over your faith, but to be helpers of your
joy ;' ¶ and all we wish is, ' by manifestation of the truth,
to commend ourselves to every man's conscience in the
sight of God.' **

3. But I hasten to advert to a *third* difficulty, which,
although I have not heard it alleged, may perhaps, silently
and unexpressed, have an influence on some minds,—viz.,
the supposition, that this meeting might interfere, in some
way or other, with those for reading prayers and the Scriptures, which are held in the English chapel. In answer to
this, it were possibly enough to remark, that we have purposely fixed on a different day and hour ; and to say, in
reference to those for whom our meetings are chiefly intended, that, among the blessings by which God lightens
our afflictions, probably one of the greatest is, that necessary retirement which gives us abundant leisure ; insomuch that I believe there is not a stranger here, who could
honestly and in conscience affirm, that want of time alone
prevents him from attending both. Other reasons there
may be—some of them perhaps conclusive—against attending the one sort or the other of these meetings ; but never
surely can our presence at the one so completely absorb
our time, as to prevent us, if we choose, from appearing at
the other. This reply, I say, might possibly be deemed
sufficient ; but I wish, in one or two sentences more, to

* 1 Thess. v. 11. † Heb. x. 25. ‡ Ps. li. 13. § Acts viii. 1-4.
‖ Acts xviii. 24. ¶ 2 Cor. i. 24. ** Ib. iv. 2.

show you, that we do not set our foot within the province occupied by these other assemblages, and consequently cannot in any way impede their fair and legitimate operation. This will be manifest, if we look at the religious exercises performed in them,—reading prayers and the Scripture lessons for the day. Now, in alluding to the first of these, I do not forget that I am addressing those, most of whom have, from their childhood, venerated the Prayer-book. Such a feeling is natural and commendable, if it be not pressed to a superstitious extreme ; if we remember, all the while, to secure to the Bible its due supremacy,—convinced that the words of eternal life challenge the chief concern of an immortal spirit, and ought to be placed on an eminence far remote from every work or compilation of man. But your regard to the Prayer-book is, I doubt not, *rational* as well as *warm*. You consider it an excellent medium for expressing the desires of a Christian congregation, and for this end you use it ; but you do not run into the extravagance of thinking that it is equally fitted for every conceivable end of worship—for expressing every variety of want, which may meet us in the ample field of the world. For example, as every form must be framed on some supposition, it is framed, as you well know, on the idea that all who use it are sincerely devout ; and hence, most obviously, there are large classes of persons,—first, the absolutely careless,—and then, those on whose minds the truth is just dawning,—those who are convinced, but not converted,—not far from the kingdom of God, yet only almost persuaded to be Christians,—to whose feelings it can only give an incidental and imperfect utterance. But again, among the events of life, there are many, of course, for which a form, if it is to be of a moderate size, can make no provision at all ; and others, such as affliction, to which it can only allude lightly and briefly. And tell me now, ye who are in trouble yourselves, or whose friends are in deadly combat with the last of enemies, if it is merely a short allusion that will satisfy the' yearnings of the heart, or if it would not soothe you more, in varied expression, suited to every changeful feeling of your souls, to carry your anxieties to the ear of your Father in heaven ? Now it is our impression, that, for all this, we want something more elastic and flexible than an unchanging form ; and, reserving to the Liturgy its proper place and its proper honours, we apprehend, that, in this more near and familiar intercourse, there will be more of that indescribable sympathy of soul with soul, which constitutes the great felicity of social devotion, if we make use of what is called extemporaneous prayer; in which, he who is to conduct the supplications of the rest, having meditated beforehand on his own wants and theirs, leaves, to the kindling impulse of the time and the place, the words in which his desires shall be clothed. In this way, we think we shall be better enabled to meet the peculiar necessities of our present circumstances; to affect our own souls, which is the first step towards affecting yours; and, by enlarging on our special difficulties and sorrows, to endeavour to come up to the meaning of the scriptural injunction, ' Pour ye out your hearts before him.'*

And now, one word respecting the other part of our service. Neither does it occupy the same ground with the reading of the Scripture lessons. We propose, not merely to read a passage of the Word of God, but to found on it some short exhortation. And surely, this will not be deemed superfluous, when you reflect, how seldom the truth which we know is duly considered; how often the letter of Scripture passes under our eye, and yet the lesson it teaches, if not urged home upon us, is overlooked or disregarded; and that, on the very principle on which we deem an exposition desirable, it has pleased God himself to give line upon line, and to institute the ordinance of preaching.

Where the *provinces* of exertion, then, are so totally distinct, there need not, surely, be any dread of interference; nay, rather, there is room for the most perfect harmony of operation. We are persuaded, that whatever benefit arises from the one will be reflected back upon the other; and, in any event, if good is done at either, we therein do rejoice, yea, and will rejoice.

4. After these specific difficulties are thus disposed of, it only remains to allude to *the general objection of human nature*, that such strictness as attending on week-day meetings, in addition to our Sabbath services, is unnecessary, —that it is carrying to an excess what is otherwise good, —that it is, in fact, being ' righteous overmuch.' † Such, I trust, is not the feeling of any one who now hears me; certainly it cannot be the feeling of any whose conscience has ever felt the weight and importance of eternity. It was not the feeling of Moses, when he said to the people

* Ps. lxii. † Eccles. vii. 16.

respecting the service of God, 'It is not a vain thing for you, because it is your life;' nor of David, when his soul rose in that fervent aspiration, 'Blessed are they that dwell in thy house; they will be *still* praising thee;' * nor of Paul, when he said, 'Let the word of Christ dwell in you richly in all wisdom;' † 'Pray always with all prayer and supplication in the Spirit.' ‡ Nor is it the working of an ingenuous mind, touched in any measure with the love of our heavenly Father, to say, 'How little may I do, and yet be safe?' but rather, 'How much can I do, that I may grow in grace and in fitness for glory?' But, indeed, where is the warrant or appearance of safety, if the hours devoted to God are counted a weariness, and the pittance of your time which so brief a service requires is given with a grudge, as a sombre and gloomy exception to the pleasant tenor of your days? Let us look, then, to our everlasting peace. The day is coming,—with some of us it even now is,—when we must be called aside, by a summons which none can resist or evade, from our usual labours and contemplations, and a still small voice will whisper to us that we *must find time to die:* and oh! were it not our wisest course now to find time to prepare for that inevitable call? Eternity, like the God who inhabiteth it, is 'not far from any one of us?' a false step, or the bursting of a little tube, may loose the silver cord, and break the golden bowl; and 'then shall the dust return to the earth as it was; and the spirit shall return unto God who gave it;' § but oh! who shall say that that spirit will be rejoicing in His presence, if it has not been so prepared on earth, as to have a taste for the songs and services of heaven?

It would be our desire, although doubtless followed out most inadequately, to make our little assemblies the scene of such a preparation. And surely we have ample encouragement in our text from Malachi : ' The Lord hearkened and heard them; and a book of remembrance was written before him for them that feared the Lord, and that thought upon his name. And they shall be mine, saith the Lord of hosts, in that day when I make up my jewels.' This promise is one that has been proved by experience. I have no right to speak of benefit that may have resulted from such meetings even here; but I may say freely, that, in the like assemblages at home, I have witnessed the glistening eye, and the heaving frame, and

* Ps. lxxxiv. † Col. iii. 16. ‡ Eph. vi. 18. § Eccles. xii. 7.

all the signs of strong emotion,—and seen the clearest
evidence, in lives devoted to God, that this was not a tran-
sient glow, but the working of a deep and pervading principle.   And 'the Lord's hand is not shortened, that it
cannot save ; neither his ear heavy, that it cannot hear.' *

And now, my friends, is it not a good and a holy work
which we have taken in hand ?   Is it not one in which we
may well claim your presence, your indulgence, your sympathy, and your prayers ?   We shall be 'with you in
weakness, and in fear, and in much trembling.'†   If the
'treasure' of the Gospel 'is in earthen vessels,' we feel
that we are the feeblest of the earthen.‡   O let us have
your prayers, that this very weakness may turn to God's
glory ; that the very circumstance of the inadequacy of
the instruments may give forth a still more effective demonstration, that 'the excellency of the power is of God ;'§
'pray for us, that the word of God may have free course
and be glorified ;' pray that we may 'obtain mercy of the
Lord to be faithful ;' ‖ pray that we may 'speak a word
in season to him that is weary ;' ¶ pray, in short, that the
Lord's presence may be in our assemblies, that His blessing may follow them, and that His kingdom may come in
power to our hearts and your own.

* Is. lix. 1.   † 1 Cor. ii. 3.   ‡ 2 Cor. iv. 7.   § 2 Thess. iii. 1.
‖ 1 Cor. vii. 25.   ¶ Is. l. 4.

THE END.

Edinburgh : Printed by JOHN JOHNSTONE, High Street.

LIST

OF

POPULAR RELIGIOUS WORKS

PUBLISHED BY

JOHN JOHNSTONE, EDINBURGH;

AND SOLD BY

R. GROOMBRIDGE, LONDON,
W. CURRY, JUNR., AND CO., DUBLIN.

POPULAR RELIGIOUS WORKS, &c.

REV. J. BUCHANAN.

The Office and Work of the Holy Spirit. By the Rev. JAMES BUCHANAN, one of the Ministers of the High Church, Edinburgh. Second Edition, fcap. 8vo, cloth, price 6s. 6d.

CONTENTS.

Part 1.—The Spirit's Work in the Conversion of Sinners
„ 2.—Illustrative Cases.
„ 3.—The Spirit's Work in the Edification of his People after their Conversion.

By the same Author.

I. Comfort in Affliction; A Series of Meditations. Tenth Edition, fcap. 8vo, 3s. 6d. cloth, lettered.

II. Improvement of Affliction; A Practical Sequel to a Series of Meditations, entitled "Comfort in Affliction." Fourth Edition, fcap. 8vo, 3s. 6d.

REV. A. BEITH.

Sorrowing yet Rejoicing; or, Narrative of Recent Successive Bereavements in a Clergyman's Family. By the Rev. ALEX. BEITH, one of the Ministers of Stirling. Fourth Edition, 1s. 6d. cloth.

AFFLICTION.

The Afflicted's Refuge; or, Prayers Adapted to Various Circumstances of Distress. Fcap. 8vo, 2s. 6d. cloth.

AFFLICTION.

Christian Fidelity in the House of Mourning. By the Rev. DAVID MITCHELL. 18mo, cloth, price 1s. 6d.

CALAMY.

The Godly Man's Ark ; or, City of Refuge in the Day of Distress. By EDMUND CALAMY, B.D., Pastor of the Church of Aldermanbury. Square 18mo, cloth, price 2s. 6d.

MEIKLE.

Solitude Sweetened. By JAMES MEIKLE, late Surgeon, Carnwath. With a Biographical Sketch of the Author. Ninth Edition. Fcap. 8vo, cloth, price 3s. 6d.

NEWTON.

Cardiphonia ; or, Utterance-of the Heart, in the Course of a Real Correspondence. By the Rev. JOHN NEWTON. With an Introductory Essay, by DAVID RUSSELL, D.D., Dundee. Fcap. 8vo, portrait, 4s. 6d. cloth.

By the same Author,

Twenty-Five Letters. *Never before Published.* Second Edition, with a Prefatory Note by the Rev. JOHN HUNTER, A.M., one of the Ministers of the Tron Church, Edinburgh. 18mo, 1s. 6d. cloth.

JACOB ABBOTT.

The Way to do Good ; or, the Christian Character Matured. By JACOB ABBOTT, Author of " The Young Christian." Second Edition, 12mo, 3s. cloth.

LADY COLQUHOUN.

The World's Religion, as contrasted with Genuine Christianity. By LADY COLQUHOUN, daughter of the late Right Hon. Sir John Sinclair, Bart. Second Edition, fcap. 8vo, 3s. 6d. cloth.

By the same Author.

I. The Kingdom of God, as to its Nature and Subjects. 12mo, 3s. 6d. cloth.

II. Impressions of the Heart, relative to the Nature and Excellency of Genuine Religion. Second Edition, 12mo, 3s. cloth.

III. Despair and Hope : exemplified in a Narrative founded on fact. Second Edition, 18mo, 6d. stitched.

REV. J. MARSHALL.

Inward Revival ; or, Motives and Hindrances to Advancement in Holiness. By the Rev. JAMES MARSHALL, formerly Minister of the Tolbooth Church, Edinburgh. Second Edition. Fcap. 8vo, 4s. 6d. cloth.

REV. E. CRAIG.

The Foundation of Christian Hope ; being a Plain and Impartial Inquiry after a safe Ground of Confidence for a Sinful Creature at the Bar of God. By the Rev. EDWARD CRAIG, A.M., of St Edmund Hall, Oxon. Fifth Edition, 32mo, 1s. cloth.

By the same Author.

Christian Circumspection ; a Brief View of the Duty of Christians to preserve themselves pure from the Irreligious Customs of this World. Fifth Edition, 18mo, 1s. stitched.

THE YOUNG.

Essential Considerations for Young Christians when Entering on the Active Period of Life. Adapted for Sabbath School Libraries. 2s. 6d. cloth.

By the same Author.

I. The Good Servant, and other Tracts; or, Examples and Warnings for Persons in Humble Life. Third Edition, 2s. 6d. cloth.

II. The Apprentice's Monitor ; containing Examples and Warnings. 2s. 6d. cloth.

DR GORDON.

Sermons by ROBERT GORDON, D.D., F.R.S.E., one of the Ministers of the High Church, Edinburgh. Fourth Edition, 8vo, 10s. 6d. cloth.

CALVIN.

A Treatise on the Sacraments of Baptism and the Lord's Supper. By JOHN CALVIN. Fcap. 8vo, 2s. 6d. cloth.

REV. J. GRIERSON.

A Doctrinal and Practical Treatise on the Lord's Supper ; comprehending copious Illustrations of the leading Doctrines of the Gospel, and of the leading Duties and varied Experience of the Christian Life. By the Rev. JAMES GRIERSON, Minister of Errol. Fcap. 8vo, 3s. 6d. cloth.

BOSTON.

A Memorial concerning Personal and Family Fasting and Humiliation, presented to Saints and Sinners ; wherein also the Nature of Personal Covenanting with God is occasionally opened. By the Rev. THOMAS BOSTON, Minister of the Gospel at Ettrick. With Prefatory Remarks by the Rev. ALEXANDER MOODY STUART, A.M., Minister of St Luke's, Edinburgh. 18mo, 1s. cloth.

REV. J. CAMPBELL.

African Light thrown on a Selection of Scripture Texts. By the late Rev. JOHN CAMPBELL, Minister of Kingsland Chapel, London, Author of "Travels in Africa," &c. Second Edition, with a Biographical Sketch of the Author. *Frontispiece*, 18mo, 2s. 6d. cloth.

REV. R. JAMIESON.

Manners and Trials of the Primitive Christians. By the Rev. ROBERT JAMIESON, Minister of Currie. Second Edition, fcap. 8vo, *frontispiece*, 5s. cloth.

DR BROWN.

Antiquities of the Jews ; carefully compiled from Authentic Sources, and their Customs illustrated from Modern Travels. *With Engravings.* By the late WILLIAM BROWN, D.D., Minister of Eskdalemuir. Second Edition, 2 vols. 8vo, 12s. cloth.

REV. D. BAGOT.

An Exposition of the Gospel of St Matthew. By the Rev. DANIEL BAGOT, B.D., Minister of St James' Episcopal Chapel, Edinburgh. To be published in Parts at 1s. each, four of which will be published in 1842, and five in the year following.

JOHN JOHNSTONE, HUNTER SQUARE, EDINBURGH.

6

THE SHORTER CATECHISM.

A Concise System of Theology : being the Shorter Catechism of the Westminster Assembly of Divines Analyzed and Explained. By ALEXANDER SMITH PATERSON, A.M., Author of a "History of the Church." With a paper on the History and Arrangement of the Shorter Catechism, by the Rev. DUNCAN MACFARLAN, Minister of Renfrew. Fcap. 8vo, price 4s. 6d.

VINCENT.

An Explanation of the Assembly's Shorter Catechism. By THOMAS VINCENT. 18mo, cloth, price 2s. 6d.

DR SYMINGTON.

Messiah the Prince ; or, The Mediatorial Dominion of Jesus Christ. By WILLIAM SYMINGTON, D.D., Glasgow. Second Edition, fcap. 8vo, 5s. cloth.

SOCINIANISM.

A Demonstration of the True and Eternal Divinity of our Lord Jesus Christ. By DIONYSIUS VAN DE WYNPERSSE, D.D., late Professor of Philosophy, Mathematics, and Astronomy, at Leyden. Second Edition, translated from the Dutch ; containing an Introduction, Appendix, Notes and Illustrations, by WILLIAM L. ALEXANDER, A.M., Minister of Argyle Square Chapel, Edinburgh. 18mo, 2s. 6d. cloth.

LESLIE.

A Short and Easy Method with the Deists, wherein the certainty of the Christian Religion is Demonstrated, by Infallible Proofs, from Four Rules. By the Rev. CHARLES LESLIE, A.M. A New Edition, with an Introductory Essay by DAVID RUSSELL, D.D., Dundee. 18mo, 2s. 6d. cloth.

CHRISTIAN EVIDENCES.

A Brief Outline of the Evidences of the Christian Religion. By ARCHIBALD ALEXANDER, D.D., Professor of Theology in the Theological Seminary of the Presbyterian Church, United States. 12mo, 1s. cloth.

LIST OF WORKS PUBLISHED BY

CHRISTIAN EVIDENCES.

Family Conversations between a Father and his Children on the Discoveries and Evidences of Christianity. 18mo, cloth, price 3s. 6d.

DR ESDAILE.

Christian Theology; or, a Connected View of the Scheme of Christianity. By JAMES ESDAILE, D.D., Minister of the East Church, Perth. 8vo, 5s. cloth.

BOWDLER.

Theological Essays. By the late JOHN BOWDLER, jun., Esq. of Lincoln's Inn, Barrister-at-Law. 18mo, cloth, price 2s. 6d.

M'EWEN.

Grace and Truth; or, The Glory and Fulness of the Redeemer displayed; in an attempt to Illustrate and Enforce the Most Remarkable Types, Figures, and Allegories of the Old Testament. By the late Rev. WILLIAM M'EWEN, Minister of the Gospel, Dundee. 18mo, 2s. 6d. cloth.

By the same Author.

Select Essays upon Doctrinal and Practical Subjects. New Edition, 12mo, 3s. 6d. cloth.

SCRIPTURE CHRONOLOGY.

Scripture Chronology, in accordance with the Hebrew Text; wherein the Dates given of the leading events between the creation and the birth of Christ, are clearly and satisfactorily proved to be the true Dates. By JAMES MACFARLANE, Perth. 12mo, 2s. 6d. cloth.

HUGH MILLER.

The Old Red Sandstone; or, New Walks in an Old Field. Second Edition, enlarged. With Plates and Geological Sections. Fcap. 8vo, 7s. 6d. cloth.

THOMAS DICK, LL.D.

On the Improvement of Society by the Diffusion of Knowledge. By THOMAS DICK, LL.D. Second Edition, improved, 12mo, 7s. 6d. boards.

JOHN JOHNSTONE, HUNTER SQUARE, EDINBURGH.

DR DUFF.

India and India Missions; including Sketches of the Gigantic System of Hinduism, both in Theory and Practice; also, Notices of some of the Principal Agencies employed in conducting the process of Indian Evangelization, &c. By ALEXANDER DUFF, D.D., Church of Scotland Mission, Calcutta. Second Edition, 12s. cloth.

By the same Author.

Missions the Chief End of the Christian Church; also, the Qualifications, Duties, and Trials of an Indian Missionary. Fourth Edition, fcap. 8vo, 2s. 6d. cloth.

THE JEWS.

The Conversion of the Jews; a Course of Lectures Delivered in Edinburgh, by the following Ministers of the Church of Scotland. In fcap. 8vo, cloth, 2s. 6d.

Rev. Dr BLACK. (*Prefatory Notice.*)	Rev. C. J. BROWN.
„ Dr MUIRHEAD.	„ HENRY GREY.
„ Dr CANDLISH.	„ ROBERT ELDER.
„ A. A. BONAR.	„ A. MOODY STUART.

JAMES HALLEY.

Memoir, with Select Remains, of the late James Halley, A.B., Student of Theology. Second Edition, fcap. 8vo, with Portrait, 5s. cloth.

MRS WILSON.

Memoirs of Mrs Wilson of Bombay; including Extracts from her Letters and Journals. By JOHN WILSON, D.D., M.R.A.S., Missionary of the Church of Scotland, Bombay. Third Edition, 7s. 6d. cloth.

FEMALE PIETY.

Memoirs of Christian Females; with an Essay on the Influences of Female Piety. By the Rev. JAMES GARDNER, A.M., M.D. Second Edition, in fcap. 8vo, with an Elegant Portrait of Mrs Hannah More, 4s. 6d. cloth.

CONTENTS.

Preliminary Essay.	Mrs Graham.
Mrs Huntingdon.	Mrs Ellis.
Lady Glenorchy.	Miss Smelt.
Miss Cuvier.	Mrs Wilson.
Mrs Judson.	Miss Reid.
Mrs Hannah More.	Mrs Winslow.

9

MRS PATERSON.

Memoir of the late Mrs Paterson, Wife of the Rev. Dr Paterson, St Petersburg, containing Extracts from her Diary and Correspondence. By the Rev. WILLIAM SWAN, Missionary at Sellingisk. Second Edition. 12mo, 3s. 6d. boards.

PLINY FISK.

Memoirs of the Rev. Pliny Fisk, A.M., late Missionary to Palestine, from the American Board of Missions. 12mo, with Portrait, 5s. bds.

LEVI PARSONS.

Memoir of the Rev. Levi Parsons, Companion of the Rev. Pliny Fisk, Missionary to Palestine. 18mo, 3s. cloth.

DODDRIDGE.

Memoirs of the Life, Character, and Writings of Philip Doddridge, D.D. By JOB ORTON; with an Introductory Essay by DAVID RUSSELL, D.D., Dundee 18mo, 2s. 6d. cloth.

BIOGRAPHY.

Sketches in Biography, designed to show the Influence of Literature on Character and Happiness. By JOHN CLAYTON, Esq. 12mo, 5s. cloth.

REV. W. M. HETHERINGTON.

A History of the Church of Scotland. From the Introduction of Christianity to 1841. By the Rev. W. M. HETHERINGTON, A.M., Minister of Torphichen. Second Edition. 8vo, cloth, 12s.

REV. T. M'CRIE.

"Sketches of Scottish Church History, embracing the period from the Reformation to the Revolution. By the Rev. THOMAS M'CRIE. With an Appendix, relative to the alleged accession of John Knox to the Conspiracy against Riccio. Second Edition. In fcap. 8vo, cloth, 6s. 6d.

JOHN JOHNSTONE, HUNTER SQUARE, EDINBURGH

CHURCH OF SCOTLAND.

A Catechism of the History of the Church of Scotland. By the Rev. BENJAMIN LAING, Colmonell, one of the Theological Professors to the Associate Synod of Original Seceders. *In the press.*

CHURCH OF SCOTLAND.

An Exposition of the Principles of the.Church of Scotland, in regard to the Admission of Pastors : A Series of Lectures by the following Clergymen. With Preface. Second Edition, in fcap. 8vo, cloth, 2s. 6d.

REV. DR CANDLISH.	REV. J. BEGG.
„ A. BENNIE.	„ A. MOODY STUART.
„ W. CUNNINGHAM.	„ R. ELDER.
„ C. J. BROWN.	„ T. GUTHRIE.

PRESBYTERY.

Manual of Presbytery ; or, A Vindication of that Form of Church Government from Scripture, and Primitive Practice ; from its Efficiency of Discipline ; and from its Identification with Learning, Civil and Religious Liberty, and Home and Foreign Missionary Enterprise. By Samuel Miller, D.D., Professor of Ecclesiastical History in the Presbyterian Theological Seminary at Princetown, New Jersey ; and the Rev. John Gordon Lorimer, Minister of St David's Parish, Glasgow.

THE DEACONSHIP.

A Treatise on the Office of Deacon, with Suggestions for its Revival in the Church of Scotland. By the Rev. J. G. Lorimer.

GENERAL ASSEMBLY.

Annals of the General Assembly of the Church of Scotland, from the Final Secession in 1739, to the Rejection of the Overture on Schism in 1776. With Appendices of Biographical Sketches, Illustrative Documents, and Notes. By the Rev. N. MORREN, A.M., Minister of the North Church, Greenock. 2 vols. 12mo, 10s. cloth.

[Each Volume is complete in itself, and may be had separately, price 5s.]

PROTESTANT CHURCH OF FRANCE.

An Historical Sketch of the Protestant Church o France, from its Origin down to the Present Day; with parallel Notices of the History of the Church of Scotland during the same period. By the Rev. J. G. LORIMER, Minister of St David's Parish, Glasgow. Fcap. 8vo, 6s. 6d. cloth.

THE COVENANTERS.

History of the Covenanters in Scotland. By WILLIAM SIME, Esq., Author of the "Histories of the Reformation," "Christian Church," "Waldenses." *A New Edition, in one Volume, in the press.*

RENWICK.

Life of the Rev. James Renwick, the last of the Scottish Martyrs. By the Author of the History of the Covenanters. 18mo, 2s. cloth.

DR M'CRIE.

Life of Thomas M'Crie, D.D., Author of "Life of John Knox," &c., &c. By his Son, the Rev. THOMAS M'CRIE. Demy 8vo, 9s. cloth, with highly finished Portrait, by Horsburgh.

DR M'CRIE.

Miscellaneous Writings, Chiefly Historical, of the late THOMAS M'CRIE, D.D. Edited by his Son. In 8vo, cloth, price 10s. 6d.

CONTENTS.

Life of Alexander Henderson.
  „ Patrick Hamilton.
  „ Francis Lambert of Avignon.
  „ Dr Andrew Rivet.
  „ Mr John Murray.
Lives of the Taborites.
Review of Milne on Presbytery and Episcopacy.
  „ Sismondi's Considerations on Geneva.
Review of Simeon on the Liturgy.
  „ Tales of my Landlord.
  „ Orme's Life of Owen.
  „ Turner's Life and Times.
Pamphlet on the Funeral of the Princess Charlotte.
———— the General Assembly 1828.
———— Females Voting in Election of Ministers.

JOHN JOHNSTONE, HUNTER SQUARE, EDINBURGH.

PRINCIPAL HILL.

View of the Constitution of the Church of Scotland. By the late GEORGE HILL, D.D., Principal of St Mary's College, St Andrews. With Appendix and Notes by ALEXANDER HILL, D.D., Professor of Divinity in the University of Glasgow. Third Edition, 12mo 3s. 6d. cloth.

ANTI-PATRONAGE.

The Select Anti-Patronage Library. This Volume comprehends a Collection of Acts of Parliament and Assembly connected with Patronage, and Treatises on the subject, by the following Authors. In demy 8vo, cloth, 3s. 6d.

LORD PRESTONGRANGE.	DR DODDRIDGE.
SIR FRANCIS GRANT.	MR CROSBIE.
SIR DAVID DALRYMPLE.	REV. JOHN CURRIE.
DR OWEN.	REV. JAMES BEGG.

REV. W. M. HETHERINGTON.

The Minister's Family. By the Rev. W. M. HETHERINGTON, A.M., Minister of Torphichen. Fourth Edition with beautiful frontispiece, 5s. cloth.

THE KENT.

A Narrative of the Loss of the Kent, East Indiaman, by Fire, in the Bay of Biscay, on 1st March 1825. Second Edition, 18mo, cloth, 1s. 6d.

THE YOUNG.

The Border Rebel ; or, Disobedient Son : A Narrative of the year 1745, founded on facts ; with an Application, containing an Admonition to Youth. With elegant frontispiece, 1s. 6d. cloth.

CATHERINE SINCLAIR.

The Nursery Plutarch, containing Lives of Julius Cæsar Nero, Titus, Domitian, Trajan. By CATHERINE SINCLAIR, Authoress of " Modern Society," " Modern Accomplishments." 18mo, cloth, 3s. 6d.

REV. D. LANDSBOROUGH.

Ayrshire Sketches ; or, Memoirs of Jeanie Charters Hugh Cunninghame, and James Baird. By the Rev D. LANDSBOROUGH, Minister of Stevenston. 18mo 6d. stitched.

AFRICAN TRAVELLERS.

Biographical Memoirs of Dr Oudney, Captain Clapperton, and Major Laing, all of whom died in attempting to Explore the Interior of Africa. By the Rev. Thos. Nelson, M.W.S. 18mo, cloth, price 2s. 6d.

THE SCOTTISH CHRISTIAN HERALD

The Scottish Christian Herald. This work is now complete in six handsome volumes, imperial 8vo, cloth, price £2. It contains Original Papers by some of the most distinguished Ministers and Office-Bearers of the Church of Scotland, all of a character admirably adapted for family reading.

THE CHRISTIAN MISCELLANY, &c.

The Christian Miscellany, and Weekly Family Expositor.

This is a Religious Periodical, generally similar in its design to the "Scottish Christian Herald," but intended to occupy a more advanced position in theological Literature. It also includes in its plan a Commentary on the Holy Scriptures, selected and arranged from the most eminent Expositors, Foreign and British. This department has a distinct typography and paging, and can, at pleasure, be bound apart from the Miscellaneous portion of the Work. The periods of publication are every Saturday morning, in Numbers at Three Halfpence, and in Monthly Parts at Ninepence. It will also, at appropriate intervals, be issued in Volumes, handsomely bound. Orders received by all Booksellers.

MISSIONARY RECORD.

Home and Foreign Missionary Record for the Church of Scotland, by Authority of the Committees of the General Assembly. Published on the 1st day of each Month. Price Threepence, unstamped ; and Fourpence, stamped and sent by post. First Series, in 8vo, bound in cloth, 10s. Second Series, Vol. I., large 4to, bound in cloth, 10s.

⁎ The Committees make the Record their stated and ordinary channel of advertising contributions and collections, and, in general, employ this Journal exclusively in communicating with the Church and the Public.

JOHN JOHNSTONE, HUNTER SQUARE, EDINBURGH.

THE EXCITEMENT.

The Excitement; or, A Book to Induce Young People to Read. Edited by the Rev. R. JAMIESON, Author of "Manners and Trials of the Primitive Christians," &c. In eight Volumes, 18mo, price 4s. 6d. each.

The Editor having carefully excluded from this work all matter of an ephemeral or temporary character, it will be found to be particularly fitted for the instruction and amusement of the young. Each volume comprises upwards of 400 pages of letter-press, and is elegantly bound, and illustrated with superior engravings on steel and wood.

CLERICAL ECONOMICS.

Clerical Economics; or Hints, Rural and Household, to Ministers and others of Limited Income. By a Clergyman of the Old School. Foolscap 8vo, cloth, 4s. *Just Published.*

YOUNG COOK'S ASSISTANT.

The Young Cook's Assistant; being a Selection of Economical Receipts and Directions, adapted to the Use of Families in the Middle Rank of Life. Edited by a Clergyman's Daughter. Fourth Thousand. Price 1s. 6d.

THE BIBLE.

Bible Narratives for the Young. By a CLERGYMAN's DAUGHTER. 32mo, 1s. 6d. cloth.

CATECHISMS AND TRACTS.

Attendance at Church. Address to those who Seldom or Never go to Church. By the Rev. ROBERT LEE, Campsie. Price 2d.

Amusements of Youth. By the Rev. HENRY GREY, St Mary's Church, Edinburgh. Price 4d.

Baptism. Help to Parents Preparatory to the Baptism of their Children. By the Rev. JOHN CHARLES. Second Edition. Price 4d.

——— Catechism on Baptism. By the Rev. HENRY GREY, Edinburgh. Fourth Edition. Price 6d.

——— Scheme of the Controversy on Baptism. Second Thousand. Price 1d.

Baptism. Vindication of Infant Baptism. By DAVID BOSTHWICK, A.M. Second British Edition. Price 6d.

Christian Evidences. Catechism of the Evidences of Revealed Religion. By Rev. Dr FERRIE. Price 2d.
———————————— Manual of the Christian Evidences. By JAMES STEELE. Price 1s.

Church of Scotland—Popular View of its Constitution. Price 1d.

Elementary Catechism. By Dr WILSON of Bombay. Price 2d.

Family Worship, Essay and Address on. By the Rev. WILLIAM BURNS, Kilsyth. Price 2d.

Gospel of St Matthew, Catechism of. By the Rev. JAMES MILLER, Monikie. Price 8d.

Holy Scripture, Catechism on the First Principles of. By Dr Russell, Dundee. Price 3d.
———————————— Epitome of. By JAMES STARK, Esq. Advocate, Ceylon. Price 1d.

Leading Doctrines and Duties of the Gospel—Fifty Questions on. Price 1d.
——— Truths of the Gospel—Three Hundred and Sixty-five Questions on. By the Rev. D. BAGOT. Price 2d.

Lord's Prayer, Catechism on. By Dr ANDERSON. Price 2d.

Mother's Catechism. By the Rev. JOHN WILLISON. Price 1d.

Old and New Testament, Series of Questions on. By the Rev. WILLIAM ANDREW. Price 1s.

Protestantism. Catechism on the Errors of the Church of Rome. By the Rev. D. BAGOT. Price 6d.

Shorter Catechism, Analysis and Explanation of. By ALEXANDER SMITH PATERSON. Price 4s. 6d.
———————————— Explanation of. By THOMAS VINCENT. Price 2s. 6d.
———————————— Three Hundred Doctrinal Questions on. By WILLIAM HAMILTON. Price 1d.

Young Children, Catechism for. By the Rev. JOHN BROWN, Haddington. Price 1d.

JOHN JOHNSTONE, HUNTER SQUARE, EDINBURGH.

SABBATH SCHOOL MAPS.

MAP OF CANAAN AND PALESTINE,

Adapted for Sabbath Schools or Bible Classes. Engraved in a clear bold style, elaborately coloured, size 4 feet 6 inches, by 3 feet 6 inches.

On Rollers, Varnished,	12s.
———— Unvarnished,	10s.

COLLEGE AND SCHOOL MAPS.

JOHNSTONS' COLLEGE AND SCHOOL MAPS.

Comprising

Eastern Hemisphere.	Asia.	England.
Western Hemisphere.	Africa	Scotland.
Europe.	America.	Ireland.

Canaan and Palestine.

Size 4 feet 6 inches, by 3 feet 6 inches.

	£	s.	d.
Price of Each Map, Rollers, Varnished,	£0	12	0
———— Unvarnished,	0	10	0
The Whole Ten in a Case,	6	6	0
———— Stand,	7	7	0
———— with Black Board,	7	17	6

MAP OF FRANCE.

Uniform with the Above,
A MAP OF FRANCE,

With the names of the principal places in English and French.

On Rollers, Varnished,	12s.
———— Unvarnished,	10s.

GEOGRAPHICAL TEXT-BOOKS.

Dr Steven's Progressive Geography, Book First, price 4d.
———— Second, 2s. 6d.

ATLASES.

			£	s.	d.
Edinburgh Cabinet Atlas, 45 Maps,			£1	11	6
———— School Atlas, 36 „			0	12	0
School Classical Atlas, 21 „			0	7	0
New Hand Atlas, 12 „			0	4	0

Check Out More Titles From HardPress Classics Series In this collection we are offering thousands of classic and hard to find books. This series spans a vast array of subjects – so you are bound to find something of interest to enjoy reading and learning about.

Subjects:
Architecture
Art
Biography & Autobiography
Body, Mind &Spirit
Children & Young Adult
Dramas
Education
Fiction
History
Language Arts & Disciplines
Law
Literary Collections
Music
Poetry
Psychology
Science
…and many more.

Visit us at www.hardpress.net